THE WORLD OF CULINARY MANAGEMENT

LEADERSHIP AND DEVELOPMENT OF HUMAN RESOURCES

FIFTH EDITION

Jerald W. Chesser

Noel C. Cullen

PEARSON

Boston   Columbus   Indianapolis   New York   San Francisco   Upper Saddle River
Amsterdam   Cape Town   Dubai   London   Madrid   Milan   Munich   Paris   Montreal   Toronto
Delhi   Mexico City   Sao Paulo   Sydney   Hong Kong   Seoul   Singapore   Taipei   Tokyo

VP, Editorial Director: Vernon Anthony
Senior Acquisitions Editor: William Lawrensen
Editorial Assistant: Lara Dimmick
Director of Marketing: David Gesell
Curriculum Marketing Manager: Thomas Hayward
Senior Marketing Coordinator: Alicia Wozniak
Marketing Assistant: Les Roberts
Associate Managing Editor: Alex Wolf
Production Editor: Alexis Biasell
Production Project Manager: Debbie Ryan
Art Director: Diane Ernsberger
Text and Cover Designer: Mary Siener
Cover Art: Erika Cespedes
Lead Media Project Manager: Karen Bretz
Full-Service Project Management: Mohinder Singh/Aptara®, Inc.
Composition: Aptara®, Inc.
Printer/Binder: Edwards Brothers Malloy
Cover Printer: Lehigh-Phoenix Color/Hagerstown
Text Font: Adobe Garamond Pro

Library of Congress Cataloging-in-Publication Data
Chesser, Jerald W.
    The world of culinary management: leadership and development of human resources /
Jerald W. Chesser, Noel C. Cullen.—5th ed.
        p. cm.
    Rev. ed. of: World of culinary supervision, training, and management / Jerald W. Chesser,
Noel C. Cullen. 4th ed. 2009.
    Includes bibliographical references and index.
    ISBN-13: 978-0-13-274774-5
    ISBN-10: 0-13-274774-X
    1. Food service management.   2. Cooks.   I. Cullen, Noel C.   II. Chesser, Jerald W. World of
culinary supervision, training, and management.   III. Title.
    TX911.3.M27C494 2013
    647.95068—dc23

                                                                            2011037438

10 9 8 7 6 5 4 3 2

PEARSON

ISBN 10:   0-13-274774-X
ISBN 13: 978-0-13-274774-5

This fifth edition of *The World of Culinary Management: Leadership and Development of Human Resources* is dedicated to my father, William "Bill" Clifford Chesser, CEC, AAC and my mother, Dorothy Jean Chesser, who by example taught me how to work, manage, and lead. They positively impacted many lives and are missed every day.

Brief Contents

Contents

Case Studies

Figures

Table

Preface

It has been 16 years since the first edition of this book was published. The changes in what it means to be a chef and how a chef is perceived both in and out of the kitchen have been extensive. When that first edition was published, in general the lines were clear: There was management, and then there was the kitchen staff, which included the chef. The chef was a supervisor, but only because he or she was responsible for the supervision of the cooks. The chef was valued for creativity, not management ability. The world of the chef has changed considerably in those 16 years.

This fifth edition has been heavily revised and expanded to reflect those changes. Today, there still may be a front and back of the house, but there is no question that the chef is a manager, not just a supervising, creating cook. The new title of this book represents what the chef is today. The chef today is still a supervisor and trainer, as is every manager. Part 1 focuses on supervision because, without effective supervision, it is not possible to achieve the quality food and service that are the lifeblood of every kitchen and ultimately the total operation. Direction, supervision, evaluation, and guidance are the underpinning of team performance. Without these there is no team, and if there is no team, there is no success. Part 2 focuses on training and development because, without these, supervision is meaningless. The chef cannot do everything, so he or she must be able to trust the culinary team to produce. This cannot take place if the team does not know what to do or how to do it, so there must be a work environment that encourages performance. A trained team that is comfortable in the work environment will achieve success.

Not all the material in parts 3 and 4 is new. Much of it was included in the previous editions, but with a different view of the chef. The focus of part 3 is management. The perspective is that of the chef as a critical part of the properties management team. Management of the property as a whole is part of the chef's world, so management of their part of that world must take all aspects of the operation into consideration. The chef no longer motivates through fear, but by building a team based on knowledge and respect. Part 4 focuses on aspects of being a leader because, to manage most effectively, one must lead. The chef must be an excellent communicator, time manager, problem solver, and decision maker. Management and leadership are not the same, but when used as a combined force, they lead to success.

The world of culinary management is extensive and is growing every day. This growth requires greater knowledge of all aspects of what it means to be a chef. The chef may be a culinarian or a culinologist but will always be a master of the art and science of culinary preparation and will always be a manager. Consequently, this new edition was created to help all current and potential chefs be the culinary managers that the responsibility of the position demands.

—Jerald W. Chesser,
Ed.D., CEC, FMP, CEC, AAC

Instructor Resources

To access supplementary materials online, instructors need to request an instructor access code. Go to www.pearsonhighered.com/irc, where you can register for an instructor access code. Within 48 hours after registering, you will receive a confirming e-mail, including an instructor access code. Once you have received your code, go to the site and log on for full instructions on downloading the materials you wish to use.

Contributors

Contributor	Sidebar Type/Title
Noble Masi, CMB, CEPC, CCE, AAC, HOF Culinary Institute of America Hyde Park, NY	What Is This Business?: The Chef in America Yesterday—Today—Tomorrow, 4
Ferdinand Metz, MBA, CMC, AAC, HOF Chair, National Advisory Board and Executive Dean Le Cordon Bleu Schools of North America	What Is This Business?: Can Anyone Ever Be Overqualified?, 9 Foreword: Hospitality Defined, xvii
Kenneth G. Wade, CEC, AAC Chef/Owner PaddyMacs Palm Beach, FL	Chef Talk: Coaching, 13
Michael Ty, CEC, AAC MT Cuisine Las Vegas, NV	Chef Talk: Team Players, 43
Keith Keogh, CEC, AAC Magic Seasoning Blends, Inc. New Orleans, LA	Chef Talk: Induction by Fire, 65
Reimund Pitz, CEC, CCE, AAC Chef Owner Le Coq Au Vin Orlando, FL	Chef Talk: Training: What's in It for You?, 74
Benjamin San Seto Chef de Cuisine Pizzeria Mozza Marina Bay Sands Singapore	Chef Talk: Patience and Discipline, 77
Victor Gielisse, Ph.D., CMC, AAC Industry Solutions Group The Culinary Institute of America Hyde Park, NY	Chef Talk: Rethinking Your Most Valuable Asset, 82
Jeffrey King Chairman Kings Seafood Company Costa Mesa, CA	What Is This Business?: Treat 'em Like Kings, 86
Aidan P. Murphy, CMC, AAC General Manager Old Warson Country Club St. Louis, MO	Chef Talk: My Way or the Highway, 105
Jacob League General Manager Hillstone Restaurant Group	What Is This Business?: One-on-One Development, 148

Contributor	Sidebar Type/Title
Dr. Robert Harrington, CEC, CCE Department of Food, Human Nutrition and Hospitality University of Arkansas Fayetteville, AK	What Is This Business?: The Chef and the "How" and "Why", 153
Tom Peer, CMC, CCE, AAC The Culinary Institute of America Hyde Park, NY	Chef Talk: Building Morale, 164
Charles Carroll, CEC, AAC Executive Chef River Oaks Country Club Houston, TX	Chef Talk: Team Building, 179
Colleen Sabrina Wong Chef Instructor Art Institute of California Hollywood, CA	Chef Talk: Transforming a Group into a Team, 183
Klaus Friedenreich, CMC, AAC Chef Instructor Le Cordon Blue College Orlando, FL	Chef Talk: Trusting Your Kitchen Team, 185 Chef Talk: Chef Leadership, 231
Dr. Carol Silkes, CEC, CCE Assistant Professor Kemmons Wilson School University of Memphis Memphis, TN	Chef Talk: Permission to Succeed, 197
Jennifer Shen-Seto Pastry Chef Wolfgang Puck CUT Singapore	Chef Talk: No Excuses, 198
Clayton Sherrod, CEC, AAC President, Chef Clayton's Food Systems, Inc. Birmingham, AL	Chef Talk: That Was Then, 200
Guy Fieri Food Network Star	What Is This Business?: The Manager in the Chef and the Chef in the Manager, 219
Jill K. Bosich, CEC, CCE Chef Instructor Orange Coast College Costa Mesa, CA	Chef Talk: Leadership Is a Privilege, 220
Richard N. Frank Chairman Lawry's Restaurants, Inc. Pasadena, CA	What Is This Business?: Co-Workers, 223
Bob Spivak Founder Grill Concepts Woodland Hills, CA	What Is This Business?: This Is Not Rocket Science, 241

Contributor	Sidebar Type/Title
Kimberly Brock Brown, CEPC, CCA, AAC Kimberly Brock Brown, LLC	What Is This Business?: Chef as Entrepreneur, 257
Bert Cutino, CEC, AAC, HBOT, HOF Co-owner, The Sardine Factory Monterey, CA	Chef Talk: Plan the Work and Work the Plan, 261
Joshua Goldman Associate Food Scientist Development and Quality Cheese and Dairy Research Kraft Foods Glenview, IL	Chef Talk: Chef: Researcher, Problem Solver, Decision Maker, 266
John D. Folse, CEC, AAC Executive Chef/Owner Chef John Folse & Co. Donaldsonville, LA	Chef Talk: Finding Gilman, 268

Reviewers

Scott Bright, The Chef's Academy
Deborah Lindsay, Keiser University, Center for Culinary Arts
Matthew Mejia, The Chef's Academy
Donald Schoffstall, Le Cordon Bleu Institute of Culinary Arts
David Weir, Daytona Beach Community College
John Witherington, Ogeechee Technical College

*Certification levels of the American Culinary Federation are:

CC:	Certified Cook	CWPC:	Certified Working Pastry Chef
CSC:	Certified Sous Chef	CEPC:	Certified Executive Pastry Chef
CCC:	Certified Chef de Cuisine	CMPC:	Certified Master Pastry Chef
CEC:	Certified Executive Chef	CCA:	Certified Culinary Administrator
CMC:	Certified Master Chef	CSCE:	Certified Secondary School Educator
PCC:	Personal Certified Chef	CCE:	Certified Culinary Educator
PCEC:	Personal Certified Executive Chef	AAC:	Member American Academy of Chefs
CPC:	Certified Pastry Culinarian	HOF:	Hall of Fame/AAC Lifetime Achievement Award

About the Authors

Jerald Chesser, Ed.D., CEC, CCE, FMP, AAC

Dr. Chesser is an internationally recognized speaker, author, and educator. He is a Professor at The Collins College of Hospitality Management, California State Polytechnic University, Pomona, one of the top hospitality management programs in the United States. Before entering academe and consulting, he spent more than a decade in restaurant operations, including ownership of a successful restaurant and off-premise catering company. He has taught at the high school, community college, and university levels. Dr. Chesser's consulting has included the Disney Development Company, Copeland of New Orleans, University of Alaska, National Restaurant Association, and American Culinary Federation. He teaches, researches, and consults in the areas of leadership, human resource development, and the culinary arts. His previous publications include *The Art and Science of Culinary Preparation*.

Dr. Chesser earned his doctorate in leadership at the University of Central Florida. He has earned certification by the National Restaurant Association as a Food Management Professional and by the American Culinary Federation as an Executive Chef and Culinary Educator. Dr. Chesser has received numerous honors including membership in the National Restaurant Association Educational Foundation's College of Diplomates and the American Academy of Chefs, and the ICHRIE Chef Herman Briethaupt and ACF Western Region Chef Educator of the Year awards.

Noel C. Cullen, Ed.D., CMC, AAC

Dr. Cullen was one of 58 American Culinary Federation Certified Master Chefs in the United States. He had over thirty years' experience in food service/hospitality as an operator and educator including executive chef, manager, university professor, and administrator. Dr. Cullen was the first chef in the United States to earn the prestigious level of CMC and a doctorate in education. Dr. Cullen was a member of the American Academy of Chefs and past president of the American Culinary Federation.

Foreword

Hospitality Defined

The world of hospitality places inordinate demands and expectations on the chef as he or she engages in the daily task of supervising and training the culinary workforce. Today, chefs are expected to provide wholesome, safe, nutritious, and great-tasting meals to their customers each and every day. Furthermore, chefs need to be able to lead a motivated staff, meet the company's financial parameters, attend to certain PR activities, and be great communicators.

In short, chefs need to be in command of many skills. However, none is more important than a fundamental appreciation of, and a sincere commitment to *hospitality*.

Our industry is defined by hospitality, a concept much talked and written about, but one that is rarely practiced in its true sense. Perhaps the most difficult task is to explain what true hospitality is really all about, yet it is based on very simple, but fundamental principles.

We should strive to extend our hospitality to members of our family, friends, co-workers, and, of course, customers, making sure that it becomes part of who we are and what we do. Hospitality cannot be turned on or off whenever one feels it is appropriate. In simple terms, hospitality requires mutual and reciprocal respect and extension of basic considerations and common courtesies. Once applied and practiced in a sincere and consistent manner, hospitality can be one powerful element that can overcome and compensate for flawed service and even for a less-than-perfect meal. Bringing this notion to an even more basic, yet comprehensive level, I would offer the following as the ultimate definition of hospitality:

> TREAT YOUR CUSTOMERS, CO-WORKERS, AND ASSOCIATES IN THE SAME MANNER AS YOUR FRIENDS THAT YOU HAVE INVITED INTO YOUR OWN HOME.

This practical, simple advice will allow you to practice and extend great hospitality, eliminating the snobbery and insincerity that often get in the way of true hospitality.

—Ferdinand Metz
Chair, National Advisory Board and Executive Dean
Le Cordon Bleu Schools of North America

part one
The World of Supervision

Chapter 1
Supervision

CHAPTER 1 Supervision
CHAPTER 2 Legal Aspects Compensation, Benefits, and Scheduling

Outline

- Introduction
- Definition of supervision
- Attributes of the successful chef supervisor
- Chef supervisory role models
- Duties and functions of the chef supervisor
- Elements of kitchen supervision
- The concept of authority
- The evolution of supervision
- Conclusions
- Summary
- Discussion questions
- Notes

OBJECTIVES

When you complete this chapter, you should be able to:

1. Identify the central position the chef supervisor occupies in assisting the management team to reach goals and achieve quality throughout the operation
2. Identify and discuss the attributes, skills, duties, and functions of the chef supervisor
3. Outline the key elements and ingredients of a desirable kitchen work environment
4. Understand the difference between culinary skills and human skills and the role each plays in the supervisory and management process
5. Indicate trends and new dimensions associated with the development of the chef supervisor
6. Recognize the role that chef supervisors play with regard to management, customers, and team members

---

Case Study: West Village Country Club

Jason Lightner has been the chef of the West Village Country Club (WVCC) for two years. He has increased the quality of the food served and the amount of food sales. Additionally, Jason has reduced the overall cost of food sold from 60 percent to 40 percent.

WVCC membership was 250 for five years before Jason became the chef. The past twelve months have seen renewed community interest in joining the club. During this period membership grew to 300 and is expected to reach 400 within the next two years.

Improvement of membership numbers and food quality with reduced food cost are the result of Jason's directly supervising preparation of every item served. Jason personally develops all menus and recipes. He checks and adjusts the flavor of every food item prepared in the kitchen. As Jason himself says, "This is my food, and the quality of every item depends on me."

The club's general manager is very pleased with the improvements Jason has brought to the kitchen at WVCC. But he has mentioned to Jason his continuing concern with the high labor cost for the kitchen staff. The general manager considers the club's annual overall staff turnover rate of 50 percent to be rather high because of the number of college students used in various service positions. He also is concerned that the turnover rate for the kitchen staff for the past twelve months has been 150 percent.

Jason tells the general manager he has dismissed only one kitchen staff member in the previous six months. Jason does not conduct separation interviews since he is certain that "staff that quit simply find the work too hard and the pace too fast." Jason tells all new hires that the baseline is simple: "It is my kitchen, my food, and my rules."

INTRODUCTION

The exact English translation of the French term **chef** is "chief" or "director." The 1988 edition of *Webster's New World Dictionary* defined "chef" as "1. a cook in charge of a kitchen, as of a restaurant; lead cook, 2. any cook." But all things change, and the role and duties of the chef are no exception. In 2010, the definition in the *Merriam-Webster Online Dictionary* (www.m-w.com/cgi-bin/dictionary) changed to "1 : a skilled cook who manages the kitchen (as of a restaurant), 2 : cook." The shift in the definition from "in charge of" to "manages" reflects the changing nature of the chef's role in the foodservice operation and the overall industry. The role of chief cook in the kitchen continues to be the foundation of the chef's responsibilities. The chef is the person responsible for the food. This is no different from the fact that keeping the financial records of the operation or company is the foundation of the financial manager's role. But what is considered the core of the positions does not reflect their true complexity. These positions are both larger and more complex. Today, the chef is expected to be not only a first-class cook who can create gastronomic masterpieces. The same chef is expected be a supervisor who can motivate and lead the kitchen team. The chef must lead the team to maximum profits and satisfied customer. All of this must be done in a fast-paced, stressful environment. To succeed, the chef today needs the finest culinary, supervision, management, and leadership skills. This text presents and discusses the elements of supervision, management, and leadership. These elements, like great recipes, are essential to the success of today's chef.

The first step to becoming a **chef supervisor** is work ethic. The individual selected to be a supervisor must first be a good worker. Beyond this first step, qualifications for the chef supervisor's job are impressive. Chefs need to be technically competent. They need to know all aspects of professional culinary practices. These practices include the processes, equipment, and quality standards. The chef needs to know the laws and regulations that govern the kitchen. These include safety and sanitation standards and labor laws. Chefs also must know the policies of their company.

In general, chef supervisors fail because they can't get others to work effectively. The failure is rarely because of their culinary skills. Chef supervisors fail because they lack good people skills. The chef supervisor is always working with others to satisfy guests. If the chef creates a workplace where trust and the Golden Rule are the standard, staff members will gives their best effort, achieving more and enjoying their work.

WHAT IS THIS BUSINESS?
THE CHEF IN AMERICA YESTERDAY—TODAY—TOMORROW

In the early days of our country, cooking was a domestic chore. Then, as the country expanded, inns were opened to accommodate travelers. When villages and towns expanded, community ovens were built, which were tended to by the village baker. The first commercial bakery opened in Plymouth, Massachusetts, in 1640 and was operated by English and European bakers. Europe had established culinary and baking guilds as well as apprentice systems for training journeymen cooks and bakers. European-trained chefs immigrated to the United States and formed ethnic chefs associations, which provided a steady stream of chefs, cooks, and bakers to hotels and restaurants in larger cities. Over time these chefs left the hotels and restaurants to open their own family businesses.

In the American home in the eighteenth, nineteenth, and early twentieth centuries, cooking was still generally a domestic chore. Families dined together each evening, with special dinners on Sundays and holidays. There was a lack of mechanical equipment and no convenience foods. Cooking and baking were very physical, requiring strength and stamina, but the joy of these dinners inspired many young men and women to develop a passion for the hospitality industry. Unlike Europe, where there was an apprentice system, work was hard to find, and most had to start as dishwashers, prep persons, or servers. In the 1930s there were only three vocational high schools teaching culinary and baking. These schools were in New York City, Chicago, and Detroit. In 1929 the American Culinary Federation was formed in New York City. The association membership once again was mostly European-trained chefs, but unlike other chefs associations, it embraced Americans who had not completed an apprenticeship. This was the first opportunity for Americans to be mentored by European-trained chefs.

After two world wars, the American household changed. During the war effort many women went to work, leaving less time for domestic chores. They purchased bread, pies, and precooked foods, and they dined in luncheonettes and restaurants more often. The five years following World War II created an economic expansion and opportunity for soldiers returning home. America experienced a new prosperity: two incomes in each household. Two-income families doing fewer domestic chores led to the growth of the food service industry; many domestic chores were replaced by purchases at restaurants, hotels, clubs, bakeries, and food markets. There is little wonder why up until 1972 cooks and bakers were listed as domestic in the dictionary of occupational trades. The American Culinary Federation was a major force in the United States Department of Labor's changing the listing in 1972 to professional.

Recognizing that the apprentice and guild system was not working in America, Francis Roth, an attorney from New Haven, Connecticut, obtained a government grant to train returning World War II Veterans. On May 22, 1946, the New Haven Restaurant School opened in New Haven, Connecticut. Three years later Katherine Angel, the wife of James Roland Angel, President of Yale University, secured five acres on the Yale Campus. It was named the Restaurant Institute of Connecticut, and in 1951 it became The Culinary Institute of America.

In the 1950s and 1960s, the U.S. population continued to grow and become more diverse. Vocational secondary schools provided strong fundamental education in the culinary arts, and postsecondary schools trained many cooks and bakers. The period from the 1970s to the year 2000 would provide great opportunities for young culinarians. Throughout America hundreds of high schools and colleges started offering a culinary education; this formal education replaced the European apprentice system. These schools taught culinary fundamentals and hospitality skills needed to keep pace with America's expanding market basket and menu diversity. The establishment of organized training programs gave professional recognition to cooks and bakers. In world competitions American teams finished consistently in the top three. Certification programs were developed to verify skill levels in cooking and baking. Colleges and universities offered advanced degrees in managerial skills, which helped to improve the work environment. Every American with a passion for cooking and baking could obtain the knowledge to become a professional chef.

Chefs in the future will face many challenges. The chef will need to develop skills in workforce management, providing a more harmonious and productive environment, less-demanding work schedules, and improved salaries for entry level workers as well as adequate benefit packages. As the chef faces more competition and a demanding public, the key to profit will be utilization of food and resources, communications, and marketing. Together with these challenges will be more opportunities. Future chefs should begin their education and work experience in grades 9–12 at a technical high school, followed by two to three years of postsecondary schooling, five years work experience, and a baccalaureate degree in hospitality. During this training period they should travel as much as possible, studying local, regional, and international market baskets and menus, and developing tasting skills and knowledge by reading when travel is not possible. Grandiose opportunities may appear early in one's career, but caution is advised; build your career with a strong foundation of culinary fundamentals and a strong work ethic. It is estimated that you will have to stay in the workforce longer and will change your job three or four times during your career, which is much different from yesterday's chefs, who often spent thirty to forty years with one company. The twenty-first century will provide great opportunity for those chefs who are properly trained.

—Chef Noble Masi, CMB, CEPC,
CCE, AAC, HOF,
Culinary Institute of America, Hyde Park, NY

DEFINITION OF SUPERVISION

Simply put, a **supervisor** is anyone in the position of directing the work of others and who has the authority that goes with this responsibility. The legal status is defined by the federal Taft-Hartley Act (1947), which states that a supervisor is

> . . . any individual having authority, in the interest of the employer, to hire, transfer, suspend, lay off, recall, promote, discharge, assign, reward or discipline other employees, or responsibility to direct them, or to adjust their grievances, or effectively to recommend such action, if in connection with the foregoing the exercise of such authority is not merely routine or clerical in nature, but requires the use of independent judgment.

The knowledge and skills required to be a successful chef supervisor fall into four broad skill categories. Those categories are personal, interpersonal, technical, and administrative.

To be a supervisor the chef needs the vision to know what to do. They need certain skills to know how to do it. The chef supervisor must have the ability to get it done by empowering other people to carry out quality standards of performance. The chef supervisor plans, organizes, communicates, trains, coaches, corrects, and leads. The chef must motivate the kitchen team to meet the company's goals and objectives. These goals and objectives are reached by supervising people in an effective and caring way. The supervisor accepts responsibility for providing a positive workplace. The chef provides the resources needed to achieve meals and service that meet and exceed customers' expectations every time.

Philip Crosby, a leading management expert, states that "in the final equation, the supervisor is the person the employee sees as the company. The type of work accomplished and the attendance maintained by employees are very much indications of their relationship with the supervisor."[1] Crosby suggests that a good supervisor can overcome, at least to some extent, the poor management practices of a weak company. At the other extreme, a weak supervisor can offset the good management practices of a good company.

Supervision is the act, not of controlling the staff members, but rather of directing, coaching, and supporting them. The chef's performance as supervisor is measured by a variety of factors. These factors include customer satisfaction and customer retention. The factors also include the kitchen staff's ability to carry out the workload to meet and exceed set standards of quality. Poor chef supervisory skills negatively affect the quality of the food produced and the work climate, all of which results in unhappy kitchen staff and customers. The outcome is high levels of employee turnover.

ATTRIBUTES OF THE SUCCESSFUL CHEF SUPERVISOR

Today's chef supervisor, in addition to being an excellent cook, must possess a strong personal inventory of personal and professional qualities. An example of the chef supervisor's *mise en place* of personal inventories is shown in Figure 1-1. Today's chef supervisor is still a take-charge individual, but approachable. The management style that works best for the chef supervisor is that of **coaching**. According to Bill Marvin, a respected restaurant consultant and author, "Coaches help bring out natural talent and measure their own success by the success achieved by their players."[2] In all good coaching, the coach, chef, tries to get the best possible performance from the team, staff, by motivating the team members. Communication and training also are critical components of coaching. The coach demonstrates respect for each team member. The coach manages, but also leads the team. The good coach maintains an acute awareness of each staff member's strengths and weaknesses. In the past, chefs were viewed as supervisors who ruled the kitchen with a rod of iron. Today the chef must lead, not just rule.

- Positive personal attitude
- Innovativeness in dealing with problems
- Honesty and sincerity
- Awareness of employee problems
- Respect and courtesy in communicating with employees
- Impeccable personal hygiene and grooming
- Technical competence
- High motivation with the ability to motivate others
- Consistency
- Assertive and action oriented
- Acceptance of diversity
- Ability to trust others
- Constant search for new ways to enhance skills
- Ability to praise others when deserved
- Leadership by example
- Team-building skills
- Loyalty to organizational goals and employees
- Ability to maintain control
- Good listening skills
- Desire to please customer
- Good persuasive skills and interest in imparting knowledge
- Love of cooking

Figure 1-1
Mise en place for the chef supervisor.

Chef supervisors need to be able to bring all these qualities to the workplace. Chefs must be able to coach and supervise under the pressures of busy meal service periods. The chef supervisor should have the ability to understand the feelings, attitudes, and motives of others. The chef must communicate effectively. Good relations with the kitchen team and all other departments in the company are critical. These attributes apply whether the chef is employed in a restaurant, hotel, institution, club, the military, education, or any other foodservice organization.

CHEF SUPERVISORY ROLE MODELS

Professionalism and ethics are essential in the chef supervisor. **Ethics** refers to the moral principles of individuals and society. **Professionalism** is the conduct or actions that characterize a profession positively. Together with professionalism, ethics is concerned with the determination of right and wrong in human behavior. The actions of the chef supervisor affect the staff being supervised and the management of the property. Equally important, the chef supervisor's actions affect the health and safety of the public being served. Although the effect of the chef supervisor's actions can be positive or negative, "Ethical behavior is recognized as resulting in good business with increased profits and reduced turnover."[3]

An **ethical code of professional practice** is necessary for both employees and supervisors. According to Jernigan, "It serves as a framework in which various other standards can be evaluated."[4] Professional practices include policies. A **policy** is a statement of how the individual is to handle specific matters. Policies are created by companies to address a number of issues. The issues include the areas of hiring or firing and confidentiality. Policies are also created to address stealing and lying. A major concern in policy making is any action that causes the loss of human dignity. Actions in this area can include malicious gossip; harassment; and racial, gender, or ethnic slurs.

The chef supervisor should establish a code of professional practice. This code must be applied fairly and without bias to all employees regardless of their position, gender, and ethnic or religious backgrounds.

History has provided us with examples of outstanding chef supervisors as role models. These chefs are known for their culinary ability and advancement of culinary art. They advanced culinary art through new gastronomic creations, techniques of cooking, improvements in kitchen design, and contributions in nutrition. Besides being culinary inspirations, they also were excellent managers and leaders. They practiced a high level of professionalism and were supervisors, trainers, and coaches. Consequently, the legacy of these chefs goes beyond their food. They are true role models for the chef of today.

Antoine Carême, one of 25 children, was born of poor parents in France in 1784. It is generally believed that he was placed in the kitchen as a scullion (kitchen helper) between the ages of 7 and 10. He taught himself how to read and write, and went on to write several books before his death at the age of 50. From his writings we get a sense of his professionalism. Describing a banquet, he provides a glimpse of the awful working conditions chefs had to endure at that time:

> Imagine yourself in a large kitchen such as that of the Foreign Minister at the moment of a great banquet [Talleyrand was Foreign Minister at the time]. There one sees twenty chefs at their urgent occupations, coming, going, moving with speed in this cauldron of heat. Look at the great mass of live charcoal, a cubic meter for the cooking of the soups, the sauces, the ragouts, the frying and the bain maries. Add to that the heap of burning coals in front of which bears a sirloin weighing 45–60 lbs, and another two for fowl and game. In this furnace everyone moves with tremendous speed; not a sound is heard; only the chef has the right to make himself heard, and at the sound of his voice everyone obeys. He concludes by saying, . . . "Honor commands, we must obey even though physical strength fails. But, it is the burning charcoal which kills us."[5]

Carême's power and influence is due not only to his writings and culinary creations, which still survive today, but also to his character and personality. His professionalism throughout his life asserted a new prestige for the chef. He was an innovator and simplifier who demonstrated all the elements of an outstanding chef leader and supervisor.

Alexis Soyer, born in 1809, lived almost exactly as long as the great Carême. Soyer was the chef at London's Reform Club for many years. While there, he was sent by the British government to Ireland during the potato famine to establish soup kitchens. He donated funds from these kitchens to charitable work. He also gained fame by traveling to the Crimea during the war there between the British, French, Russians, and Ottoman Turks. While in the Crimea, he worked with the famous nurse Florence Nightingale to improve food preparation for the troops. In addition, he authored cookbooks priced for the poorer classes. He invented a military cooking stove that was still in use during World War II. Soyer was an outstanding example of a chef leader. He could hold his own among the professional class of his time by his personal qualities as much as by his culinary skills. He helped to further enhance the image of the chef through his writings and his superb organizational skills and leadership abilities.

Auguste Escoffier, known as the "King of Chefs" and the "Chef of Kings," dominated the first quarter of the twentieth century. He continues to influence chefs and the culinary arts to this day. Escoffier is perhaps still the greatest role model for chefs as a culinarian. He was a chef supervisor and coach who cared about his staff. He was a man whose talents dovetailed into the trends of his times.

Economic and social forces were changing in the early part of the twentieth century, as were the dining and drinking habits of society. Escoffier was in tune with the

- Moved the kitchen out of its traditional location in the basement
- Created the *partie* system
- Insisted on the highest standards of personal hygiene from all staff
- Required that cooks wear the newly fashioned jacket and check pants
- Discouraged his staff from smoking and drinking
- Advocate of education
- Strongly supported schooling for employees
- Proponent of lifelong learning
- Began the standardization of recipes

Figure 1-2
Beliefs and innovations of Escoffier.

needs of his time. He was prepared to go with trends and appreciated the importance of anticipating them. He refined and simplified classic cuisine, and he also created dishes that have become part of classic cuisine.

Escoffier was a pioneer in the movement toward what Chef Casey Sinkledam would later term "simple but elegant." He believed in the simple concept that food should look and taste like food. Escoffier applied his beliefs to his kitchen and brought about change that helped to shape the modern kitchen. It was he who created the "partie system." This system streamlined the work flow and processes of the foodservice industry. Some of his beliefs and innovations are shown in Figure 1-2.

Escoffier's book *Le Guide Culinaire* is still one of the most widely respected textbooks for professional chefs. In the foreword of his text he states:

". . . the more one learns the more one sees the need to learn more and that study, as well as broadening the mind of the craftsman, provides an easy way of perfecting himself in the practice of our art."[6]

Having started his career at the age of 12 (in 1859), Escoffier retired from active duty at the Carlton in London in 1921. He was then 74 years old and had practiced his art for over 62 years.

Ferdinand Metz has influenced how food is prepared around the globe today. Chef Metz was president of the Culinary Institute of America (CIA) from 1980 to 2001. He initiated the development of extensive educational and training programs for aspiring culinarians in the United States and around the world. He was a leader in the establishment of apprenticeship and certification in the United States. In 2010, Chef Metz became chairman of the National Advisory Board and Executive Dean at Le Cordon Bleu Schools of North America.

Chef Metz, through his work at the CIA and his activities in the American Culinary Federation, the National Restaurant Association Educational Foundation, the World Association of Chefs Societies, and other organizations, has been a major factor in the elevation of the culinary profession around the world. He was the manager of the American Culinary Olympic Team and led it to three consecutive world championships. In 1995, *Nation's Restaurant News* named Chef Metz as one of the fifty most influential people in the industry. He has, by example, established that the chef is a professional, an educator, and a business person.

Chef Metz has been recognized in many ways for his contributions to the profession. He is the recipient of both the James Beard and the American Culinary Federation Lifetime Achievement Awards and is a member of the National Restaurant Association Educational Foundation's College of Diplomates. As an author and speaker, he continues to be a leader in the culinary profession.

WHAT IS THIS BUSINESS?
CAN ANYONE EVER BE OVERQUALIFIED?

The obvious answer to this question is, of course, a resounding NO. An individual may sometimes have more qualifications than a current responsibility demands, but surely can never be overqualified in anticipation of future career opportunities. Consequently, it would seem prudent to take advantage of every opportunity that presents itself, whether it is convenient at the time or not.

This is easier said than done, but it is exactly the path that the author of this text, Dr. Jerald Chesser, and I took.

Dr. Chesser realized early on that today's chefs need more credentials, both in the area of experience as well as academics. I am sure that it was not easy for the author, a certified chef on several levels, to earn an Ed.D., which made him unique among his peers.

In my case, when I joined the H.J. Heinz Company's R&D department, I enjoyed, for the first time in my life, regular "office" hours. Rather than becoming spoiled by this newfound luxury, I enrolled at the University of Pittsburgh and earned a baccalaureate and a master's degree in business administration over a seven-year period.

Nonetheless, I did not neglect my responsibilities at Heinz and to the Pittsburgh Chefs Association, as we established the national models for today's Certification, Apprenticeship, and Master Chef certification programs. In addition, managing the U.S. Culinary Olympic Team and my own Gourmet Cooking School understandably kept my plate full.

As the result of all these activities, in the early 1980s I was the only person in the United States who was a Certified Master Chef and had an MBA. These credentials and others gave me the opportunity to lead the R&D department of a global company and later to assume the presidency of the Culinary Institute of America, which I held for over 22 years. My earning of additional credentials was never motivated by the goal of heading up the most prestigious culinary school in the country; rather, it was the uniqueness of my qualifications that qualified me for that position.

Students who have the opportunity to combine a specialized craft with academic credentials make themselves more valuable in their chosen field and gain a broader and more inclusive perspective for themselves. It is not by accident that many academic institutions today have come to value the concept of a SPECIALIZED LIBERAL ARTS program, which recognizes the need for specific skills combined with academic credentials.

—Ferdinand Metz, MBA, CMC, AAC, HOF
Executive Dean, Le Cordon Bleu Schools of North America

Paul Bocuse is considered one of the finest chefs of the twentieth century. He continues in the twenty-first century to influence cuisine and food preparation. He was one of the founders of the *nouvelle cuisine* movement in France in the 1970s. This cuisine is simpler and lower in calories than the traditional *haute cuisine*. *Nouvelle cuisine* stresses the importance of fresh ingredients of the highest quality. Chef Bocuse has influenced the preparation of food through a chain of brasseries (restaurants) under his license.

Chef Bocuse was one of the first chefs to make public appearances away from his restaurant to promote the preparation of food. He also has authored numerous books. In 1987 he established the Bocuse d'Or. The Bocuse d'Or is considered one of the most prestigious culinary awards in the world today. Through his extensive endeavors, Chef Bocuse has had a major impact on culinarians of today.

To be a leader in any profession, it is necessary to model a high standard of ethics and professional practice. Food workers who lack ethics and professionalism are a threat. They are a threat to the image of the foodservice industry. More importantly, they are a threat to the health and safety of the public. True culinary professionalism will always embrace high ethical standards.

DUTIES AND FUNCTIONS OF THE CHEF SUPERVISOR

In the past, chef supervisors reported mainly to the food and beverage manager. In many foodservice establishments, this manager supervised all food and beverage operations. Kitchen operations were a major portion of this manager's responsibilities. The food and beverage manager, or some higher level of management, usually evaluated the chef supervisor. The criteria for evaluation were limited to achieving a targeted food cost percent and producing meals smoothly with a minimum of customer complaints. Provided that these criteria were achieved, the manner in which they were achieved was left up to the chef. The manager made all other major decisions. These included menu positioning as well as personnel decisions dealing with recruitment, orientation, training, and termination. Today, the responsibilities of both the chef and manager have changed. The duties of the chef as a supervisor have expanded to include personnel decisions.

The modern chef exercises greater decision-making power. With the power to make decisions comes greater responsibility. The chef must be more than a highly skilled culinarian. The chef must be a supervisor. This means the chef must be a coach who develops people. The chef also must be a team builder. Today's chef is part of the management team of the operation.

Traditionally, the chef supervisor was viewed as the person who supervised the foodservice operation from the back door to the front door. The supervisor's primary duty was overseeing the receipt of food products at the back door and then their processing into a customer meal at the front door. Quality human resources management involving the kitchen staff as a team was not a major concern. Consequently, this system was **authoritarian** by nature. Directives and orders were given with little or no input from employees and even less interest in what the customers had to say. The modern chef supervisor, however, is a team leader who exhibits a different style of management. This style of management is still focused on the kitchen but goes beyond food preparation.

The chef supervisor as an unreasonable, temperamental artist, as historically portrayed, has no place in the modern foodservice industry. In fact, this type of conduct never has had a place there, nor will it be tolerated by management or staff today. Foodservice workers, like other workers, need to be recognized as contributing team members. They want to know what their chef supervisor expects of them. As in other areas of industry, kitchen employees need a workplace where communication is frequent and encouraged. The employee needs a work place in which they can develop a sense of belonging. Even-handed and fair treatment is required from the chef supervisor. Employees want to give their best, so it's up to the chef supervisor to provide a work climate that helps them do so. This is vital because a chef supervisor's success depends on his or her staff.

The principal driving force behind the modern chef is customer satisfaction. Today's chef manages the culinary operation from the front door to the back door rather than the other way around. One of the main reasons customers stop coming to a foodservice establishment is an attitude of indifference by the staff. It makes little sense to prepare food that customers don't want. The chef should be aware of customers' preferences and be trained in all the contributing elements of customer satisfaction.

Supervising the functions involved in food production comprises many elements, some new, and others not. Many of these elements, such as rationalization, downsizing, risk management, yield management, management by objective, and so on, have swung with the pendulum of different management fads over the years. Several of them, however, remain part of a chef supervisor's arsenal of skills.

ELEMENTS OF KITCHEN SUPERVISION

Supervising

Supervision is concerned with the most effective and timely use of personnel and materials to achieve goals. The goals of the chef supervisor focus on customer satisfaction and retention. These goals are achieved by maintaining a highly motivated, well-trained kitchen team.

- Preparing new employee induction/orientation programs
- Assessing training needs
- Preparing training objectives
- Developing standards of performance
- Implementing standards of total quality
- Ongoing and continuous training and team building
- Coaching and correcting employees
- Setting high standards of personal hygiene and grooming
- Setting excellent standards of conduct and fairness
- Developing and encouraging teamwork
- Providing decisive leadership
- Building and fostering professional pride
- Providing timely employee feedback on performance
- Encouraging a desire to meet and exceed customer expectations
- Demonstrating a total quality respect for all kitchen team members

Figure 1-3
Elements of the chef supervisor's duties.

A major part of being a supervisor is clearing away obstacles and providing the resources the team needs to accomplish the declared goals and objectives. The goals and objectives must be clear and well defined. Another part of being a supervisor is the recruiting and interviewing of potential kitchen team members. Other elements of the chef supervisor's general duties are shown in Figure 1-3. In future chapters you will study the various elements of supervision.

Planning

Following the Allied Forces' successful invasion of Europe during World War II, it was suggested to General Dwight D. Eisenhower, the supreme commander of the successful invading forces, that he must have had an outstanding plan to have carried out such a massive operation. The operation involved moving thousands of men and equipment with all the ancillary support of materials and men. His response to this suggestion was most enlightening: "The plan is nothing, but planning is everything."[7]

A **plan** can be defined as a carefully considered and detailed program of action to achieve an end. The development of a plan that can be communicated and then executed requires three steps. The three steps are information gathering, analysis of the information, and development of the program of action. The process requires the supervisor to stop, look, and listen. This allows a broader and more long-term view of the current situation and potential future situation. Planning is very different from "firefighting." **Firefighting** is the solving of problems as they arise without consideration of the base cause of the problems. Firefighting does not achieve long-term goals. To plan, the supervisor must make the time to plan.

The chef supervisor obviously needs to plan menus, but this is only part of the chef supervisor's planning responsibilities. Extensive planning is required to run a smooth, efficient foodservice operation. The major areas of planning for the chef supervisor include:

- Setting and communicating standards of performance
- Communicating clear job expectations
- Determining training needs
- Planning and forecasting workloads
- Preparing employee work schedules

- Ascertaining guest satisfaction levels
- Planning equipment repair and replacements
- Determining food and supply inventories
- Developing employee empowerment programs
- Planning future personnel levels
- Providing effective communication with team members and other departments
- Conducting employee performance appraisals

The chef supervisor's execution of each of these areas of planning will have an impact on the success of the team and the operation.

Organizing

A quality plan is the basis for good organization. Good organization is needed to carry out a plan. One of the chef supervisor's key roles is the organizing of people and materials to succeed in completing the plan. This happens through good organizational ability on the part of the chef supervisor. Carrying out the plan requires using the available resources and being prepared to adapt as circumstances and conditions warrant. Typical organizational goals of a kitchen department include:

- Organizing the kitchen team to:
  - produce and serve meals in the most efficient, economical, and effective fashion
  - utilize each team member within a limited time period and within criteria of effort and productivity
- Defining job tasks, analyses, and descriptions
- Preparing task lists to accomplish the planned goals
- Determining relationships with each member of the kitchen team together with management, other departments, and customers
- Organizing support areas of purchasing, receiving, storage, and stewarding
- Organizing training sessions
- Organizing and implementing employee empowerment and reward systems
- Organizing and implementing recycling programs

Coaching

Coaching is the guiding, supporting, and correcting of kitchen staff to perform their jobs in a way compatible with the organization's goals and objectives. It means creating a workplace in which staff members feel comfortable enough to give their best. Good coaching requires excellent communication and leadership skills. More importantly, coaching requires chef supervisors who trust people. To succeed as a coach, a chef supervisor should be consistent and not subject to wild mood swings. The chef supervisor must work to be fair at all times. The chef supervisor must be firm in dealing with performance issues, when appropriate, yet still be approachable and friendly. As the link between management and staff members, the chef supervisor needs to believe in the "team" concept. A good coaching style involves:

- A positive people attitude
- An interest in helping people attain personal goals
- Respect for the dignity of every individual in the team
- Sincerity, honesty, fairness, and impartiality
- Sensitivity and respect for different cultures
- Strong ethical and moral values
- An emphasis on the future rather than the past
- Praise where praise is due
- Correction of mistakes without apportioning blame

Effective supervision requires adaptability combined with quality coaching. This combination will allow the team to succeed and consistently achieve guest satisfaction.

Team Building

Kitchen employees can be developed into teams with the help of a committed chef supervisor. In an effective kitchen team, each member has an assigned role. When the members integrate their skills to build on strengths and minimize weaknesses, foodservice quality objectives are assured. On the other hand, when members of the kitchen staff are poorly led and work as individuals, they often will fail. Unfortunately, many chef supervisors today fail to recognize their roles as team builders. In the past, many have not understood how to transform their employees into productive teams.

Teamwork is effective at all levels. It is just as important among top executives as among kitchen employees. If the chef supervisor does not place a high value on teamwork, it will not occur. Teamwork takes conscious effort to develop and continuous effort to maintain. Part of this maintenance is recognition of team performance through celebration of positive performance. There also must be acknowledgment of negative performance and assistance in correcting it. A team that is properly trained and is working in a positive environment will require less direct supervision. The team will not need to be micro-managed. Central to team building is investment in the individual and the team. The chef supervisor who ensures that the team has the training, equipment, and guidance to succeed will in fact experience success.

Communication

Communication is a basic and essential element of the supervision process. Supervision often breaks down or fails because of poor communication. All elements of supervision and management require effective communication. The challenge that must be

---

CHEF TALK
"COACHING"

Building a successful kitchen team requires a great deal of patience and a lot of time and effort. Ten years ago, when I took over at Harpoon Louie's (6 million dollars a year in sales), I found a kitchen staff without a single professional chef on board. My first step was to recruit four experienced chefs who had worked with me before and understood what needed to be done.

With the four on board, a foundation was set. The professional chef's uniform was mandatory for all kitchen cooks. The fryer cooks, broiler cooks, and all other cooks were terminated, and those who were interested in becoming professional chefs were rehired as apprentices. No specialized positions were offered until such time as all the cooks had become competent in all areas of the kitchen.

Hiring procedures were developed and implemented. Crucial to these new procedures was the hiring of kitchen team members who had a real and genuine interest in cooking. We started our formal apprenticeship program soon afterward under the auspices of the American Culinary Federation Educational Institute.

Constant coaching, in-house cooking classes, and encouragement of our apprentices to compete in professional chef competitions were key to bonding the team together. Once the team was in place and working, employee retention became a priority. As common in other establishments, financial reward alone does not guarantee retention. It is vital to be sympathetic to the needs of the team, which can be very demanding, but with careful motivation a team spirit can be maintained.

Respect is key. It has a tremendous bearing on what type of coach you are. Unskilled employees in the kitchen are a vital part of the foodservice operations. How these team members are treated has a dramatic impact on their performance level. The coach must be sure to communicate with these team members on a regular basis—coaching, correcting, and offering words of encouragement. Chefs who have to wash their own pots know how important their team members are and have a great deal of respect for them. I very clearly see myself as a coach rather than a manager. Today's kitchen staff should be led rather than managed or directed. Without a team approach at our restaurant, we would not be successful.

—Kenneth G. Wade, CEC, AAC, Chef/Owner, PaddyMacs, Palm Beach, FL

addressed is the difference that often exists between what is said and what is heard. The communication process involves a sender and a receiver exchanging and understanding information so that the information can be received and understood.

Communication is the foundation for understanding, cooperation, and action. A good communication system maintains a two-way flow of ideas, opinions, information, and decisions. The first step in any effort to open communication is to establish and maintain a climate that encourages the free exchange of ideas. It is the umbrella under which all effective supervision lies.

Delegation

Delegation means granting to a kitchen team member the authority to oversee specific tasks and responsibilities. This includes letting other team members know that these responsibilities have been delegated to this team member. Just telling a team member to perform a task is not delegation; it is assigning work. Assigning work may be sufficient for simple, short-term jobs, but more complex tasks that require a sustained effort should be delegated.

Before delegating, the chef supervisor should answer the following questions:

- Does the team member understand the purpose of the task?
- Is the value of the task recognized by the team member?
- Is the workload too much for just one person?
- Has the employee been provided with detailed, step-by-step instructions?
- Has the employee been given the resources needed to accomplish the task?
- How will satisfactory completion of the tasks be evaluated and measured?

Chef supervisors should not "delegate" those portions of their work they consider unpleasant, unimportant, or risky. Kitchen team members are seldom deceived by the chef supervisor's efforts to "dress up" the task. What usually results from such a practice is resentment, and the team member's motivation to do the task will decrease. The end result is often a team member trying to avoid or off-load the task.

In addition, before delegating, it is useful to consider:

- Is there acceptance and understanding of the task?
- Has a reason for the delegation been given?
- Is the task being delegated a worthwhile and whole task?
- Can the team member be trusted and encouraged to do the job correctly?
- Have checkpoints been built in to check progress?
- Has knowledge been shared by pinpointing possible problems?
- Has information been withheld that could have simplified and speeded up the task?
- Have sufficient training, encouragement, coaching, and leadership been provided to make the team member look good and succeed?

Delegation by the chef supervisor encourages cooperation among kitchen team members. It demonstrates trust in the team while building morale. The advantage of delegating is that the workload is spread in a planned, orderly way. It allows more time for creating and planning. The chef supervisor who tries to do everything personally will not succeed. The support of the kitchen team is essential. It is impossible for a chef supervisor to prepare, cook, and present every meal every day. The chef supervisor who fails to delegate to other team members will be frustrated, unproductive, and viewed as a weak leader by the entire kitchen team.

Empowerment and Ownership

Empowerment is the process of enabling people to do what they have been trained for and are qualified to do. Empowerment leads to a feeling of ownership. A team member who has a feeling of ownership—a personal stake in the operation—will work harder to make the operation a success. Empowering kitchen team members to take more initiative is an important part of team building. It is a basic piece of quality supervision and management. There is no better way to create a shared vision and to generate commitment and loyalty than through empowerment and the feeling of ownership. The goal is a team member who has "buy-in." This is when the team member feels they have had a part in creating the vision of the company. They believe there is respect for their ideas. The team member feels the chef supervisor recognizes their contribution to the company's success. The "buy-in" will lead to continuous improvement and innovation.

In 1992 and in 1999, the Ritz-Carlton Hotel Company won the Malcolm Baldrige National Quality Award. The Ritz-Carlton is the only hotel company to date (2011) to have been awarded this prize. Part of their winning strategy in 1992 was called "applied employee empowerment." According to Horst Shulze, the Ritz-Carlton's chief operating officer, "all our employees are empowered to do whatever it takes to provide instant pacification. No matter what their normal duties are, other employees must assist if aid is requested by a fellow worker responding to a guest's complaint or wish."[8] When the Ritz-Carlton won the award in 1999, as part of the company's employee empowerment program, every employee was empowered to spend up to $2000 to immediately correct a problem or handle a complaint.[9]

The biggest challenge to the concept of empowerment and ownership is its acceptance by chef supervisors. The position of chef has long been associated with power and control. This concept is changing now and will continue to change in the future. Team building and employee "buy-in" have become key components of supervision and management throughout the hospitality industry and in many kitchens.

Sanitation

Food safety is clearly an important issue for the chef supervisor. According to a Centers for Disease Control and Prevention (CDCP) study, in 2007 there were 1097 foodborne illness outbreaks resulting in 21,244 cases of foodborne illness and 18 deaths.[10] This study only addressed outbreaks, which means incidents where two or more people were involved. In a previous report, the CDCP indicated that over 6 million people become ill from contaminated food annually in the United States, and almost 80 percent of these illnesses occur at foodservice establishments. Sanitation must be a front-of-the-mind consideration for everyone involved in the preparation and service of food. Supervisors must have up-to-date knowledge of sanitation regulations and procedures, both local and national.

One food safety and self-inspection system that the chef supervisor should be thoroughly familiar with is the **Hazard Analysis Critical Control Point**, more commonly known as **HACCP**. There are many chances in the flow of food preparation and service for food to become contaminated. The HACCP system targets these areas. By emphasizing high-risk foods and handling procedures, the chef supervisor can reduce the risk of food contamination. You can learn more about HACCP at the Food and Drug Administration website, http://www.cfsan.fda.gov/~lrd/haccp.html.

It is important for the chef supervisor to adopt a proactive position regarding sanitation. All foodservice workers are potential disease spreaders. This fact requires the chef supervisor to analyze the procedures involved in every aspect of the operation. These include food receiving, preparation, cooking, and storage of food leftovers. The baseline must be effective supervision of sanitation. The chef supervisor needs to look at the foodservice operation through a customer's eye, determining what sanitation messages are being sent and regularly checking to make sure the kitchen team is clean and well groomed. Initial training and regular refresh courses in the prevention of food contamination need to be provided. This important aspect of the duties of the chef supervisor requires constant attention.

Safety

One goal of excellent foodservice operation is to reduce the possibility of accidents in the kitchen. Accident prevention works best when it involves the participation and cooperation of all kitchen team members. A safety program should have incentives to encourage the entire team to work safely. Rewards may be given to kitchen team members who remain accident-free. The issue of safety needs to be incorporated into orientation and training programs. Its importance needs to be stressed and emphasized on a continuous basis. Supervisors must have up-to-date knowledge of safety policies and Occupational Safety and Health Administration (OSHA) policies affecting the operation.

Technology

The chef supervisor must stay ahead of technological advances in equipment and machinery in order to be competitive and focused. Innovations in labor-saving devices and training devices appear each year. Computer-managed information programs for the kitchen, which allow the chef supervisor to give greater focus to all aspects of supervision, are improved constantly.

Leadership

Leadership styles and skills are vital to making all the factors and elements of supervision in the kitchen work. These two areas have a major impact on the quality of supervision.

THE CONCEPT OF AUTHORITY

The chef supervisor is the formal leader of the group because of the **authority** of the position. A chef's supervisory success, however, depends on more than this source of authority. Success as a supervisor depends on many skills. A high level of team-building skill is critical to the ability of the chef supervisor. It is this skill that makes it possible to increase the kitchen's team productivity and job satisfaction. When team-building skills are applied rather than just the authority of position, employees cooperate more with each other and with other departments. Staff members develop better interpersonal relationships, and team spirit is generated. As John Maxwell states in his book on leadership, "The only thing a title can buy is a little time either to increase your level of influence with others or erase it."[11]

The proper and effective use of authority:

- Requires an obedience in which employees retain their freedom
- Strikes a balance between authority and individual freedom
- Leads individuals toward growth
- Involves practical judgment skills
- Acts as a uniting element of a group's common goals
- Enhances cooperative efforts
- Reserves the right and power to make decisions

For authority to be genuine, chef supervisors exercising that authority must know what they are requesting of team members and why they are making those requests. Authority for the sake of power is useless. The chef supervisor must seek to inspire desired outcomes from each person. Requests or demands made on employees without good reason often lead to anger and frustration on the part of both the employee and the chef supervisor. Remember, kitchen team members will respond more freely to a request than they will to an order.

THE EVOLUTION OF SUPERVISION

Supervision has evolved over the past century. This evolution was based to a great extent on knowledge gained initially from two sources: the Hawthorne studies and the Likert studies.

The Hawthorne Studies

Begun in the 1920s, the Hawthorne studies represented an effort to determine what effect hours of work, periods of rest, and lighting might have on worker fatigue and productivity. These experiments were conducted by university professors Elton Mayo, Fritz Roethlisberger, and J. W. Dickson at the Western Electric Company's Hawthorne Works near Chicago, Illinois. These studies represented one of the first endeavors to evaluate employee productivity. The Hawthorne studies revealed that the attitudes employees had toward management, their work group, and the work itself significantly affected their productivity. Initially, the results of the research on the small study group baffled the researchers. Despite altering the work environment and measuring productivity against this changing environment (reducing rest periods and eliminating rest time), the productivity of the study group increased continuously. The group had fewer sick days than did other workers who were not in the research group.

The leaders of the research group concluded that productivity increased, not as a result of any of their contrived stimuli, but rather as a result of the absence of any authoritarian supervision and of the interest shown in employees by the researchers. The mere fact that the workers were being studied was sufficient for them to improve their productivity. This phenomenon is still referred to by researchers as the **Hawthorne effect**: Change will occur simply because people know they are being studied, rather than as a result of some form of treatment. The most important conclusion of the Hawthorne studies, however, was that people respond better when they have a sense of belonging.

The findings of the Hawthorne studies produced a new direction for "people management." As a result of these studies, greater emphasis was placed on managing employees, with concern for them as individuals. The studies also focused attention on the need for managers and supervisors to improve their communication skills and become more sensitive to employees' needs and feelings. This new movement also emphasized the need to develop more participative, employee-centered supervision.

Likert Studies

In the 1940s, Renis Likert conducted research into the creation of a productive and desirable work climate. He observed four approaches to supervision and leadership.[12] The first type was an authoritarian approach that was potentially explosive. It placed high pressure on subordinates through work standards and obtained compliance through fear. This approach resulted in high productivity over short periods, but low productivity and high absenteeism over longer periods. The second approach was authoritarian but benevolent in nature. The third approach was a consultative supervisor/employee approach. The fourth approach was group participation in which the supervisor was supportive and used group methods of supervision, including group decision making. The last three approaches yielded high productivity, low waste, and low costs, along with low absenteeism and low employee turnover.

Likert also developed the "linking pin" concept that focused on coordinating efforts through layers of middle management. It provided a formal, structured approach. Central to its philosophy was the idea that each level of management is a member of a multifunctional team that includes the next upward level.

Supervision in kitchens, and often in restaurants in general, has been authoritarian in nature. The Hawthorne and Likert research make it clear that authoritarian-style leadership and supervision are not the most effective. Authoritarian conduct by the supervisor does not deliver productivity. It does not create the positive workplace that results in high productivity of quality products and great guest service. Today's chef supervisor must be what Merritt calls a *Theory Y manager*.[13] This is a manager who believes that people not only want to do a good job but also thrive when supported and encouraged to grow.

CONCLUSIONS

The end of the twentieth century was a very exciting time for the U.S. foodservice industry. The economy was strong, with rapid job growth. These good times brought about a change in American dining habits and a higher level of gastronomic sophistication. People were traveling more and consequently gained more exposure to different cuisines. The chef as a leader, supervisor, and manager became the norm rather than the exception.

This professional evolution was supported by the growth of culinary education programs in the United States from a handful to hundreds. Culinary education matured and encompassed all levels from K–12 to university. This growth was fueled by the glamour and prestige that began to be associated with the culinary profession and the chef. There was a corresponding increase in professional associations for chefs. These associations, such as the American Culinary Federation, Research Chefs Association, International Association of Culinary Professionals, American Personal and Private Chef Association, and others, encouraged the exchange of ideas and information. They promoted life-long learning and professional development through education and certification programs.

The successful chef now had to possess additional skills, along with a new attitude to food production that had to be customer-driven and focused on quality. The chef became a supervisor and leader. They became someone who created a motivational kitchen environment with a team culture. Chefs recognized the need for trained and educated team members and supported the growth of programs for culinary training and education in the United States.

The successful chef in the first decade of the twenty-first century is a supervisor and leader as well as a good culinarian. Today's chef values training, education, diversity, individual initiative, and team cohesiveness. The chef of today has evolved from a domestic to a professional and from a chief to a manager. This evolution is not complete. As the food industry changes, the role of the chef will continue to evolve. Those who constantly pursue knowledge will help to shape the changes rather than just react to the changes that are always part of progress.

Chef supervisors have responsibilities to senior management, customers, and other team members. Understanding the different elements of the chef supervisor's role will make it easier to refocus efforts toward creating a motivational environment in the kitchen. Experience has shown that establishing a team culture in the kitchen results in a feeling of ownership by the team members, which is the foundation for a quality-conscious staff.

As you study the rest of this text, remember that the goal is to be the best possible chef supervisor, and this requires far more than just cooking good food.

SUMMARY

The modern chef supervisor's skill sets include the abilities to coach and lead the entire kitchen team by creating a motivational environment. Successful chef supervisors see themselves as facilitators and enablers whose job is to develop the kitchen team. This means demonstrating attributes that include an understanding of feelings and attitudes that motivate the entire kitchen team. The attributes that a successful chef supervisor demonstrates are shown in Figure 1-4.

- Practice a code of ethics and administer this code fairly and without bias to all kitchen team members
- Emulate the outstanding chef role models that history has provided
- Be a customer satisfaction–driven professional
- Know, understand, and apply the elements of supervision and know how these elements interrelate with the foodservice organization's goals, the other departments, and the kitchen team
- Know and understand the various steps in planning, organizing, coaching, team building, communicating, delegating, empowering, safety, sanitation, leadership, and technology
- Separate and know the concepts of authority, power, and leadership

Figure 1-4
Attributes of the successful chef supervisor.

The professional development of a culinarian, particularly one who desires to be a chef, has evolved from purely the skills of the craft to inclusion of the principles of supervision, management, and leadership. This evolution has occurred against the emerging development of the human resources management movement, from Hawthorne to Likert.

DISCUSSION QUESTIONS

1. Define the following chapter key terms:
   a. Chef
   b. Chef supervisor
   c. Supervisor
   d. Coaching
   e. Ethics
   f. Professionalism
   g. Ethical code of professional practice
   h. Policy
   i. Authoritarian
   j. Supervision
   k. Plan
   l. Firefighting
   m. Communication
   n. Delegation
   o. Empowerment
   p. HACCP
   q. Authority
   r. Hawthorne effect

2. List and explain the functions of the chef supervisor's job.
3. What skills and attributes do you consider important for the chef supervisor's success?
4. Discuss the Hawthorne and Likert studies and their importance to learning how to be a chef supervisor.
5. Why is an ethical code of conduct critical to a chef supervisor's job?
6. What is meant by the concept of front-door to back-door management as it relates to the chef supervisor's job?
7. What are the elements of kitchen supervision? Describe them.
8. What are the benefits of team building and empowerment within the foodservice industry?
9. What is the concept of authority?
10. What is meant by the evolution of the chef with regard to supervisory positions?
11. How does the chef supervisor's role affect management, team members, and customer satisfaction?

NOTES

1. Philip Crosby, *Quality Is Free* (New York: McGraw-Hill, 1978), 111.
2. Bill Marvin, *Coaching Skills* http://www.restaurantdoctor.com/articles/coaching.html#ixzz1HMhqtqWr
3. Christine Lynn, *Teaching Ethics* (November, 2007). www2.nau.edu/~clj5/Ethics/Teaching%20Ethics.doc
4. Anna Katherine Jernigan, *The Effective Foodservice Supervisor* (Rockville, MD: Aspen, 1989), 213.
5. *Larousse Gastronomique* (London: Hamlyn, 1971), 303.
6. August Escoffier, *Le Guide Culinaire* (New York: Mayflower Books, 1921), x.

7. Peggy Anderson, ed., *Great Quotes from Great Leaders* (Lombard, IL: Carrier Press, 1989), 52.

8. Ritz Carlton publicity pamphlet, The Ritz Carlton Co., Boston, MA, 1993.

9. Ibid.

10. Centers for Disease Control and Prevention, *Morbidity and Mortality Weekly Report: Surveillance for Foodborne Disease Outbreaks—United States, 2007.* 59(31): 973–979, http://www.cdc.gov/mmwr/preview/mmwrhtml/mm5931a1.htm?s_cid=mm5931a1_w

11. John C. Maxwell, *The 21 Irrefutable Laws of Leadership: Follow Them and People Will Follow You* (Nashville, TN: Thomas Nelson Publishers, 1998), 14.

12. Arthur Sherman, George Bohlander, and Herbert Crudden, *Managing Human Resources,* 8th ed. (Cincinnati, OH: South-Western, 1988), 352.

13. Dr. Edward Merritt, Strategic *Leadership: Essential Concepts* (Chula Vista, CA: Aventine Press, 2008).

Chapter 2
Legal Aspects

OBJECTIVES

When you complete this chapter, you should be able to:

1. Discuss and describe laws relative to the relationship between employers and unions
2. Discuss and describe laws related to fair labor standards
3. Discuss and describe the laws administered by the Equal Employment Opportunity Commission
4. Discuss and describe the Americans with Disabilities Act
5. Discuss and describe laws related to immigration

Case Study: Paul's Bar & Grill

Paul's Bar & Grill is a bar and restaurant located in the Good Night Inn in downtown St. Clair. It is operated by the Paul Bryant Group, which has other properties in a number of the downtown hotels. The business has over 100 full-time employees.

Camilla worked full-time at the Paul's Bar & Grill for 18 months as a line cook. She became pregnant and requested from her supervisor a 12-week leave of absence beginning 4 weeks before her due date. The supervisor granted the leave.

Camilla left her job 4 weeks before her due date as agreed. The delivery went well, and she had a healthy baby girl. Two weeks before her leave was to end she called the supervisor and informed him she would be returning to work as agreed. The supervisor informed her that she could come back to work, but the only job he had open was a dishwasher position at a lower wage. Camilla thanked him and hung up.

The Paul Bryant Group received a notice from John Liu, an attorney, that Camilla was filling a lawsuit against the company.

Based on what you have learned from previous chapters and the content of this chapter, answer the following questions.

- What basis might Camilla have for a lawsuit against the Paul Bryant Group?
- What role did supervision/management play in this situation?
- What specific steps could have been taken to avoid the current situation?
- What, specifically, can be done to overcome the challenges and generate motion in a positive direction for the Paul Bryant Group?

INTRODUCTION

As stated in the previous chapter, "Chef supervisors have responsibilities to senior management, customers, and other team members. Understanding the different elements of the chef supervisor's role will make it easier to refocus efforts toward creating a motivational environment in the kitchen." An element of great importance is the law. A chef supervisor, while not a lawyer, must be sufficiently familiar with the law to ensure that the rights of the employee and the employer are protected. What is commonly referred to as **labor law** has existed in the United States from the establishment of the country. In 1791, Philadelphia carpenters successfully went on strike for a 10-hour work day and overtime pay. Then, almost fifty years later, in 1840, President Van Buren declared a 10-hour work day for federal employees on public works. This is just one historic example of how movements in society can be reflected in government policy and law. It is in the last few decades, however, that the number of labor laws has drastically increased. Today's chef supervisor must understand and have a solid knowledge of the multiple laws that now govern employees and employers in the United States. The laws discussed in this chapter are only the most prominent ones. They are not all the laws relative to labor and employers, and new laws are constantly being instituted. Consequently, the chef supervisor must stay current to be effective.

THE LAWS[1]

National Labor Relations Act (Wagner Act) (1935)

This act was created to establish a national policy of encouraging collective bargaining, guaranteeing certain employee rights, and detailing specific employer unfair labor practices. The act set up the **National Labor Relations Board** (NLRB) to enforce these provisions. The NLRB has the power to investigate, dismiss charges or hold hearings, issue cease and desist orders, or pursue cases via Circuit Courts of Appeals or the U.S. Supreme Court. The National Labor Relations Act (NLRA) applies to private employers, their employees, and unions.

Labor-Management Relations Act (Taft-Hartley Act) (1947)

This act is an expansion and refinement of the NLRA. The act established control of labor disputes on a new basis by enlarging the NLRB and providing that the union or the employer must, before terminating a collective-bargaining agreement, serve notice on the other party and on a government mediation service. The government was empowered to obtain an 80-day injunction against any strike that it deemed a peril to national health or safety. The act also prohibited jurisdictional strikes (disputes between unions over which should act as the bargaining agent for the employees) and secondary boycotts (boycotts against an already organized company doing business with another company that a union is trying to organize), declared that it did not extend protection to workers on wildcat strikes, outlawed the closed shop, and permitted the union shop only on a vote of a majority of the employees. Most of the collective bargaining provisions were retained, with the extra provision that a union, before using the facilities of the LRB, must file with the U.S. Dept. of Labor financial reports and affidavits that the union officers are not Communists.

Labor-Management Reporting and Disclosure Act (Landrum-Griffin) (1959)

This act provided additional regulation of unions. It also guaranteed certain rights to all union members. These rights, referred to as the union members' "Bill of Rights," are:

- Equal rights to participate in union activities
- Freedom of speech and assembly
- Voice in setting rates of dues, fees, and assessments
- Protection of the right to sue
- Safeguards against improper discipline

The Office of Labor-Management Standards (OLMS) of the U.S. Department of Labor administers and enforces most provisions of the LMRDA.

These laws, while not strictly related to unions, make it clear that supervision in a unionized operation requires knowledge beyond that needed for a nonunion operation. Supervision in the broadest sense is the same, no matter what the operation, but because supervision is localized to a particular property and company, the knowledge required can change. Union representation of the workforce is a variable that requires additional knowledge for effective supervision.

Fair Labor Standards Act (1938)

The Fair Labor Standards Act (FLSA), as amended by 29 United States Code (USC) β201 et seq., 29 Code of Federal Regulations (CFR) Parts 510–794,[2] establishes minimum wage, overtime pay, recordkeeping, and child labor standards affecting full-time and part-time workers in the private sector and in federal, state, and local governments. The FLSA is administered by the Employment Standards Administration's Wage and Hour Division within the U.S. Department of Labor. The act contains numerous sections and specifications. Some of the most common and broadly applied ones are discussed below.

- Covered, nonexempt workers are entitled to a minimum wage (currently $7.25 per hour, effective July 24, 2009).
- Nonexempt workers (generally defined as hourly personnel) must be paid overtime pay at a rate of not less than one and one-half times their regular rates of pay after 40 hours of work in a workweek.
- Tipped employees are individuals engaged in occupations in which they customarily and regularly receive more than $30 a month in tips. The employer may consider tips as part of wages, or the employer must, at the current time, pay at least $2.13 an hour in direct wages. The employer must be able to verify that the combination of direct wages and tips meets or exceeds the minimum wage. If it does not, the employer is required to make up the difference.

- A minimum wage of less than $4.25 (as of 2010) is permitted for employees under 20 years of age during their first 90 consecutive calendar days of employment. This is termed the **Youth Wage**. A Youth Wage employee cannot be hired to replace a regular minimum wage employee.
- The FLSA child labor provisions are designed to protect the educational opportunities of minors and prohibit their employment in jobs and under conditions detrimental to their health or well-being. The provisions include restrictions on hours of work for minors under 16 and lists of hazardous occupations, both farm and nonfarm jobs, declared by the Secretary of Labor to be too dangerous for minors to perform.
- Some employees are exempt from both the minimum wage and overtime pay provisions. Those exempted include:
  - Executive, administrative, and professional employees (including teachers and academic administrative personnel in elementary and secondary schools), outside sales employees, and employees in certain computer-related occupations (as defined in DOL regulations);
  - Employees of certain seasonal amusement or recreational establishments. Some employees are exempt from the overtime pay provisions, or from both the minimum wage and overtime pay provisions.
- The Patient Protection and Affordable Care Act ("PPACA"), signed into law on March 23, 2010 (P.L. 111-148), amended Section 7 of the FLSA to provide a break time requirement for nursing mothers.
- According to the FLSA, the workweek is a period of 168 hours during 7 consecutive 24-hour periods. It may begin on any day of the week and at any hour of the day established by the employer. Generally, for purposes of minimum wage and overtime payment, each workweek stands alone; there can be no averaging of two or more workweeks. Employee coverage, compliance with wage payment requirements, and the application of most exemptions are determined on a workweek basis.
- According to the FLSA, covered employees must be paid for all hours worked in a workweek. In general, "hours worked" includes all time an employee must be on duty, either on the employer's premises or at any other prescribed place of work, from the beginning of the first principal activity of the workday to the end of the last principal work activity of the workday. Also included is any additional time the employee is allowed (i.e., suffered or permitted) to work.
- The Equal Pay Act (1963) is part of the Fair Labor Standards Act. It prohibits differential wages paid to men and women doing substantially the same work. If both sexes are doing the same work with similar skills, responsibility, working conditions, and effort, the pay must be equal.

Title VII of the Civil Rights Act (1964)

Title VII of the Civil Rights Act (1964) is the principal federal law relating to most types of employment discrimination. The purpose of Title VII is to give everyone an equal chance to obtain employment. The law has a number of objectives; specifically, it:

- Outlaws certain discriminatory employment practices
- Creates a federal agency to enforce the law and give it regulatory powers
- Sets penalties for violators of the law
- Requires state laws to uphold Title VII
- Requires that certain records be maintained by designated persons or agencies
- Does not alter state or federal veterans' preference laws

Title VII prohibits employment discrimination based on race, religion, sex, color, or national origin. Employers are also prohibited from discriminatory practices regarding:

- Recruiting and hiring
- Job advertising
- Ability and experience
- Occupational qualification
- Testing
- Prehire inquiries
- Employment status
- Compensation
- Merit, incentive, or seniority plans
- Insurance, retirement, and welfare plans
- Promotion and seniority
- Dress and appearance
- Leave of absence benefits
- Discharge
- Retirement
- Union membership
- Persons opposed to discriminatory practices or exercising their rights under Title VII

Title VII applies to all employers who have more than 15 employees. Employers who do not comply with the law are subject to court-decreed affirmative action programs and may be required to pay back pay. The act is administered by the Equal Employment Opportunity Commission (EEOC).

Age Discrimination in Employment Act (1967, 1978, 1986)

The Age Discrimination in Employment Act (ADEA) promotes the employment of older persons based on ability rather than age. The act prohibits arbitrary age discrimination in employment of workers 40 years and older, and it helps employers and workers resolve age-related employment problems. The ADEA applies to private employers with 20 or more workers and to all government agencies regardless of number of employees. The act also applies to employment agencies and unions with 25 or more members. Failure to comply with the ADEA can lead to court-decreed affirmative action programs, back pay, fines up to $10,000, and possible imprisonment. The act is administered by the EEOC.

Occupational Safety and Health Act (1970)

The Occupational Safety and Health Act created regulations and enforcement practices to render the work environment safe and healthy for workers. Most employees in the United States come under OSHA's jurisdiction. OSHA covers private sector employers and employees in all 50 states, the District of Columbia, and other U.S. jurisdictions either directly through Federal OSHA or through an OSHA-approved state program. State-run health and safety programs must be at least as effective as the Federal OSHA program. OSHA standards are rules that describe the methods that employers must use to protect their employees from hazards. There are OSHA standards for Construction work, Maritime operations, and General Industry, which is the set that applies to most worksites. These standards limit the amount of hazardous chemicals workers can be exposed to, require the use of certain safe practices and equipment, and require employers to monitor hazards and keep records of workplace injuries and illnesses. Failure to comply with the act can result in fines up to $100,000 per violation. OSHA is administered by the Occupational Safety and Health Administration in the Department of Labor.

Immigration Reform and Control Act (1986)

The Immigration Reform and Control Act (IRCA) prohibits employers from knowingly hiring, recruiting, or referring for a fee any alien who is unauthorized to work. As a result of this law, all employers are required to verify both the identity and employment eligibility of all regular, temporary, casual, and student employees hired after November 6, 1986, and complete and retain a one-page form (INS Form I-9) documenting this verification. Failure to comply with these requirements may result in both civil and criminal liability with the imposition of substantial fines ranging from $100 to $1,000 per hire, as well as possible imprisonment for a pattern or practice of noncompliance. Most importantly, failure to verify a new employee's identity and employment eligibility will result in the termination of employment for that employee. United States Citizenship and Immigration Services is responsible for implementing this law.

Americans with Disabilities Act (1990) with Amendments (2008)

The Americans with Disabilities Act (ADA) provides broad nondiscrimination protection for individuals in employment, public services, public accommodations, and services operated by private entities, transportation, and telecommunications. Title I states that no entity covered by this act shall discriminate against a qualified individual because of a disability with regard to a job application procedure or in the hiring, advancement, or discharge of employees, employee compensation, job training, and other terms, conditions, and privileges of employment.

The ADA defines a disability as:

- a physical or mental impairment that substantially limits one or more major life activities of such individual;
- a record of such an impairment; or
- being regarded as having such an impairment (An individual meets the requirement of "being regarded as having such an impairment" if the individual establishes that he or she has been subjected to an action prohibited under this chapter because of an actual or perceived physical or mental impairment whether or not the impairment limits or is perceived to limit a major life activity.).

It is important to note that the act specifically states, "The definition of disability in this chapter shall be construed in favor of broad coverage of individuals under this chapter, to the maximum extent permitted by the terms of this chapter."

Failure to comply with the ADA can result in injunctive relief and back pay but not compensatory and punitive damages. The ADA is administered by the EEOC.

Civil Rights Act (1991)

The Civil Rights Act of 1991 extends punitive damages and jury trials to victims of employment discrimination based on the employee's sex, religion, disability, as well as race. Under previous acts employees could only seek back pay. The result of not complying with this act can be punitive damages at the rates of $50,000 for businesses with 100 or fewer employees; $100,000 for firms with 101 to 500 workers; and a maximum limit of $300,000 for businesses with over 500 employees. This act is administered by the EEOC.

Family Medical Leave Act (1993)

The Family Medical Leave Act permits employees to take up to 12 weeks of unpaid leave per year from work for the birth or adoption of a child; for the case of a seriously ill child, spouse, or parent; or for a serious illness afflicting the worker. Employers must guarantee the worker can return to the same or a comparable job. Employers must also continue health care coverage during the leave period. During the leave time workers are not eligible for unemployment or other government compensation. This law applies to employers that have 50 or more employees within a 75-mile radius. Employees who have not worked at least one year and have not worked 1,250 hours or 25 hours a week in the previous 12 months are not covered by the law. The act is administered by the EEOC.

CONCLUSIONS

There are few things that evolve as rapidly as the law. There are also few things that can have as devastating an effect on a business. Today is the age of transparency. This transparency may be initiated by an individual or company, or it may be initiated by others. It is easy today to quickly achieve wide distribution of personal and company information. Keep this in mind when considering your actions as a supervisor.

As a chef supervisor you must be familiar with the law in order to balance your actions with the law. In the past the question was, "How will this action look in the headlines (newspaper) tomorrow morning?" Today the question is, "How will this action look on the web within the next hour?" Laws generally are created in response to a demonstrated need for reinforcement of a society's standard of behavior. But the first "law" that a chef supervisor should put into force, known as the **Golden Rule**, is not actually a law in the above-described sense. The Golden Rule is better regarded as a formula for creating a positive environment that leads to success for all. Always remember, first and foremost: "Do unto others as you would have them do unto you."

SUMMARY

The chef supervisor's skill sets must include knowledge of laws relative to the employee and employer. These laws include those related to the relations between the employer and unions. The employees have the right to decide if they want a group such as a union to represent them. This decision, the formation of a representative group such as a union, the manner in which the representative group takes action and the employer's actions in relation to the representative group all are subject to federal law. The laws addressing fair labor standards address minimum wage, overtime pay, employment records, and child labor. Equal employment opportunity is safeguarded by numerous laws, and these laws are administered by the Equal Opportunity Employment Commission. The rights of disabled individuals are the focus of the Americans with Disabilities Act. The safety and health of the worker is the focus of the Occupational Safety and Health Act. The law is constantly changing. The role of the chef supervisor is to protect the rights of both the employee and the employer. To meet this responsibility, the chef supervisor's knowledge of the law must constantly be updated.

DISCUSSION QUESTIONS

1. Define the key terms:
   a. Labor law
   b. National Labor Relations Board
   c. Youth Wage
   d. Golden Rule
2. List the laws that address the relationship between the employer and unions.
3. State three specific directives pertaining the formation and function of a union in the workplace.
4. List the laws administered by the EEOC.
5. Discuss the Family Medical Leave Act.
6. What was the purpose of the Civil Rights Act of 1964 (Title VII) and the Civil Rights Act of 1991?
7. Discuss the Occupational Safety and Health Act.
8. Discuss the specifics of three laws related to fair labor standards.
9. Discuss the Immigration Reform and Control Act.

NOTES

1. *Employment Law Guide*, United States Department of Labor, http://www.dol.gov/elaws/elg/.

2. *United States Code*, United States Government Printing Office, http://www.gpoaccess.gov/uscode/.

Chapter 3
Recruiting and Selecting Team Members

OBJECTIVES

When you complete this chapter, you should be able to:

1. List the methods for completion of a job analysis
2. Describe the steps in conducting a job analysis
3. Write a job description
4. Write a job specification
5. Identify the uses of job descriptions
6. Identify the uses of a job specification
7. Define various recruitment techniques employed to attract a pool of qualified job candidates
8. Describe the legal issues associated with recruiting and selecting job applicants
9. Understand the steps in screening potential new team members
10. Describe different types of interviews used to screen applicants
11. List the steps to be considered when interviewing potential team members
12. State appropriate and inappropriate questioning techniques
13. Understand elements associated with the hiring decision-making process

Case Study: Adair Catering

Mr. Adair operates Adair Catering, a catering company that does only off-premise catering. The level of business varies widely, so he employs only a few full-time employees. The majority of staff members are on-call employees who work when needed. Most have other jobs, and many of them have other full-time jobs.

Today has been a very bad day. Two dishwashers and one driver did not show up for work. One lead cook came to work drunk and had to be sent home. Mr. Adair has pots and pans stacking up. He has deliveries that need to be made. He needs to closely monitor three full-service lunches in three different locations because several of the on-call leads and servers could not work today. The full-time employers of those staff members are also experiencing extremely high volume, and so they are working at those jobs.

There is a bright spot in the morning. One of the current dishwashers, Ray, has a friend, Joe, who can both wash dishes and drive the company trucks, since he has a chauffeur's license. Ray has worked for Mr. Adair for a year and has been a very dependable worker. His recommendation of Joe carries a lot of weight.

Ray calls Joe, who arrives thirty minutes later to meet with Mr. Adair. Joe is clean and neat; in fact, his shirt and pants are pressed. Joe assures Mr. Adair that he would really like a chance to work for him. Mr. Adair checks his driver's license, which is a current chauffeur's license. When asked when he can start, Joe says, "Immediately." Mr. Adair hires Joe and gives him the keys to the delivery truck along with instructions for the deliveries. He tells Joe that when he gets back, he is to help Ray with pots and pans and other kitchen cleaning duties. Mr. Adair tells Joe that they will discuss his potential status as a full-time staff member tomorrow.

The next day, Mr. Adair tells Joe that he is very pleased with his work and he would like to take him on as a full-time employee as a combination driver/dishwasher. Joe accepts, and he is added to the payroll. Joe's work is exemplary, and he is able to handle the deliveries without any problem.

Two weeks later, Joe does not show up for work. Mr. Adair asks Ray if he knows why Joe did not show up for work. Ray says that Joe is in jail. Mr. Adair asks why he is in jail, and Ray says for driving without a license and forgery. Mr. Adair says, "Driving without a license! But he had a chauffeur's license. I saw the license." Ray says, "That's why they are also charging him with forgery. Apparently the license was a fake."

Based on what you have learned from previous chapters and the content of this chapter, answer the following questions.

- What is the overall reason for the challenges that occurred at Adair Catering?
- What are the primary causal agents for the challenges that occurred at Adair Catering?
- What role did leadership and supervision/management play in the challenges that occurred at Adair Catering?
- What specific steps could have been taken to avoid the challenges that occurred at Adair Catering?
- What, specifically, can be done to avoid a repeat of the challenges for Adair Catering?

INTRODUCTION

A key part of supervision is finding and hiring the best people for the job. Recruiting and hiring decisions must reflect the vision and values of the company. Hiring the right people builds the culture of the company. When the right people are hired, the result is quality in performance and operations. People make the difference between success and failure.

The process of recruiting and hiring staff begins with job analysis. To hire the right person, the activities, responsibilities, and working conditions of the position must be clear. It is the match between the individual and the position that determines the quality of performance on the job. A good match is not possible without a job description that clearly states the specifics for the position. The specifics of the position are determined through a job analysis.

There are a number of laws and regulations that protect the job seeker and the company. These laws and regulations directly impact the recruiting and hiring process. The way recruiting and hiring are done varies from company to company. In some companies the supervisor is directly responsible for this process. In other companies the recruiting and hiring are done by the human resource/personnel department. In both situations the role of chef supervisor is critical, as is that of all members of the management team. Staff recruitment and selection is a responsibility shared by all members of the management. All members of management are responsible for knowing and complying with labor laws and regulations.

The recruiting and hiring process may be managed by a human resources or personnel department. This does not mean the chef is not part of the process. The final decision to hire should be made by the chef supervisor. The chef supervisor has the best understanding of the needs of the kitchen. The chef supervisor is building a team. New hires who know they were personally selected by the chef supervisor will be more committed to the team.

JOB ANALYSIS

Job analysis is the determination of the activities, responsibilities, and working conditions of a position. It also is a process used to determine the skills and knowledge required to do the job. The first step in job analysis is information gathering. This can be done in several ways. These include a position audit, self-analysis, survey, and observation. An **audit of position output** is conducted by the human resources or personnel department. The product produced or jobs completed are compiled over a period of time. **Self-analysis** is completed by a current position holder. The individual is asked to keep a log of all their activities and responsibilities over a period of time. It can also be valuable to conduct a survey of the individual's holding similar positions in other locations or companies. This would be done by developing a questionnaire directed to gaining information about what they do on the job. Another method of information gathering is **direct observation**. The observer monitors the activities of an individual or individuals in the position over a period of time. In all cases where the information is gathered over a period of time, the time needs to be sufficient to capture enough information to accurately reflect the position.

The most effective information gathering combines the methods described in the previous paragraph. Each method has weaknesses. An audit of position outcome provides a narrow picture of the position. It does not indicate activities such as coaching and training. It also provides little information about working conditions. The activities, skills, and knowledge may not be directly reflected in the individual's product output. The job analysis is intended to capture all aspects of the position. This is best done by using multiple methods of information gathering.

Once the information has been gathered, the next step is to analyze the information. The information gathered is analyzed to answer the following questions.

- What does the individual in the current position actually do?
- What are the responsibilities of the individual in the current position?
- What specific skills are needed to carry out the activities and responsibilities of the current position?
- What type of knowledge is needed to carry out the activities and responsibilities of the position?
- What are the working conditions for the position?
- If there is an existing job description and specification, are the answers to the above questions a match with its content?
- Is what is currently done by the position what the company needs the position to do?

Once these questions have been answered, it is then possible to write an accurate job description and specification.

JOB DESCRIPTION AND SPECIFICATION

Job descriptions are used to clearly state the activities, responsibilities, and working conditions of a position. The job description also specifies the knowledge and skills desired and required of the person in the position. The job description is like a good recipe. The recipe helps the chef assemble the ingredients and states the time and temperature required to complete the dish, ensuring quality. The job description does the same for the chef supervisor in the hiring process. It is a key tool in choosing the right person. A well-developed job description is the foundation of the recruiting, selection, and performance appraisal sequence. As shown in Figure 3-1, the sequence begins with job analysis.

Based on the information in the job analysis, the job description is developed. The job description must be carefully developed. It is considered a legal document in disputes between the employee and the employer pertaining to the performance of job duties. The job description for a position should be reviewed and updated regularly to ensure that it correctly reflects the requirements for the position. A clear job description is the foundation of quality performance by the employee. The employee must clearly understand what they are expected to do in order to do a job well. An up-to-date job description is also critical to performance evaluation. In order for performance evaluation to be meaningful, it must be based on what the staff member was told they were to do. The job description is the primary means of making it clear to everyone what a position does. The skills, knowledge, and physical requirements of a position are called the **job specification**. This is part of the job description but can also be used as a separate document. The clarity and accuracy of the job specification will determine the quality of the match of the person to the position. In a job specification, two types of qualifications can be stated. The first type of qualification is termed required. A **required qualification** is something that the individual must possess to carry out the activities and responsibilities of the position. A **desired qualification** is one that the individual does not have to possess to do the job. Often, desired qualifications are those that make the individual a candidate for greater growth in the position and the company. An example of a qualification that is commonly required is ServSafe certification. An example of a qualification that is often desired is an associate degree in culinary arts. The details of a job description can be seen in Figure 3-2.

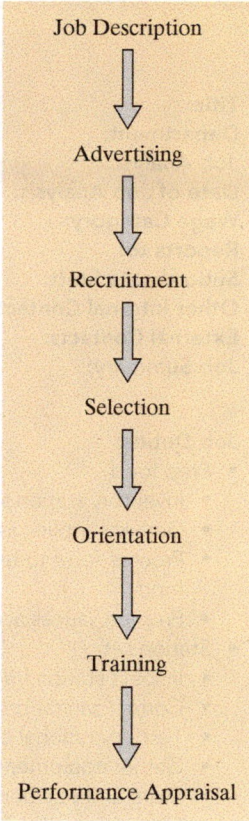

Job Description

↓

Advertising

↓

Recruitment

↓

Selection

↓

Orientation

↓

Training

↓

Performance Appraisal

Figure 3-1
Recruiting/training/
performance sequence.

Job Description

Title:	Line Cook
Department:	Culinary
Job Analyst:	Chef Ortega
Date of Job Analysis:	6/21/11
Wage Category:	Hourly
Reports to:	Evening Sous Chef
Subordinate Staff:	Not Applicable
Other Internal Contacts:	Kitchen personnel and service staff
External Contacts:	Not Applicable
Job Summary:	Perform food preparation and presentation to specification and to order, set up and maintain work station, prep food as directed

Job Duties:
- Prep food
  - Inventory station stock levels and equipment
  - Gather supplies as needed to return station to par for service period
  - Process food to level necessary to meet requirements of the station for quality and timely preparation and presentation of food
  - Prepare sauces according to recipe, properly cool, and store
- Station set
  - Inspect station for sanitation and safety issues
  - Correct sanitation and safety issues
  - Test operational condition of major equipment
  - Gather equipment required to return station to ready-state for service period
  - Store and position prepped supplies
  - Organize station for efficient work flow
- Food preparation to order
  - Mastery of standards for all menu items assigned to station
  - Quality preparation and presentation of all items ordered
    - To specification
    - In a prescribed time for each item
  - Minimal waste (maintain waste report)
  - Maintenance of sanitary and organized station at all times
- Station changeover and sanitation
  - Return station to order
  - Stock station according to standard
  - Correct sanitation and safety issues
  - Submit waste report to Line Supervisor
  - Report equipment issues to Line Supervisor
- Other duties as assigned

Working Conditions:
Kitchen setting, exposure to cleaning materials (protective equipment and MSD sheets provided)

Job Specifications:
- Required
  - High school graduate
  - Minimum of 2 years experience working in a restaurant food preparation
  - Demonstrated knowledge of basic knife cuts
  - Demonstrated knowledge of classical sauce preparation
  - ServSafe certified
  - U.S. citizen
  - Ability to stand for extended periods with minimal breaks
  - Ability to lift 25 lb unassisted
- Preferred
  - Certificate or degree in culinary arts or ACF certification
  - English/French speaker

Figure 3-2
Job description.

RECRUITING

Recruiting involves seeking and attracting a diverse pool of qualified candidates for a position. The more applicants there are for a position, the better chance the chef supervisor has of selecting the right person. The key to successful recruiting is to begin the process well in advance of any openings occurring in the team. Part of this process is building a positive company reputation and culture. It has often been said that a foodservice organization's reputation determines the outcome of the recruiting process. The reputation of the company, the chef, and the workplace are factors that have an impact on the quality of job applicants.

There are many ways to begin searching for new team members. Recruiting can be formal or informal. It can be done internally or externally. Some of the most reliable methods of recruiting include:

- Advertising using electronic media
- Asking friends, customers, or suppliers
- Seeking candidates at culinary colleges and local chefs' associations
- Reviewing past applicants
- Attending job fairs
- Networking with other foodservice organizations

In some areas of the United States, the public employment service is also a good source for recruiting. Private employment agencies provide another route. When using private employment agencies, the new team member sometimes pays the agency, but in most cases it is the employer who pays. Charges can range from 10 to 50 percent of the employee's first month's or first year's salary.

Networking is generally a positive recruiting source. It can yield good results but can also cause problems. If a team member is recommended by a colleague but turns out to be unsatisfactory and must be "let go," the colleague who made the recommendation may be unhappy or angry about the outcome. Whatever method is used, it must always be in compliance with the law.

Obviously, the best recruiting philosophy is to seek out quality people. **Active recruiting** is the basis on which good chef supervisors acquire the best team members. They work on attracting talented individuals rather than hoping that qualified people will appear. This process of recruiting says to a potential team member, "You are someone special and I want you on my team."

Recruiting people who respond to quality operational goals is the basis for culinary success. **Esprit de corps**, the spirit of the team members that inspires dedication and devotion to the team's goal, is critical to building a strong team. A strong team is critical to achieving quality at each step. When the best possible "neatness of fit" occurs between people and organization, the chef supervisor will have recruited an asset to the kitchen and company, not just a "warm body."

Turnover of staff costs the company the money spent in recruiting and training the staff member. Recruiting qualified people that are a good match to the company's culture reduces turnover. The hire that is a good match stays longer. Whatever the recruiting method, the goal is to achieve the best match of individual and position.

LEGAL IMPLICATIONS

It is important that chef supervisors and all management consider the legal aspects of recruitment and selection. Title VII of the Civil Rights Act (1964) is the principal federal law relating to most types of employment discrimination. Title VII prohibits employment discrimination based on race, religion, sex, color, or national origin. In recruiting and selection, therefore, the employer must ensure that no action taken in the process was discriminatory. The ad below, for example, could easily lead to charges of discrimination.

> Wanted waitress, 18–22 years old, unmarried, must have a working car, non-Christian preferred. Apply in person at the Not Bright Restaurant.

The correctly worded ad would be:

> Wanted server, must be able to walk and stand for extended periods of time and lift 20 pounds unassisted. Apply in person at the Smart Way Restaurant.

The first ad contained numerous requirements, but none were **Bona Fide Occupational Qualifications** (BFOQ). Age, marital status, personal information, and religion do not determine an individual's ability to do a job. Sometimes factors such as gender may be considered a BFOQ. An example of gender as a BFOQ is requiring that the attendant for the men's locker room at the golf club be male. In the second ad the employer has declared walking, standing, and lifting as BFOQs. The employer must be prepared to prove that these are BFOQs.

SCREENING

The recruiting process yields applicants whose qualifications must be assessed against the requirements of the job and the culture of the company. **Screening** is the initial step in selecting the new staff member. It is based on a comparison of the application materials and the requirements of the job stated in the job description. Screening also includes an initial impression of the applicant's potential fit with the company's culture. Screening needs to be done carefully. The selection of new staff members has a long-term impact on team performance. Careful screening results in better hiring. The staff and the guest benefit from a careful selection process. One of the chef supervisor's most important responsibilities is staff selection. They should fully understand the objectives and policies relative to evaluating and selecting new staff members.

The goal of screening is to generate an initial pool of potential staff members. These are the best fit with the job requirements and the rate of pay available.

Screening and selection in some instances may also be affected by union contracts. Union contracts often require that all in-house applicants for a position be interviewed. Additionally, a union contract may require that consideration be given to seniority with the company. In a unionized workplace the chef supervisor must know the terms of the contract. Failure to comply with the provisions of the contract can lead to the union disputing the hiring decision. This can delay the filling of the position and also creates ill will between the union and management.

In matching people and positions, complete, clear, and unambiguous job description and specification reduce the influence of ethnic and gender stereotypes. These tools help the chef supervisor differentiate between qualified and unqualified individuals based on proper criteria. There are other steps that can be taken to reduce the influence of ethnic and gender stereotypes.

Most organizations require application forms to be completed, because they provide a variety of information about the potential staff member. As with interviews, the Equal Employment Opportunity Commission (EEOC) and the courts have found that many questions asked on application forms disproportionately reject females and minorities and often are not job-related. To keep in line with this legal requirement, application forms should be developed with great care and revised as necessary.

The information on the application form is generally used as a basis for further exploration of the applicant's background. It should be designed to elicit as much information as possible that will help predict job success. An example job application is provided in Appendix A. The application should always require the signature of the applicant indicating that all information provided is accurate. In the screening process, an incomplete application should be a matter of concern. In most situations an incomplete application means that the individual is not eligible for interview. Even if an applicant has provided a resume, it is still important that application forms be completed early in the application process.

The resume is a standard means for an applicant to initially present their information to the potential employer. A resume does not replace an application. The strength and the weakness of the resume is that, when well written, it always presents the individual in the most positive manner. The straightforward questions of the application provide the information in a more basic fashion. The value of the resume lies in the broader information about the applicant that may not be requested on the resume. A company is responsible for the actions of an employee who represents the company. This dictates that the company carefully check the background of potential staff members. For the hiring of kitchen staff, the most common **background check** is contacting references and previous employers. Kitchens that serve high-security facilities such as government installations or prisons may require more in-depth background checks.

Doing a background check is often reserved for applicants who have been selected for the interview pool. The initial step is verification of the applicant's employment history. Permission to contact previous employers should be requested on the application. Failure by an applicant to give permission to contact a previous employer should not automatically be considered a cause to remove them from the applicant pool. If the applicant is a good match in all other ways, however, it may be worth asking them why this permission was not given. Most previous employers, when contacted, will provide only verification of employment. Companies generally will not comment on job performance. This situation is the result of lawsuits by former employees who disputed comments made by their previous company.

The primary sources for information on the applicant's previous job performance are references. The applicant should be asked to provide references that can and will comment on their job performance. On the application the applicant should be asked to grant permission for the references to be contacted.

When doing background checks, remember that the information should be job-related. The information requested and received about the applicant should be documented. Individuals have a legal right to examine letters of reference about themselves (unless they have waived the right to do so or the documents were protected by the Privacy Act of 1974 or by state laws). Written documentation should exist outlining that the employment decision was based on relevant information.[1]

INTERVIEWING

The most crucial step in selecting potential staff members is the face-to-face interview. An **interview** is a conversation or verbal interaction between two people (in this case, the chef supervisor and the applicant). The goal is to evaluate compatibility for a particular reason. It is a process for choosing the applicant most suited for the staff position to be filled. The interview has three main purposes:

1. To validate previously submitted information
2. To discover those skills and attitudes necessary to achieve "neatness of fit" for the position
3. To predict the successful integration of the applicant into the company's culture

When meeting somebody for the first time, it is natural to react to him or her in some way. Sometimes this reaction goes further and some definite judgments are made based only on the first impression. If this happens, the interviewer will usually tend, often without realizing it, to listen to and observe the person selectively. This means the interviewer sees and hears only what confirms the first impression. The interviewer filters out anything that contradicts that initial impression.

First impressions are based largely on nonverbal cues: what is seen, what is said, and how it is said. Nonverbal cues are based almost entirely on reliving old memories. They are based, therefore, not on the person, but on the memories of others in the past. The interviewer must work to overcome these tendencies. The goal is to see persons as they are, not in the light of memory-based perception.

There is no best way to interview. Interviews can be structured or unstructured, or they may be conducted in groups. Three interview types are commonly used in the foodservice industry.

- *Structured interviews* consist of a series of carefully designed and structured questions asked of each job applicant by the interviewer. This type of interview is based on a clear set of job specifications. In this type of interview, the interviewer maintains control of the interview by systematically asking prepared questions. An advantage of using a structured interview is that it provides the same criteria for all interviews.
- *Unstructured interviews*, as the name implies, require very little preparation on the part of the interviewer. These types of interviews are conducted without a predetermined checklist of questions. Open-ended questions are used instead. This type of interview may pose problems of subjectivity and bias on the part of the interviewer; however, unstructured interviews can provide a more relaxed atmosphere for interviewees.
- *Group interviews* are interviews in which several applicants are questioned together in a group discussion. They typically involve a structured and unstructured question format.

Additional types of interviews are shown in Figure 3-3.

Although interviews are the most widely used method to select staff members, they can create a host of problems. One of the most significant is that interviews are subject to the same legal requirements of validity and reliability as other steps in the recruitment and selection process. The interview also should follow EEOC guidelines. Interview questions should be tied to job descriptions, which should detail only the characteristics of the position. The basic thrust of equal employment legislation is straightforward: Do not discriminate against people on the basis of their race, color, sex, religion, or national origin. Subtle interpretations of the laws, however, make this area one of the most actively pursued in the courts. If the interview questions stick to job-related items, are objective, and are applied consistently to all applicants—men,

- Board interviews
- Stress interviews
- Counseling interviews
- Evaluation or job appraisal interviews
- Exit interviews

Figure 3-3
Additional interview types.

women, persons of all racial and all national groups—then the interviewer will most certainly stay within the law.

Interviewing Guidelines

By putting the potential staff member at ease, the interviewer is more likely to get a true picture of the applicant's skills, abilities, and attitudes.

The interview should take place in a pleasant and nonthreatening environment. Begin the interview by welcoming the applicant warmly. An applicant who is at ease will be more likely to answer questions spontaneously. Introduce yourself by name and title. Ask the applicant his or her preferred name and use it throughout the interview. Prepare the atmosphere by initiating a brief conversation on issues unrelated to the interview. Establish and maintain rapport with applicants by displaying sincere interest in them and by listening carefully. Indicate the intention to take notes or complete an evaluation form, and be sure to extend this opportunity to the applicant. Strive to understand what is only suggested or implied. A good listener's mind is alert, and his or her face and posture reflect this.

Some interviewers tend to talk too much. According to Bill Marvin, "Most interviewers talk half of the time or more during an interview, but it is the candidate who should be talking 80 or 90 percent of the time. After all, how can you learn about an applicant if you do all the talking?"[2]

Focus on the questions and the applicant's responses to questions. Listen for observations beyond the content required to answer the question. Watch the body language of the applicant. All of these provide clues to that person's attitude and feelings. Answer fully and frankly the applicant's questions. Use questions effectively to elicit truthful answers. Questions should be phrased as objectively as possible, without an indication of the desired response. During the interview, separate facts from inferences. Use open-ended questions that give the applicant an opportunity to talk and share information about past work experiences, training, or lifestyle. Things to avoid doing in an interview are shown in Figure 3-4.

An interviewer who is not getting honest answers to carefully prepared questions may hire the wrong person. To become an effective interviewer, the dynamics of verbal and nonverbal communication must be mastered so that dishonest applicants can be easily spotted. About 80 percent of communication is nonverbal rather than verbal,

- Avoid biases and traps. This includes favoring people who have interests, backgrounds, or experiences similar to those of the interviewer.
- Avoid allowing an impressive attitude to overshadow the need to ask essential questions about skills and knowledge.
- Avoid the influence of "beautyism." Discrimination against unattractive persons is a persistent and pervasive form of employment discrimination.
- Avoid the "halo effect," judging an individual favorably or unfavorably on the basis of one strong point (or weak point) on which high (or low) value has been placed.
- Avoid allowing first impressions (good or bad) to overrule the information gathered from the interview.
- Avoid making a judgment on the basis of preinterview material and either spending the entire time trying to verify the material or simply rendering the interview pointless.
- Avoid making a decision too soon.
- Avoid the temptation of talking too much.

Figure 3-4
Things to avoid during an interview.

- Put the applicant at ease.
- Focus attention on the applicant's responses to questions.
- Use open-ended questions.
- Avoid biases that may affect judgment.
- Avoid the halo effect.
- Don't allow first impressions to overrule information gathered from the interview.
- Know what questions are inappropriate and those that are permissible.

Figure 3-5
Guidelines for effective interviewing.

and that 80 percent is manifest in a person's face, particularly in the eyes. An interviewer should be able to recognize the subtle nonverbal cues that indicate an attempt to deceive. Few applicants can lie without feeling tightness in the stomach, as well as displaying some involuntary change in facial expression or diverting the eyes from the interviewer.[3] Verbal clues that sometimes can indicate deception include remarks such as "to tell the truth," "to be perfectly honest," or "I wouldn't tell most people this." Sometimes verbal and nonverbal cues are combined, for example, an "honest to God" remark accompanied by a major break in eye contact, a shift in body orientation, or a movement of a hand to the face.

Be sure to obtain all of the information needed before ending the interview. Keep in mind the qualities needed for the job. Cover all major skills that are needed on the job. As a final step in the interview process, ask the applicant if there are further questions or more information to be discussed before closing the interview. Guidelines for effective interviewing are shown in Figure 3-5.

Interview Questions

To evaluate the qualifications of potential staff members, the chef supervisor must ask a series of questions. Certain types of questions, however, violate EEOC guidelines. Other types of questions are inappropriate, but inexperienced interviewers may ask them unwittingly. Following are some examples of appropriate and inappropriate questions.

Name

Inappropriate: Inquiries about names that would indicate the applicant's lineage, ancestry, national origin, or descent. Inquiry about the previous name of an applicant whose name has been changed by court order or otherwise. Inquiries about preferred courtesy title, Mr., Mrs., and Ms.

Permissible inquiries: "Have you worked for this organization under a different name?" "Is any additional information relative to change of name, use of an assumed name, or nickname necessary to enable a check on your work and educational record? If yes, please explain."

Marital Status

Inappropriate: "Are you married, divorced, or separated?"

Permissible inquiries: Whether the applicant can meet specific work schedules or has activities, commitments, or responsibilities that may hinder the meeting or work attendance requirements.

Age

Inappropriate: "How old are you?"

Permissible inquiries: Requiring proof of age in the form of a work permit or a certificate of age if the applicant is a minor. If it is necessary to know that someone is over a certain age for legal reasons, this question could better be stated, "Are you 21 or over?"

National Origin

Inappropriate: "Are you native born or naturalized?" "Do you have proof of your citizenship?" "What was your birthplace?" "Where were your parents born?"

Permissible inquiries: If it is necessary to know if someone is a U.S. citizen for a job, this question could be asked directly, without asking anything that might reveal national origin. If it is necessary to require proof of citizenship or immigrant status, employment can be offered on the condition that proof is supplied.

Mental or Physical Handicap

Inappropriate: "Do you have or have you ever had a life-threatening disease?" Questions regarding treatment for alcohol or drug abuse or an on-the-job injury. "Have you ever been treated for a mental condition?"

Permissible inquiries: For employers subject to the provisions of the Rehabilitation Act of 1973 and the Americans with Disabilities Act of 1990, applicants may be invited to indicate how and to what extent they are handicapped. All applicants can be asked if they are able to carry out all necessary job assignments and perform them in a safe manner. The employer must indicate that compliance with the invitation is voluntary or that the information is being sought only to remedy discrimination or provide opportunities for the handicapped.

Religion

Inappropriate: "What is your religious affiliation?" "What clubs/associations are you a member of?" "Can you work Saturdays or Sundays?"

Permissible inquiries: None. However, an applicant may be advised concerning normal hours and days of work required by the job, to avoid possible conflict with religious or other personal convictions.

Conviction, Arrest, and Court Records

Inappropriate: Any inquiries relating to arrests. Any inquiry into or request for a person's arrest, court, or conviction record if not substantially related to functions and responsibilities of the particular job in question.

Permissible inquiries: Inquiry into actual convictions that relate reasonably to fitness to perform an actual job.

Military Record

Inappropriate: The type of discharge.

Permissible inquiries: Type of education and experience in the service as it relates to a particular job.

Credit Rating

Inappropriate: Any questions concerning credit rating, charge accounts, ownership of car, etc.

Permissible inquiries: None.

The following questions can provoke responses that help determine a person's motivation, initiative, insight, and planning abilities.

On Motivation

"How will this job help you get what you want?"

"What have you done to prepare yourself for a better job?"

The underlying intent of these types of questions is to determine the applicant's priorities and how motivated he or she may be.

On Initiative

"How did you get into this line of work?"

"When have you felt like giving up on a task? Tell me about it."

The intention here is to determine if the person is a self-starter or can complete an unpleasant assignment.

On Insight

"What is the most useful criticism you have received?"

"From whom? Tell me about it."

"What is the most useless?"

From answers to these questions, it is possible to develop an understanding of the applicant's ability to take constructive action on weaknesses and determine how the applicant can take criticism.

On Planning

"Tell me how you spend a typical day."

"If you were the boss, how would you run your present job?"

Reactions to these questions may tell how easily the applicant will fit into your corporate culture and team. They also will help elicit whether they have a vision or can get bogged down by details.

General Questions

"Tell me about yourself."

"What practical experience have you had in this area?"

"What is your major strength? Weakness?"

"What types of people annoy you?"

"What have you done that shows initiative and action?"

"How do you spend your spare time?"

"What personal characteristics do you feel are necessary for success in the foodservice industry?"

"Where would you like to be in one year?"

"Why do you want to work for us?"

"Why do you want to leave your present job?"

Questions About the Foodservice Organization

"What do you know about our organization?"

"Why do you want to work for us?"

"Why would you like this particular job?"

"How can you benefit our organization?"

"What experience(s) have you had that suit you for our organization?"

"What position would you like to hold with us in five years? In ten years?"

"What interests you about our organization?"

"What kind of chef supervisor do you prefer?"

"What do you feel determines a person's progress in a good organization?"

"What are your ideas about how the foodservice industry operates today?"

In addition to verbal and nonverbal responses during the interview, much can be learned from the actions and appearance of the applicant. These actions include:

- Arriving early for the interview
- Being alert and responsive
- Being dressed appropriately
- Being well groomed, with clean hair and nails
- Making good eye contact
- Listening carefully
- Speaking well of other people
- Sticking to the point

Obviously, the person who arrives late for an interview, is inappropriately dressed and unclean, looks away, complains about other people, or exhibits inappropriate responses presents a negative image. The interview session provides the chef supervisor with an opportunity to form an impression about the applicant's abilities and general disposition and to make a reasoned judgment on the applicant's suitability for the kitchen team.

MAKING THE DECISION

In reviewing all the information from the screening, background check, and interview, the chef supervisor must ask: Is this the person I want for my team, and is he or she qualified and suitable? When references are checked to verify the accuracy of the presented application and resume materials. It must be remembered that reference checking assumes that the past will indicate the future and that performance in one job has some continuity with the next. This is not always the case. Often, what interviewers see is what they will get, and leopards don't change their spots. The applicants will never look or behave better than they have throughout the evaluation process.

Determine the applicant's temperament. How well will this person fit into the kitchen team? Can this person be trained and developed? What is his or her energy level? The foodservice industry has demanding, busy service periods. Is the applicant a team player? If all of the applicant's hobbies or interests center around individual activities such as reading or listening to music or other solitary activities, this might be an applicant who prefers being alone. Applicants from a background that includes team activities often will have a grasp of the imperatives of teamwork. In a kitchen team, ideal members are those who are "people-oriented."

Remember also that a foodservice organization can hire only what it can afford. If the team vacancy that exists pays less than the potential team member is worth, and if

- Compensation: The rate of pay available affects the degree of selectivity.
- Labor relations: Unions may influence who is selected.
- Training and development: Training costs in terms of time and expense may be reduced or increased.

Figure 3-6
Other factors in the hiring decision.

this person has no immediate promotional opportunities to advance into, then this person most certainly will soon be looking for a better-paid position elsewhere.

Obviously, most of the team positions that chef supervisors are called on to fill are for cooks. Therefore, a simple cooking test may be appropriate. Much can be learned of an applicant by asking him or her to cook a simple and inexpensive dish. This test can quantify the applicant's skill level much more than an impressive résumé containing a list of awards won at food shows ever will. It also will demonstrate the applicant's energy level, organizational abilities, application of safety and sanitation procedures, use of correct equipment, and attitude toward customer service. All of this information can be gathered from having the applicant make a dish as simple as an omelet.

As is usual with many aspects of decision making regarding hiring new team members, not all of the applicants will fit into each component of the job specification: A chef supervisor may like everything about them, but in one or two areas they fail to match the specifications. Sometimes it is necessary to evaluate the risk of hiring against what is generally known as "can do" and "will do" factors. "Can do" concerns the individual's knowledge, skills, and attitudes. "Will do" concerns the person's motivation, interests, and personality characteristics. Some element of risk is involved when the elements of "can do" are not entirely fulfilled. Experienced chef supervisors can calculate the risk by determining that training and development will fix the "can do" part, because the "will do" elements outweigh other factors. Therefore, the availability of training and development may permit the hiring of potential team members who can be made qualified. Other factors in the hiring decision are shown in Figure 3-6.

SUMMARY

Recruiting and selection procedures that are well developed and applied assist in hiring the best possible candidates for the kitchen team. Chef supervisors must be aware of the legal issues involved in hiring a team member. Well-developed hiring procedures aid the chef supervisor in observing all of the laws pertaining to hiring personnel. Additionally, the chef supervisor must always remember that they can hire only what the organization can afford.

Ultimately, recruiting and hiring decisions should be based on two questions:

- Will this person fit into our team?
- Does he or she have the skills and knowledge needed?

The "neatness of fit" between the foodservice organization and the potential new team member determines future turnover. The reduction in turnover achieved with a good fit decreases training costs. Knowing the sources and methods of recruiting is key to succeeding in the right fit in the hiring process.

Job descriptions should be used to format the essential and desirable skills of new team members. The EEOC criteria with regard to employment applicants must be followed strictly so that all applicants are afforded the same employment opportunities. Discrimination in employment opportunity is illegal, and ignorance of the various laws is no defense.

CHEF TALK
"TEAM PLAYERS"

One of my most difficult tasks as an executive chef is hiring the right players for my kitchen team. Because we have a strong team philosophy at our hotel, we go to great lengths to get the best possible people. I therefore look for individuals who can fit our high standards.

Among the qualities I consider important in potential new kitchen employees are, of course, experience and how the candidates present themselves for interview. But more importantly, I look for that special "hospitality attitude." For me that's a critical quality. People who possess hospitality attitudes are usually those who also will make good team players. These attitudes are not hard to tease out. I simply ask potential employees who the most important person is in the hotel. If their answer indicates that it is the guest, chances are they understand the concept of hospitality.

Previous work experience in similar establishments is not the only deciding factor in the hiring process. If the person's disposition is positive, that can be a good reason to invest in developing and training that person.

Key to putting a great team together is "keeping them together." Therefore, investing in the existing team ensures that there is as little turnover as possible.

We employ a variety of screening processes before we get to the interview stage. Even then, not everyone who comes for an interview will be determined to be suitable. For the interview I involve my existing team members. I seek their opinions and encourage them to participate in the interviewing of new members; after all, they will have to embrace them if they are selected. We share our opinions on the candidates and collectively we evaluate their suitability.

Experience has taught me that some employment candidates can "talk a great game," but when it comes to actually cooking, they are left wanting. Administering a cooking test can tell you a lot, not only about candidates' cooking skills but also about vital approaches to safety and sanitation.

—Michael Ty, CEC, AAC,
MT Cuisine, LLC, Las Vegas, NV

Careful and effective screening of applicants will reduce the risk of selecting unsuitable team members. Screening requires the chef supervisor to actively check references.

Interviewing permits face-to-face evaluation of potential new team members. Therefore, interviewing skills are necessary, along with an understanding of the various types of interview processes.

The decision to hire an applicant is based on an evaluation of the information gathered through the application form, the screening stage, and the face-to-face interview. Additionally, a cooking test may be appropriate to determine skill levels. Elements of the decision to hire are based on this information, recognizing that past performance does not always predict future performance.

The chef supervisor has an important role to play and should be the final decision maker in the process of selecting new team members.

DISCUSSION QUESTIONS

1. Define the following chapter key terms:
   a. Job analysis
   b. Audit of position output
   c. Self-analysis
   d. Direct observation
   e. Job description
   f. Job specification
   g. Required qualification
   h. Desired qualification
   i. Recruiting
   j. Active recruiting
   k. Esprit de corps
   l. Bona fide occupational qualification
   m. Screening
   n. Background check
   o. Interview

2. Why is a "job analysis" conducted?

3. Why are job descriptions used?

4. What methods are most commonly used in the foodservice industry to recruit new team members?

5. What is active recruiting?

6. How can seeking out "qualified" persons contribute to reducing costs?

7. What are the guidelines of the Equal Employment Opportunity Commission as they apply to the recruitment and selection of employees?

8. Why should great care be taken in designing job application forms?

9. Why can inadequate reference checking lead to high employee turnover?

10. Why is the face-to-face interview the most crucial step in selecting potential team members?

11. What are the primary differences between a structured and an unstructured interview?

12. Why are open-ended questions used during a job interview?

13. What are five questioning areas an interviewer should not engage in during a job interview?

14. How might a chef supervisor ascertain the skill level of a cook applicant?

NOTES

1. E. R. Worthington and Anita E. Worthington, *People Investment* (Grant's Pass, OR: Oasis Press, 1993), 108.

2. Bill Marvin, *The Foolproof Foodservice Selection System* (New York: John Wiley, 1993), 5.

3. Robert F. Wilson, *Conducting Better Job Interviews* (New York: Barron's, 1991), 25.

Chapter 4
Compensation, Benefits, and Scheduling

OBJECTIVES

When you complete this chapter, you should be able to:

1. Discuss the relationship of compensation and motivation
2. List the steps in determining job worth
3. Summarize the principles of compensation structure
4. List the types of incentive programs
5. Discuss the value of incentive programs
6. Identify the benefits common in restaurant operations
7. Discuss the value of employee benefits
8. Define what an Employee Assistance Program is
9. State the steps in scheduling employees
10. Write a staff schedule

Case Study: B & J's Restaurant

Mother's Day is B & J's Restaurant's busiest day of the year. The restaurant has seating for 350 guests. On a normal Sunday the restaurant serves a total of 1200 guests. Five years ago the original owners of B & J's restaurant, Ben and Jen, decided to try something different on Mother's Day. On Mother's Day the restaurant converted to all buffet service. The Mother's Day buffets were an instant success and have continued every year with the number of guests served increasing every year. B & J's has become well known for its elaborate Mother's Day breakfast, brunch, and dinner buffet.

The Mother's Day buffets also became something that all of the restaurant's staff eagerly anticipated. The tradition had been established the first year, when Ben and Jen invited the immediate family members of all staff to be their guests for the breakfast buffet. A staggered schedule was even established that allowed staff members to have 45 minutes to eat with their families.

At last year's buffet, between 8 A.M. and 8 P.M., the restaurant served 2800 guests, 150 of which were staff and their family members, up from 2550 the previous year. Ben and Jen decided to retire shortly after last year's Mother's Day buffet and sold the restaurant. The goal of the new owners this year is to increase the number of paying guests by 15 percent for a total of 3048 paying guests. They have reviewed the previous year's Mother's Day sales and profitability. It is clear to them that the impact of the free meals for the staff member's families on profitability and extra labor cost for the special scheduling has to be stopped. The cost is just too high.

The key to success on Mother's Day at B & J's has always been planning and execution of the plan, grounded in a foundation of teamwork. Planning for the buffets began the week after Mother's Day. Ben and Jen had started the planning process with the Mother's Day team (better known as the MDT) of the managers and chef before leaving. After their departure the new owners, Mike and Priscilla, took over the planning personally. They quickly made it known to the previous members of the MDT that there would be no "family comps or staff members eating with family" on the upcoming Mother's Day.

Mike and Priscilla know that, to succeed in their goal on Mother's Day, the level of teamwork throughout the restaurant must be high. They are one month away from the big day and worried. Everything they have tried to maintain and increase the level of team work has failed. The staff just does not seem to have any enthusiasm for either the day-to-day business or the upcoming "big day." Several staff members have indicated that they are not willing to work overtime to do prep for or on Mother's Day. Mike and Priscilla have even heard rumors that members of the management team, including the chef, are looking at jobs with other restaurants.

Based on what you have learned from previous chapters and the content of this chapter, answer the following questions.

- What is the overall reason for the challenges occurring in B & J's Restaurant?
- What are the primary causal agents for the challenges occurring in B & J's Restaurant?
- What role did supervision/management play in the decline in B & J's Restaurant?
- What specific steps could have been taken to avoid the current situation occurring in B & J's Restaurant?
- What, specifically, can be done to overcome the challenges and generate motion in a positive direction for B & J's Restaurant?

INTRODUCTION

Compensation, benefits, and schedule are three areas of importance in supervision and human resource management. Compensation is not considered a motivator, but it is central to an employee's morale. Restaurant management, including the chef, has to balance the level of compensation for the employees with the operation's ability to meet its bottom line. Being the highest-paying employer will make it easier to find staff, but it may also put the company out of business.

Benefits are not the norm for restaurant employees. According to a study conducted by the Restaurant Opportunities Centers, 87.7% of restaurant employees in major metropolitan areas reported not having paid sick days and 90% reported not having health insurance.[1] This has become a major issue for the restaurant industry. The challenge, again, is one of balancing cost with the ability to keep the operation open.

The restaurant industry is not normally thought of as an incentive-based employer. This is a misleading perception. Wait staff are often asked to upsell. To encourage upselling, the staff member is often given an incentive. It is also possible to use incentives to encourage performance in the kitchen.

Having the right number of staff on hand at the right time is critical to the success of the business. Poor scheduling impacts the quality of food and service delivered to the guest. It also impacts the morale of the staff. Trying to do too much with too little can be as costly as overstaffing.

The chef supervisor is a manager and a member of the management team. As such, the chef supervisor must be prepared to deal with all aspects of human resource management. This includes compensation, benefits, and scheduling.

FOUNDATIONS OF COMPENSATION

Compensation is the pay an individual receives for doing a job. Compensation can take many forms. This includes barter, such as when an individual does a job and receives some type of good in return. Also, individuals can work for food and lodging. The most common form of payment in the restaurant industry is money. The individual performs assigned duties for a set length of time and in return receives money, commonly termed pay, wages, or salary.

The amount of compensation will vary with the type of job. Jobs requiring little to no experience, knowledge, or skill receive the lowest pay. Jobs requiring the highest levels of experience, knowledge, and skill receive the highest pay. The position's level of pay is also affected by the position's level of responsibilities and decision making.

Compensation Classifications

Compensation is further divided into hourly wage and salary. An employee receiving an **hourly wage** is paid only for the number of hours worked. An example is Josef and Bill, both of whom are paid $11.00 per hour. Last week Josef worked 25 hours, and he was paid $275 before deductions (we will discuss these shortly). Bill worked 40 hours last week, and he was paid $484 before deductions. On the other hand, Yen Li and Yolanda are managers and are paid a **salary** of $750 per week before deductions. Managers take turns working "long" and "short" schedules each week. Last week Yen Li worked the "long" schedule of 52 hours, while Yolanda worked the "short" schedule of 44 hours. Each manager was paid $750 for the week.

Under the Fair Labor Standards Act (FLSA), there are two compensation classifications: exempt and nonexempt. The **exempt** classification refers to employees that do not receive additional pay for overtime. Both salaried and hourly employees can be classified as exempt, but it is usually salaried employees that have this classification. The current standards for exempt status that apply to the restaurant and foodservice industry are shown in Figure 4-1 as an excerpt from the U.S. Department of Labor Wage and Hour Division Fact Sheet 17A.[2] The current standards for overtime pay and **nonexempt** personnel that apply to the restaurant and foodservice industry are shown in Figure 4-2 as an excerpt from the U.S. Department of Labor Wage and Hour Division Fact Sheet 14.[3] These standards are revised often, so it is best to check the current law at www.dol.gov/whd/. It is important to note that individual states generally have their own regulations relating to overtime pay. The chef supervisor must be up to date on all of the regulations. Failure to pay overtime when it should be paid can result in major fines costing the company far more than the overtime pay.

The *FLSA* requires that most employees in the United States be paid at least the *federal minimum wage* for all hours worked and *overtime* pay at time and one-half the regular rate of pay for all hours worked over 40 hours in a workweek.

However, Section 13(a)(1) of the FLSA provides an exemption from both *minimum wage* and *overtime pay* for employees employed as bona fide executive, administrative, professional and outside sales employees. Section 13(a)(1) and Section 13(a)(17) also exempt certain computer employees. To qualify for exemption, employees generally must meet certain tests regarding their job duties and be paid on a salary basis at not less than $455 per week. Job titles do not determine exempt status. In order for an exemption to apply, an employee's specific job duties and salary must meet all the requirements of the Department's regulations.

See other fact sheets in this series for more information on the exemptions for *executive*, *administrative*, *professional*, *computer* and *outside sales* employees, and for more information on the salary basis requirement.

Executive Exemption

To qualify for the executive employee exemption, all of the following tests must be met:

- The employee must be compensated on a *salary* basis (as defined in the regulations) at a rate not less than $455 per week;
- The employee's primary duty must be managing the enterprise, or managing a customarily recognized department or subdivision of the enterprise;
- The employee must customarily and regularly direct the work of at least two or more other full-time employees or their equivalent; and
- The employee must have the authority to hire or fire other employees, or the employee's suggestions and recommendations as to the hiring, firing, advancement, promotion or any other change of status of other employees must be given particular weight.

Administrative Exemptions

To qualify for the administrative employee exemption, all of the following tests must be met:

- The employee must be compensated on a *salary* or fee basis (as defined in the regulations) at a rate not less than $455 per week;
- The employee's primary duty must be the performance of office or non-manual work directly related to the management or general business operations of the employer or the employer's customers; and
- The employee's primary duty includes the exercise of discretion and independent judgment with respect to matters of significance.

Figure 4-1
FLSA exempt classification.

COMPENSATION STRUCTURE
Job Worth

The first step in determining a compensation structure is establishing job worth. **Job worth** is the value placed on the work and responsibilities assigned to a position and the experience, knowledge, and skills required to carry out the work and responsibilities. Establishing job worth begins with the job analysis, which leads to the job description. Once it is clear what the position does and what is needed to succeed in the position, there are two primary ways to determine the value: external and internal equity. The desired outcome is a pay structure that reflects the market value of positions and creates equity across positions in the company.

The establishment of job worth is a complex undertaking. The ability of companies to conduct the research and analysis needed to properly carry out the work is limited. In most cases an outside consultant is used. Methods used to establish job worth

Fact Sheet #14: Coverage Under the Fair Labor Standards Act (FLSA)

This fact sheet provides general information concerning coverage under the *FLSA*.

The FLSA is the Federal law which sets *minimum wage, overtime, recordkeeping,* and *youth employment standards*.

The minimum wage for covered nonexempt workers is not less than $7.25 per hour effective July 24, 2009. With only some exceptions, overtime ("time and one-half") must be paid for work over forty hours a week. Child labor regulations prohibit persons younger than eighteen years old from working in certain jobs and additionally sets rules concerning the hours and times employees under sixteen years of age may work.

More than 130 million American workers are protected (or "covered") by the FLSA, which is enforced by the Wage and Hour Division of the U.S. Department of Labor.

There are two ways in which an employee can be covered by the law: "enterprise coverage" and "individual coverage."

Enterprise Coverage

Employees who work for certain businesses or organizations (or "enterprises") are covered by the FLSA. These enterprises, which must have at least two employees, are:

(1) those that have an annual dollar volume of sales or business done of at least $500,000
(2) hospitals, businesses providing medical or nursing care for residents, schools and preschools, and government agencies

Individual Coverage

Even when there is no enterprise coverage, employees are protected by the FLSA if their work regularly involves them in commerce between States ("interstate commerce"). The FLSA covers individual workers who are "engaged in commerce or in the production of goods for commerce."

Examples of employees who are involved in interstate commerce include those who: produce goods (such as a worker assembling components in a factory or a secretary typing letters in an office) that will be sent out of state, regularly make telephone calls to persons located in other States, handle records of interstate transactions, travel to other States on their jobs, and do janitorial work in buildings where goods are produced for shipment outside the State.

Also, domestic service workers (such as housekeepers, full-time babysitters, and cooks) are normally covered by the law.

Figure 4-2
FLSA—Nonexempt classification.

include the ranking method, classification method, point method, and factor comparison method. Each method involves an in-depth analysis of what is termed compensable factors. A **compensable factor** is one that the company values and is willing to pay for. Examples of a compensable factor include education, skills, experience, and position responsibilities. The company probably will be willing to pay for a college degree for a management position, but not for a dishwasher position.

The **ranking method** is typically the ranking of positions by a group of managers based on the difficulty of the work, skill required, or possibly importance to the organization. For example, positions would be ranked from least difficult to most difficult. The **classification method** is also called "job grading." This method is often used by government agencies. Positions are classified at set levels, which have established pay ranges. Classifications for federal employees, the GS (General Scale) ratings, include:

- Clerical and nonsupervisory personnel (GS1 to GS4)
- Management trainees (GS5 to GS10)
- General management and highly specialized jobs (GS11 to GS15)

The **point method** assigns a point value to each position based on set criteria. The development of the criteria is a complex process, but once it is done, the method is easy to use. The factor comparison method is based on identifying key jobs in the company. Once the key jobs are identified, the wage for these positions becomes the benchmark for all other positions.

Compensation Package

The establishment of the worth of a position is part of creating a **compensation structure** for the company. A company's compensation structure reflects its mission, values, and goals. A well-structured compensation structure encourages high morale, loyalty, and quality performance. The compensation structure is not just pay, it is a package. This package includes pay, benefits, and incentives.

BENEFITS

Benefits are part of a comprehensive compensation structure. **Benefits** can generally be classified in four broad categories: mandatory, optional/voluntary, retirement, and miscellaneous. Mandatory benefits are those mandated by the state or federal government. There are three primary mandatory benefits that most nongovernmental employers must provide. These are Social Security, Workers Compensation, and Unemployment Compensation.

Social Security was established in 1935 by the Federal Insurance Contribution Act. The purpose of **Social Security** is to provide financial security for all employers, employees, and their dependents through retirement and disability income and survivor benefits. In 2011, the employer contributed 6.2% and the employee contributed 4.2% of the employee's pay per year to the taxable maximum. The 2011 rate of contribution by the employee was actually 2% below the standard. The standard is 6.2% for both the employer and the employee.[4]

The **taxable maximum** is the contribution and benefits base set by the federal government.[5] The contribution and benefits base for Social Security in 2011 was $106,800. The taxable maximum can change. Changes in the taxable maximum are generally tied to increases in the "average wage index." For example, the taxable maximum was $102,000 in 2008 and was adjusted to $106,800 in 2009 with no change in 2010 or 2011.[6]

Related to Social Security is the **Medicare** Hospital Insurance program, which is intended to provide the same type of security for health care. The employer also contributes 1.45% of the employee's pay to Medicare, but there is no contribution base limit for this contribution.[7]

Both Social Security and Medicare benefits are available to the employee at retirement if they have met the age requirement. The eligible age for retirement and benefit amount based on birth year for 2011[8] is shown in Figure 4-3. These benefits are also available to employees who have become disabled and the survivors of employees that have passed away.

Workers compensation provides for the medical care and disability pay of individuals injured in the workplace. The amount the employer pays for this benefit will vary with the claims rate of the employer. The fewer the claims the employer has, the lower the rate for the insurance. Workers compensation insurance may be provided by the state, private insurance companies, or restaurant associations. Many states allow companies to self-insure. This means that the company creates a fund that is available to pay in case of injury. Companies that self-insure generally have to have their funding certified by someone in state government and submit to audit by the state.[9]

Age To Receive Full Social Security Benefits	
Year of Birth	Full Retirement Age
1937 or earlier	65
1938	65 and 2 months
1939	65 and 4 months
1940	65 and 6 months
1941	65 and 8 months
1942	65 and 10 months
1943–1954	66
1955	66 and 2 months
1956	66 and 4 months
1957	66 and 6 months
1958	66 and 8 months
1959	66 and 10 months
1960 and later	67

The earliest a person can start receiving Social Security retirement benefits will remain age 62.[5]

Figure 4-3
Social Security benefits.

"The Social Security Act of 1935 (Public Law 74-271) created the Federal-State Unemployment Compensation (UC) Program. The program has two main objectives: (1) to provide temporary and partial wage replacement to involuntarily unemployed workers who were recently employed; and (2) to help stabilize the economy during recessions. The U.S. Department of Labor oversees the system, but each State administers its own program."[10] This benefit is generally paid by the state to qualified individuals. The overall purpose of the federal-state unemployment compensation is to provide minimal support to unemployed individuals while they find new employment. The unemployment insurance fund in a state is generally, at least partially, funded by a tax on employers based on their number of employees and claim rate. Again, as with workers compensation, the fewer the claims, the lower the rate paid by the employer.

Common optional benefits include paid sick days, paid vacation days, health insurance, life insurance, dental insurance, and paid holidays. The cost associated with each of these benefits can be significant. According to the U.S. Department of Labor, as of December 2010, on average total employee compensation broke down to 70.8% for wages and 29.2% for benefits.[11] This means that for every dollar spent on wages, an additional forty-one cents was spent for benefits. This means that the employee who is paid the federal minimum wage of $7.25 per hour is actually receiving $10.23 in compensation. Benefits are costly but generate positive outcomes. "Results indicate that among the industry groupings examined, firms that offer more benefits have lower employee turnover."[12] The cost of turnover is high. Turnover involves training cost and affects quality of service. Providing these types of benefits can increase employee loyalty.

According to the 9th Annual Survey of Employee Benefits Survey,[13] these outcomes include increased employee loyalty. These benefits can be funded 100% by the employer or provided on a cost share basis. A cost share program is one in which both the employer and the employee pay a portion of the cost of the benefit.

Retirement benefits can add to the stability of the company's workforce. "Benefits continue to attract and retain employees, and the importance of benefits to employees across all generations will only increase over the coming year," Ron Leopold (vice president of MetLife) predicted. "Employees and employers acknowledge the importance of salaries and health benefits to employee loyalty. But other benefits are important drivers of loyalty as well," Leopold said, "especially retirement benefits and nonmedical benefits, including life, dental and disability insurance. Yet, only about 37 percent of employers recognize this."[14] There are two primary types of retirement plans: contributory and noncontributory. A **contributory** retirement plan is one in which the employer and employee contribute to the plan. An example would be the employer matching every $1.00 contributed by the employee with $2.00. This is the most popular type of retirement plan today. A **noncontributory** plan is one in which only the employer contributes to the plan. In both types of plans, the funds invested in the plan are tax-deferred income. Tax-deferred income is income that will be taxed when the funds are taken out of the plan. Generally this is done at retirement, and the tax rate for the individual is lower than at the time of investment. There are specific guidelines for the handling and withdrawing of funds from a retirement plan. The Employee Retirement Income Security Act of 1974 established guidelines to which the employer must adhere.

The terms vested or vesting are of importance when discussing retirement plans. Vesting is a provision generally applied to retirement plans to encourage employees to stay with a company for an extended period of time. The act of becoming **vested** in a retirement plan means that the individual contributes to the plan (and works for the company) for a specific length of time. Employees who leave the company and stop contributing to the plan before the specified length of time will receive back what they have put into the plan, but they will not receive any funds contributed by the company. The length of time to achieve vesting varies from company to company and plan to plan.

Miscellaneous benefits often include free or discounted meals, educational scholarships, and flexible work schedules. In the foodservice business it is common to provide some type of meal benefit. In settings such as private clubs or fine dining restaurants, this often is in the form of a "family meal." The family meal is prepared for all employees and served before the start of a service period such as dinner. In other settings, such as quick service or full service restaurants, it is common for an employee working a 6- to 8-hour shift to be given a meal or provided the opportunity to purchase a meal at a discount rate.

It is becoming more common for employers to offer assistance to employees who are pursuing education or training. This assistance may be a scholarship award based on work performance. The assistance may also be in the form of a reimbursement plan. The employee, upon successfully completing course work, obtains reimbursement of the cost of the course or training from the company. These types of programs generate employee loyalty. They also can be a cornerstone of a program to develop a pool of in-house employees suitable for advancement. "Education benefits have long been associated with full-time workers who want to move up within their companies with advanced degrees. But, eager to recruit and retain employees, local businesses such as Bill Miller Bar-B-Q are beefing up their investment in higher education and training even for young, part-time employees."[15]

In the restaurant industry, flexible work schedules are not as easily provided as in other types of businesses. In general, a flexible work schedule means that a company allows employees to adapt their work schedule to their other life responsibilities. This might include individuals who work from home to allow them to take care of children or an elderly parent. This is probably not realistic for a restaurant. What is realistic is asking employees what hours are best for them to work and taking this into consideration when creating a work schedule.

INCENTIVE PROGRAMS

Incentive programs can be an important part of a compensation package or can simply be a moral builder depending on the type of program. An **incentive** is something that encourages the employee to take action. An **incentive program** is a program that encourages employees to achieve specific goals set by the company. The program is built on rewards for achieving those goals. This type of program is a common part of a management (including the chef and possibly the sous chef) compensation package. Generally the program is structured around the achievement of a specific food and/or labor cost target and/or a profit level for the operation. The reward for achieving the goal set may be a bonus or profit sharing. The level of bonus or profit sharing generally is scaled according to the level of the employee. For example, the chef would receive more than the sous chef, but the chef would receive less than the general manager. This may also extend to the other staff in the front and back of the house. If a property achieves a specified goal, there may be a bonus for all team members.

Another common type of incentive program in the restaurant business is sales based. An example is creating a reward for the server who sells the most wine or desserts. Generally these types of programs are intended to accomplish too goals. The incentive is designed to increase overall sales. The incentive is also designed to drive sales of a particular part of the menu or menu item. This can be an excellent way to bring customer notice to a new item or a standard item that has slipped in sales.

EMPLOYEE ASSISTANCE PROGRAMS

Employee Assistance Programs are considered to be a benefit, but they benefit both the employee and the employer. An **Employee Assistance Program (EAP)** is intended to help employees deal with personal problems that could adversely affect the employee's work performance, health, and well-being. EAPs focus on issues such as personal crises. These situations could include a death in the family, abuse of the employee by someone either inside or outside the company, or financial hardship. Drug and alcohol abuse also are a major focus of EAPs. The EAP provides short-term counseling and refers the employee to professionals and agencies that can give them long-term assistance. The EAP is part of the company, but must be able to deal with issues confidentially. Because the EAP can deal with issues confidentially, it may also be the go-to place for what is termed whistle blowing. **Whistle blowing** is when an employee feels there is an inappropriate or unsafe activity is taking place that should be reported, but fears they could lose their job for being the one who reports the activity.

The number of companies that provide EAPs is increasing. These programs allow companies to assist long-term employees through difficult times so they continue to be an asset to the company.

SCHEDULING

Scheduling is the action of establishing the flow of staff over a set period of time for a property based on the projected need for personnel at a specific time. A staff schedule can contribute to the company's profit or loss. Scheduling more staff than are needed

Employee Schedule
Week Of June 23rd- June 29th

SPMH- 53
Projected Total Sales $26,129

	M-23rd	Tue-24th	Wd-25th	Tr-26th	Fr-27th	Sat-28th	Sun-29th	Total per
X1Serv	10:30–1:30 5:30–9:30	X	9:30–1:30 5:30–9:30	X	10:30–1:30 5:30–9:30	X	10:30–1:30 5:30–9:30	29
X2Serv	X	9:30–1:30 5:30–9:30	X	10:30–1:30 5:30–9:30	X	10:30–1:30 5:30–9:30	X	22
X3Serv	5:30–9:30	X	5:30–9:30	X	5:30–9:30	X	5:30–9:30	16
X4Serv	10:30–1:30 5:30–9:30	X	10:30–2:00 5:30–9:30	X	10:30–1:30 5:30–9:30	X	10:30–1:30 5:30–9:30	28.5
X5Serv	X	5:30–9:30	X	5:30–9:30	X	5:30–9:30	X	12
X6Serv	5:30–9:30	5:30–9:30	5:30–9:30	5:30–9:30	5:30–9:30	X	5:30–9:30	24
X7Serv	9:30–2:30	X	X	9:30–2:30	9:30–2:30	9:30–2:30	9:30–2:30	25
X8Serv	X	10:30–2:00 5:30–9:30	X	10:30–1:30 5:30–9:30	X	10:30–1:30 5:30–9:30	X	21.5
X8Host	X	11:30–1:30 6:00–9:00	X	11:30–1:30 6:00–9:00	X	5:30–9:30	11:30–1:30 6:00–9:00	19
X9Host	11:30–1:30 6:00–9:00	X	11:30–1:30 6:00–9:00	X	11:30–1:30 6:00–9:00	11:30–1:30 6:00–9:00	X	20
X10LC	X	10:30–1:30 5:30–9:30	X	10:30–1:30 5:30–9:30	X	10:30–1:30 5:30–9:30	X	21
X11LC	6:00–2:00	X	X	6:00–2:00	6:00–2:00	6:00–2:00	6:00–2:00	40
X12LC	2:00–10:00	X	X	2:00–10:00	2:00–10:00	2:00–10:00	2:00–10:00	40
X13LC	10:00–3:00 6:30–9:30	6:00–2:00	6:00–2:00	X	X	10:00–3:00 6:30–9:30	10:00–3:00 6:30–9:30	40
X14LC	X	5:30–9:30	5:30–9:30	5:30–9:30	5:30–9:30	5:30–9:30	5:30–9:30	24
X15LC	X	2:00–10:00	2:00–10:00	10:00–3:00 6:30–9:30	10:00–3:00 6:30–9:30	X	X	30
X16DW	11:00–2:00 6:00–10:00	X	X	11:00–2:00 6:00–10:00	11:00–2:00 6:00–10:00	11:00–2:00 6:00–10:00	11:00–2:00 6:00–10:00	35
X17DW	6:00–10:00	11:00–2:00 6:00–10:00	11:00–2:00 6:00–10:00	X	X	6:00–10:00	6:00–10:00	26
X18DW	6:00–10:00	6:00–10:00	6:00–10:00	6:00–10:00	6:00–10:00	X	X	20
								493
Total Day	71	64.5	59.5	78	71	78	71	493

Figure 4-4
Employee schedule.

to provide the level of service and production output for a period of time increases labor expense unnecessarily.

Developing a schedule requires information such as sales projections and output standards. **Sales projections** are based on sales histories. A sales history is the result of keeping track of sales. To develop a schedule, the previous sales for the same or a similar time of year, month, day, and even hour should be reviewed. This information is considered along with weather predictions, the current economic climate, and any special circumstances.

For example, when building a staff schedule for the week of June 23–29, the scheduler looked at the sales for the period in the previous three years. A single year can be used, but it is more accurate to look at multiple years to predict sales for the coming year at that time. The sales looked at are not just dollar sales. Also considered are the number of guests served, the type of food served, and the times of day for the sales. The scheduler also considers that overall sales have been down for the past 12 months on average by about 5% from the previous year. The downward trend of sales looks like it will be balanced for the week being scheduled because a special festival is scheduled that is expected to bring a 15% temporary increase in sales. All of this information makes it possible for the scheduler to make an educated estimate of sales for the period in question.

The sales are now predicted, but the number of staff members needed to take care of that level of business must still be determined. This is decided based on the standards of the operation for production and service, which can also be called **output standards**. The standards will vary depending on the type of property, but the question is always the same: How many guests can a service staff member serve and still deliver the standard of service established for the restaurant? How many line cooks and other kitchen staff are needed to deliver the number of products that will be needed at the level of quality established for the restaurant? These questions can easily be applied to any business. For example, how many housekeepers are necessary to clean the projected number of rooms in the hotel at the established level of quality?

Companies use a variety of methods for scheduling in an effort to control both quality and costs. One of the more common methods is called **sales-per-man-hour**. Sales-per-man-hour, when applied to scheduling, is the dollar amount of sales that one hour of labor is expected to generate. This one hour of labor is generally hourly labor, not salaried management. A company often will set a standard for sales-per-man-hour by, for example, scheduling no more than 1 hour of labor for every $55 in projected sales. Under this standard, if the projected sales for a day are $3,200, no more than 58.18 hours of labor time can be scheduled. The scheduler, or manager, must determine where to apply the hours available. An example of a schedule that utilizes sales-per-man-hour is shown in Figure 4-4.

SUMMARY

While many of the details addressed in this chapter may be delegated to a human resource department in a larger operation, the full management team, including the chef supervisor, should be involved. Compensation benefits and scheduling are critically important to the continued operation of any business. In today's world, profit margins often are slim. This makes consideration, planning, and execution in this area of even greater importance. The goal is always to attract and retain the finest possible staff. Compensation, benefits, and scheduling play an important part in accomplishing this goal.

DISCUSSION QUESTIONS

1. Define the following chapter key terms:
   a. Compensation
   b. Hourly wage
   c. Salary
   d. Exempt personnel
   e. Nonexempt personnel
   f. Job worth
   g. Compensable factor
   h. Ranking method
   i. Classification method
   j. Point method
   k. Compensation structure
   l. Benefits
   m. Social Security
   n. Taxable maximum
   o. Medicare
   p. Contributory
   q. Noncontributory
   r. Vested
   s. Incentive
   t. Incentive program
   u. Employee Assistance Program (EAP)
   v. Whistle blowing
   w. Scheduling
   x. Sales projections
   y. Output standards
   z. Sales-per-man-hour
2. Discuss the relationship between compensation and motivation.
3. What are the steps to determining job worth?
4. List three examples of incentive programs that might be used in a restaurant.
5. Discuss the value of benefits?
6. What are the steps involved in scheduling?
7. What is Social Security?
8. What is Medicare?
9. Using the example provided in Figure 4-3 as a model, write a 7-day staff schedule based on sales-per-man-hour of $38 and total sales for the seven days of $30,134.

NOTES

1. http://www.rocunited.org/research-resources/reports/roc-serving-while-sick/, (September 30, 2010) Restaurant Opportunities Centers United.

2. http://www.dol.gov/whd/regs/compliance/fairpay/fs17a_overview.pdf, (revised July, 2008) United States Department of Labor, Wage and Hour Division.

3. http://www.dol.gov/whd/regs/compliance/whdfs14.htm, (revised July, 2009) United States Department of Labor, Wage and Hour Division.

4. http://www.ssa.gov/oact/cola/cbb.html, (last reviewed December 29, 2010) Social Security Administration.

5. Ibid.

6. Ibid.

7. Ibid.

8. http://www.ows.doleta.gov/unemploy/uifactsheet.asp, (updated January 13, 2010) United States Department of Labor.

9. http://www.dir.ca.gov/sip/sip.html, (2011) California Department of Industrial Relations.

10. http://www.policyalmanac.org/social_welfare/archive/unemployment_compensation.shtml, Almanac of Policy Issues.

11. http://www.bls.gov/news.release/ecec.nr0.htm, (March 9, 2011) United States Department of Labor, Bureau of Labor Statistics.

12. http://wydoe.state.wy.us/lmi/0203/a2.htm, (2003) The Wyoming Department of Employment, Research & Planning.

13. John Scorza, "Benefits Can Boost Employee Loyalty," (April 1, 2011) http://www.shrm.org/hrdisciplines/benefits/Articles/Pages/Benefits_Loyalty.aspx, Society for Human Resource Management.

14. Ibid.

15. Lisa Y. Taylor, "Recipe for Retention," *San Antonio Business Journal*, October 10, 2004. http://www.enewsbuilder.net/peoplereport/e_article000326611.cfm?x=b11,0,w

part two
The World of Training and Development

Chapter 5
Orientation

OBJECTIVES

When you complete this chapter, you should be able to:

1. Differentiate between induction and orientation training programs
2. Identify the elements and essential information that form part of induction and orientation training
3. Describe methods of communicating induction and orientation programs and outline how they can benefit the foodservice organization and the new team member
4. Describe topics for inclusion in kitchen orientation training programs
5. Explain the value of follow-up and evaluation of induction and orientation training

Case Study: Rock Hill Inn

Lisa was extremely glad that she had been hired as an apprentice at the prestigious Rock Hill Inn. She felt that her successful completion of the three-year apprenticeship would lead to opportunities in the finest restaurants around the country. Lisa had wanted to be a chef ever since she first began to help her mother in the kitchen. Starting at the age of 12, one of her greatest treats was to prepare food for her family and friends. She was eager to learn the "right way" to prepare food.

On her first day, Lisa reported to Executive Chef Lang at 8 A.M., and Chef Lang immediately sent her to the Human Resource office to complete paperwork. After she completed the necessary paperwork, one of the Human Resource officers quickly reviewed the benefits package. She was also given an employee handbook and instructed to read it carefully so that she would be familiar with the various company policies. After signing a form acknowledging that she had received a copy of the handbook, Lisa was told to report to Chef Lang. It was 9:30 A.M.

Chef Lang explained to Lisa that as an apprentice she would be rotated through various areas of the kitchen and would receive training from virtually all the cooks and chefs. He gave her a training manual and a training journal. Chef Lang instructed her to familiarize herself with the manual and to ask her first supervising chef how to keep a record of her training in the journal. He said that he reviewed each apprentice's journal on a weekly basis. Chef Lang explained that Lisa's first assignment would be the banquet kitchen because it was an excellent place to learn and refine her basic skills. He said she could expect to be in the banquet kitchen for 6 to 8 weeks. He also told Lisa that generally on Mondays he gathered all the apprentices (a total of 12) together to discuss how their training was progressing and any concerns they might have.

Chef Lang escorted Lisa to the banquet kitchen, where he introduced her to the banquet chef, Hank. It was 10:15 A.M. When Chef Lang left, Hank told Lisa that he was extremely busy and would meet with her later. He introduced her to two other apprentices, Jim and Gale, who were prepping for that evening's banquet. Hank told the apprentices to give Lisa some work to do and told her he would speak to her when things slowed down. Lisa noticed that Jim and Gale gave each other a "Yeah right!" look as Hank walked away.

Gale told Lisa that she could start by peeling and fine dicing fifty pounds of onion. She showed Lisa where the cutting boards were located and where to work. As she walked away she told Lisa, "Welcome to the grunt squad." Later, when Lisa was about half finished with the onions, Jim told here that the onions now needed to be thin sliced rather than diced and that she had to start over.

Jim told Lisa to put the diced onion in containers, label it, and place it in the walk-in refrigerator "because someone would use it for something." It was 11:30 A.M. He also told her that before she started cutting onions again, they would go get some lunch in the employee dining room. During lunch, Gale and Jim told Lisa all about being an apprentice or, as they called it, a "grunt" at the Rock Hill Inn. She asked how long they had been at the Inn, and they each said "four months." She asked why they were still in the banquet kitchen since Chef Lang had told her she would be there only 4 to 8 weeks. Jim and Gale said that the training schedule in the manual was rarely followed and that Chef Lang had never reviewed their training journals. Lisa asked if the schedule and journals were discussed in the Monday meetings, and they said there had not been a Monday meeting in three months. Jim and Gale made it clear to Lisa that they were both looking to leave the Inn as soon as they could get another position because they did not feel they were learning anything. They said that all they ever did was cut and chop things and sweep and mop floors.

After lunch, Lisa started peeling and slicing onions. It was 12:15 P.M. Lisa finished peeling and slicing the onions and then cleaned the area where she had been working. Jim then told her to sweep out the store rooms and walk-in refrigerators associated with the banquet kitchen. At 5:30 P.M. Hank came by and told her that she could leave for the day and that he would meet with her at 7:30 A.M. the next day, give her a work schedule, and discuss her duties with her. He asked her what she thought of being part of the team at the Rock Hill Inn and she said, "It's ok, I guess." Hank told Lisa that she'd better get a more enthusiastic and positive attitude or she would not last long at the Inn.

Based on what you have learned from previous chapters and the content of this chapter, answer the following questions.

- What is the overall reason for Lisa's perceived lack of enthusiasm and positive attitude?
- What are the primary causal agents for Lisa's perceived lack of enthusiasm and positive attitude?
- What role did leadership and supervision/management play in Lisa's perceived lack of enthusiasm and positive attitude?
- What specific steps could have been taken to avoid Lisa's perceived lack of enthusiasm and positive attitude?
- What, specifically, can be done by the Rock Hill Inn to avoid a repeat of Lisa's perceived lack of enthusiasm and positive attitude by future apprentices?

INTRODUCTION

A new team member's first impressions about his or her job can make all the difference. Orientation is the foundation for attitudes that may stay in place as long as that team member remains in the foodservice organization. Orientation describes the types of training given to a new kitchen team member. It provides information about the job and working conditions, and covers the main activities and duties in which the new team member will be involved. Orientation clarifies the area of training in which the new team member will be instructed and the levels of performance expected. Orientation also involves socialization, which includes the culture, mission, and philosophy of the organization. Socialization is only part of orientation, but a very distinct part. It also provides a systematic plan to accomplish these goals. By providing an orientation program, the chef supervisor communicates to new employees what is expected of them and how their jobs fit into the overall operation. It also helps employees fit into their jobs faster, be more productive and satisfied, and realize that the supervisor cares. Also, remember that how employees treat customers often reflects how they are treated by management.[1]

ORIENTATION

Orientation is a systematic method to acquaint the new team member with all aspects of the new job. Orientation can be defined as a two-way informational and introductory session conducted by the employer to educate and excite all participants.[2] Its purpose is to make the new team member an effective contributor to the kitchen team in the shortest time available.

New team members receive orientation from their fellow team members and from the organization. The orientation received from fellow team members is usually unplanned and unofficial, and it often provides the new team member with misleading and inaccurate information. This is one reason why the official orientation provided by the foodservice organization is so important. An effective orientation program has an immediate and lasting impact on the new team member and can make the difference between a new team member's success or failure. Studies have identified a strong correlation between customer satisfaction and the employee's view of service quality. When employees view an organization's human resources policies favorably, customers tend to view the quality of service they receive favorably.[3]

It is ultimately the responsibility of the chef supervisor to carry out induction and orientation training. Each new team member brings to the workplace his or her own

Figure 5-1
Planned orientation ROI.

> - All new team members will receive information to allow them to fit into the kitchen as quickly as possible.
> - The new team member is working productively from the first day.
> - The new team member is assigned duties and is informed of the quality standards required.
> - The new team member will be more inclined to have a sense of belonging and will consequently be motivated.
> - The new team member will be more inclined to be confident and loyal.
> - The scene is set for further training.
> - Job expectations are fulfilled.

set of values. The new employee's values and attitudes may be quite different from those of the supervisor and other employees. The background of the new employee will have some effect on the way this person relates to the supervisor and to the new job.[4] In view of this, orientation training should be prepared with the same attention to detail as any other training program. It can be one of the best and most complete training investments that the foodservice organization makes.

The highest proportion of employee turnover occurs within the first 30 days. This is due largely to poor or nonexistent orientation training. The **return on investment** (ROI) from a planned approach to orientation takes many forms, as shown in Figure 5-1. The type of operation in which the kitchen is located affects who does the training and the format of the training. Regardless of the type or size of operation, orientation training is critical to employee success and reduction of turnover.

In the large restaurant or hotel, the training may take place in a formal setting and is highly structured. There are a large number of team members to be oriented to the company, the property, and their specific department. The consistency of the program is based on materials developed strictly for that purpose, particularly at the company and property levels. The initial part of the program may be conducted by the human resource department and cover information about the company and property for all new team members. The orientation of the new team members of the various departments would be conducted in those departments, including the kitchen. The orientation of the new kitchen team members would be conducted by the chef supervisor following the general orientation. In a chain property, there are generally standardized orientation materials for each department. If materials are not available, they would be developed by the chef supervisor in conjunction with the human resource department. In larger properties, the total orientation generally will take a half to a full day.

The first three days for the new team member at work is a critical time and will have a definite effect on his or her future performance. The first day is an opportunity to set a positive tone, which can avoid problems that might occur later.[5]

In smaller properties where there is no human resource person in house, the orientation is generally conducted by the chef supervisor with possible input from the general manager. Materials would be developed by the chef supervisor with input from the general manager. Conduct of the orientation becomes more of a challenge in the smaller property because often the need for the new team member in production is immediate. This need must be recognized as a reality of the operation. The chef supervisor who is quality focused will not allow the orientation to be sidelined because of the need. The ROI on the orientation training is too great and its impact on future quality too certain to dismiss it because of time challenges. In the small operation, the mark of

Figure 5-2
Orientation and the smaller property.

- Schedule orientation time as part of the new team members' first day and first week.
- Prioritize orientation information into 3–4 levels and spread the information over shorter orientation sessions throughout the new team member's first week.
- Create orientation materials that can be used repeatedly.
- Develop a handbook for the basic information that a kitchen team member needs to know and require the new team member to read the handbook before reporting for duty the first day.

the excellent chef supervisor will be their scheduling of time for, and conducting orientation training for all new team members. Suggestions for conducting orientation training in smaller, time-challenged operations are shown in Figure 5-2.

The topics presented in the training plan should be based on the needs of the organization and the new team member. Generally, the foodservice organization is concerned with meeting the needs of its customers, making a profit, satisfying team member needs, and being socially responsible. New team members, on the other hand, are generally more interested in pay, benefits, and specific terms and conditions of employment. A good balance between the foodservice organization and the new team member's needs is essential if the orientation program is to be successful.

Arrangements should be made to tour the foodservice facilities. In addition, comprehensive orientation kits should be prepared for all new team members and should include the type of information shown in Figure 5-3.

The chef supervisor might want to conclude the explanation of the orientation handbook policies and procedures by reviewing the most important points. Additionally,

CHEF TALK
"MY FIRST DAY"

It will remain with me forever, my first day in the kitchen. As an innocent young apprentice chef filled with expectations of my future in the culinary profession, armed with my new chef uniforms and my meager set of chef's knives, I began my "orientation" to the chef's profession, which I still love to this day. However, my first day on the job as an apprentice chef at Jury's Hotel in Dublin, Ireland, was anything but a pleasant experience. Induction and orientation training sessions were unheard of back then. In fact, the only information I was provided with was a duty roster in which I was listed as the "new body." Nobody had bothered to even find out what my name was. The roster, as I remember, was an 11-day cycle spread over 2 weeks. It was broken down into 7 late days, 6 early days, with every second Sunday off and a day off each week. Late days began at 9 A.M., off at 3 P.M., return at 6 P.M., until 10:30 P.M. Early days were 9 A.M. to 6 P.M.

On my first day I reported to the "back office" for a time card. I was directed to the male changing room. After considerable effort, I eventually found this room. When I got there, there was no available locker to store my street clothes after I had changed into my chef uniform. I reported to the head

chef and introduced myself to him. He barely acknowledged my presence, and with a grunt waved me toward the sous chef, who assigned me to the garde manger department. The chef garde manger's method of induction and orientation was to give nicknames and engage constantly in ridicule. At the end of my first period that day, I returned to the locker room to discover that my street clothes had disappeared. I had to cycle home that afternoon in my chef uniform. My parents were furious. They wanted me to remain at home and to consider some other profession. In any event, I did go back to the hotel that evening. Orientation was by the sink-or-swim method by the other chef apprentices. This was probably the worst type of orientation anyone could receive. As a result of that first day, I formed attitudes about the organization that took many years to undo. If I had been inducted and orientated in a planned and sequential way, I know I would have been a much more productive worker. I have often wondered since then how many potential "Escoffiers" were turned off simply because of poor initial orientation or no orientation training at all.

—Noel C. Cullen, Ed.D., CMC, AAC

Figure 5-3
Orientation kit content.

- Map of the foodservice organization's facilities
- Organizational chart
- Organization's policies and procedures handbook, which typically features information and guidance on the following topics:
  - Safety and sanitation procedures
  - Uniforms, dress code, and grooming policies
  - Union policies (if applicable)
  - Payroll procedures
  - Vacation, public and religious holiday policies
  - Group health insurance
  - Meals and break policies
  - Pension/savings plan
  - Attendance, hours of work
  - Incentive programs
  - Performance evaluations
  - Emergency procedures
  - Promotion policy
  - Harassment policy
  - Employee assistance programs
  - Security department's authority
  - Disciplinary rules and actions
  - Key telephone numbers
  - Training programs

the forms that the new team member will need to complete should be highlighted within the orientation. *Reassure new employees. Let them know you are confident they can do the job and that they will get all the support they need from the team.*

Many foodservice organizations require team members to complete a questionnaire on the policy notebook. The questionnaire is not graded, but it is checked. Others require passing a test on safety and sanitation, emergencies, hazardous materials handling, and harassment policies. This shows whether there are areas of the notebook that are unclear and need further explanation. The policy notebook will contain policies on topics such as vacations, holidays, sick leave, absenteeism, tardiness, health examinations, accidents, safety, parking regulations, disciplinary actions, grievance procedures, health and group insurance, and other policies and benefits.

SOCIALIZATION

Socialization implies the absorbing of a new team member into the culture of the foodservice organization. It is separated deliberately from other orientation as a focus. Orientation tends to be process oriented. Socialization is more culture and attitude oriented. Training targeted to socialization will cover issues such as customer focus, philosophy, team focus, mission statement, corporate culture, commitment to goals, concepts of empowerment, and individuals' attitudes toward these goals. Socialization does not need to cover specific job details, since its purpose is to evoke feelings and generate commitment. The chef supervisor conducting the socialization should sell the organization's philosophy along with security, caring, and peace of mind by talking in general terms about benefits, recognition programs, and salary policies. New team members want to be part of a successful organization.

Socialization begins on the first day the team member begins the new job. It takes place formally through training. It takes place informally as the new staff member becomes immersed in the environment of the workplace.

While written policies concerning these issues are contained in an orientation kit, most induction training is conducted by the team. It is not just a series of slogans, but a calculated rationale that is lived by each member of the team daily. Socialization may begin with training, but it matures with time and experience. When an employee leaves an organization, needless staffing expenses are incurred and service to customers is likely to decline. Potentially good employees may be "turned off" through improper orientation and poor training.[6]

When tactfully and correctly implemented, socialization will result in a committed team member armed with the expectations of the mission of the organization.

DURATION OF ORIENTATION TRAINING

It is impossible for a new team member to absorb in one long session all of the information in the foodservice organization's orientation program. **Brief sessions** should be used. These may last up to two hours, and be spread over several days. This increases the likelihood that the new team member will understand and retain the information presented. Frequently, when new team members arrive in the kitchen, they are handed a departmental procedures handbook and are told to read the material and to ask any questions they may have. Task and station orientation should be well planned and conducted by the chef supervisor using appropriate menu and recipe guidance.

It is important to introduce the new team member to the other kitchen team members on the first day. During these introductions each team member's function and position within the team should be indicated and an explanation of how each one fits into the department should be given. Ensure that employees are told about company goals and visions and their role in the dream.[7]

As with any training, time is involved: the new team member's and the chef supervisor's. Orientation training, however, is a quality investment of time. It is one that can contribute to effective integration of the new team member and set the foundation for a long association with the organization.

CONDUCTING ORIENTATION TRAINING

If the chef supervisor does not communicate and deliver the orientation program, other team members will. This may not be the type of orientation you wish the new person to receive. Unplanned orientation can be harmful. Existing team members can paint an unfavorable and untrue picture of the kitchen operation. Most people will have a tendency to relate and listen to those they feel are their peers, rather than the supervisor. Therefore, it is important that the first impressions of the organization be created by the chef supervisor within the framework of real work situations.

New team members come with a certain amount of anxiety. They will have feelings of insecurity about their ability to do the job and fit into the team. The type of positive work environment the chef supervisor creates can reduce these anxieties and increase a feeling of worth and belonging in new team members. It is much better to invest in training at this stage because team members will become productive in a shorter period of time.

In communication, an open style should be adopted. Speak to the team member in a manner that indicates "we picked each other." Speak clearly and directly as one human being to another. Provide any background information he or she will

CHEF TALK
"INDUCTION BY FIRE"

Being a country boy with little exposure to the European culinary scene, I was a prime candidate for induction ceremonies that I later found out took place in almost every kitchen. The first night on the hot line, while setting up garnishes for the self-professed "king of the broiler," I ran out of oval platters, which were the only appropriate frame for the masterpieces coming hot and sizzling from the "master."

After being duly reprimanded for allowing the platters to run out, I was told to hastily retrieve platters from the dish room. Upon entering the dish room, I discovered there were no oval platters. With the screams of the broiler chef getting louder, I ran back to inform him of the situation. He glared at me and told me to go to the storeroom and get a "plate stretcher." Not thinking, I ran to the storeroom. I was directed to a cabinet, opened it, and rifled through

it, not even knowing what I was looking for. Suddenly it dawned on me. Plate stretcher! I turned and walked out of the storeroom to the laughs and howls of those who witnessed what I had just done. From that moment on I was adopted into the kitchen brigade and no longer felt an outsider. Rightly or wrongly, this method of passing through the gate to the inner circle of acceptance still goes on today. In the pressured, highly technical world of culinary art, humor and acceptance go hand in hand. It is a necessity to laugh together, to perform together, to depend on each other. That's a team. And it's always apparent (from the food served) if there is a team in the kitchen.

—Keith Keogh, CEC, AAC,
Magic Seasonings Blends, Inc., New Orleans, LA.

need. Explain any technical terms and avoid using kitchen jargon. Too much information at one time is as bad as too little. Provide information in manageable parts. Without making it obvious, repeat anything that is important for the team member to remember. Use open questions as much as possible. Listening to the new member during the orientation is important, not just because of what might be learned, but because it means a lot to the new team member. The intention is to communicate, not to intimidate, during this phase. Avoid "talking down" from a position of power. Show respect for the individual. A little awareness and genuine kindness go a long way. Develop an orientation program that not only goes over the rules but also stresses a "spirit of hospitality."[8]

Perception plays an important role in communication during an orientation session. It can help immensely, but it also can devastate the most sincere effort to communicate effectively. The fact is that people often hear only what they want to hear. Knowing this, the chef supervisor should keep trying until the correct feedback is received. The negative aspect of this is that it can cause the new team member to become defensive, which will hinder the communication process. Problems in perception often are caused by differences in ethnic or cultural backgrounds, different educational levels, and difficulties with the particular language used. The cultural background of people has a strong influence on the communication process, which includes nonverbal and verbal communication. Investing time to start the new team member on the correct path will make things easier for the chef supervisor.

FOLLOW-UP AND EVALUATION

Formal and systematic evaluation of the orientation training program is essential. New team members should receive a set of contingency plans and contacts in the event they need further clarification or assistance to ensure their careful induction and orientation into the foodservice organization. The chef supervisor should regularly check on how well the team members are doing and answer any questions that may have arisen after their initial induction and orientation. A formal scheduled follow-up should take place within one month after the team members become part of the kitchen team. The orientation training plan should be reviewed at least once a year. The purpose of this evaluation is to determine if the plan is meeting the foodservice organization's and new team members' needs. The evaluation is critical to improving the current program.

Feedback from new team members is one method of evaluating the induction and orientation program. This can be achieved by asking new team members to complete unsigned questionnaires or by conducting in-depth interviews. Feedback of this type enables the chef supervisor and the foodservice organization to adapt and modify the program. Induction and orientation training programs for new team members take priority in development and implementation; once completed, work on other training aspects can begin. The first day on the job is an opportunity for the chef supervisor and the foodservice organization to set a positive tone and thereby avoid problems that might occur later. The way a new kitchen team member is treated during the orientation period conveys an impression of the chef supervisor and the organization as having a well-planned, well-executed orientation program.

SUMMARY

Orientation training programs are vital to assimilating new team members into the foodservice organization's philosophy. They also provide for a clear understanding of what team members' jobs are and the level and standards of quality performance expected.

Socialization is a distinct part of orientation. It covers issues of corporate culture, philosophy, mission, customer focus, concepts of individual empowerment, and expected team member attitudes. Socialization is eventually conducted by the entire team. Orientation training is the umbrella under which socialization takes place. The purpose of the orientation training plan is to systematically and sequentially orient the new team member to the job, the kitchen, and the other team members. This approach enables him or her to effectively contribute to the organization in the shortest possible time. The first 30 days of the new team member's tenure in the job are vital. It is during this period that most employee turnover occurs, due largely to poor orientation training.

Orientation training should include an information kit that enables the new team member to fit smoothly into the foodservice organization. It is the chef supervisor's duty to ensure that the new member is armed with

the necessary information to understand rules and procedures. Orientation training should take place over a period of time in a planned way, rather than as one long session. Formal and systematic follow-up should be planned. If the chef supervisor does not conduct the orientation of the new team member, others will. Unplanned orientation, including socialization, usually results in the new person having a negative view of the new job, the organization, and the chef supervisor.

The communication style of the chef supervisor during orientation should be open and concentrate on removing anxiety and building feelings of security in the new team member. Topics for the orientation training sessions should include the kitchen department functions, team members' duties and responsibilities, pay and benefits, rules and procedures of the organization, and a tour of the entire organization.

Formal evaluation of the orientation training program should take place annually to ensure it meets with the needs and requirements of the organization and its future employees. A systematic follow-up to the initial orientation should take place within at least one month to check on new team members' comfort with their new position.

DISCUSSION QUESTIONS

1. Define the following chapter key terms:

   a. Orientation
   b. Socialization
   c. Return on investment
   d. Brief sessions
   e. Perception
   f. Formal and systematic evaluation
   g. Feedback

2. Discuss the difference between general orientation and socialization?

3. Why is an orientation training program important?

4. Why does the highest proportion of team member turnover in the kitchen occur within the first 30 days?

5. What 10 critical items should form part of an orientation packet for new kitchen team members?

6. What are the advantages of receiving feedback on an orientation training program?

7. What are the effects of unplanned socialization and orientation with regard to new kitchen team members?

8. How long after the initial orientation should systematic follow-up take place?

NOTES

1. Karen Eich Drummond, *The Restaurant Training Program* (New York: John Wiley, 1992), 1.

2. Vincent H. Eade, *Human Resources Management in the Hospitality Industry* (Scottsdale, AZ: Garsuch Sciarisbrick, 1993), 173.

3. Cliff Barbee and Valerie Bott, "Customer Treatment as a Mirror of Employee Treatment," *Advanced Management Journal,* Spring 1991, 31.

4. Anna Katherine Jernigan, *The Effective Food Service Supervisor* (Rockville, MD: Aspen Publications, 1989).

5. Marion E. Haynes, *Stepping up to Supervisor* (Los Altos, CA: Crisp Publications, 1990), 76.

6. Herman Zaccarelli, *Training Managers to Train* (Los Altos, CA: Crisp Publications, 1988), 56.

7. Jeff Weinstein, "Personnel Success," *Restaurants & Institutions,* December 1992, 113.

8. John J. Hogan, "Turnover and What To Do About It," *Cornell HRA Quarterly,* February 1992, 41.

Chapter 6
Training and Quality

OBJECTIVES

When you complete this chapter, you should be able to:

1. State the connection between training and quality
2. Describe the contribution of training to the organization's long-term health and well-being
3. Describe a systems approach to training and explain how training interacts with the quality goals of the foodservice organization
4. Define the types of training models and their strengths and weaknesses and describe situations appropriate for each method
5. List the major categories of learning, and explain how they influence the rate of learning
6. Understand the concept of andragogy and outline the challenges in this area for the chef supervisor
7. Identify factors that inhibit learning

Case Study: Juniper Crest Country Club

Juniper Crest Country Club is located in a city of 35,000. Metro Oil, the city's largest employer, dominates the city's economy and the economic well-being of the club. Metro Oil is one of the largest oil companies in the world, and Juniper Crest is the home of Metro Oil's International headquarters. Metro Oil is generous in its support of the club because the "Club" is the only place in the city that they can "properly" entertain the individuals from around the world that visit the company on a daily basis. The reason for the large membership is the number of people that hold memberships by virtue of their position with Metro Oil.

The executives of Metro Oil, many of whom are on the Club's Executive Board, and all of whom are club members, have begun expressing their dissatisfaction with the food served at the club. These individuals, as do most of the club members, regularly travel the nation and the world on behalf of Metro Oil. Through their travels they are exposed to many cuisines and trends in cuisine. They have well-developed palates and enjoy the variety and change they experience when traveling. This has presented an ongoing challenge for the club's management. The club for many years has maintained a reputation for well-prepared, high-quality food with its long-standing menu of steaks, chops, local freshwater fish, and traditional local dishes. Management's efforts over the years to change the menu, including those of the chef, have been frustrated by a lack of trained personnel in the local area and an inability to attract trained culinarians to Juniper Crest. The club has consistently offered above-average wages to attract individuals from outside the area, but the lack of a career path has still kept the club from attracting trained, skilled culinarians.

The Executive Board in its last meeting informed the General Manager and the Chef that they wanted changes made in the menu within six months or they would look for a new management team for the club. The General Manager and the Chef immediately worked to develop a plan to make the mandated changes. As the first step, the General Manager and the Chef, with the approval and support of the Board, did a whirlwind tour of the major culinary pacesetting cities in the United States. In a two-week period they traveled to San Francisco, New Orleans, Chicago, and New York. They spent two days visiting and eating at the top restaurants in each city. Additionally, they spent an extra day in Chicago, New York, and San Francisco, consulting with faculty from the prestigious culinary schools in those areas.

The General Manager and Chef utilized the information and experience from their trip to develop a new menu that incorporated different cuisines, new types of dishes and presentations, and new ingredients, but that still contained the club's most popular traditional items. The challenge was to train the existing staff to prepare the new items at the same quality level that had always been the hallmark of the Club's traditional food.

The training needed to familiarize the culinary team with the cuisines and products, including their storage and handling, was introduced as well as how to prepare the dishes. An aggressive timeline was developed for the training, and it was determined that the culinary team members would be paid for participating in the mandatory training.

The General Manager and the Chef knew that integrating the training into the Club's normal operation would be a major challenge. The operation of the kitchen had to continue with no reduction in quality while the training was taking place. Additionally, although the extent of the planned changes had not been formally announced, the culinary team's resistance to change was clearly evident. Many team members had already questioned the value of training that would not increase their wages or increase their opportunities for advancement.

Based on what you have learned from previous chapters and the content of this chapter, answer the following questions.

- What is the overall reason for the challenges occurring at the Juniper Crest Country Club?
- What are the primary causal agents for the challenges occurring in the Juniper Crest Country Club's culinary department?

- What role did leadership and supervision/management play in the challenges occurring in the Juniper Crest Country Club's culinary department?
- What specific steps could have been taken to avoid the current situation in the Juniper Crest Country Club's culinary department?
- What, specifically, can be done to overcome the training challenges and to generate motion in a positive direction for the Juniper Crest Country Club's culinary department?

INTRODUCTION

Quality is the key to success in any business. A critical factor in achieving success is training. The impact that training has on the quality of every facet of the operation is almost limitless. A partial listing of the facets of the operation affected by training includes:

- How well team members do their job
- The quality of the product and service received by the guest
- The efficiency and effectiveness of communication internally and externally
- The safety of the food served
- The safety of the work environment

Quality management and quality team member performance cannot be achieved without training. Without a strong and committed investment in training, the kitchen team will not be successful.

TRAINING IS AN INVESTMENT

Training is an investment. It is an infrastructure investment that leads to a tangible return on investment. Philip Crosby, in his book *Quality is Free*, argues that achieving quality costs nothing. He points out that the real cost of quality is doing things wrong—the cost of waste.[1] The ultimate aim of quality in the kitchen is to eliminate waste and to avoid doing things wrong at any stage in the culinary process. Therefore, if every stage is done correctly and conforms to the quality standard, then costs are not incurred and real value is accrued. Figure 6-1 shows the return on investment for training.

Figure 6-1
ROI: Training is an investment.

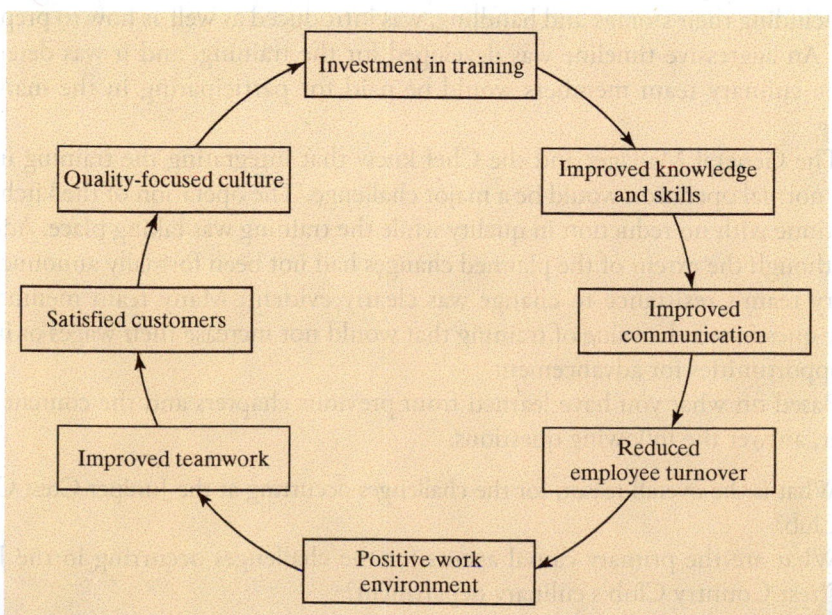

Commitment to quality and the training required to achieve it must come from the top levels of the organization. It should be communicated clearly and consistently. The commitment must be reflected in all of the organization's actions including recruitment, pay, recognition, promotion, and training. The challenge that must be met is establishing appropriate attitudes and values within the kitchen team and throughout the entire foodservice organization. Ultimately, quality will not be achieved unless there is a long-term strategy of continuous development and training of people within the kitchen. The real challenge is making it all happen. The aim of training is to provide services and products both internally and externally that meet and, it is hoped, exceed customer expectations every time. The company must deliver what was promised. The kitchen team and all staff need to be aware of what is acceptable and what is not from the customer's point of view.

Training is an investment in the long-term health and well-being of the organization.

A SYSTEMS APPROACH TO TRAINING

Training is a learning process that involves the acquisition of skills, concepts, rules, and attitudes so as to increase the performance of each team member. Training is not education. Training is the process of integrating personal and organizational goals. Training is used to close the gap between current and desired performance of individual kitchen team members. It also is about helping people learn and develop.

Training can be treated as a **total systems approach**, as a cycle with interrelated elements. These elements closely parallel the steps that a person uses to solve a problem. Five steps, shown in Figure 6-2, are generally considered to be part of this closed-loop continuous process.

1. *Analysis of training needs.* This step is sometimes called **needs analysis** and has two main purposes: to determine what is needed in the first place, and to ensure that the training that does occur is based on sound requirements.[2] Therefore, the needs analysis process is the most important step in developing a training program because all other activities involved in the design, delivery, and evaluation stem from this process. A needs analysis typically contains the following steps:

a. Identify performance problems
b. Identify knowledge, skills, and attitudes to perform the job
c. Assess team members' knowledge and skill
d. Determine methods of gathering data
e. Gather data
f. Analyze data
g. Prepare training plans based on data

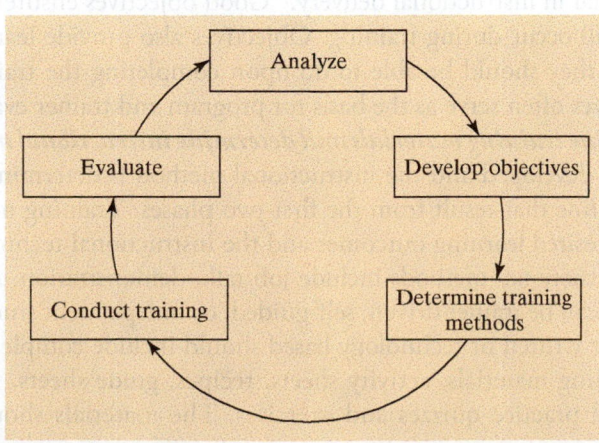

Figure 6-2
The training process.

The needs analysis assists in determining the difference between present performance and desired performance, that is, the gap between what is and what ought to be. "Performance problems might be reflected in high employee turnover, a decline in productivity, grievances, poor teamwork, and/or customer complaints. If this is the case, the following questions should arise as part of the needs analysis":[3]

- What are the specific problems?
- What exactly is the desired outcome of training?
- What would the effect of *no* training be?
- Is training the best method of resolving the problems?

Once the problem or problems have been identified and have been determined to be related to training, the next step in the needs analysis process is to:

- Identify the knowledge, skills, and attitudes essential to performing the job.
- Assess individual team members. Analyze their strengths as well as their weaknesses. These strengths and weaknesses are measured against the specific job requirements identified in the needs analysis step.
- Design an instrument or method of gathering information. The basic rule of thumb in a systematic approach is to collect only the information needed to design the training program.

Principal methods of data collection in the kitchen are:

- *Observation:* The process of observation involves observing team members—their work routines and behaviors and how each person interacts within the team.
- *Interviews:* The face-to-face interview is also a useful method of gathering information on training gaps. The interview technique, like the observation process, can employ informal interviews to discuss problems or issues related to training.
- *Work samples:* Samples of work produced by the team member can be evaluated by having the individual prepare and cook a dish from the menu.

Once the data have been collected, it must be analyzed so that specific training plans and strategies may be formulated.

The training plan should be prioritized on the basis of the needs analysis. The basic purpose of the needs analysis segment of a systematic approach to training is to uncover the quality gaps—that is, what is preventing a quality dining experience. Needs analysis also is about utilizing scarce resources of time, money, and people so as to maximize the training effort in a planned, systematic, and sequential way.

2. *Training objectives.* Systematic and sequential planning of the training program is critical to its success. The development of precise and measurable training objectives is crucial in instructional delivery.[4] Good objectives ensure that learners are aware of what will occur during training. Objectives also provide learners with information on what they should be able to do upon completing the training session. In addition, objectives often serve as the basis for program and trainer evaluation.

3. *Determine training materials and determine instructional method.* Training materials are developed and the instructional method is determined based on the training plan outline that result from the first two phases. Training materials must be matched to the desired learning outcomes and the instructional technique selected for the training. Instructional methods include job talk, demonstration, role-play, or lecture. Instruction can be trainer driven, self-guided, or independent study. Instructional materials whether written or technology based should include complete student materials such as reading materials, activity sheets, recipes, guide sheets, reference sheets, assignments, and practice quizzes and exercises. The materials should also include instructor lesson plans, tests and quizzes with answers, exercises and assignments with answers, equipment lists, recipes, and timelines. The technology used for instruction and instructional materials is rapidly expanding and changing and currently includes videos, CD, DVD, and online and other computer-based instructional programs. Only the time spent on the training itself is greater than the amount of time spent on developing the training materials. The quality of the training materials contributes substantially to the overall quality of the training.

4. Conduct the training. This is where all the preparation pays off. The chef trainer's role here is to instruct, motivate, lead, enable, and facilitate learning. In addition to serving as a training instructor, the chef supervisor should facilitate the logistics involved in the training sessions.

The first few minutes of any training session are critical. The introduction should capture the interest of the entire kitchen team. The chef supervisor as a trainer has a considerable advantage in that he or she has an existing rapport with the group, which should help get the object of the training session across smoothly. However, different topics that are important to the success of the organization should be introduced to provide variety. This will help to generate additional interest. Successfully delivering the introduction will ensure that each team member is prepared to receive instruction.

5. Evaluate the training. Instruction is designed to bring about the learning of several kinds of skills. The outcomes of this planned training are learner performances that show that various types of additional knowledge, skills, and attitudes have been acquired. The chef trainer needs a system to determine how effective the training has been. Learner performance needs to be assessed and learning checked to determine whether the designed instruction has met the training objectives. Evaluation is an essential component of training. It is often neglected because the chef trainer is not sufficiently adept at measuring learner performance. Materials that are used continuously need to be assessed so that improvements may be made. In simple terms, in evaluation the trainer asks, "Did the planned changes occur?" Without evaluation it's impossible to quantify the results of the training plan. Methods of evaluation include:

- Instructor evaluation of the training outcome when each segment is completed
- Learner evaluation of the course (What skills do I possess now that I did not have prior to training?)
- Third-party evaluation by guests or other work centers
- Field evaluation to determine whether the learners are performing well in the roles for which the training was to have prepared them (Can the learners perform the skills at the level desired?)

Field evaluation is the most suitable method to determine training effectiveness in the kitchen. Learners may be assessed on the job by the chef supervisor. Coaching on the job is also facilitated through this method of evaluation. Evaluation is part of the continuous loop that feeds back into the cycle.[5]

TYPES OF TRAINING

There are many types of training. Each has its own relative strengths and weaknesses. The following training methods are appropriate for training in a culinary environment. The characteristics of each method and its strengths and weaknesses are shown so that each may be evaluated relative to the appropriateness of the training mission.

Job talk is a speech by the chef supervisor with limited opportunities for open discussion.

- **Strengths**
  - Clear and direct method of presentation

CHEF TALK
TRAINING: "WHAT'S IN IT FOR YOU?"

In rough economic times, nothing comes under fire more than a training budget. It's an easy budgetary target. The alternative is just not to do any training.

But training is extremely important for the success of any foodservice operation. Without it, the leader cannot motivate other members of the kitchen to achieve high-quality standards and cooking skills. Training is about setting quality objectives and then showing people how to perform these tasks to the required standards. More and more, foodservice organizations are focusing on training the kitchen team.

Is it easy? No! There is often strong resistance from management because of a fear of giving up power and control. Where enlightened organizations have invested in training, their kitchen employees' success has followed. Training, in my view, not only is the path to success for the company but also sends a message to the individual being trained. Very often employees in training programs will remark, "If this company is investing in me, then they must value me as an employee." This sense of belonging, engendered through training, encourages greater effort by the individual.

There are all sorts of "buzz words" associated with training: empowerment, participative management, self-directed work teams, and others. What it all means is respecting the abilities of individual kitchen employees and giving them the tools to do their jobs. Involve the employees in deciding what training is necessary. Ask for their input and then proceed slowly. It's really a win-win formula for success. You end up with a more productive team involved and participating in the successful accomplishment of the foodservice organization's goals.

—Reimund Pitz, CEC, CCE, AAC, Chef Owner,
Le Coq Au Vin, Orlando, FL

- Good for large groups
- Materials can be provided to each member in advance to help with preparation
- Chef supervisor has control over time
- Inexpensive training method
- Little or no equipment is necessary

- **Weaknesses**

- Information is not easily assimilated
- Appeals to one sense only (hearing); therefore, overloading may occur
- Group can become easily bored
- Difficult to assess if your "message" has been understood and accepted by the team
- Difficult to pace to the learning rate of each team member

Team meetings (group discussions) generally include a speech by the chef supervisor with a lot of participation and interaction with the team. The meetings always require leadership. Team meetings are particularly useful for teams with mixed experience levels.

- **Strengths**
- Good for a small number of people
- All team members have the opportunity to present their ideas
- More ideas can be generated
- Good for total quality principles
- Quality gaps can be identified
- Effective for continuous improvements within the foodservice organization

- **Weaknesses**

- Team may get away from the subject matter
- Chef supervisor may be inexperienced at guiding or leading the discussions
- Possibility of one strong individual dominating the meeting

Role playing is the creation of a realistic situation and having team members assume the parts of specific personalities in the situation. Their actions are based on the roles assigned to them. Emphasis is not on problem solving. A role play draws upon the participants' experiences and knowledge and forces them to apply theory to practice.[6] It is effective for attitude awareness training.

- **Strengths**
  - Good if the situation is similar to the actual work situation
  - Team members receive feedback that gives them confidence
  - Good for interpersonal skills
  - Teaches team members how to act in real situations
  - Can be used to highlight sensitive topics such as personal hygiene and/or poor interpersonal habits

- **Weaknesses**
  - Team members are not actors
  - Role playing sometimes is not taken seriously
  - Some situations cannot be implemented in role playing
  - Uncontrolled role plays may not lead to any results
  - Requires that both incorrect and correct methods being role played be described

Demonstration is the use of actual equipment and ingredients to demonstrate an action. This is the most effective method for instructing culinary manipulative skills. Demonstrations make use of the learner's visual sense.

- **Strengths**
  - Has great visual impact
  - Instruction can be built step by step
  - Ensures that instruction is given in sequence
  - Difficult tasks may be shown in easy stages
  - Makes use of the natural inclination to imitate
  - Best if preceded by study assignment

- **Weaknesses**
  - Suitable for relatively small groups
  - Requires a lot of preparation
  - Pace is often too fast
  - Learners often watch the demonstrator rather than the demonstration
  - Should be avoided unless adequate time has been allowed for preparation and practice beforehand

A **case study** is a written narrative description of a real situation faced by chefs. Team members are required to propose one or more suitable solutions and/or make appropriate decisions.

- **Strengths**
  - Individual cases can be very interesting
  - Involves the team members in a lot of discussions and interactions since there is no absolute solution
  - Develops kitchen team members' ability to communicate and encourages active participation
  - Develops the ability to analyze factors that influence decision making

- **Weaknesses**
  - A slow method of training
  - Often difficult to select appropriate case studies for specific training problems
  - Requires a high level of skill by both chef supervisor and team members
  - Can sometimes be boring for team participants

Apprenticeship training is a culinary apprentice's work under the guidance of skilled chefs. The culinary apprentice rotates through all kitchen departments in a planned sequential way. According to the American Culinary Federation, "the apprentice [chef] completes 6,000 hours of on-the-job training as well as the related theory courses, usually over a three year period."[7]

- **Strengths**
  - Learner develops culinary skills while working
  - Promotes understanding of the actual work skills required
  - Can involve extensive training over a period of years
- **Weaknesses**
  - Takes a long time
  - Chef mentor changes may adversely impact continuity of learning, along with quality/quantity of skill development

On-the-job training (OJT) is training conducted on the job using actual work situations with which the kitchen team member is involved.

- **Strengths**
  - Can be individualized to suit the learning pace of the individual
  - Provides immediate job application for the new team member
  - Integrates the new individual into the team
- **Weaknesses**
  - Requires a good deal of preparation and application by the chef supervisor
  - Sequencing of on-the-job training must be planned and then recorded
  - Not all skills are addressed within one establishment

HOW PEOPLE LEARN

No two people learn at the same rate. Some team members will pick up new skills very quickly, while others will require repeated instruction and supervised practice. There are several ways to classify types of learning, but all of them basically fall into what are called "domains." These domains consist of the following four categories: cognitive, psychomotor, affective, and interpersonal skills.[8]

Cognitive: This refers to knowledge learning and includes the mental skills of classifying, identifying, detecting, and making decisions. This type of learning is experienced through self-paced individual interactive programs. The cognitive domain includes learner-controlled instruction, which is sometimes called self-instruction.

Psychomotor: These are the manipulative, or physical, skills that require the learner to *do* something. Within the kitchen, psychomotor skills are found everywhere. Culinary art requires many manipulative skills, from knife skills to whipping, chopping, or shredding.

Affective: These skills reflect attitudes, values, and interests of the kitchen team. Personal leadership, such as the chef supervisor as coach of the kitchen team, is one way to facilitate attitudinal learning. Attitudes can be learned. Good attitudes are vital in the foodservice industry. However, affective or attitudinal training is more difficult to do than any other method of training, because attitudes are so difficult to measure.

Interpersonal Skills: Learning involves interaction among people. These skills are crucial to supporting total quality in the foodservice industry. They are

---

CHEF TALK
PATIENCE AND DISCIPLINE

The success or failure of a team can be traced back to a team's growth, and the effectiveness of its training regimen. I have never known this to be truer than when I arrived in Singapore to open a restaurant for an American-based company. We were faced with many challenges in coming to a foreign market. Among these were sourcing our product, adapting to environmental differences, and training a staff that had a varied range of cultural backgrounds.

I had spent the previous eight months understanding, and training in the concept that I was hired to open in Singapore. Not only did I have to understand the product inside and out, I also had to learn the company culture and develop as a manager in order to train others to operate the concept successfully.

The first thing I had to do was to hone my own management style. I took from my past mentors, using what I felt was the most effective for me, and developed my own approach.

I remember working in my first professional kitchen. The Executive Chef was a nurturer. She was committed to her cooks' personal and professional growth. She was the mother of the kitchen, and we were her children. We all worked so as to not disappoint her, but we would also try and get away with things when she was not looking. She had an ease about her that made you comfortable, she was always focused on the task at hand, and she produced results by running her team like a family unit. From her I learned **patience**.

My next Chef was a dictator. He was effective, but in a different way. He demanded excellence from his cooks, and we produced out of fear. We were a well-oiled machine, we went into battle every night, and we worked like a military unit, executing with precision and deft. From him I learned to develop my own standards and, most importantly, the meaning of **discipline**.

By the time I had reached my next kitchen, I had already begun to develop as a manager and was crafting my own training style. I learned to be direct and honest. I learned the importance of coaching and developing cooks.

I look back at my past mentors and accept that my style is a result of their training influences on me. I have learned that the importance of training is to produce not only a certain result or product and service, but also an entire generation of people who will look to you as a mentor and guide for their own paths. The responsibility is enormous, and one that I do not take lightly.

When training my own cooks, I have recognized that some people want to be told what to do, while others require more coaching. The challenge is figuring out what each individual will respond to best, so I can get the most out of every cook. One style doesn't always work. Sometimes this requires patience, and sometimes it requires a demand for discipline. The challenge is being able to adapt.

—Benjamin San Seto, Chef de Cuisine, Pizzeria Mozza, Marina Bay Sands, Singapore

---

people-centered skills that involve the ability to relate effectively with others. Examples include teamwork, counseling techniques, administrative skills, salesmanship, discussion activities, and customer relations.[9]

Most learned capabilities actually contain elements of all domains. They entail voluntary display (affective) of some observable action (psychomotor) that indicates possession of some mental skill (cognitive) and working with other people and through people so as to meet customer needs (interpersonal).

We learn through our senses: seeing, hearing, touching, smelling, and tasting. The most important training sense is seeing, but when giving instruction, as many of the five senses as possible should be used to relay the message. Show things as often as possible. For example, when demonstrating sauce preparation, the method is explained (learning), skills are demonstrated (seeing), the desired texture is determined (touching), and finally the sauce is sampled (tasting).

Culinary skills instruction has a major advantage in that it can make use of the learner's five senses.

Instructional techniques may be divided into two areas: passive and active techniques. Passive techniques require little or no activity from the learner. It is therefore difficult to assess what learning has taken place. Passive instructional techniques involve:

- *Telling:* The use of words to explain the subject matter.
- *Showing:* Trainers perform the activity.
- *Illustrating:* The use of visual materials to demonstrate the procedure.

Figure 6-3
Retention and learning
activities.

Training experts generally agree that we retain:

- 20 percent of what we hear
- 50 percent of what we hear and see
- 70 percent of what we hear, see, and say
- 90 percent of what we hear, see, say, and do

Active techniques require the learner to participate by saying or doing something:

- *Question and answer:* Checking through communication to see if information is understood.
- *Participation:* Involvement by the learner through actions.
- *Discussion:* Learners are involved through verbal communication.
- *Practical exercises:* Learners practice the techniques.

The best training techniques for culinary instruction are obviously "active." They allow the chef supervisor to check if learning has taken place.

Most of the training in the kitchen involves hearing, seeing, saying, and doing, which indicates that this is the desired training method for all skills instruction. Figure 6-3 shows the retention level associated with these learning activities. These methods involve breaking down training into steps that are paced to the learner's ability so that he or she can assimilate this new information. By using this method, difficult tasks can be shown in easy stages. The unknown becomes known. Training is about helping people learn and develop. It should center on the team member, and there are no reasons why it should not be enjoyable: "Individuals learn best when they choose what to learn—that is, when they learn things that interest them, which they find personally satisfying, and when the learning environment is in harmony with their own particular learning preference or style."[10]

ADULT LEARNING

Andragogy is the concept of adult education. At the heart of this concept is the assumption that adults *want* to learn. Adults prefer training sessions that will assist them in the successful completion of their daily work tasks. Therefore, instruction should be designed relative to the needs of each participant.[11] If the need or relevance of the training topic is not evident to adult team members from the start, they may soon become disenchanted with the training process. To meet this adult need, the objectives of the training session should be stated and linked to job performance in the introduction stage of the training program or module. For the most part, adults enter training with a high degree of interest and motivation. Motivation can be improved and channeled by the chef supervisor, who can provide clear instructional goals. Adults learn by doing. They want to get involved. Adults relate their learning to what they already know. This presents a challenge for the chef supervisor to incorporate participative activities into training such as hands-on work, discussions, or projects. A variety of training topics and methods tends to stimulate and open all five of the team members' senses.

The need for positive feedback is characteristic of all learners. Adults, especially, prefer to know how their efforts measure up when compared with the objectives of the training program. Additionally, adult learners may have certain reservations when it comes to training; among these are doubts about their ability to learn and a fear of failure.

Each training session should be opened with a good introductory activity that will put everyone at ease. Adults prefer to be treated as individuals who have unique and particular talents, and they prefer an informal environment.

Learning flourishes in a nonintimidating win-win setting without grades. Facilitators of the adult learning process can be described as change agents. The role of the chef supervisor as a change agent is to present information or skills in an environment that is conducive to learning, and the learner's role is to take the information (or skills) and apply it in the best way.

The establishment of a positive training environment hinges on understanding the characteristics of adult learners. The dynamics of the training process are dependent upon the instructor having a clear understanding of these characteristics. For adults, training should be a highly motivating experience, after which they should be inspired and committed to trying out new ideas and approaches. Effective adult training should be relevant, practical, inspirational, dynamic, informative, and solution centered.

BARRIERS TO LEARNING

Fatigue is a condition that prevents learning. It reduces the physical and mental ability to accept and assimilate new information. It is therefore essential that training be planned and implemented at appropriate times. It should not be conducted at the end of work shifts. Monotony also is a problem. If the chef supervisor finds the training boring, the team members also will probably find it boring. It is important for the chef supervisor to keep the sessions lively and interesting. While the information is routine for the chef supervisor, it may not be so for the team member.

Distractions inhibit training. Time for training should be planned to avoid work-related distractions. People are usually tense when confronted with the unknown. It is up to the chef supervisor to create a positive training environment that is motivational and encourages quality performance.

Before the actual training begins, in addition to physical considerations of how, when, and where the training will take place, the team members must be analyzed to determine the following:

- What are their prior culinary work experiences, knowledge, and skills?
- What types of job duties must they perform?

A careful match must be made between what tasks each team member currently performs and what the training is preparing them for.

Before commencing the training session, review the training objectives. This review will focus the chef instructor on the intended purposes of the training program and its desired outcomes. The development of the presentation is the next step. This includes the session topics and highlighting the learning activities designed to reinforce the learning. It is important at this stage to realize that excellent training session design does not guarantee excellent outcomes in terms of training.

Questions to consider with regard to creating the training environment include the smooth transition from a work-driven atmosphere in the kitchen to a training-driven atmosphere. Training sessions need not take up large chunks of the workday. They can range from 30-minute to 2-hour sessions, but they must be on an ongoing basis. What is vital is that each training period be totally uninterrupted by the requirements of work.

Plans should include arrangements for meals or coffee breaks during the session periods. Time allocation must be strictly adhered to when it is made part of the training plan. Where will the training take place? Even the most dynamic chef trainer can fail in poorly prepared facilities. Whether training is to be conducted on site or off site, the facilities should be satisfactory:

- If the room to be used is too warm or too small, a poor instructional climate will result.
- Is lighting adequate? Can the room be darkened to show visuals, yet still allow participants to take notes?
- Is the required audio/video and demonstration equipment in working order?
- Is there a writing board or flip chart available with marking pens or chalk?

Starting Right

Training sessions that begin correctly, in a positive environment, generally have a better chance of finishing well than those that start badly. If the first training session begins properly, the chef trainer will feel good about the session. Much more learning will probably take place. First impressions can be long-lasting ones, and the first training session sets the tone for the rest of the training program.

Preparation

There are several reasons why preparation is necessary:

1. It ensures that no essential detail is omitted.
2. Instruction can be arranged systematically.
3. Topics can be assessed to determine their relevance to overall objectives and organizational vision.
4. The chef supervisor's thinking can be directed to match the training needs of individual team members, and individual needs can be addressed to allow for different competency levels.
5. Unnecessary overlapping and repetition of topics can be avoided.
6. The amount and type of learner involvement is decided beforehand.
7. It ensures that maximum benefit is derived from the time allocated for instruction.
8. Most importantly, it helps to strengthen the chef supervisor's confidence in himself or herself as a trainer.

Adequate preparation often serves as a refresher and helps chef supervisors do their job more effectively.

On-the-Job Training

The unpredictable nature of the foodservice industry often makes it difficult to plan for training. In addition to the structured training sessions, every possible advantage should be taken for total quality training. The following are some guidelines for fitting training into the day-to-day routine:

- Take advantage of downtime to give short pieces of training instruction or review previous training topics. If downtime can be predicted, plan to use it for training.
- If possible, schedule team members with similar training needs to be in the kitchen at the same time so that these needs can be addressed more effectively.
- Chef supervisors should use their own work as quality standard setting demonstrations. Have team members watch while explaining critical elements during the demonstration.
- Take advantage of crises and problems to give on-the-spot correction and explanation of the correct way to perform tasks.
- Assign work that will allow each team member to practice new skills as soon as possible after instruction.

- Fit training in whenever possible. If only 5 or 10 minutes is available, cover a portion of the task.
- Keep simple records to track the training you have given, to whom, and whether or not the training was successful.
- In addition, other experienced team members may be used as co-trainers. However, the chef supervisor is ultimately responsible for the culinary training.

By integrating training on the job, the chef supervisor is watching for gaps between the required quality and the way that each team member is performing, while giving praise and encouragement to the team.

CONCLUSIONS

Investment in training is investment in the health and well-being of the organization. It is an investment in the future. Success cannot be achieved without it. Therefore, the modern chef supervisor, in addition to the other necessary skills of supervision, must be a first-class trainer.

Training is a process, and it has various forms. It is the systematic application of:

- Analyzing training needs
- Developing training objectives
- Determining appropriate training methods
- Conducting and evaluating training

There are many types of training. The training methods that have proved most suitable for culinary training are job talks, demonstration, role-play, case study, apprenticeship training, and on-the-job training. Each has strengths and weaknesses. Experienced chef supervisors can assess the training needs and determine the most appropriate training methods. The secret is to develop skill in using a variety of these training tools. The most critical roles of the chef supervisor as trainer are counseling team members through the learning process and being a subject matter expert, teacher, and motivator of all team members as they rotate through the training process.

Understanding how people learn is key to effective training. No two people learn at the same rate or in the same way. There will be peaks and valleys in individual team members' progress.

Training sessions should be stimulating and inspiring and be separate from the usual work schedule. The environment in which the training session is to be conducted should be one that is conducive to learning. The duration and timing of training are important. Training must be planned in a sequential and logical way and should not last too long. Dynamic presentations will always ward off monotony and fatigue.

SUMMARY

- Training is the cornerstone of success for the organization at large and the kitchen team as a unit.
- Training should be viewed as a total systems approach; the steps are (1) determining training needs, (2) developing training objectives, (3) determining appropriate methods, (4) conducting the training, and (5) evaluating the training.
- Types of training used for foodservice training include job talks, team meetings, role-playing, demonstrations, case studies, apprenticeship training, and on-the-job training.
- People learn at different rates and in different ways. Essentially, learning falls into the categories of cognitive, psychomotor, affective, and interpersonal; these are referred to as domains. Additionally, training is conducted through either active or passive training techniques.

CHEF TALK
"RETHINKING YOUR MOST VALUABLE ASSET"

Today, the hospitality industry is as dynamic as ever, full of rapid changes and opportunities to use newly learned skills. Therefore, productive training is more critical than ever.

While the concept of training is straightforward and quite basic, the true challenge is applying it to the ever-changing issues that arise on a daily or weekly basis. Well-trained kitchen team members are crucial to the culinary operation. Part of this is understanding how team members relate to the product or services you provide and realizing that their values are not necessarily the same as yours. Remember, important elements that you may consider motivating factors could be regarded as simple satisfiers in a team member's eyes.

As an exercise, view your operation from an employee's perspective. Remember, you have the ability to control how your employees interpret your culinary operation. If their definition of what your business is all about does not concur with yours, you are likely to be vulnerable, because they are the main link with how your customer perceives your business. Chef leaders who are involved with their employees on a daily basis encourage spontaneous communication that creates an atmosphere that can increase their ability to think and respond to the needs of their customers.

—Victor Gielisse, Ph.D., CMC, AAC
The Culinary Institute of America, Hyde Park, NY

- Andragogy is the concept of adult education. Adults learn by doing. They want to learn, are motivated, and relate training to what they already know. Positive feedback is a characteristic of adult learning. Learning for adults flourishes in a nonthreatening environment where grading is absent.

- Training must be presented in an environment conducive to learning and at a time when the kitchen team member is ready to receive it.
- The modern chef supervisor must constantly invest in training the team to have success.

DISCUSSION QUESTIONS

1. Define the following chapter key terms:
   a. Training
   b. Total systems approach
   c. Needs analysis
   d. Job talk
   e. Team meeting
   f. Role play
   g. Demonstration
   h. Case study
   i. Apprenticeship
   j. OJT
   k. Cognitive
   l. Psychomotor
   m. Affective
   n. Interpersonal skills
   o. Andragogy
2. What is the difference between training and education?
3. What are the steps involved in a systems approach to training?

4. Before training can commence, a needs analysis is conducted. What is the purpose of this step?
5. What are the strengths and weaknesses of "job talk" as a training method? When should it be used?
6. Why is demonstration as a training technique appropriate for skills training in the kitchen?
7. What are the learning domains of cognitive and psychomotor? How may they be applied to training in the kitchen?
8. What are the advantages and disadvantages of passive and active training techniques?
9. Adults learn by doing. What training challenges does this present to the chef supervisor?
10. What are the important factors that the chef supervisor should ensure in order to remove training barriers?
11. In planning training sessions, what physical factors should be considered?

NOTES

1. Philip B. Crosby, *Quality is Free, The Art of Making Quality Certain* (New York: Wiley, 1989).

2. Richard L. Sullivan, Jerry R. Wircenski, Susan S. Arnold, and Michelle D. Sarkeess, *Practical Manual for the Design, Delivery, and Evaluation of Training* (Rockville, MD: Aspen, 1990), CD 1.

3. Ibid., p. CD 2.

4. Ibid., p. CD 37.

5. Tom W. Goad, *Delivering Effective Training* (San Diego, CA: Pfeiffer & Co., 1982), 169.

6. Lois B. Hart, *Training Methods That Work* (London: Crisp, 1991), 65.

7. American Culinary Federation (ACF), *Apprenticeship Operations Manual* (St. Augustine, FL: ACF, 1985), 21.

8. Robert Heinich, Michael Molenda, and James D. Russell, *Instructional Media and the New Technologies of Instruction* (New York: Macmillan, 1989), 41.

9. Ibid., p. 42.

10. Brian Thomas, *Total Quality Training: The Quality Culture and Quality Trainer* (Berkshire, England: McGraw-Hill, 1992), 73.

11. Dugan Laird, *Approaches to Training and Development* (Reading, MA: Addison-Wesley, 1985), 25.

Chapter 7
Training Objectives and Planning

Outline

- Introduction
- Definitions
- Hierarchy of objectives
- Training lesson plans
- Characteristics of a training session
- Steps in planning training sessions
- Conclusions
- Summary
- Discussion questions

OBJECTIVES

When you complete this chapter, you should be able to:

1. Describe the components of good objectives and write a performance objective that contains each of these components
2. Identify the hierarchical elements that reflect how team members learn and the associated behaviors
3. List the rationale for preparing performance objectives
4. Identify and outline steps in preparing training plans and sessions
5. State the purpose and application of a lesson plan

Case Study: Hamilton House Restaurant

The Hamilton family established the Hamilton House Restaurant in 1993. The time was right for the Hamilton family's entry into the restaurant marketplace. The country atmosphere and good country cooking offered by their restaurant were an instant hit. The restaurant became so popular that the family decided to build a second restaurant in 1996, a third in 1999, and a fourth in 2002. Each of the restaurants was within the same part of the state, and a member of the Hamilton family managed each. Each of the Hamilton House Restaurants was a success. The Hamilton family had succeeded in exporting to other properties the concept and product that made the original property a success with no loss of quality or consistency.

The Hamilton family held their weekly business meeting on Monday afternoon in the offices at the original store. The purpose of the meetings was to report on store activities, discuss challenges at the various stores, and plan for the future of the Hamilton House Restaurants. At the last meeting the decision was made to proceed with a plan to aggressively expand the Hamilton House Restaurants as a chain. The goal was to keep the chain as a family-held enterprise. The goal was set to open three properties in the next twelve months and six properties per year each of the following three years. Months of discussion and site research had taken place in the months leading up to the final decision. The financing had been arranged, the sites selected, and preliminary construction schedules developed for the first three properties. The discussion in every meeting returned to the one question that concerned the family the most: Who would run the new Hamilton House Restaurants? The family was out of family members to place in units as general managers. In fact, they knew that with the opening of the ninth property, only two years in the future, they would need all of the family members available for operations and development at the company level.

Based on what you have learned from previous chapters and the content of this chapter, answer the following questions.

- What are the overall challenges involved in providing management and staff for the new Hamilton House Restaurants?
- What type of information will the family need to begin effectively addressing these challenges?
- What specific steps does the Hamilton family need to take to develop effective training programs for the new restaurants?
- What specific steps would you take to develop a training program for future Hamilton House Restaurants' culinary team members?
- Based on what you know about the management and organization of a Hamilton House Restaurant, what do you consider to be the greatest strength and the greatest weakness in the development of a training program?

INTRODUCTION

Learning is gaining knowledge, experience, and understanding.[1] It is the modification of behavior based on past and present experience. Learning often results in an activity that can be observed, measured, and recorded. To ensure that the learner gains the desired knowledge, experience, and understanding requires that training be structured. Training that is well structured and executed will lead to the intended behavior modification.

Part of structuring training is the development of learning objectives. **Learning objectives** are intended not to limit what a team member learns, but to provide a minimum level of expected achievement. Learning objectives in any of the learning domains discussed in the previous chapter may be adapted to the abilities of the individual learner.

Learning objectives are also called *performance objectives* or *behavioral objectives*. Whatever terminology is used, it is the concept that counts. The concept is that stating objectives for whatever type of training is undertaken in the kitchen will ensure that all efforts are directed to achieving only the desired results. The objective allows the chef supervisor or other trainer to tell if the training objectives have been achieved. Team members' performance is compared to the standard set by the objective to measure their mastery. The objectives guide both the trainer and trainee in the training process.

WHAT IS THIS BUSINESS?
"TREAT 'EM LIKE KINGS"

Guest service counts, and for far more than getting a good tip. It starts the moment a person steps *toward* our door and away from all else. That simple decision—to walk our way—sets in motion a relationship. The direction that relationship subsequently takes hinges on guest service. Swinging on the same hinge is the success or failure of the company. Guest service and corporate success are inseparable.

This bone-deep dedication to excellence in guest service must be taught to every crewmember. Good training yields good results—consistently. Consistency is critical. Regardless of the restaurant or the meal, we guarantee that every guest, on every visit, will enjoy his or her experience. We stand by this guarantee because we live by our crewmembers.

Great training begins with great hiring. The soul of guest service is hard to instill, but if it's there it's hard to miss. We look for this virtue when hiring entry-level staff, managers, and executives. We start with the best ingredients, so to speak.

After being hired, everyone receives training—indoctrination, actually. Our training creates and maintains our company culture, with its unique values, language, and expectations. The foundation of all our training is that every guest is, first and foremost, a guest in our own home.

Putting guests first works only when the whole team works together. We marry the value of our guests with valuing our colleagues through the "circle of responsibility" concept. This simple concept has powerful implications for the culture of our company: "If we're not there for each other, our guests won't be there for us."

The concepts of guest service and individual and team responsibility are interwoven throughout all aspects of our training and operations at every restaurant.

Our training is divided into two different tracks: crewmember training and management training. Each track is divided into two phases: classroom and practicum. Crewmembers are trained to become Ambassadors of Seafood: friendly in their demeanor, confident in their knowledge, secure in their advice, anticipatory in their service, and enthusiastic in their duties. Managers learn by doing the jobs of every person they will supervise. They come to see the restaurant through the eyes of the crewmembers by working shoulder-to-shoulder beside them, learning from them. Management training imparts empathy, team cohesion, open communication, and commitment to quality at every level. What is learned in both phases and in both tracks becomes the basis of our company-wide culture.

The teaching atmosphere is oriented toward adult learners. We utilize a "Tell, Show, Do, Review" approach to ensure that all learning styles are accommodated. It is safe, stress-free, hands-on, and fun. There are no uncomfortable surprises. Assessments are a combination of written quizzes, oral explanations, and live demonstrations. Classroom work is reinforced by four real-life practicums conducted during actual shifts and observed by certified workgroup trainers. By investing early and heavily in the professional development of our crewmembers, our long-term objective is greater retention and better promotion within the company.

In purely monetary terms, it costs more to recruit good employees than to nurture good employees. Treat your staff well and they will do likewise. Treat them poorly and they will become someone else's asset. Service that is second to none starts with excellent employees.

What's our secret at King's Seafood Company? We treat 'em like a King.

—Jeffrey King, Chairman,
Kings Seafood Company,
Costa Mesa, CA

A statement of objectives may be viewed as an agreement between the kitchen team and the chef supervisor, whose responsibility as an instructor is to provide training and coaching in a positive environment. The team member's responsibility is to listen and work hard in the training sessions.

Problems of quality in the kitchen can be redefined as objectives that can be used to develop plans for training. Critical to all objective preparation is stating what the team member *will be able to do* after completing a training session. Objectives should build the training needs of each team member in a logical and systematic way.[2]

DEFINITIONS

Three **basic components** make up performance objectives:

- The performance of the task.
- The conditions under which the task is to be performed.
- The criteria or standards to which performance of the task will be compared.

Expressed another way, objectives are an unambiguous statement of what the learner will be able to do as a result of some training. These can also be referred to as "enabling" objectives, which state what the team member is going to learn that will enable him or her to perform a task.

Within the stated objectives, the facilities, tools, equipment, and constraints under which the objective is performed should be included. The level of performance in terms of time, accuracy, and completeness of the tasks is also described. The statement of objectives must also have measurable attributes that should be observable in the team member upon completion of training. Otherwise, it is impossible to determine whether or not the training program is meeting the stated objectives.

The essence of a good objective is the description of a measurable performance. According to Robert Mager, a complete objective will have three parts:[3]

1. **Performance:** Use an action verb followed by the object of the action.
2. **Conditions:** Specify what the team member will be given to complete the task and under what conditions the task will be completed.
3. **Standards:** State the standard against which the performance will be evaluated, and the level of mastery required.

Examples of training objectives for the kitchen team are shown in Figure 7-1. These are precise statements. They make a futuristic promise to the team members indicating what they will be able to do when they complete a training session.

Tasks consist of a single action verb and an object. The verb may represent the cognitive, affective, psychomotor, or interpersonal domain. A task should have a definite beginning point and should be independent of other tasks. For example, the task "understand sauce making" is meaningless. What does *understand* mean? Where does it start? Similarly, the chef supervisor would have a difficult time observing the task "appreciate" in the importance of good sauce making.

Goals are statements of intent in the learning process. Goals are overall statements or general aims for a training program. They provide the chef supervisor with a general idea of what a given training session should achieve. Goals and objectives differ as follows:

- Goals may be written to help select the area of knowledge and skills and may contain *immeasurable* verbs.
- Goals written as "knowing" or "understanding" do not provide specific actions that team members should perform to show that learning has occurred. This makes evaluation of the results of training difficult.

Since attitudes are difficult to measure, we write attitude "goals." Barbee and Bott state: "Training in the hospitality industry involves more than just the technical skills common in other industries. Interpersonal skills are as important, if not more so."[4] At times, with attitude goals it is difficult to find precise words for the objective.

- Upon completion of the training session on sauce making, the kitchen team member will be able to correctly prepare within 10 minutes 2 quarts of Hollandaise sauce from the recipe provided using the kitchen blender following all safety/sanitation procedures indicated within the lesson.
- After completion of the training session on quick breads, the kitchen team member will be able to properly prepare and bake 5 specified quick breads from the assigned list using the dough mixer and baking oven while observing correct timing and temperature.

Figure 7-1
Example objectives for the kitchen team.

However, objectives should always communicate the same intent to all people. One way of testing whether a written objective clearly defines a desired outcome is to answer the following two questions:

- How exactly do you intend the training to change the learner?
- How exactly will you know if the change has occurred?

A final criterion for a set of training objectives is to ask yourself if you would be fully satisfied if the team members achieved only the stated performance objectives and nothing else.

Objectives must be examined as a complete set of topics, levels, and skills of the overall training plan. Some of the more subtle objectives concerning attitudes or even the more complex kinds of understanding may be missing. Whenever possible, these subtle objectives should be included.

Objectives must be attainable. While this may seem an obvious point, the objectives must be assessed carefully in relation to the knowledge, background, and expectations of the team along with the resources available and the duration of the training session.

Objectives for training should fall into the category of skills and knowledge the team member "needs to know" rather than what may be "nice to know." In searching for the neatness of fit between the culinary quality training plan and the team member's needs, performance objectives must contain the essentials that the person needs to know first and those that are desirable second.

HIERARCHY OF OBJECTIVES

Objectives should be prepared in a hierarchy that reflects how a person learns and associates behavior within each **level of learning**:

1. *Knowledge:* This refers to remembering previously learned materials.
2. *Comprehension:* This is defined as the ability to grasp the meaning of the materials.
3. *Application:* This refers to the ability to use learned material in new and concrete situations.
4. *Synthesis:* This is separating ideas into component parts and examining relationships.
5. *Evaluation:* This involves judging by using self-produced criteria or established standards.[5]

The flow of the hierarchy is shown in Figure 7-2.

The following is a list of action verbs used in preparing performance objectives. The areas that concern most kitchen training objectives are the first three: knowledge, comprehension, and application.

Action Verbs

1. *Knowledge:* define, state, list, name, write, recall, recognize, label, underline, reflect, measure, reproduce.
2. *Comprehension:* identify, justify, select, indicate, illustrate, represent, name, formulate, explain, judge, contrast, classify.
3. *Application:* predict, select, assess, explain, choose, find, show, demonstrate, construct, compute, use, perform.
4. *Synthesis:* combine, restate, summarize, argue, discuss, organize, derive, select, relate, generalize, conclude.
5. *Evaluation:* judge, evaluate, determine, recognize, support, defend, attack, criticize, identify, avoid, select, choose.

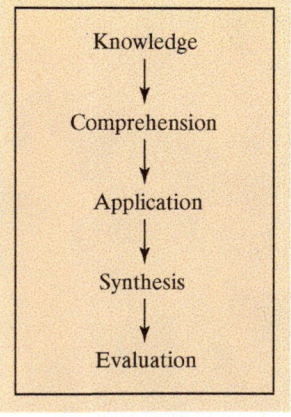

Figure 7-2
Hierarchy of objectives.

Complete objectives state *standards* of performance and the conditions under which performance is to be evaluated. Objectives can be best described as:

- An intent about what the team members will be able to do when they have successfully completed a learning experience.
- An intent communicated by describing a proposed change in a team member.
- Precise statements of desired learning outcomes.
- A worthwhile, nontrivial learning activity, unambiguously stated, that is necessary to both the team member and the culinary operation and is perceived as a benefit for the team member to progress in his or her job.

Performance objectives are written in the compilation of training plans because they:

- Limit the scope of training tasks
- Remove ambiguities and difficulties of interpretation
- Ensure that measurement is possible
- Define the desired level of attainment and depth of treatment of each topic area
- Provide a basis for the selection of appropriate materials, content, and training methods
- Ensure that no essential details are left out
- Organize training instruction systematically
- Avoid unnecessary overlapping and repetition of training information
- Ensure maximum benefit from the often limited training time available in the kitchen
- Strengthen the chef supervisor's confidence in the instructional role

TRAINING LESSON PLANS

Just as training objectives serve as a road map and a check to see if training is accomplished, the training lesson plan guides the chef supervisor through the process of instruction that causes training to occur. A **lesson plan** may be thought of as a combination of speaker's notes, recipes, and scripts. It is an outline of everything that is to happen during the training event.

In the case of individual team member instruction, the lesson plan serves as the lesson specification from which text is derived. One of the requirements for being prepared is to have a lesson plan. Even if the training is a short 30-minute presentation, a plan is essential. Learning is stimulated and aided when the chef supervisor can present a coherent and sequential series of training sessions, each of which has a clear-cut training objective.

The **four-step training method** has been widely utilized in training in the kitchen. These four steps have been tried and found to be a successful pattern around which every training session can be planned and instructed. These four steps are:

1. Preparation.
2. Presentation.
3. Application.
4. Evaluation.

CHARACTERISTICS OF A TRAINING SESSION

To be effective, a training session:

- must be a complete unit of learning. What is to be learned should be made apparent to the team members in the title of the session.

- should contain new material exclusive of review or some other training topic, previously instructed material for reinforcement, and new material for progression. Sullivan states: "Our primary duty is to teach our staff something new every day. Training is a philosophy not a department."[6]
- should be adapted to the needs of the team member. The material should be within the capabilities of the team member and it should be consistent with the needs of the team in keeping with the purpose of the training and according to the progress of the entire kitchen operation.
- should be reasonable in scope. It should be balanced, interesting, and neither too simple nor too complex.
- have a clear-cut beginning, a presentation, and an end. The language of the chef instructor should enable the team member to follow, comprehend the presentation, and finally absorb the material with a feeling of understanding and accomplishment.
- should require a measurable standard of achievement in terms of high-quality standards of performance. High-quality standards of performance should start at the beginning and continue throughout each training session.

Types of Training Lessons

The type of training session presented will depend on the type of lesson, and it is from these materials that the chef supervisor will develop training topics.

Manual skills lesson is a type of instruction in which the chef supervisor instructs team members in using physical skills to perform the manual phases of a culinary skill. The skill lesson is generally taught by demonstration. To further simplify and clarify the intent of any skill lesson, the following question should be asked: "Am I going to teach the team member how to do something?" If the answer is yes, then the lesson will be a skill lesson.

Informational lesson is a type of instruction in which the team member is instructed in the theory and basic fundamentals of the area being taught. The area covered by a "theory" lesson appears to be broader than that covered by the skill lesson because so many subtopics can be included. This type of lesson is also referred to as "job talks."

STEPS IN PLANNING TRAINING SESSIONS

Careful and thorough preparation is essential to successful instruction. The effectiveness of the other stages of instruction will depend on how well the chef has selected training tasks and adapted this training material to the special needs, abilities, and interests of the kitchen team; arranged for equipment and materials needed; planned for activities; and anticipated problems. Many chef supervisors often feel there is never enough time for adequate planning. One solution to this problem is to use a systematic procedure in the preparation of training sessions. The following is a simple, yet effective procedure, as you will see when we build a training session on the Frenching of a lamb rack.

Step 1: The objectives.   This is the starting point for all planning of training activities. The chef instructor must realize from the start just what can be accomplished and the limits of time. (The objective, when well developed and written, will serve also as a tool to evaluate the training.)

> *The time for the Frenching demo will be limited to 15 minutes with a 10–15-minute follow-up supervised practice. The objectives for the demo are given below.*
> *Upon completion of this demo the team member will be:*
> - *able to demonstrate the ability to French a 204A lamb rack.*
> - *able to demonstrate the ability to cut the Frenched rack into chops.*

- *able to identify:*
  - *fat cap,*
  - *lifter meat.*
- *aware of the use of trim from a lamb rack.*
- *aware of the characteristics of a lamb hotel rack.*

Step 2: Analysis of the training topic.   This involves determining the specific objectives, skills, knowledge, or techniques the team member must learn for successful performance of the task. For example, the objective of a training session may be the use of the meat thermometer. An analysis of this subject, or breaking it down into instructional steps, would result in these teaching points: Describe a meat thermometer; show and explain the thermometer; demonstrate how to read the thermometer; and have team members measure internal temperature with the thermometer and sanitize after use. Each step would have subpoints in the presentation, but in the analysis only the major instructional steps required to accomplish the training are considered.

> *The steps in producing Frenched lamb chops are:*
> 1. *Remove fat cap*
> 2. *Split membrane on rib (1.5 to 4 inches trim)*
> 3. *Push or cut rib free of membrane and surrounding muscle and fat*
> 4. *Trim to eye*
> 5. *Frenched chop—Cut chop*

Step 3: Equipment, facilities, and training aids.   Requirements for and availability of training aids, equipment, training areas, and facilities need to be considered. Advance notice may be required to obtain training films, videos, or other media. Frequently chef supervisors must improvise, and this often takes time. Last-minute arrangements for training aids or equipment usually result in slipshod instruction. The ingredients used for demonstrations must be selected and checked well in advance for quality and portion size.

> *The facility to be used for the Frenching demo is the prep table close to the protein cooler. The group will be limited to four team members so that each will be able to have a clear view of the procedure. The ingredients needed for the demo are limited to 5 prime, 204A hotel lamb racks. The lamb racks used for the demo and practice session will be part of the standard diner prep. The equipment list for the demo is: cutting board with anti-slip mat; boning knife; steel; sanitation bucket with sanitizing liquid; 4 side towels, 1 in the sanitation bucket, 3 dry; 2 - ½ sheet pans with parchment paper liner, 1 for cut chops and 1 for trim; and a lamb chart, if available. The equipment list for the practice session is 4 cutting boards with anti-slip mats; 4 boning knives; 1 steel; 2 sanitation buckets with sanitizing liquid; 6 side towels, 2 in the sanitation buckets, 4 dry. The practice chops and trim will go on the ½ sheet pans used for the demo.*

Step 4: Availability of time.   If time is short, the training subject matter should be limited to the items essential for accomplishment of the training objectives. If time is available, more team participation can be used and more supporting material can be included.

> *Time for the demo is limited and cannot be allowed to interfere with dinner prep. Two members of the lunch protein prep team at the end of their shift and two members of the dinner protein prep team at the beginning will participate in the demo, and this will be repeated as needed to train all appropriate team members. Having the chops prepared will assist in the dinner prep. The demo and practice are to be held to a maximum of 30 minutes.*

Step 5: Training condition.   Instruction must be flexible enough to remain effective even when obstacles to training arise. The basis of such flexibility is careful planning.

The schedule for the Frenching demo and practice session will be:

2:30 P.M.	*Introduction: today's lesson and objectives*
2:32 P.M.	*Introduction hotel rack (204A): description, placement in carcass, characteristics*
2:35 P.M.	*Fabrication of rack: Frenching technique*
	Fabrication of rack: use of trim
2:40 P.M.	*Fabrication of rack: cut rib chop*
2:45 – 3:00 P.M.	*Practice session/Q&A*

Each team leader that has team members attending is to schedule work to allow for the absence of the team members. In case of interruption due to operational challenges, the lesson will be rescheduled to the earliest possible date.

Step 6: Select and organize material.   Identify essential manipulative skills and related knowledge, then organize the materials for demonstration. Examples and stories can be used to make the lesson presentation or skill demonstration more interesting and meaningful. They should be related to the overall quality objectives of the foodservice organization and should be used whenever possible.

The purpose of this lesson is to ensure consistency of the quality of one of the restaurant's top-selling menu items, Moroccan Grilled Lamb Chops. The follow-up to this demo will be a demo on the proper seasoning and cooking of the chops and pan gravy. The use of a live demo will most effectively communicate the knowledge and skills to the team members. The team members will specifically learn and/or refine their ability to French a lamb rack and produce consistent Frenched chops. The team members will also be introduced to or review the use of the trim from the chops. A secondary benefit will be refinement of team members' use of the boning knife and steel. The information and skills presented in the demo will be immediately reinforced with supervised practice. The use of a lamb chart to indicate the location for the 204A hotel rack on the lamb carcass would be helpful, but is not mandatory. No other materials or teaching aids will be used due to the confined space and short time period for the demo. If, at a later date, it is decided to make this a demo for a large group of team members, the use of closed circuit video cameras and PowerPoint would be highly recommended additions to the demo.

The lesson plan ensures that the training session will be complete. It shows what material is to be instructed, in what order, and what procedures and training methods will be used. Each training lesson plan is an outline for one segment of the training plan. The purposes of a training plan are shown in Figure 7-3.

- Ensures a wiser selection of material and a more complete coverage of the topic and assists the chef supervisor in focusing on training objectives
- Assists in the presentation of training material in the proper sequence for effective learning
- Ensures that proper consideration is given to each part of the plan, that essential points are included, and that irrelevant material is omitted
- Provides time control
- Provides an outline of the training methods and procedures to be used in the instruction
- Assists in the proper use of presentation media technology
- Serves as a record of training provided to each team member
- Refreshes the chef supervisor's memory and keeps topics current

Figure 7-3
Purposes of the Lesson Plan.

- Must focus on one main thing to be learned
- Must contain something new
- Must not present too much material at one time
- Must be suited to team members and their past experiences
- Team members must derive satisfaction
- Achievement should be measurable

Figure 7-4
Requirements of a good training lesson plan.

The lesson plan should be reviewed each time it is used. Few chef supervisors are gifted with such phenomenal memories that they do not need to refresh themselves on what is to be taught and how the training is to be conducted. This review will help keep the training progression smooth and effective. The requirements of a good training lesson plan are shown in Figure 7-4.

Once a lesson plan has been completed, it should be thought of as a dynamic entity. Each time it is used, determine how it can be improved. Make notes each time the training lesson plan is used. It is a tool to help prepare for effective training.

CONCLUSIONS

Training is critical to the success of any operation. In the kitchen, training is the key to quality and consistency. For proper training, it is necessary to determine the training's objective. The objective must be clear to both the trainer and trainee. The objective must be measurable and attainable. The training plan makes it possible to achieve the objectives. Achievement of the objectives will make it possible to achieve the goals of the operation.

SUMMARY

Training objectives are the starting point in an overall plan for continuous improvements in the kitchen:

- They facilitate objective instruction and define the task performance.
- They are an unambiguous statement of what the team member will be able to do as a result of training.
- They provide criteria, standards, and conditions under which different tasks are to be accomplished.
- They allow for measurement of the training.
- They provide the basis for determining the *essential* and *desirable* training objectives.
- They separate tasks between knowing and doing.
- They provide time control, organize training systematically, and avoid unnecessary overlapping.
- Training plans are a road map to guide the chef supervisor through the process of training.

- Training plans require four steps: preparation, presentation, application, and evaluation.
- Each training session must be a complete unit of learning and should contain some old material for connection along with some new material.
- Training plans are classified as (1) manual skills and (2) the informational areas of the training topic.
- Training lesson plan outlines are prepared to ensure complete treatment of the training objectives.
- The needs and capabilities of the kitchen team should be important considerations of the training plan.
- Equipment and material needs for the training session must be planned for and secured before beginning the training session.

DISCUSSION QUESTIONS

1. Define the following chapter key terms:
   a. Learning
   b. Learning objectives
   c. Basic components
   d. Goals
   e. Level of learning
   f. Complete objectives
   g. Lesson plan
   h. Four-step training method
   i. Manual skills lesson
   j. Informational lesson
2. Why is it necessary to prepare explicit objectives?
3. What are the three basic components that make up a performance objective?
4. Why is the essence of a good objective the description of a measurable performance?
5. What are the primary differences between goals and objectives as they relate to training?
6. Why are action verbs used in the preparation of performance objectives?
7. What are the four essential characteristics of a well-planned training session?
8. What method of instruction is generally considered appropriate for culinary skills?
9. What is the purpose of lesson plans as they pertain to training?
10. What are the requirements of well-developed training lesson plans?

NOTES

1. Lois B. Hart, *Training Methods That Work* (London: Crisp, 1991), 15.

2. Robert F. Mager, *Preparing Instructional Objectives*, 2nd ed. (Belmont, CA: Fearon, 1971).

3. Ibid.

4. Cliff Barbee and Valerie Bott, "Customer Treatment as a Mirror of Employee Treatment," *Advanced Management Journal*, Spring 1991, 31.

5. Benjamin S. Bloom, *Taxonomy of Educational Objectives: Book 1* (New York: Longman, 1977).

6. Jim Sullivan, "Making It Stick: How To Eliminate Teflon Training," *Nation's Restaurant News*, April 1993, 22.

Chapter 8
Training Methods

OBJECTIVES

When you complete this chapter, you should be able to:

1. List the major techniques of training used for instructing within the kitchen
2. Explain which training techniques can be used to achieve specific learning objectives
3. Understand and describe the elements of training reinforcement
4. Identify negative training methods and state their effect
5. Identify characteristics of those team members with potential for development
6. Specify designs for evaluating training

Case Study: China Delight

The Hanon Restaurant Group began with the Select Seafood Restaurant in 1963. In January 1995, the company had 1191 restaurants around the world. These included 660 Select Seafood Restaurants, 480 Italian Palace Restaurants, and fifty-one China Delight Restaurants. They were the largest, most successful, and most stable restaurant company in the world. On March 1, 1995, Hannon Restaurant Group shocked Wall Street and the restaurant industry when, without any prior announcement, they simultaneously closed all fifty-one China Delight properties. On the afternoon of March 1, 1995, the company released the following statement:

> "Hannon Restaurant Group has made the strategic decision to discontinue the China Delight Restaurant concept. The company has been unable to address recurring challenges in the area of food quality and consistency, service quality and workforce stability."

Hanon Group had determined during the initial conceptualization of the China Delight Restaurants that serving authentic Chinese cuisine would be one of the cornerstones of the concept. To achieve this goal, Chinese were hired as general managers, and the majority of the kitchen staff was Chinese. Managers, assistant managers, wait staff, and other personnel were not necessarily Chinese.

The management and operation of the China Delight Restaurants was built on the model that had been used so successfully for the Select Seafood and Italian Palace Restaurants. This model recognized the importance of the general manager and other members of the management team, but with close control from the corporate office. An operations manual was developed that effectively addressed every eventuality. Managers did not have to guess how to handle most issues; they simply had to refer to the manual. All sales, purchasing, and payroll information was forwarded to the corporate office on a daily basis. This information was analyzed, and guidance was provided to the management from the corporate office daily regarding the operation. All menu and recipe development was done at the corporate level and then distributed to the properties. Stringent guidelines were in place for the preparation of the food and sanitation in the facility. This tightly controlled model had been very successful for the company for many years. Their experience with over one thousand restaurants had yielded a wealth of knowledge and insight into the management and operation of restaurants. The model worked well in the first few units that were created close to the corporate offices and initially opened by a team of Chinese and Chinese-speaking managers from other Hanon properties.

Based on the strength of the model and the success of the first few properties, the company rapidly expanded the China Delight Restaurants, building fifty-one in less than five years. The model did not continue to work. Expansion only compounded the problems that began to appear when the company had to hire individuals from outside the company to be general managers. The new general managers all had strong management backgrounds in the operation of similar-type restaurants. Since there had never been a chain of this type before, however, almost none had experience in operating a chain restaurant. To assist them in the transition to the concept, they were put through a well-designed three-month training program to teach them the Hanon way and culture. This program was used as the starting point for all Hanon management personnel. Additionally, the managers were given one week of intensive training in the operation and systems specific to the China Delight Restaurants. The training program did not achieve the desired results.

The general managers did not submit their information in a timely fashion, and did not pay attention to the input provided by the corporate office. Shoppers reported major differences in the menu items from one property to another. The sanitation levels in the properties were far below those of the other Hanon restaurants. Customer traffic at the properties began strongly but slowly crept downward. Guests complained of slow service, and the properties' food cost percentage was consistently out of line.

The regional managers, when asked why they could not get control of the properties, consistently referred to the managers as too entrepreneurial. One district manager stated, "They act like they own the business and can run it any way they want." The district managers also reported a disruptive level of friction between the front and back of the house. The district managers freely admitted that they had little ability to directly address problems in the back of the house because the majority of the cooks did not have a good command of English and did not speak any Chinese dialect. All communication was through the general managers in the properties. The communications problem was compounded in the properties that had non-Chinese members in the management teams. These management team members, hired by the corporation and assigned to the property, complained of being excluded from the actual operation of the restaurant by the managers who spoke Chinese. They also reported that they were unable to communicate with the kitchen staff.

The president of China Delight characterized the speed-of-service issue as the application of western restaurant management principles to an oriental restaurant operation. He stated that speed of service in the restaurant was directly related to the number of woks in the kitchen: "One wok, one cook, one dish!" A Hanon Restaurant Group vice president stated, "Going from three or four units to fifty was the kiss of death."

Based on what you have learned from previous chapters and the content of this chapter, answer the following questions.

- What is the overall reason for the failure of China Delight Restaurants?
- What are the primary causal agents for the failure of China Delight Restaurants?
- What role did leadership and supervision/management play in the failure of China Delight Restaurants?
- What specific steps could have been taken to avoid the failure of China Delight Restaurants?
- What, specifically, can be done by Hanon Restaurant Group to avoid a repeat of the China Delight Restaurant failure with their next concept rollout?

INTRODUCTION

All modern learning theories stress involvement by the learner. Learners should have a degree of ownership of the learning process. **Training** is therefore a learning process that involves the gaining of skills, concepts, rules, or attitudes that serve to increase the performance of the kitchen team. The gains are made more quickly by the learner through methods that actively involve them. Using individualized or group-training techniques can accomplish training and retraining. This chapter will explore the instructional techniques and methods that best serve members of the kitchen team.

People grow to a point where they are ready for new responsibilities beyond their initial assignments. When this happens, the foodservice organization can help them to develop and adjust to new roles. The goal is for team members to grow to understand all the elements necessary to continuously improve themselves and the organization. Training is the critical factor. Training all employees, with special attention to hourly employees, will enable the kitchen to recruit and retain workers and keep a well-run foodservice establishment afloat and realizing its potential even in hard times.[1]

SPECIFIC TRAINING METHODS

Job Talks

Job talks are a method of instruction whereby the chef supervisor provides verbal information about a particular job. These are typically used in the kitchen when the chef supervisor is presenting information concepts and theories that are found in the cognitive learning domain. They are delivered by way of an illustrated lecture and may be supplemented with a variety of instructional materials such as slides, transparencies, projected computer displays, flip charts, instruction sheets, and/or videotapes. Job talks

Figure 8-1
Job talk strengths and weaknesses.

Job Talk Strengths
- Get the message across to a large group
- Chef can communicate enthusiasm for subject matter
- Cover material not otherwise available
- Chef supervisor can serve as effective role model
- Nonthreatening to the individual team member
- Chef supervisor controls the material, time involved
- Not necessary to plan group involvement

Weaknesses
- Often do not allow for feedback from the team
- Passive methods of training
- Difficult to maintain listeners' interest
- Appeal to one sense only—hearing (unless illustrated)
- Overloading may occur
- Difficult to assess if the "message" has been understood
- Success depends on public speaking ability of chef
- Unsuitable for certain higher forms of learning such as analysis and evaluation

are, by definition, words spoken by the chef supervisor. This medium is a verbal one, offering a passive, nonstimulating experience for the kitchen team member, unless the chef supervisor has unusual vocal talent. Interesting examples as well as colorful and persuasive language are needed to illustrate the job talk.[2] Job talks offer many advantages to the chef supervisor. They can be an effective method of reaching mixed groups of learners. Job talks can ensure that a large amount of information is delivered in a relatively short period of time. The strengths and weaknesses of job talks are shown in Figure 8-1.

The goal of the chef supervisor when conducting a job talk is to make the strongest possible connection with the team members and thereby achieve the highest possible level of understanding of the material presented. There are several keys to achieving this "maximum value" from job talks. The chef supervisor needs to make sure the team members see the relevancy of the subject matter to their jobs or professional development and advancement. Relevancy is a driver of the team member's interest in the subject matter. Team members' level of comprehension and mastery resulting from the job talk is tied to their level of interest in the subject.

Relevancy alone will not deliver success in a job talk. The chef supervisor must be an effective presenter/communicator. The chef supervisor must demonstrate enthusiasm for the subject matter. The chef supervisor can connect on a more personal level by calling team members by their names, displaying a sense of humor, moving around to achieve "eye contact" with each team member, engaging the team members with questions, and providing positive feedback. The chef supervisor should be a model in terms of dress, appearance, support for the quality objectives, and enthusiasm for the training program and by helping each team member grow and succeed.

There are three parts to the structure of a job talk. In the *introduction,* state what you are going to talk about and why. Start positively; go over previous information pertaining to the job talk. In the *presentation,* avoid reading word for word; use key words to revolve around. Develop the talk from the known to the unknown, from the simple to the more difficult. Build information in a logical way. Try to develop a picture in the team member's mind. Media technology may be used to emphasize and support the job talk. Vary your tone of voice, observe each person, and don't fix your gaze on a "challenging" individual. Avoid rushing the job talk, and attempt to pace it to the learning rate of the group. Do not allow too many long pauses. In the *summary,*

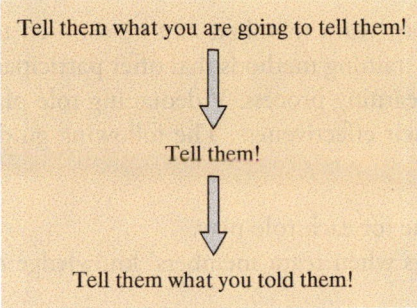

Figure 8-2 Tell them.

restate the key points of the job talk. Allow time for team members to ask questions. Use questions to determine what learning has taken place. Praise the team for their interest and link forward to the next job talk or training session.

Schedule job talks close to when the knowledge and skills will be used by each team member. Break the job talk down into fairly simple steps, then progress through each step until the entire job is learned. This provides an opportunity for the team member to experience success along the way, to remain interested, and to be motivated to learn the job. Team members can be overwhelmed if too much information is presented all at once, and this will cause frustration.

When a highly experienced person attempts to instruct the details of a job, significant points may be omitted, assumptions may be made that "everyone knows that," or some detail is so routine that it is overlooked. Do not assume anything. Concentrating on the key points should help simplify the job talk. If the job talk preparation process is complete, then repeating and emphasizing key points becomes easy to do. The tried-and-true method of preparing job talks and all presentations, "Tell them!", is shown in Figure 8-2.

Role Play

In **role-plays**, team members simulate or act out a real or hypothetical situation in order to acquire the skills needed to manage the interpersonal dynamics of that situation. The strengths and weaknesses of role-play are shown in Figure 8-3.

This training method can be used to build skill and confidence. It is usually followed by discussion and analysis among the kitchen team participants. Team members are asked to act out certain roles in order for others to be able to practice how to handle certain problems. The idea is for the team members to learn from playing out the

Figure 8-3
Role-play strengths and weaknesses.

Role Play Strengths
- Team members are directly involved in the training
- Highlights key attitudinal issues
- Develops awareness of other people's feelings
- Similarity between role-play and work situations becomes clear to team members
- Team members receive instant feedback that gives them confidence
- Good for interpersonal skills
- Allows team members to "see" problem areas as they exist

Weaknesses
- Require a lot of preparation
- Suitable only for small groups
- Sometimes not taken seriously by team members
- Require close monitoring and control by the chef supervisor

assigned roles. In this way, team members can be exposed to both sides of an issue. Role-plays are one of the training methods that offer participants the opportunity to be actively involved in the learning process. Videotaping role-plays allows for review and evaluation to improve their effectiveness. The following guidelines are recommended for role-plays:

- Allow plenty of time for each role-play.
- Introduce role-plays when team members' knowledge of the subject will assure success.
- Fully explain the purpose of the role-play (outline training objective) as well as the expected results.
- Always demonstrate role-plays before team members try them.
- Keep the tone of the training session "serious."
- Invite the team member to choose a particular role; seek attitude changes during the role-play.
- Coach and correct team members during and following enactment of the role-play.
- Give positive reinforcement and praise and link forward to further training.

Total immersion in the learning process can be achieved by using a role-play. It is particularly useful for awareness training with regard to customer satisfaction and may also be used to demonstrate correct and appropriate interpersonal transactions. If done with enthusiasm by the chef supervisor, it can become a very effective method of training.

Role-plays may be highly structured, with the roles well defined, or they may allow the team members who are playing the roles a great deal of flexibility in acting them out.[3] Role-plays cast participants into real-life situations. Real-life situations within the kitchen take on special meaning when dealing with personal sanitation, grooming, and hygiene. Sensitive topics such as these are ideal subject matter for role-plays. Crucial to the success of these sessions are prior explanation of the training objective and follow-up discussions on the role-play content. In this way, sensitive topics can be treated as part of a group role-play with critical sensitive elements being highlighted. Remember, role-plays work only if the participants are able to let go of their inhibitions, feel empathy for the roles they are asked to play, and really get into the situation. The chef supervisor's ability to understand team members' attitudes toward role-play training ideally will enable him or her to improve personal awareness of individual shortcomings.

Training in the foodservice industry involves more than just technical skills. Interpersonal skills are just as important, if not more so. Chef supervisors must not assume that team members know how to treat customers or other members in the foodservice organization in a polite and friendly manner. Instructing interpersonal skills by using role-plays is an efficient training method that results in increased motivation. Although role-plays do not, by themselves, guarantee that the desired behavior will be used on the job, they do provide examples of expected behavior. This method of training should be used with care and is most appropriate when the social competence of the team member is low.

Demonstration

Demonstration as a training method is very effective in skills training. By showing team members how to perform a task while explaining the procedure, the chef supervisor enables the kitchen team members to use more than one sense and one learning mode at the same time. Team members can listen to the chef supervisor while observing the proper performance steps of the task or skill being demonstrated. Follow-up

> **Demonstration Strengths**
> - Great visual impact
> - Instruction can be built step by step, given in sequence
> - Difficult steps or tasks can be broken down into easy stages
> - Makes use of the natural inclination to imitate
> - Most effective method of instructing a skill
> - Emphasis on safety/sanitation practices can be included
> - Food product quality and specifications can be observed
> - Required job skills or tasks may be repeated/reinforced
>
> **Weaknesses**
> - Only suitable for relatively small groups
> - Great deal of preparation is required
> - Pace of demonstration is often too fast
> - Team members may watch the demonstrator rather than what is being done

Figure 8-4
Demonstration strengths and weaknesses.

activity on the job then allows the team member to practice while being coached and corrected by the chef supervisor. The strengths and weaknesses of demonstrations are shown in Figure 8-4.

In a demonstration, actual kitchen equipment is used to illustrate the steps involved in the task. Demonstration alone makes use primarily of the team member's visual sense. The team member may hear and/or smell, which reinforces learning. Keys to an effective demonstration are:

- Ensure that all actions can be seen easily.
- Arrange all food ingredients, equipment, and tools needed for the demonstration in advance.
- Introduce the demonstration by reviewing previously instructed information and/or skills that are relevant to the demonstration.
- Introduce any technical/culinary terms that are relevant to the demonstration, particularly new terms.
- Demonstrate the manipulative skill or task in a way that closely resembles the actual kitchen environment and clarify why the skill is important.
- Stress food safety and sanitation.
- Check for understanding during the demonstration by asking team members questions.

The potential for a demonstration's success in bringing team members to the desired level of understanding or mastery can be improved by some simple actions. Use supporting materials such as a procedure sheet to reinforce the performance steps being demonstrated. Keep the demonstration focused and short, preferably 15 to 30 minutes. Closely follow the demonstration with supervised practice and/or an assignment related to the demonstration to reinforce the information presented. During and after the demonstration, show your interest in the team members' understanding and mastery by asking questions and providing positive feedback.

The chef supervisor should avoid demonstration as a training method unless practiced beforehand and adequate time for preparation and checking of equipment and food materials has been allowed. The demonstration can be reinforced with an effective review and summary.[4]

A common mistake is to complete a demonstration and ask whether each team member feels he or she can perform the steps or understand the basic skills involved. The usual response in this situation is silence or affirmative nods. An excellent summary technique is to ask the team member to repeat the demonstration while the chef supervisor or another team member reads each of the steps. After the second demonstration, the individual is ready to practice the steps.

Demonstrations are especially suitable for skills training (psychomotor objectives) but can also be used as modeling to illustrate interpersonal, interviewing, or communication skills. Within the kitchen, demonstration is by far the single most effective method for instructing culinary art: the preparation, cooking, and presentation of menu items. As a method, it has the benefit of utilizing all five senses of the team member, and no other training method affords this total sensual integration.

Effective questioning and reinforcement techniques are employed during and after the demonstration to encourage team members to think about the training topic. In addition, questioning helps to maintain the individual's interest. It provides the chef supervisor with feedback regarding team members' understanding of the topic and allows for feedback to strengthen the training climate in the kitchen.

Case Study

The **case study method** of training presents to the kitchen team real or hypothetical situations for them to analyze. Ideally, the case study should force the team member to think through problems, propose solutions and choose among them, and analyze the consequences of the decision. Case studies are a popular way to get the team involved so that discussion and resolutions of problems may be brought down to the level of concreteness. The strengths and weaknesses of case studies are shown in Figure 8-5.

In traditional case studies, team members receive a printed description of a problem situation. The description contains sufficient details so that the individual can make recommendations for appropriate corrective actions. Areas in which the use of case studies is particularly appropriate as a training method in the kitchen include analysis of safety and sanitation procedures, teamwork, workflow, work organization, customer relations, and quality in all areas of organization.

While many cases exist under these headings, it is possible for resourceful chef supervisors to create their own. Additionally, team members can be encouraged to write their own case studies from past real-life situations, and these may then be shared with the rest of the kitchen team. To increase total participation, team members may be split into small "buzz groups." When there are fewer people in each group, individuals are more inclined to participate at higher levels than they would be in only one large discussion group.

To facilitate and enable success with case study training methods, the technique of structured discussions is used. Structured discussions are conversations between team

Figure 8-5
Case study strengths and weaknesses.

Case Study Strengths
- Emphasize the analysis of a situation typical of a training need
- May improve the team members' communication skills
- Expose team members to true-to-life problems in the kitchen
- May inspire interest in otherwise theoretical and abstract training materials

Weaknesses
- Focus on past and static considerations
- Analysis often lacks emotional involvement on the part of the team member and therefore can become unrealistic in terms of what the team member would actually do in the situation
- There are time limits on analysis and discussion

members aimed at specific learning objectives. These objectives distinguish structured discussions from more social conversations. The learning objective for the case study analysis should be announced in advance. Structure in the ensuing discussions can be facilitated by the use of an agenda with time controls. Agendas and timetables developed by the team afford ownership of the session to the kitchen team.

Attempting to conduct a structured discussion when team members have had a limited exposure to the case study topic often will result in little or no interaction and an ineffective discussion. Creating an effective structured discussion begins with the environment. The chef supervisor must create an environment for the discussion that encourages not only engagement and interaction of the team members but also ensures respect for all participants. This means ensuring that no team member will be ridiculed or rejected for expressing their thoughts on the subject under discussion. Provision of guidelines for conducting the discussion is critical to establishing an environment that will lead to truly open dialogue.

As with any training method, relevancy of the subject matter is a key to success. The chef supervisor must bring into focus for the team members the relevancy of the issue being discussed and provide positive reinforcement. The chef supervisor should act as a catalyst in the discussion, encouraging participation and stimulating discussion when lulls occur. The chef supervisor must not dominate the discussion.

Structured discussions are appropriate for use with case studies. They should have predetermined objectives. The chef supervisor must ensure that team members do not bring a negative viewpoint to these objectives. When used with case study analysis, structured discussions can be a motivating and useful training method in the kitchen.

On-The-Job Training

On-the-job training is the most commonly used method to train kitchen team members. It is not necessarily the best training method for culinary standards of quality. The chef supervisor usually conducts it, and it has the advantage of providing "hands-on" experience under normal conditions. Although on-the-job training (OJT) is commonly used in the kitchen, it also is one of the most poorly implemented methods of training. Common drawbacks of OJT include:

- Lack of a well-structured training environment
- Poor chef supervisor training skills
- Omission of a well-defined high-quality job performance criterion

On-the-job training can be successful when the chef supervisor as trainer has an objective, a plan, and the knowledge that quality and continuous improvements can only be implemented on the job.

One benefit of OJT is that it provides immediate application and satisfaction for the new team member who may often be anxious and fearful. The chef supervisor can determine which training method is most suitable for instructing different job duties. Additionally, for retraining or cross training, different methods and techniques and/or combinations of these methods may be appropriate.

Steps and Structure of OJT

1. *Introduction*
   - Introduce what the team member *will be able to do* at the end of the session.
   - Indicate why the team member is to learn.
   - Discuss how this training relates to what the team member already knows.
   - Demonstrate equipment to be used during the training session.
   - Explain the steps involved in the task and the overall purpose.

2. *Presentation*

- Highlight key points.
- Demonstrate the procedure in sequential order.
- Explain the what, why, who, when, how, and where.
- Use training aids where appropriate.
- Instruct at a pace that allows the team member to understand the task.

3. *Summary*

- Demonstrate the task a second time, if necessary; repeat the key points and steps.
- Encourage questions on points of clarification.
- Give specific feedback.
- Give praise when due.
- When satisfied that learning has occurred, move to the next step.

4. *Practice*

- Team members practice under supervision.
- Ask questions to assess team members' understanding.
- Coach and correct team members.
- Praise when correct quality standards have been achieved.

5. *Follow-up*

- The team member puts into practice what has been instructed under supervision.
- Encourage further questions from the team member.
- Decide on follow-up talk.
- Show how every job relates to the importance of every other job and that failure of one affects the value of all of the others.

6. *Coaching*

- Allow all team members to become involved with the procedures they will use.
- Conduct correction interviews in private.
- Permit team members to evaluate their own performance.
- Allow ample time for skill development.
- Use open questions to establish work problems.
- Provide positive reinforcement.

The first step of coaching is to observe team members doing their job. If they are doing the job well, don't hesitate to tell them. Everyone likes to be praised; try to catch team members doing good things.

Training is progressive and it must be continuous. Repetition is the key to learning. Therefore, it is important that the chef supervisor demonstrate a good deal of patience. If there appears to be a problem with some aspect of the team members' performance, check the following:

- Are they fully aware of what is supposed to be done?
- Do they have adequate equipment and materials to perform the task?
- Did they receive adequate feedback during the practice stage?

The next step is to confront, not criticize, the team member's poor performance. **Confronting** is a positive process used to correct job performance problems. Chef supervisors who confront are more interested in helping team members feel confident about improving future performance, rather than making them feel inadequate and guilty about past performance. Praise in public, correct in private. Training means directing the growth of an individual.[5] In the quality kitchen environment, cross training is important. **Cross training** prepares individual team members to fill in as needed on jobs. This is also an excellent method of eliminating job monotony and fatigue.

Another advantage of cross training is that it makes flexibility possible; for example, when one team member is absent, another can perform that job.

Apprenticeship Training

Apprenticeship training is designed to provide young chefs entering the culinary profession with a comprehensive training in the practical and theoretical aspects of work required in a highly skilled profession. Apprenticeship programs combine OJT and classroom training with a skilled and experienced chef conducting the OJT during the apprenticeship period. The purpose of this training is to learn practical culinary skills on the job. Apprentices learn the theoretical side of the culinary profession in classes they attend outside the job. Subjects covered in classroom training are safety, sanitation, communication skills, mathematics, supervisory management, law, food cost control procedures, purchasing, and nutrition.

The culinary apprenticeship program in the United States is sponsored by the American Culinary Federation in cooperation with local chapters of that organization. It is the only national apprenticeship training program for chefs and operates in cooperation with the U.S. Department of Labor, Bureau of Apprenticeship and Training (BAT). The apprenticeship program also operates in conjunction with local postsecondary schools and colleges providing culinary theory courses.[6]

The culinary apprentice completes 6000 hours of OJT as well as theory-related courses, usually over a three-year period. Wages paid to apprentices usually begin at half those paid to fully trained chefs. However, wages are generally advanced rapidly at six-month intervals. The BAT has established the following minimum standards for apprenticeship programs:

1. Nondiscrimination in all phases of apprenticeship employment and training.
2. Organized instruction designed to provide the apprentice with knowledge in technical subjects related to the trade or skill.

CHEF TALK
"MY WAY OR THE HIGHWAY"

To train means to form by instruction, discipline, or drill. In the kitchen, chefs are involved primarily in training two types of culinarians: the apprentice chef (who is inexperienced in the area of culinary art) and the cook (who may have had many years of experience with other establishments). From my personal experience, each culinarian should be handled differently when it comes to training.

In comparing the apprentice chef and the cook from a training standpoint, I feel most chefs would prefer to train apprentice chefs. The rationale is that the apprentice is new, has no preset ideas or bad habits, and is usually eager to learn. It doesn't take much for the chef to convince the apprentice of how things should be done. Let's face it: All of us chefs have different ideas on how things should be done. So with an apprentice, it basically boils down to what we as chefs are willing to commit to this person, and that should be everything we know about cooking and how to run a kitchen.

The experienced cook may have served an apprenticeship with another chef, or may be a graduate of a culinary school or of the "School of Hard Knocks." Either way, they are most assuredly going to do things differently from you.

How do you train such a cook? When I first became a supervisory chef, I thought it would be simple. My technique, in all honesty, was "my way or the highway." As I gained experience, I learned how to work with and train these individuals. In fact, sometimes I ended up as the trainee. Training becomes a watching process. I would watch new cooks in action, observing their skill levels, techniques, work methods, and the final product. When they prepared something that was different from our standards, I would compare both methods and discuss which method was better. If theirs made sense, we would change to that method, and vice versa. If the end result was the same, and there was no difference in the cost or time factor, then either method could be used.

It is difficult to train persons if they are uncomfortable with the training method. I discovered that by utilizing an open training style and involving the cooks, they become more open to my suggestions because they realize their input is valued.

—Aidan P. Murphy, CMC, AAC,
General Manager, Old Warson
Country Club, St. Louis, MO

3. A schedule of work processes in which an apprentice is to receive training and experience on the job.
4. A progressively increasing schedule of wages.
5. Proper supervision of OJT with adequate facilities to train apprentices.
6. Periodic evaluation of the apprentice's progress on both job performance and related instructions.
7. Recognition for successful completion.

Upon graduation the apprentice receives a Department of Labor certificate and/or a certificate of the American Culinary Federation and is admitted as a member of that organization.

TRAINING REINFORCEMENT

People strive to achieve objectives they have set for themselves. The most frequently identified objectives of kitchen team members are job security, rewarding work, recognition, status, responsibility, and achievement. If training assists team members in achieving these objectives, then the learning process is greatly facilitated. When training provides greater opportunities for job advancement, team members will be highly motivated because they can see that greater rewards and job security will likely result. Knowledge of results (feedback) influences the training/learning process. Keeping team members informed of their progress as measured against a quality improvement standard helps in setting goals for what remains to be learned. The ongoing process of analyzing progress and setting new objectives greatly enhances learning.

Reinforcement theory states that behavior appearing to lead to a positive consequence tends to be repeated, while behavior appearing to lead to a negative consequence tends not to be repeated. A positive consequence is rewarded.[7] Praise and recognition are two of the most important rewards used in training. Each segment of training should be sequentially organized so that the individual can see not only its purpose, but also how it fits into the overall quality training program.

Perfect practice makes perfect, and bad practice will not make perfect. This is applicable to training in the kitchen. Repeating a job task several times develops facility in performing it. Practice and repetition almost always lead to effective training.

NEGATIVE TRAINING METHODS

It is impossible to implement standards of quality food production if chef supervisors do not actively engage in training their team. Yet it is not uncommon to observe poor or no training in some kitchens. Many chef supervisors assume that experience in a previous job takes the place of training. They assume that new team members know how to do the job to the quality standards that have been set. There is also a misguided assumption that once a team member is hired, he or she will learn the job from other team members. Known as the **buddy system**, this is rooted in the mistaken belief that other team members can train the new team member, often while still doing their jobs. Probably the most common negative training method is the one that allows the person leaving the job to train the person who will take over the job. Other negative training methods are:

Spectator method. The new team member does not have the right to do anything and can only watch others. This is boring for the individual, produces nothing, and simply prolongs the training period.

Unskilled labor method. The team member can perform only trivial jobs, for example, cleaning up or getting coffee. Nothing is learned, and the team member feels useless and is not stimulated by the job.

Do-it-yourself method. New team members are left on their own to "sink or swim." This method can be successful with individuals who catch on quickly and who like to show off their capabilities. The downside to this method is the risk that a new team member will develop bad habits, and this can harm team spirit. Later, these team members are usually unwilling to pass on to others what they know.

DEVELOPING THE TEAM MEMBER WITH POTENTIAL

Training deals with the immediate concerns of the kitchen team; development deals with recognizing team members who possess obvious talent for leadership roles. Developing individual team members into capable chef supervisors of the future is key to the continuous improvements necessary to provide better-quality food and service to customers. The team member with potential for growth needs nurturing and encouragement.

Human resources development is generally a combination of OJT and educational opportunities that will help a team member develop into a more productive and responsible member of the foodservice organization. Although there are no foolproof methods of determining who has the greatest potential for development, Figure 8-6 shows some of the observable characteristics that help identify potential leaders.

There are two important steps in developing a team member:

1. A series of jobs through which a team member can be promoted.
2. Opportunities to receive training beyond each job for each team member who shows potential for leadership.

Each job can be an opportunity for the team members to prepare for something better. **Internal job mobility** means that team members have a chance to grow, and the foodservice organization has a reliable source of labor without the high cost of turnover and of training someone new.

TRAINING EVALUATION

Evaluation is necessary to determine whether training in the kitchen has had an impact on improving team members' knowledge, skills and attitudes, and job performance related to total quality. Evaluation of training is part of the cycle of the training process. Without it, chef supervisors are unable to determine whether they have been simply "spinning their wheels."

Evaluating is the final step before reviewing and renewing training objectives and before starting the process again. Training is a very dynamic process. Its elements

- Are able to cope with problems and seek help when it is needed
- Are able to act without supervisory direction
- Are open-minded, calm, and tolerant
- Accept responsibility for their actions and don't try to blame others
- Maintain a level disposition
- Display high energy levels

Figure 8-6
Characteristics of potential leaders.

Figure 8-7
Evaluation questions for the
impact of training.

- Did training make a difference?
- Is the team member able to perform the skills presented during the training session?
- What effect has training had on team attitudes?
- Were interpersonal skills improved?
- Were the resulting changes in team members worth the investment in training?
- Did team members provide suggestions for improving the training sessions?
- Did training correct identified problems?
- Were deficiencies related to method of training, content, format, and delivery identified?
- What recommendations are there for improvement?

Figure 8-7
Evaluation questions for the impact of training.

cannot be left alone for long without their possibly becoming stagnant, outdated, inaccurate, or even harmful to the total quality efforts of the organization. Additionally, team members do not always learn precisely what the training was intended to teach them. Evaluating the impact of training on kitchen team job performance revolves around finding the answers to the right questions. Examples of those questions are shown in Figure 8-7.

The answers to these questions should be sought from the participants. Additionally, external input should be sought regarding the success of the training. If most of the feedback is positive, it can be assumed that the training was effective. If specific concerns were expressed, the data must then be compared to other methods of evaluation.

The kitchen team members who received training are the most obvious source of data regarding the impact of training. Through the **evaluation process**, team members are asked to express their opinions and make observations about the effectiveness of the training. In addition to asking them to respond to specific questions related to tasks addressed within the training program, a number of general questions can be built into a survey instrument that will provide valuable information. Typically, participants are asked to complete a questionnaire with regard to the training they received. These questionnaires may be quite elaborate or simple. Figure 8-8 shows a simple example detailing elementary questions to be asked.

This type of training participant evaluation is not too tedious to complete and is easy to follow. This "form type" of evaluation should be used at the end of the training session or segment of a teaching program. It is important that evaluations of this type not be overused. Evaluation tests can be administered at any appropriate time or whenever they will help. The reasons for testing are essentially the same as the reasons for asking questions.

When training is effective, team members completing a training program are able to perform the skills or apply the knowledge necessary to correct quality or implement correct standards. Evaluation also monitors the team members' performance OJT as well as the entire training process. Continuous monitoring and feedback ensure that

Figure 8-8
Example training participant questionnaire.

- Are job elements different from those taught during training?
- Was the benefit from training worth the effort spent?
- Were the course objectives explained clearly?
- Did the instructor demonstrate technical knowledge?
- Were the training topics sequenced logically?
- Were all your questions and concerns regarding training answered?
- Were facilities adequate and suitable for training?

the training process is successful and that the chef supervisor is able to fulfill the roles and responsibilities required in the design, delivery, and evaluation of training.

CONCLUSIONS

The success of any operation is the result of team members delivering what is promised to the guest. This task requires that the team member have the skills and knowledge to perform to the standard. A team member that consistently performs to the standard is the outcome of training. Once this is achieved with the team member, the goal must be to retain that individual.

Retaining the individual requires more than just training for today. The chef supervisor needs to be watching his team members to determine who would benefit from training that will eventually move them forward. It is this nurturing of the team members that will develop loyalty, job satisfaction, and retention. This action also builds a stronger workforce that will help grow the business.

SUMMARY

Attaining maximum involvement of the kitchen team member in the training process is one of the greatest objectives of the chef supervisor. People learn best by doing.

Specific training methods suitable for the implementation of training in a culinary environment include the following.

Job talks, which by definition are a one-way process by the chef supervisor, can be boring and unproductive unless considerably enhanced and supported by stimulating visuals, good preparation, and interesting delivery.

Role-play participants are asked to act out certain roles in order for other learners to be able to practice how to handle certain problems. In this way, participants can be exposed to both sides of the role-play issue. It offers full participation in the training process by the kitchen team member.

Demonstration is a widely used training method in the kitchen. It offers the chef supervisor a method to carefully and slowly instruct skills. Team members can then practice under supervision while the chef supervisor coaches and corrects.

Case study team members develop solutions and approaches to situations that are presented by means of written cases. Proposed and actual solutions and their results are discussed.

On-the-job training is the most widely used method following demonstration. This is a combination of all methods of training and retraining. In this method the team member is placed into the real work situation and trained to do the different parts of the job by

an experienced team member or the chef supervisor. It includes the following steps: introduction, presentation, summary, practice, follow-up, and coaching.

Apprenticeship training in the kitchen is organized according to guidelines and structures set forth by the American Culinary Federation Educational Institute and the U.S. Department of Labor. Apprenticeship offers the foodservice establishment a long-term training program that can provide a long-term commitment from those in the program.

Reinforcement training theory is based on studies showing that behavior that leads to a positive consequence tends to be repeated, while behavior that leads to a negative consequence tends not to be repeated. Praise and recognition are two of the most positive elements of reinforcement training.

Negative training methods involve skills that the chef supervisor assumes team members either bring to the job or learn from others on the job. The results of negative training are that team members learn bad habits and are unaware of objectives or the quality vision of the kitchen team.

Developing the team member with potential is necessary to identify future leaders. Characteristics of these potential leaders manifest themselves in high energy levels. These people are problem solvers. Promotions and further training opportunities are ways to develop these potential leaders.

Evaluation of training is necessary to determine the success of the planned training. Evaluation is the final step in the training process. It provides the basis for a review of the objectives and applied methods.

DISCUSSION QUESTIONS

1. Define the following chapter key terms:
   a. Training
   b. Job talk
   c. Role-play
   d. Demonstration
   e. Case study method
   f. On-the-job training
   g. Confronting
   h. Cross training
   i. Apprenticeship
   j. Reinforcement theory
   k. Buddy system
   l. Internal job mobility
   m. Evaluation
   n. Evaluation process

2. What are the merits of using case study as a specific training technique in the kitchen?

3. What are the main disadvantages to apprenticeship training?

4. Why is on-the-job training sometimes considered to be one of the most poorly implemented training techniques in the kitchen?

5. In your opinion, what training technique(s) is most suited to implementing total quality management?

6. Describe reinforcement theory. How can reinforcement facilitate quality improvements?

7. What are negative training methods? What is their impact on new team members?

8. What team member characteristics demonstrate potential for further development?

9. Why is evaluation of training programs necessary?

10. What are the links between training objectives and training evaluation?

NOTES

1. Francine A. Herman and Martha E. Miller, "Training for Hospitality," *Training & Development*, September 1991.

2. Robert B. Maddux, *Team Building: An Exercise in Leadership* (Los Altos, CA: Crisp, 1992), 33.

3. Lois B. Hart, *Training Methods That Work* (London: Crisp, 1991), 70.

4. Herman Zaccarelli, *Training Managers to Train* (Los Altos, CA: Crisp, 1988), 48.

5. John Bank, *The Essence of Total Quality Management* (New York: Prentice-Hall, 1992).

6. American Culinary Federation, *Apprenticeship Operations Manual* (St. Augustine, FL, 1985).

7. B. F. Skinner, *About Behaviorism* (New York: Alfred Knopf, 1974).

Chapter 9
Instructional Delivery

OBJECTIVES

When you complete this chapter, you should be able to:

1. Describe the factors that contribute to an effective training presentation
2. Identify elements conducive to creating a professional training atmosphere
3. Describe methods used to achieve an effective presentation comfort level
4. Understand the appropriate communication style used for effective training
5. Describe the steps appropriate to training a diverse kitchen team
6. Recognize the differences between open and closed questioning techniques
7. Define the dynamics of group behaviors and the activities associated with kitchen team training

Case Study: Cypress Cove Resort

Cypress Cove Resort is an upscale resort that operates year round, but generates 70 percent of its annual revenue between Memorial Day and Labor Day. The resort operates with a skeletal year-round staff. Seasonal staff are hired to accommodate the guests during the high season. Most of the seasonal staff members are college students, including interns from a number of college hospitality and culinary programs around the United States. Most of these workers arrive for training one week before Memorial Day.

Don Hanson joined the Cypress in January as executive chef. The previous chef had been with Cypress for three years and left for a position with a larger resort. Before leaving, the previous chef provided Don with the training schedule, manuals, and other materials that had been developed over the years to train the seasonal staff that would be part of the Cypress culinary team.

Don was previously the sous chef in a hotel similar in size to the Cypress. As sous chef, Don had done some one-on-one specialized training for a few culinary team members. Don's executive chef, however, did any large-scale training that was required while Don oversaw the day-to-day operation of the kitchens. The training that Don had done involved very little formal preparation. He had merely noticed that a team member needed assistance with perfecting a particular skill and arranged a time to work with the team member on that skill.

Don admitted to himself that he enjoyed the one-on-one training that he had done, but the thought of conducting a full week of training for thirty people was intimidating. During the winter and spring, Don reviewed the materials and training schedules the previous chef had given him. He made very few changes because he was sure that the materials had been created by people who knew more about "that sort of thing" than he did. The training objectives sounded "alright," and he figured if they were not quite on target it would not really matter. He did introduce new recipes and remove old recipes to accommodate changes he had made to the Cypress menu. Don considered the timeline to be reasonable. If anything, he felt that too much time was allowed for lecture, demonstration, and question-and-answer sessions. He thought trainees should just have the opportunity to "get in there and practice doing it."

When Labor Day arrived, all of the year-round culinary staff said that it had been one of the most difficult seasons they had ever had. "The seasonal folks just did not seem to be able to get the hang of it." Don had the same thought that had been recurring to him throughout the season: "These college kids just do not get it! They will never make it in the industry!"

Based on what you have learned from previous chapters and the content of this chapter, answer the following questions.

- What is the overall reason for the challenges that occurred at the Cypress Cove Resort?
- What are the primary causal agents for the challenges that occurred at the Cypress Cove Resort?
- What role did leadership and supervision/management play in the challenges that occurred at the Cypress Cove Resort?
- What specific steps could have been taken to avoid the challenges that occurred at the Cypress Cove Resort?
- What, specifically, can be done to avoid a repeat of the challenges next year for the Cypress Cove Resort?

INTRODUCTION

Every time a chef supervisor enters the training room, what follows should be a dynamic and effective training session. An effective presentation can be the most exciting and rewarding aspect of the chef supervisor's job. The time invested in determining the needs analysis and preparing training objectives pays off. In this process the chef supervisor becomes an instructor and learns to interact, discuss, question, and work with the kitchen team to reach the training objectives. Chef supervisors who are able to maintain team member interest with a dynamic delivery using a variety of instructional techniques are more likely to be successful in helping the kitchen team succeed.

The **purpose of instruction** is to communicate knowledge and skills from the chef supervisor to the team member. It is successful only when, at the end of the training, the individual team member can safely perform skilled activity to the required standard. It is essential that the chef supervisor choose the instructional method most suited to the training topic and the needs of the team member. Do the following before proceeding with training:

- Specify to the team what needs to be learned.
- Decide on training priorities.
- Decide appropriate techniques of training.
- Specify when and how often training can take place.
- Decide on how much instruction can be given at one time.
- Decide over what period of time training will take place.

Every presentation should begin with an interesting introduction to capture the kitchen team's interest and to prepare them for learning. Good introductions will prepare the team members, boost their confidence, and set the stage for a positive learning environment. Dugan Laird states, "In professional instruction, learning processes are not blurred by an instructor's awkwardness or amateurism. Professionalism is often based on the mastery of a few teaching techniques."[1]

CHEF TALK
"TEACHING OLD DOGS NEW TRICKS"

A lesson I learned many years ago about improving the standard of cooking and food presentation involved a major personal commitment and investment in training my kitchen brigade.

The Shelbourne Hotel is a first-class hotel located on Dublin's famous St. Stephen's Green. It is one of the oldest, most celebrated hotels in Ireland. When I came to it as only its fourth executive chef in 100 years, I found a traditional kitchen designed on the old labor-intensive "partie system." Its cooking philosophy was deeply embedded in the traditions of classical cuisine. My arrival there coincided with the advent of the cuisine nouvelle period of the early 1980s.

One of the major goals set for me by management was to introduce a new style of cooking in line with the modern approach and style of cuisine that reflected the needs of the discerning, health-conscious customer of the 1980s. As a young enthusiastic chef, this was a challenge I was happy to accept. The a la carte menu that was in place when I arrived had not changed in many years. The repertoire of dishes included on this menu was rather limited, and my attempts to introduce new dishes and simpler methods of preparation and presentation were resisted by the older, more conservative chefs. Change was therefore necessary to bring the cuisine up to date.

Before any new dish was introduced, I had to develop an overall training plan for the traditional brigade, one that would meet with each person's schedule. Great consideration was given to the training methods to be used. The method I felt best suited my training goals was the demonstration training technique.

The problem I faced was how to convince the kitchen staff to attend my training sessions voluntarily. No budget was available to facilitate the training on company time. Because of trade union rules, I could not compel any of the chefs to attend these sessions. However, I decided to go full speed ahead with my plans. I selected Saturday mornings as the most appropriate training time and informed the kitchen brigade of my planned training sessions. For the first session, three apprentice chefs showed up, which, needless to say, was disappointing. Despite this initial disappointment, I continued with the training sessions each Saturday morning.

Key to my training philosophy and plan was my approach. I would demonstrate the preparation, cooking, and presentation of new dishes to be featured on our new menu along with explaining the relevant techniques of preparation. I did the work, and then with careful coaching and correcting on the job, the session participants grew in confidence and developed professionally. Demonstrating these new techniques showed the participants the benefits of the training sessions. Training made their jobs easier and provided them with additional culinary skills.

I believe a positive training atmosphere was set, one that was anxiety free, entertaining, and educational. What started out with three apprentices eventually grew to full participation by the kitchen brigade. When the older chefs learned of the training style adopted, they began to attend. They felt comfortable and unthreatened.

My training sessions did not happen accidentally. They were planned step by step. Careful planning made the training sessions work. The most worthwhile measurements of investing in culinary training are the increased skills and improved attitudes of those receiving the training, and that has an impact on customer satisfaction. I am happy to say this happened at the Shelbourne. Within six months we had higher standards of professional practice from all our chefs, including the "old dogs." Training works, and the greatest compliment I received as a chef trainer was when the older chefs "bought into" my culinary philosophy and thanked me for sharing with them new skills that gave them a renewed pride in the culinary profession.

—Noel Cullen, Ed.D., CMC, AAC

The **training session introduction** may be used to review the objectives, restate the culinary mission, and describe the activities that will be occurring during the training session. During the introduction step, it is necessary to ensure that all of the team members participating in the training session are aware of what the chef supervisor is trying to achieve by the training and what is expected of them as a result of the training. The first five minutes of the training session can be the most important. Start off the session with an icebreaker, the purpose of which is to relax everybody.

GETTING STARTED

Appearance is very important. Choose your attire carefully. The best attire for the chef is, of course, a clean, crisp, smart chef coat. This helps the chef to bond with the kitchen team members. Overdressing can cause alienation from the group: "Be respectful. Right or wrong, some listeners will make judgments about your message based on their interpretation of the respect you are showing by your choice of dress."[2] The training environment is the same as the normal working environment of the kitchen team. A general rule to follow is, the more formal the training session, the more formal the attire.

Be conscious of **body language**. Good posture is important. Use body language that expresses confidence and that enhances the training presentation. Maintaining eye contact is essential. Put enthusiasm in your voice, speak clearly, and don't start with an apology for being there. Create a comfortable atmosphere. There is no reason why a warm, friendly atmosphere cannot be created and maintained throughout the training session. Try to establish this at the beginning. Other helpful suggestions for conducting a training session are shown in Figure 9-1.

YOUR COMFORT LEVEL

The key to your success as a presenter is finding your comfort level. It is natural to be a little nervous just before beginning, but extreme nervousness generally has a source, and that source is generally not being well prepared. The greater your familiarity with

Figure 9-1
Suggestions for conducting a training session.

- Use effective facial expressions.
- Use and maintain eye contact.
- Move around the room and gesture.
- Use gestures that are not distracting.
- Communicate with the team members in the training session on a personal level.
- Vary tone and pitch of voice.
- Emphasize key points and use relevant examples.
- Be certain to talk to, not at, the kitchen team.
- Select and use appropriate media technology.
- Make logical, smooth transitions between topics.
- Give clear directions for all subsequent activities.
- Greet all team members as they arrive for the training session.
- Be available during breaks to visit with each member to answer individual questions.
- Be available after the training session to answer any additional questions or to discuss concerns.
- Provide clear oral and written instructions for all assignments and activities.
- Maintain alertness.

the information you're presenting, the more comfortable you will be. To be fully prepared, you must practice. Practice your presentation and make sure you are familiar with all of the material you will be presenting.

Chefs are busy people, so finding time to **practice** can be difficult, but it must be done. A common suggestion to executives is that they plan time into their day for planning. As a chef, you must also plan time for training development and preparation into your day. The importance of training is tremendous, and your ability to achieve excellence as a trainer is equally important. Approach training team members with the same dedication that you approach developing menu items. You would never put an item on the menu without testing it first. A training session should have no less attention.

Generally, when you take the time and do the preparation, you will find that your comfort level and nervousness are not an issue. If you do begin to feel nervous, however, slow down and be more deliberate. This is a good way to avoid becoming tongue-tied. Also, strive not to worry about it. As Becker and Becker stated, "'Don't worry about it', this may actually be the best advice. Worry is like a rocking chair. It gives you something to do but it doesn't get you anywhere. Don't worry—do something about your fears."[3] In this case, rehearsing until you are confident that you are ready will help enormously. Mentally walk through the training session from beginning to end, picturing in your mind everything that you expect to happen.

EFFECTIVE INTERPERSONAL COMMUNICATION

Simplicity is the key to effective communication in the training setting. Simple, clear language usually is all that is required. Using terminology and jargon causes problems. Use culinary terms with which the team members are familiar. This can build rapport within the group but must be handled carefully. The intention is to communicate, not to intimidate or impress. Therefore, the team will not be insulted if simple language is used.

Communicate on a personal level with each team member and take action to ensure they all understand what is being said and demonstrated. When new terms are first introduced, work with the team members on the pronunciation and spelling of the terms. Deliver important concepts and points slowly and cover less important material at a faster pace. Improve team member understanding by using appropriate gestures and visual aids to illustrate what you are saying.

As a trainer, as you should as a supervisor, show that you believe in the potential of each team member and are sincerely interested in the success of each team member. This is done by taking an active interest in the learner's progress. Create an active rather than a passive learning environment by involving team members in the learning process. Ask the team members questions and for input pertaining to the demonstration or information session to reinforce what is being presented. This will also assist you in determining whether team members are gaining an acceptable level of understanding of what is being presented.

As the training session progresses, gauge the attention level of the participants. Be prepared to change direction or involve the team quickly in order to get back on track. Open communication throughout the workplace is important to having effective teams. This includes training. Facilitate open communication by inviting the team to participate in identifying training that will provide continuous improvements in training plans. As a trainer/presenter, there are things that you should avoid because they can be barriers to effective communication. Examples of these actions are shown in Figure 9-2.

Figure 9-2
Actions to avoid as a trainer/
presenter/communicator.

- Eliminate "er," "ah," "ok," "you know what I mean," and similar nervous expressions from your vocabulary.
- Avoid long monologues. Make your presentation as natural as possible. Break up your speaking with other activities. Ask questions.
- Do not appear to be reading aloud. An outline is better than a complete script.
- Avoid all "-isms" (ageism, sexism, racism).
- Avoid using slang.
- Avoid "talking down" to the team.
- Avoid undesirable habits, such as fumbling with your hair, picking at your face, or cleaning your nails.

Imagery is an important part of the communication process. When speech is used to create a picture or scene, that image helps facilitate learning. Perception also plays an important part in interpersonal communication. It can either help or destroy the most sincere effort to communicate. People often hear only what they want to hear. Problems in perception can be caused by team members with dissimilar attitudes, different cultural or educational backgrounds, and difficulty with the language used.

The cultural background of kitchen team members has a strong influence on their receptiveness to new information. This includes verbal and nonverbal communication. A big consideration in nonverbal communication is distance.[4] The distance that people maintain when communicating has been determined as follows:

- Intimate Distance
  - Close phase: close physical contact
  - Far phase: 6 to 18 inches; not considered proper in public by Euro-Americans
- Personal Distance
  - Close phase: 1 to 2 feet; comfortable if the people know one another
  - Far phase: 2 to 4 feet; arm's length
- Social Distance
  - Close phase: 4 to 7 feet; impersonal business
  - Far phase: 7 to 12 feet; more formal communication
- Public Distance
  - Close phase: 12 to 25 feet; can get away
  - Far phase: 25 feet or more; set around important public figures

The distance that is accepted is based on the relationship between people involved and the circumstances. Depending on the physical nature of the training environment and the type of training to be given, the chef supervisor and the kitchen team's personalities can be categorized within the personal and social distance scales.

TRAINING AND DIVERSITY

According to the U.S. Bureau of Labor Statistics, women and minorities will make up the largest percentage growth in the work force early in the twenty-first century. In a 1991 report, the U.S. Department of Labor Bureau of Statistics predicted that the number of white males in the workforce would drop to 39.4 percent, down from 48.9 percent in 1976.[5] According to Richard Koonce in 2001, ". . . only about 15 percent of new entrants into the American workforce are white males. The rest is a mix of Hispanics, African Americans, Vietnamese, Chinese, Russians, Europeans, and others."[6]

American culture is becoming increasingly diverse. It is no longer a melting pot where new ethnic groups attempt to leave their original cultures behind them: "A more accurate image is a tossed salad, where various ingredients remain distinct even as they are mixed together."[7] Embracing cultural diversity in the kitchen requires the chef supervisor to adopt training skills and styles that are sensitive to valuing the differences within the kitchen team. Diversity in training is no longer just about correcting behavior in relation to racial discrimination and sexual harassment.[8] Training should embrace the diversity of the team and work to increase the capability of the team through that diversity.

Diversity includes everyone. It is not something that is defined by race or gender. It extends to age, education, lifestyle, sexual orientation, geographic origin, exempt and nonexempt status, physical abilities, religion, and where a person lives. There are also subcultures within any one of these categories. In practice, however, the word *diversity* has become synonymous with "people" who are other than white men.[9] "Companies recognize the importance of creating workplaces that look like their marketplaces and that don't discriminate based on race, age, gender, ethnic background, religion, or sexual orientation," according to Koonce.[10]

When viewed from a quality standpoint, cultural diversity in the foodservice industry is an advantage. **Cultural diversity** is an advantage that is a natural extension of the multinational nature of many kitchen teams. The naturally occurring diverse points of view can breathe life into a culinary operation. A diverse kitchen team can offer better customer service because the team reflects the differing needs and preferences of those who make up the foodservice establishment customers. Key to developing this potential for better customer service is training. Diversity training and assisting cross-cultural communication can improve cooperation in multinational work teams.[11] What is required, according to R. Roosevelt Thomas, Jr., is "a new way of thinking about diversity, not as an us/them kind of problem to be solved but as a resource to be managed."[12]

The foundation for training and teamwork in a culturally diverse kitchen is valuing and appreciating *all* the differences within the team. This can be achieved by:

- Fostering awareness and acceptance of individual differences
- Helping team members understand their own feelings and attitudes about people who are different
- Exploring how differences might be tapped as assets in the kitchen
- Enhancing relations between people who are different
- Finding or inventing ways for each team member to collaborate

Thomas also stated, "You can manage diversity without valuing differences, but you can't manage diversity without understanding differences."[13] Tapping the team's full potential is about *empowerment*, and success depends on the ability to empower the entire workforce. Acceptance, tolerance, and understanding, however, are not by themselves enough to create an empowered team. To empower a diverse kitchen team to reach their full potential, training is needed. It is therefore important to understand the cultural values, attitudes, and beliefs of the team and the uniqueness this brings to the kitchen.

GETTING THE TEAM INVOLVED

Vital to the efforts of all quality improvement training sessions is getting each kitchen team member involved. The quality and the quantity of learning and continuous improvement are directly proportional to the degree of involvement by the kitchen team. Most people **learn by doing**. Key to the success of this method is to shift responsibility for learning to the team member. This technique is sometimes referred to as learner-controlled or self-paced instruction. Interacting with the team in this way requires the skills of a group facilitator. **Team activities** such as discussion, role-plays, or case studies provide an opportunity for team members to explore topics, interact with each other, and share information by expressing their views and responding to each other's ideas and opinions. While these group activities may be perceived as informal by the team, as an instruction method they need to be carefully planned. The role of a **group facilitator** consists of managing group discussions and group processes so that individuals learn and group members feel that the experience is positive.

Typical activities for a facilitator include group activities in which quality improvements are assessed. In group discussions where all team members feel committed to the quality improvement actions, there exists an enhanced awareness of team efforts. Participation by all team members is facilitated. The members are invited to present their viewpoints, levels of knowledge, and attitudes regarding various topics of culinary quality. Group activities stimulate thinking, create enthusiasm, and assist in analyzing different approaches to food preparation. The environment and characteristics of good team involvement are:

- Informal relaxed atmosphere
- Willingness to act as a group, communicate, and listen to each other
- Willingness to share new ideas
- Willingness to focus on differences about concepts, not about team members
- Readiness for action once a course of action has been arrived at through consensus

Questioning is a tried-and-true method for getting each team member involved. Questions arouse interest in the team member. They stimulate thinking, keep the team members on track, solicit information, and get individual team members involved. Questions can be classified in at least two ways. It is necessary to understand both types in order to become successful using the technique. Questions are categorized as open/closed and direct/indirect questions. Other descriptions of these question types are overhead, direct, relay, and return.[14]

Open questions are the most suited to group discussions. They arouse interest, stimulate creative thinking, keep the chef supervisor and team on track, and provoke feedback. If overused, however, questioning may send a message that the chef supervisor lacks confidence. Overuse of questioning can suggest to the team that constant reassurance is needed on topic matters being discussed. Open questions are questions asked of the entire training group. After each answer, the question is repeated to generate more answers. These types of questions are typically used to open discussions, introduce new topics, and give each team member a chance to comment. Open questions are recommended, as they arouse interest and encourage the team member to think creatively.

Closed questions, no matter how carefully they are asked, require only one answer. They don't contribute to advancing discussion or encourage the development of new ideas or concepts.

Direct questions are used to call on individuals for specific information and may be used to involve a team member who has not participated in the discussion. Directing questions to specific team members also helps to even out the distribution. **Indirect or rhetorical questions** can be used to avoid giving an opinion on a topic but encourage team members' opinions. Indirect questions are aimed at the entire team and can be useful for brainstorming.

Examples of each of the types of questions are shown in Figure 9-3.

Effective questioning means knowing how to seek information and stimulate insight. A question is defined as an inquiry designed to test, stimulate thought, or clarify. Questions can serve as an ongoing assessment of the learning taking place. As often as possible, use questions that allow the learner to respond.[15] When team members

Figure 9-3
Question type examples.

Examples of Open Questions
- What do you ask for in quality food presentation?
- How would you explain why this is so?
- Can anyone suggest a better method?
- What do you think would happen if _____?

Examples of Closed Questions
- Can anyone tell me who has ultimate responsibility in the kitchen?
- What are the ingredients for this recipe?
- How many methods of cooking fish are there?
- What is the order of preparation of this dish?

Examples of Direct Questions
- Jennifer, now that we have discussed our new menu composition, what other items should we include?
- Frank, how do you feel about the training program within the kitchen?
- Scott, tell me how you would prepare chili?
- Jude, what would you do to improve foodservice quality?

Examples of Indirect Questions
- The question that calls for an opinion—what are the team's views?
- How does the team view the new menu?
- Can anyone suggest new ways?
- What other methods might we try?

respond correctly, the chef supervisor can feel confident that the information or topic matter has been received. Questioning also provides the opportunity for dealing with any concerns individual members have before proceeding with training.

The primary purpose of questioning is to encourage team members to think about the training session topic, but involving the team through questioning also helps to maintain their interest and attention. Specific uses for questions in training include:

- Establishment of learners' level of knowledge
- Check learning and understanding
- Reinforce information
- Summarize information
- Maintain learner engagement
- Stimulate dialogue among team members

In general, the trainer/presenter should:

- Keep things simple
- Maintain eye contact
- Be aware of tone of voice and body language
- Maintain awareness of team emotions

Brainstorming

While **brainstorming** is a means of generating new ideas, it can be made to work effectively only within a formal structure in which every participating kitchen team member must know and understand.

- A brainstorming session should be limited to a defined place and time. It is useful to precede it with a 10-minute warm-up session on a totally unrelated and even trivial subject. Plan 30 minutes on the real session objective. It should stop on time even if it is in full flight.

- The session should be held in a relaxed atmosphere. The team must be encouraged and motivated to generate *their* ideas; evaluation of the ideas generated is strictly avoided during the sessions.
- The procedure requires each team member to come forth with new ideas no matter how extreme they seem. Team members should not switch off to other people's ideas and wait for a chance to have theirs included, but rather should develop the other members' ideas.

The functionaries during these sessions are the chairperson (who need not be the chef supervisor) and the note taker. The chairperson's functions are:

- Defining the objective or problem at the outset
- Being independent of the issues that arise and resisting interference or domination
- Directing the discussion and keeping it on track
- Acting to control input from everyone at once, helping the less vociferous to be heard
- Contributing to idea generation
- Stopping any form of evaluation during the session
- Involving each team member and providing positive feedback to encourage more team member input

The note taker's functions are:

- Writing down ideas as they are generated
- Reviewing written suggestions and stimulating additional ideas

Using brainstorming in a structured way is an excellent method of resolving problems within the kitchen. It is also an excellent way of identifying training gaps. Getting the people involved is one of the best methods to facilitate training. It is the single most positive contributor to successful training.

UNDERSTANDING GROUP BEHAVIORS

Within groups, people often act out roles that are closely related to their individual personalities. Each person plays out a particular role or assumes a certain mental posture during training. Chef supervisors should be aware of these various roles. These roles can be divided into building and supportive roles, self-centered roles, and task roles. Team members within each category may be subdivided into more specific roles.

The **building and supportive role** can be subdivided into the supporter, who is the one that praises and agrees with team members. The supporter goes along with the team. The harmonizer mediates differences between team members. The tension reliever cracks jokes and works to brings out humor in the team. The facilitator works to open channels for communication.

The **self-centered role** can be subdivided into the blocker, who constantly raises objections and revisits topics when others have moved on. The aggressor constantly expresses ill will and makes sarcastic remarks. The recognition seeker calls attention to himself or herself during the training session. The dominator tries to run the session by giving orders, interrupting, and attempting to get his or her own way. The apathetic member simply does not participate in team activities.

The **task role** is the problem solver and task performer.

Other roles include those of the **initiator,** who proposes new ideas, goals, and procedures. The **information seeker** seeks facts and additional information before making decisions. The **information giver** offers facts and information. The **opinion seeker** seeks clarification of the values involved. The **opinion giver** constantly states his or her personal opinions. The **clarifier** elaborates on ideas offered by other team members. The **coordinator** brings together ideas offered by the team. The **energizer** prods the team to a greater level of activity.[16]

By carefully listening and watching the various verbal and nonverbal clues, each of the described roles may be observed. Recognizing these behaviors is the first step in developing a method of coping with them. Each team training session will take on a culture and personality of its own. A most serious lapse is when a chef supervisor appears to be taking over. This alienates the other team members, who may consequently lose sight of the objective of the training session. The opposite is also a problem. An inexperienced chef supervisor new to the training role often defers to a dominant type. This action has the effect of alienating the group, causing them to lose confidence in the chef supervisor. Another signal to watch for is the question that does not relate to the topic under discussion. This may be an indication of boredom or a team member who is having difficulty.

Team building and maintenance relies greatly on team/group activities such as meetings, discussions, and training. Understanding the dynamics of the group enables the chef supervisor to recognize and deal with them. Each team training session will almost certainly have a selection of these various personality types. Expect to have them, but learn to cope with them. Continuous improvements within the kitchen cannot be made by one person. It takes the entire kitchen team. This is where the chef supervisor demonstrates leadership skills by overcoming these personality obstacles.

SUMMARY

Vital to effective training is the understanding of all the elements that can lead to its success. Good introductions by the chef supervisor facilitate the training process. The first five minutes of the training session set the scene for the training that will follow. Attention to detail ensures success with training. Among the important elements of this process are:

- Explaining the objectives of the training sessions
- Capturing the kitchen team's interest and preparing them for training
- Being cognizant of the message being sent through appearance and individual demeanor
- Creating a warm, friendly atmosphere, which facilitates training
- Being prepared and comfortable

- Using effective, clear interpersonal communication skills, avoiding the use of jargon
- Recognizing the nonverbal and distance aspects of communication
- Understanding the advantages of a diverse team in the kitchen and actively fostering training toward empowerment
- Recognizing the dynamics of group behavior and the role of the chef supervisor as team facilitator
- Using correct and appropriate questioning techniques
- Facilitating and planning the kitchen team's brainstorming sessions
- Understanding the dynamics of group behaviors, arranging meetings to elicit feedback, and identifying training gaps

DISCUSSION QUESTIONS

1. Define the following chapter key terms:

   a. Purpose of instruction
   b. Training session introduction
   c. Appearance
   d. Body language
   e. Practice
   f. Imagery
   g. Diversity
   h. Cultural diversity
   i. Learn by doing
   j. Team activities
   k. Group facilitator

l. Questioning

m. Types of questions: open/closed/direct/indirect/rhetorical

n. Brainstorming

o. Types of roles: building and supportive; self-centered; task; initiator; information seeker; information giver; opinion seeker; opinion giver; clarifier; coordinator; energizer

2. Why is it important to outline to all team members what is expected of them as a result of training?

3. What are the methods that can be employed to deal with nervousness?

4. What are the four levels of distance that team members often maintain when communicating?

5. What are the significant elements to be considered for training a diverse kitchen team?

6. What are the key points that contribute to getting team involvement in training?

7. What are the closed, open, and directed questioning techniques?

8. What are the primary uses and benefits of brainstorming as a training technique?

9. Within groups, each member plays out a certain role. What are the three categories into which these roles fall?

NOTES

1. Dugan Laird, *Approaches to Training and Development* (Reading, MA: Addison-Wesley, 1985), 76.

2. Dennis Becker and Paula Borkum Becker, *Powerful Presentation Skills* (Boston, MA: Mirror Press, 1994), 65.

3. Ibid., p. 33.

4. Edward T. Hall, *The Hidden Dimension* (New York: Doubleday, 1966).

5. U.S. Department of Labor Bureau of Statistics (Washington, DC, 1991).

6. Richard Koonce, "Redefining Diversity: It's not just the right thing to do. It also makes good business sense." *Training & Development*, December, 2001, www.findarticles.com/cf_ntrstnws/m4467/12_55/83045836/print.jhtml, p. 2.

7. Sally J. Walton, *Cultural Diversity in the Workplace* (New York: Irwin, 1994), v.

8. Richard Koonce, "Redefining Diversity: It's not just the right thing to do. It also makes good business sense." *Training & Development*, December, 2001, www.findarticles.com/cf_ntrstnws/m4467/12_55/83045836/print.jhtml, p. 1.

9. Julia Christensen, "The Diversity Dynamic: Implications for Organizations in 2005," *Hospitality Research Journal*, Vol. 17, No. 1 (1993), 70.

10. Richard Koonce, "Redefining Diversity: It's not just the right thing to do. It also makes good business sense." *Training & Development*, December, 2001, www.findarticles.com/cf_ntrstnws/m4467/12_55/83045836/print.jhtml, p. 1.

11. Ibid., p. 4.

12. R. Roosevelt Thomas, *Beyond Race and Gender* (New York: AMACON, 1991), 10.

13. Ibid., p. 169.

14. David Wheelhouse, *Managing Human Resources in the Hospitality Industry* (East Lansing, MI: Educational Institute of the American Hotel and Motel Association, 1989), 170.

15. Bruce B. Tepper, *The New Supervisor Skills For Success* (Boston, MA: Mirror Press, 1994), 85.

16. Richard L. Sullivan, Jerry R. Wircenski, Susan S. Arnold, and Michelle D. Sarkeess, *Practical Manual for the Design, Delivery, and Evaluation of Training* (Rockville, MD: Aspen, 1990), 37.

Chapter 10
Performance Appraisal

Outline

- Introduction
- Evaluating performance
- Methods of evaluation
- Appraisal interviews
- Compensation
- Summary
- Discussion questions

OBJECTIVES

When you complete this chapter, you should be able to:

1. State the elements upon which chef supervisors evaluate team member performance within the kitchen
2. Describe the benefits and the impact of performance appraisals on the development of the kitchen team
3. Outline important methods of team member evaluation
4. Describe the prior steps of appraisal interviews and outline the steps in conducting these interviews
5. Outline the procedures for evaluating weak team-member performance

Case Study: Canyon Bluff Resort

Canyon Bluff Resort's personnel policies require that all personnel be given a formal performance evaluation each year. Mike Harris, executive chef, feels it is best to do all performance evaluation at the same time each year, so every February 1 he begins doing employee evaluations. To complete the evaluations, he meets with two employees each day for three weeks. This year he has scheduled a full 15 minutes for each meeting.

Chef Harris completes the evaluation form provided by Human Resources for each employee prior to the meeting. Occasionally, he refers to the employee's personnel file if he remembers an incident involving the employee. Generally, he depends on his excellent memory to complete the form. Since the form has a graphic rating scale, he rarely makes written comments about the employee's performance unless he remembers something exceptional about the staff member.

Chef Harris feels strongly that, for employees to succeed in retaining their positions at Canyon Bluff, their work has to be satisfactory, so most employees receive a satisfactory rating in each category every year. Chef Harris also feels that the evaluations really have little purpose other than to comply with company policy. He has been doing performance evaluations for the kitchen staff every year for the six years he has been at Canyon Bluff, and he has not seen any changes result from the evaluations. He does not expect the results to be any different this year. Chef Harris does consider the annual meeting with the employees to be an opportunity to ask how their families are doing and give them a pat on the back.

Based on what you have learned from previous chapters and the content of this chapter, answer the following question.

- Do you believe that the annual performance evaluation of kitchen staff at the Canyon Bluff Resort contributes to growth and improvement of the individual or the operation? Explain your answer, including the following:
  - Overall reason
  - Primary causal agents
  - Role of leadership and supervision/management
  - Specific steps that either have been taken or should be taken to achieve a positive result of the process

INTRODUCTION

Performance appraisal is the systematic process of developing criteria for job performance. This involves outlining criteria to team members along with assessing team members' job performance relative to the criteria and communicating the results to the team members.[1]

Many chef supervisors look upon performance appraisals as an unpleasant task. However, performance appraisals present the chef supervisor with opportunities to make valuable contributions not only to the team, but also to each individual member, thus improving the culinary operation. It is not unusual for chef supervisors who rise from the ranks to find it uncomfortable to evaluate another team member's performance.

Performance appraisal and evaluation is an ongoing responsibility. All chef supervisors are required to consider how well members of the kitchen team are doing their jobs. Through appraisal, decisions may be made on who should be recommended for promotion, transfer, reassignment, further training, salary increases, or even termination. One of the most important aspects, however, is encouraging team-member performance improvement. In this regard, performance appraisals are used to communicate to team members how they are doing and to suggest needed changes in behavior, attitude, skills, or knowledge. This type of feedback clarifies for each team member the job task and overall quality expectations held by the chef supervisor. Additionally, appraisals often serve to validate the selection procedures used during the recruitment stage.

Performance appraisals should be conducted periodically to let team members know how they are doing and to outline to them whether their performance is satisfactory or unsatisfactory. This typically is done through an appraisal interview.

- Quality and amount of work performed
- Adherence to sanitation or safety procedures
- Adherence to food cost control procedures
- Quality of culinary skill
- Personal grooming or appearance
- Attendance
- Cooperation
- Ability to work unsupervised
- Initiative
- Knowledge of rules and company procedures
- Involvement as a team player
- Leadership potential

Figure 10-1
Example areas of performance evaluation.

EVALUATING PERFORMANCE

Performance evaluation is never an end in itself. It is the preliminary step prior to conducting meaningful feedback discussions, making appropriate administrative recommendations, and determining where performance improvement is required. Evaluation of team members includes work productivity and quality, dependability, team interactions, initiative, and leadership performance. Example areas of performance evaluation are shown in Figure 10-1.

Generally, people are interested in how they are viewed by the chef supervisor. In the absence of specific feedback, team members often form their own conclusions by comparing their experiences with those of others around them. This can sometimes lead to wrong conclusions. Clearing up doubt or uncertainty is a major purpose of the performance appraisal:[2]

> A productive appraisal, along with providing a review of the employee's work, serves as a work session between supervisor and employee in which you take the time and effort to meet with an individual employee and set new goals and objectives for the coming year. A productive appraisal recognizes that *people* are the most valuable resource of any organization.

The benefits of a good performance appraisal are shown in Figure 10-2.

Performance appraisals also provide written records to substantiate actions. Therefore, they can serve as an information and team member feedback system. More and more administrative decisions taken by management are being subjected to review by outside parties. To verify the appropriateness of decisions made, it is necessary to

- Team members learn what their strengths and weaknesses are within the team.
- New goals and objectives are agreed upon between the chef supervisor and team member.
- The relationship between the chef supervisor and the team member is brought to a new level.
- The team member becomes an active participant in the team objectives.
- The team may be restructured for maximum efficiency.
- The team member's commitment to the team is renewed.
- New training needs are identified.
- Time is set aside for discussing issues other than money.
- Team members feel they are taken seriously as individuals.

Figure 10-2
Benefits of performance appraisal.

document all meetings for review purposes. Performance appraisals serve as excellent records. Such documentation can also serve to confirm understandings between the chef supervisor and the team member.

METHODS OF EVALUATION

An evaluation decision is made by comparison. Whatever is being evaluated is compared to something else, and it exceeds or equals or falls short in comparison.[3] There are many methods of evaluation. Each has its merits. Indeed, many foodservice organizations use more than one. The following four methods are those commonly used in the evaluation of kitchen team members in both small and large operations.

The **essay appraisal**, in its simplest form, requires the chef supervisor to write a paragraph or more covering a team member's individual strengths and weaknesses and his or her potential for further development. A major weakness of this method is its inconsistency in length and content. Essay evaluations are difficult to combine or compare.

The **graphic rating scale** typically evaluates a team member on the quality and quantity of work—outstanding, above average, or unsatisfactory—and on a variety of other factors that vary but usually include traits like reliability and cooperation.

The **critical-incident appraisal** requires the chef supervisor to maintain a log of critical incidents of positive or negative behavior. So, for appraisal purposes, the discussion with the team member is based on actual behavior. One of the challenges posed by this method is that it requires the chef supervisor to write down incidents on a regular basis. The benefit of this method is its avoidance of appraising based on only the most recent performance, which is always top-of-mind.

The **behaviorally anchored rating scales** (commonly referred to as *BARSs*) require the prior conducting of a job analysis that identifies performance behavior appropriate for different levels. The BARS method is objective. Each team member is rated against a predetermined specific set of behaviors identified on a job-by-job basis. The downside to this evaluation method is that it can be costly to initiate and time consuming for the chef supervisor.

Even though there are a variety of performance appraisal methods to choose from, it is still possible to end up with inaccurate information on the kitchen team. To avoid this, chef supervisors should be trained in the techniques of performance appraisals. A common error in the performance appraisal process is the **halo effect** (discussed in Chapter 3). This occurs when the evaluator allows a single prominent characteristic of a team member to influence his or her judgment. Personal preferences, prejudices, and biases also can cause errors in performance appraisals. Chef supervisors with biases or prejudices tend to look for team member behaviors that conform to their biases. Figure 10-3 is a simple generic example of a graphic rating scale.

APPRAISAL INTERVIEWS

The performance appraisal process is not complete until there is a conference between the team member and chef supervisor. This interview allows discussion about the period since the last appraisal. It typically reviews the previous year and sets a course for the coming year. These discussions help answer such questions as: "How am I doing?" "Where can I go from here?" and "How do I get there?" The first step in beginning an appraisal interview is to give the team member a few days' notice of the interview date so that he or she may prepare for it. Chef supervisors should preview relevant data for the interview during this time period. A time and a place that will be private and free from interruptions should be selected for the interview.

Figure 10-3
Graphic rating scale performance evaluation.

Team member: John Smith
Job Title: Kitchen Team Member
Department: Kitchen

Check all items relevant to team member's position. Rate each item on a scale of 1–5.
Circle number at right:

1 = Needs much improvement
2 = Needs some improvement
3 = Satisfactory
4 = Very good
5 = Excellent

Part I: General work habits and attitude

Sanitation and safety	1	2	3	4	5
Attendance and punctuality	1	2	3	4	5
Meets deadlines	1	2	3	4	5
Cooperates with team members	1	2	3	4	5
Accepts suggestions	1	2	3	4	5
Uses equipment properly	1	2	3	4	5
Prioritizes work well	1	2	3	4	5

Part II: Job Performance

Quality of work	1	2	3	4	5
Ability to solve problems	1	2	3	4	5
Uses original ideas	1	2	3	4	5
Communications ability	1	2	3	4	5
Time management	1	2	3	4	5
Hands-on skills	1	2	3	4	5
Interpersonal skills	1	2	3	4	5
Ability to work on a team	1	2	3	4	5

The chef supervisor must work to create a positive feel during the interview. Traditionally, team members view a performance appraisal with some level of fear. The process is generally regarded by team members as an ordeal they must go through before they can find out whether or not they will receive a negative or positive evaluation. The goal should be to create a spirit of teamwork and collaborative problem solving.

Start the interview by creating the impression that the interview is considered very important. Next, help the team member feel that the interview is a valuable, constructive, cooperative process by placing emphasis on his or her development. Avoid any impression that the interview was arranged only for the purposes of warning or reprimanding. Assure the team member that its purpose is to give constructive and objective feedback.

The interview portion of the performance appraisal should consist of a thorough review of the team member's goals for the appraisal period, the degree to which these goals were accomplished, and the setting of new goals for the subsequent period. The discussion should be based on observed behavior and performance, not on the team member's personal characteristics. Team members accept criticism when it is based on fact rather than vague remarks. This is where the *actual* appraisal evaluation method is used. This may be the BARS method, a graphic rating scale, or a critical-incident appraisal method. Try to keep the interview friendly, natural, and informal. Remember, the interview is also used to give positive feedback.

The conduct of an effective appraisal requires attention to five areas: *mise en place*, environment, focus and engagement, closure, and documentation. Before the interview the chef supervisor must do their **mise en place**. As a culinarian, you know that *mise en place* means everything in its place. In the kitchen, this is the gathering of ingredients and supplies and doing pre-prep to ensure that preparation and service go smoothly and to avoid last-minute scrambling for needed items. Preparing for an appraisal interview differs only in what is being gathered. The chef supervisor must:

- Ensure that all relevant data concerning the team member is available.
- Select for the interview only those accomplishments and problems relevant to the discussion.

The success of the interview is directly affected by the **environment** established by the chef supervisor.

- Arrange the meeting area so that the evaluator and the team member can sit face to face, without a desk between them, or can sit at the same side of the desk.
- Make the area comfortable, with the right temperature and comfortable chairs.
- Create a nonthreatening environment and display a supportive attitude.

The **focus** established by the chef supervisor must be on the behavior rather than the individual. Additionally, the greater the **engagement** of the team member in the interview, the more likely it is that the outcome of the interview will lead to improved performance.

- Focus feedback on the behavior rather than on the individual.
- Get the team member to commit to future goals and set benchmarks for accomplishment.
- Ask team members for their opinions on work-related issues. Interviews are two-way streets. Encourage continued conversation.
- Allow for individual differences in the ratings. Don't compare an average but competent team member with a superstar.
- Evaluate honestly and carefully. Don't say, "I don't like your attitude." It is more appropriate to say, "Your behavior shows that you seem to resent doing the work that is asked of you. If that is true, you need to change your behavior." Give specific examples.
- Some questions encourage, while others limit. State questions so that the team member will think and give detailed responses. Generally, avoid closed-ended questions that require yes or no answers. Actively listen and avoid forming conclusions on too little data.
- An interview cannot be conducted only as a series of questions. It is appropriate for the chef supervisor to add thoughts on the various topics discussed. This will be either confirmation or clarification of the team member's understanding of the points discussed. Always allow the team member ample time to respond to any questions posed.

Closure is a critical step in the interview. It should be viewed as solidifying what the expectations are for future performance. When all the points that were planned have been covered, close the discussion. Three important issues need to be addressed at this stage:

- Summarize the key points and check for team members' understanding. Invite them also to summarize.

- Compare the points agreed upon.
- Team members should have a chance to review their problems and outline any concerns or work-related problems that they may have.

After the end of the interview, the chef supervisor must **document** the interview by writing a brief summary of the discussion. This should include **action plans** that make it clear what actions are expected of the employee. These plans are based on specific **action points**. Action points are the specific performance factors targeted for improvement. The chef supervisor and team member should both sign the plan, indicating that it was not only discussed but understood. If it was agreed to do anything during the course of the interview, follow through. Something that was agreed to but not acted upon can have a serious impact on the team member's morale. It sends a message that the chef supervisor does not care. Follow-up is important with all team members, but when dealing with weak team members it is crucial. These members need continued guidance and support from the chef supervisor. The goal is always to grow the employee. This is achieved only when direction and guidance are given.

Documenting appraisal interviews serves a secondary purpose. It can also be used to protect the chef supervisor and the foodservice organization against accusations of bias or improper behavior by an individual, by another manager, or in a lawsuit: "Any incidents that are out of the ordinary or that involve a significant clash of tempers or personalities should be included in the documentation."[4] The documentation of the interview should be finalized by allowing the team member to review and sign the report on the interview. The signature line should have next to it the statement that the team member's signature is acknowledgement solely of their having seen the document, not of their agreeing with the document.

Conducting the performance appraisal of a poorly performing team member can be particularly challenging. Performance appraisals do not always bring good news to a team member. Good and bad employees alike must be told how they are doing. Handling the bad news requires some special techniques:[5]

- Have the relevant documentation available to demonstrate previous discussion on poor performance.
- Give specific examples of where work failed to match set quality standards. Show where work failed to match the work of other team members.
- Prepare a list of changes the team member is to make in his or her performance.
- Be positive about each team member's ability to improve. Arrange for further training sessions.
- Set short-term goals that are within the ability of the individual. Progressively build upon successes.
- Be honest with team members. Spell out clearly what they have to do to improve and outline the consequences if they do not improve.
- Make a short-term agreement with the team member on measurable performance improvements set against a specific time period. Agree to meet again after the short time period to assess progress.

End the meeting on a positive note. Point out the team member's accomplishments. Reaffirm a willingness to continue to work with the team member until he or she reaches a satisfactory performance level. It is vital to get the team member's attention if performance is unsatisfactory. Chef supervisors should not gloss over prior performance and go easy on the team member. The team member may see what the chef supervisor may view as a tough review as an acceptable appraisal unless the unsatisfactory behavior is clearly stated.

COMPENSATION

It is natural for the employee to associate directly compensation and performance evaluation. The discussion of pay, however, should be separated from the performance appraisal interview. Productive performance appraisals focus entirely on issues of strengths and weaknesses and the development of new goals and objectives. Once money becomes part of the discussion, interest in improvement tends to dissipate. If the team member does bring up the question of money during the appraisal interview, state that this will be discussed later and that now the interview will concentrate on performance only.

While pay should be discussed in a separate conference with the employee, the connection between performance appraisal and pay must exist. Policy for pay increases that is tied to performance appraisal should be established. Compensation after initial employment is generally classified as either cost-of-living or merit pay increases. **Cost-of-living pay increases** are not based on performance. They are adjustments based on the purchasing power of money in the market place. This purchasing power can increase because of changes in the economy. **Merit pay increases** are based on an employee's performance. When a merit format is used, employees who perform at the highest level receive the greatest pay increase.

SUMMARY

A sound performance appraisal system draws on both the chef supervisor and the team member. Together they negotiate performance expectations for the future. Through appraisal, decisions may be made on who should be recommended for promotion, transfer, reassignment, further training, salary increases, or termination. Performance appraisals are used to communicate to team members their strengths and weaknesses in their job performance. Together with the chef supervisor, plans for future development can be made. Performance appraisals should be conducted periodically. These usually include aspects of work quality, attitude, and cooperation.

When used correctly and appropriately, performance evaluations may be an asset in identifying gaps in the training stage and act as information-gathering systems and morale boosters for the kitchen team.

Performance evaluation methods vary: supervisor-produced essays, graphic rating scales, critical incident appraisals, and BARSs. Every effort should be made to eliminate areas of bias and prejudice when evaluating team members.

Appraisal interviews are used to inform the team member of acceptable or unacceptable behavior. They should contain a thorough review of the team member's performance outlined during a matter-of-fact, friendly interview. When the interview is concluded, both parties "sign off" on agreed goals. Issues discussed and agreed upon should be documented.

DISCUSSION QUESTIONS

1. Define the following chapter key terms:

    a. Performance appraisal
    b. Essay appraisal
    c. Graphic rating scale appraisal
    d. Critical-incident appraisal
    e. Behavioral anchored rating scale appraisal
    f. Halo effect
    g. *Mise en place*
    h. Interview environment
    i. Interview focus
    j. Interview engagement
    k. Interview closure
    l. Interview documentation
    m. Action plan
    n. Action point
    o. Cost-of-living pay increase
    p. Merit pay increase

2. What are the positive outcomes of team member performance appraisals?

3. How can performance appraisals be used to validate selection procedures?

4. What elements of team member performance are usually evaluated?

5. What are the benefits of performance appraisals relative to working relations between the chef supervisor, the foodservice organization, and the individual team member?

6. Why is it appropriate to maintain a written record of performance appraisal interviews?

7. Describe the procedures commonly used for conducting appraisal interviews.

8. What important factors should be considered for conducting appraisal interviews?

9. What are the three important issues to be addressed at the conclusion of the interview?

10. How should the question of compensation be treated by the chef supervisor during the interview?

11. What is the methodology used to appraise weaker team members?

NOTES

1. Donald W. Myers, Wallace R. Johnson, and Glenn Pearce, "The Role of Interaction Theory in Approval Feedback," *SAM Advanced Management Journal,* Summer 1991, 28.

2. Marion E. Haynes, *Stepping up to Supervisor* (Los Altos, CA: 1990), 84.

3. Randi Toler Sachs, *Productive Performance Appraisals* (New York: AMACOM, 1992), 5.

4. Ibid., p. 43.

5. Alfred W. Travers, *Supervision, Techniques and New Dimensions* (Englewood Cliffs, NJ: Prentice-Hall, 1993), 181.

Chapter 11
Work Environment

OBJECTIVES

When you complete this chapter, you should be able to:

1. Identify the issues that contribute to team member frustration
2. Describe steps to deal effectively with team member complaints
3. Define the connections between motivation and job satisfaction
4. Outline the basic steps in health, safety, and accident prevention in the kitchen
5. State the advantages and disadvantages of counseling and know when to intervene or refer team members for outside help
6. Identify the benefits of employee assistance programs and their impact on team member wellness

Case Study: Texas Moon Restaurant

The Texas Moon is considered by most of its employees to be an excellent place to work. Competition for open positions at the restaurant is fierce. The Texas Moon has extremely stringent selection criteria for all positions, but its reputation as one of the best places to work ensures that there is always a large pool of applicants for any opening. It is considered to be the finest restaurant in the state.

The Texas Moon has sixty-five staff members and ten managers including the executive chef and two sous chefs. All Texas Moon employees are fulltime. The Texas Moon is open 365 days per year, seven days per week. Staff members work a 5- to 6-day week with a total of 40 hours, and managers work a 6-day week with a total of 48 hours. Employees receive health benefits after six months with the restaurant. The health benefits are subsidized by the restaurant at the rate of 50 percent for both individual and family policies. Staff members receive one week of paid vacation per year after one year of service, and two weeks of paid vacation per year after five years of service. Managers receive two weeks of paid vacation per year after one year of service, and three weeks of paid vacation per year after five years of service. Additionally, managers receive two personal holidays per year. Employees also earn sick-leave at the rate of half a day per month after one year of service.

The Texas Moon management believes that outstanding performance should be recognized and rewarded. Employees earn performance recognition points toward involvement in an annual cuisine and culture trip as well as for other performance recognition rewards such as tickets to local attractions and movie tickets which are awarded annually. In last year's trip to Mexico, the six staff members and five managers who went became a developmental team for new menu items for the next year. Performance recognition points are awarded by managers and department heads for outstanding performance based on criteria developed by each department head. Managers are automatically included in a trip every other year. Managers do not participate in the other performance recognition awards. Managers receive a cash bonus if financial targets are achieved.

The Texas Moon has an established method for the scheduling of vacation days. The minimum vacation time that can be used at one time is one week and the maximum is two weeks. Vacation scheduling is managed within each department. The calendar clearly shows the number of employees that may be on vacation at the same time during each week of the year. Texas Moon treats holidays such as Christmas, Thanksgiving, Rosh Hashanah, and the Fourth of July the same as any other day in the year.

The Culinary Department has always based vacation scheduling on seniority. Beginning the first week in September a vacation calendar is circulated in each department according to seniority. The Texas Moon Restaurant has fourteen full-time line and prep cooks. Three of the line cooks and two of the prep cooks have been with the restaurant for more than seven years each. For the past three years the three line cooks and two prep cooks with the greatest seniority have selected vacation dates that included the major holidays. The other line and prep cooks have no opportunity to select holiday dates as part of their vacation dates and resentment has steadily grown in the past few years over the scheduling of vacations.

John, a line cook, has been with Texas Moon for 18 months. John was recognized for his outstanding performance and was one of the six staff members selected to travel to Costa Rica this year.

John mentioned the vacation scheduling to Tracey, one of the five managers, during the trip to Costa Rica. He stated that he was considering leaving Texas Moon because he considered the scheduling of vacations in the Culinary Department to be unfair and inequitable. He also indicated that other team members in the Culinary Department were looking for positions with other restaurants because of the department's vacation scheduling.

Tracey asked each of the other five staff members on the trip—one from the Culinary Department, two from the Guest Service Department, and two from the Sales Department—how they felt about the scheduling of vacations in their department. All of the staff members indicated that seniority was the basis for scheduling and they felt it created inequities and discontent. All of the staff members stated that they felt the system was designed to reward longevity, not performance.

Tracey organized an open discussion of the issue with the other four managers and all of the staff members during the trip. The five managers returned from the trip convinced that the general manager (not present on the trip) needed to address the issue of vacation scheduling to avoid the loss of valuable staff members.

Based on what you have learned from previous chapters and the content of this chapter, answer the following questions.

- What is the overall reason for the challenges occurring in the Texas Moon Restaurant?
- What are the primary causal agents for the challenges occurring in the Texas Moon Restaurant?
- What specific steps could have been taken to avoid the current situation occurring in the Texas Moon Restaurant?
- What, specifically, can be done to overcome the challenges and generate motion in a positive direction for the Texas Moon Restaurant?

INTRODUCTION

The performance of team members is affected by many factors, and some of the most important and most-frequently abused of those factors relate to the work environment. The nature of the work environment, positive versus negative, has a major impact on team member performance and development. A **positive work environment** generates a more positive attitude among team members and leads to higher levels of quality.

A positive environment can be achieved only when the foundation has been established to support that type of environment. The chef supervisor's ability to address conflicts is critical to a positive work environment and a positive attitude among team members. The goal in a positive work environment is to prevent conflict between team members, or between team members and management. The reality is that there will always be some conflict. The maintenance of a positive environment requires quick and effective conflict resolution.

Also key to a positive environment is the **physical work environment**. Employers are required by the Occupational Safety and Health Act (OSHA) to provide a safe work environment. The company and the chef supervisor as the representative of the company are responsible for meeting the requirements of the law. Complying with the law does contribute to a positive work environment. However, the greatest contribution to a positive work environment is achieved when the company, including the chef supervisor, sincerely cares about the safety of team members.

The other foundational piece for a positive work environment is that of employee wellness. Safety addresses the physical safety of the team member. The concept of "**employee wellness**" addresses both the psychological and physical well-being of the team member.

A well-laid foundation combined with a clearly delivered message of concern for the well-being of the employee will help to minimize team-member frustration. The result will be team-member job satisfaction. The goal of the chef supervisor should be to create and maintain a positive work environment. The result of pursuing this goal will be quality team-member performance and high levels of guest satisfaction.

JOB SATISFACTION

Like motivation, **job satisfaction** means different things to different people. At its highest level, it is the kitchen team member who derives happiness from the knowledge that the foodservice customer had an outstanding dining experience. Generally, the satisfaction that individuals receive depends on the extent to which the job and everything associated with it meets their needs and wants.

- The "**wants**" are items the individual feels will deliver satisfaction. The wants are perceived differently within the team and are based on differences in age, educational level, sex, health, family relationships, personality, and other factors. They are often of an intrinsic nature.
- Typically, "**needs**" represent tangible rewards such as pay and benefits.

Job satisfaction has been shown to be closely linked to turnover and absenteeism. The higher an individual's satisfaction, the less likely it is that he or she will leave the organization. According to *People Report* in November 2006, the average annual turnover rate for hourly employees in the restaurant industry was 107 percent.[1] This represents an unacceptable level by any set of measurements. The link between turnover and satisfaction in the foodservice industry indicates that many employees are unhappy. Is it pay or working conditions? Maintaining quality in all aspects in the kitchen requires a team that is stable and satisfied. Replacing a kitchen team member is time consuming and expensive. Replacement has a direct impact on product quality delivered to the guest due to the ramp-up time required for a new team member to achieve complete mastery of processes and procedures. It is far better and more cost effective to invest in current team members than to constantly hire and train new people.

Replacement costs cover three areas: separation costs for the departing employee, recruiting and hiring a replacement, and the time and training costs of the new hire. Total replacement costs are two to three times the monthly salary of the departing team member.

The intangibles of a dissatisfied kitchen team member are potentially more costly. This includes the effect on morale within the team and its impact on customer satisfaction, and the missed opportunities to utilize the team member's talent and potential to grow.

Job satisfaction is affected by all of the elements discussed in this chapter. Chef supervisors should invest in the kitchen team through excellent supervisory skills and by providing conditions within the kitchen that provide the basis for job satisfaction. Mentally challenging work with which each individual can cope successfully is of primary importance. Ideally, each member should love food and have a strong sense of culinary professionalism. The atmosphere in the kitchen should be open and nonthreatening, led by a firm but friendly supervisor who seeks input and support from the

---

CHEF TALK
"HOSTILE ENVIRONMENT"

There was a time when chefs believed it necessary to act out the often-portrayed image of the crazy, unreasonable, temperamental chef. This disposition often manifested itself in undesirable traits such as shouting, throwing things around the kitchen, and arguing loudly with waiters, other chefs, and managers. The kitchen area was a hostile domain. These old-style chefs were not approachable; they were aloof and generally indifferent to employees. I particularly remember, as an apprentice chef, that I "knew my place" as a lowly trainee and was expected not to converse with those higher than me. In fact, open communication was not the order of the day. The pecking order was through the supervisory layers: chef, chef de partie, sous chef, and, finally, the head chef. Heaven forbid if you had to ask for time off within your scheduled time. I came to work scared and left scared for the first year of my apprenticeship. Back then, the head chef had practically the power of life or death over each member of the kitchen staff. I believe that if the work climate in the kitchen then had been more conducive to communication, I would have learned a lot more and probably could have contributed a lot more to the operational goals. That head chef was eventually dismissed, and the day he left, the kitchen staff had a party.

—Noel C. Cullen, Ed.D., CMC, AAC

Figure 11-1
Typical sources of frustration.

- Hostile chef supervisors
- Monotonous tasks
- Unpleasant working conditions
- Economic insecurity
- Unfair work assignments
- Abuse of established working procedures
- Lack of orientation training
- Being ignored

team and by whom each team member is valued. Satisfaction is not about winning popularity contests; rather, it is about the creation of a team and an environment in which the individual is respected. Most studies in the area of job satisfaction conclude that a link exists between satisfaction and performance. The role that the chef supervisor plays in this link is crucial.

FRUSTRATION

When examined, the working day of a kitchen team member will reveal that not all needs are satisfied fully. Members may be prevented from reaching a particular goal or objective, or there may be conflicting goals. Either condition may produce a state of dissatisfaction and tension that prevents a harmonious team spirit in the kitchen. Chef supervisors should understand the forces and factors that contribute to tension and dissatisfaction. Barriers to achieving individual goals produce a frustrating condition. A list of typical sources of frustration is shown in Figure 11-1.

A frustrated individual may respond by engaging in disruptive behavior. The distance between frustration and aggression is a short one. **Aggression** typically involves verbal or physical attacks against the person or persons perceived to be the cause of the frustration. Chef supervisors have a responsibility to be sensitive to the warning signs in this area. Not all sources of frustration are under the direct control of the supervisor. However, an awareness of potential areas of frustration and a sincere effort to handle them effectively through better organization, planning, and communication can help to remove many of the conditions that cause frustration.

When individuals sense that they are in danger, they may experience a feeling of **anxiety**. In contrast to fear, anxiety results when the source of danger cannot be identified. The physical symptoms of anxiety are similar to those associated with fear: nausea, trembling, a pounding heart, and dryness in the throat. Anxiety is a form of stress that is emotionally and physically harmful. Anxiety may account for various kitchen team members' behaviors that are often misunderstood or misinterpreted, particularly in individuals of different backgrounds and cultures. Anxiety is also frequently caused by the prospect of change. This anxiety often can be misinterpreted by supervisors as team members' being difficult rather than simply frightened.

COMPLAINTS

Complaints are an indication of discontent among the kitchen team. The chef supervisor is key to addressing complaints before they develop into something they are not and become even more difficult to resolve. Speedy resolution of grievances and complaints is part of a positive, well-led kitchen work environment. Wise handling of complaints affords the greatest opportunity to win kitchen team members' respect and to gain their confidence.

Most interpersonal conflicts in the foodservice industry have been between dining-room and kitchen team members. A traditional animosity has always existed between these two groups. Chefs view themselves as the skills-oriented aristocrats of the foodservice organization. Service personnel are viewed by chefs as the lesser participants in the big scheme of things. Ironically, and this may come as a big surprise to many chefs, dining-room team members also view themselves as aristocrats and the most important people in the organization. They have a low opinion of chefs. Of course, although both positions are ridiculous, they are a great source of conflict. Departments that conflict or fail to focus on the objective of customer satisfaction will doom the entire foodservice organization to failure. Every member of the organization must be a committed team player totally focused on continuous improvements that facilitate the provision of high-quality food and service; both are inextricably intertwined.

Complaints from team members concerning other team members come to the forefront very quickly. Most people don't hesitate to complain about each other. It is a normal human phenomenon. Complaints about other people can be presented in a highly emotional way or in a cool, calculating manner. But usually they are delivered with a great deal of emotion, which colors the facts involved. This can make it difficult to determine the real problem as opposed to the symptoms.

In all cases, the issue should be dealt with as soon as possible. The longer the complaint remains unresolved, the more other people get involved and the more the quality of the work is affected. The quality of work has an immediate impact on customer satisfaction. If the chef supervisor has difficulty in resolving the complaint, further help may be sought from senior management. The main point is that there should be some avenue by which the complaining kitchen team member can obtain a full and fair hearing, particularly if he or she is dissatisfied with the decision of the chef supervisor.

The "ideal" resolution of complaints avoids a "**one loses and one wins**" scenario and leads to a "**win-win**" scenario. A "win-win" scenario is achieved by the team member's participation in resolving the issue together with the chef supervisor. One of the most useful approaches is the application of a systematic approach to resolving complaints, as shown in Figure 11-2.

The following steps can lead to a satisfactory resolution and investigation of the complaint:

- Check the team member's record in detail. Look for evidence of tardiness or absenteeism. Get the facts. Perhaps there are hidden reasons for seeking attention by complaining.
- Attempt to understand why the team member has made the complaint and what his or her feelings are. Allow the individual to "vent." Let him or her communicate freely and without interruption. Watch for body language and observe facial expressions.
- When other persons are involved, check for accuracy of information.
- Avoid an argumentative disposition when hearing the complaint.
- Keep senior management informed.
- Admit a supervisory mistake. Do not try to conceal it if you have caused the complaint.
- Record the formal complaint; do not depend on memory. Be specific: Include day, date, time, place, those involved, the type of complaint, and any other relevant facts.
- Prepare a written statement that includes the resulting decision and the rationale for this decision.
- Establish facts and a definition of the complaint with the team member. Seek solutions, exhausting all avenues. Finally, bring the resolution to a mutually agreeable set of terms that includes steps for avoiding future problems in the area of the complaint.

Figure 11-2
Systematic Approach to Resolving Complaints.

Complaints are sometimes used by kitchen team members to gain attention and to send messages regarding unfair wage scales, poor working conditions, and discriminatory actions against team members on the basis of ethnic origin, gender, or sexual preference. The individual making the complaint is entitled to a fair hearing. Complaints that are not handled promptly and decisively can lead to problems of arbitration with labor unions. By bringing the complaint or problem to a win-win situation, the chef supervisor deals with the immediate problem. However, win-win solutions can involve a promise to solve the complaint through higher authority. What is important in dealing with complaints is that the chef supervisor recognizes that the old-style theory X type supervisor has been replaced with a theory Y type, which in some instances represents a major shift in attitude for the chef supervisor. It replaces the notion that complaining kitchen team members are adversaries and it focuses on solutions, assuming that both parties are aiming for the same goals. The win-win approach is consistent with an environment that encourages continuous improvement of product and service. In the foodservice industry, positive, motivated, happy team members are critical to success.

SAFE WORK ENVIRONMENT

Foodservice employers are required by law to provide working conditions that do not impair the safety or health of kitchen employees or indeed of any other unit or department member. Therefore, they must provide an environment that protects employees from physical hazards, unhealthy conditions, and unsafe or dangerous practices by other kitchen team members. Effective health and safety practices promote a positive work climate in the kitchen by providing for the physical and emotional well-being of all team members as well as enhancing their economic security.

Safety hazards in the foodservice industry range from the use of knives and power-driven equipment to slippery floors and chemical cleaning materials. These hazards can produce accidents resulting in individuals' falling, cutting themselves, burning themselves, receiving an electric shock, scalding themselves, or worse. These accidents occur because of ignorance of safety procedures and carelessness.

In the late 1960s, Congress became increasingly concerned that each year job-related accidents accounted for more than 14,000 deaths and nearly 2.5 million disabilities.[2] Eventually, these concerns led to the passage of the **Occupational Safety and Health Act** (OSHA) in 1970. The Act was designed to "assure so far as possible every working man and woman in the nation safe and healthful working conditions and to preserve our human resources." One of the responsibilities of OSHA is to develop and enforce mandatory job safety and health standards. These standards cover workplace issues of machinery and equipment, materials, power sources, processing, protective clothing, first aid, and administrative requirements. OSHA also requires that supervisors train and inform employees of any known safety hazard in the kitchen. The **Hazard Communication Standard** (HCS) requires employers to inform employees what chemicals they are working with and to detail their risks and what can be done to limit these risks. HCS compliance is achieved through training programs and detailed labeling on or near chemical containers. **Material Safety Data Sheets** (MSDS) are part of this standard. A system of priorities for workplace inspections (which includes kitchens) has been established by OSHA:[3]

- Inspection of imminent danger situations
- Investigation of catastrophes, fatalities, and accidents resulting in hospitalization of five or more employees

- Investigation of valid employee complaints of alleged violation of standards or of unsafe or unhealthful working conditions
- Follow-up inspections to determine if previously cited violations have been corrected

The current OSHA regulations are available online at http://www.osha.gov/pls/oshaweb/owasrch.search_form?p_doc_type=STANDARDS&p_toc_level=1&p_keyvalue=1910.[4] OSHA provides a free on-site consultation service that helps employers identify hazardous conditions and corrective measures. According to the new law, a minimum fine of $5,000 is mandatory for intentional violations with a maximum fine of $70,000 for intentional or repeat violations. A maximum fine of $7,000 applies for all other violations, including failure by an employer to post the required OSHA notice.[5]

One of the best methods for identifying potential hazards in the kitchen is to simply consult the team. Have them develop a list of accident prevention measures. They see hazards in and around the kitchen every day.

Chef supervisors may unintentionally reinforce unsafe acts by not correcting them when they are first observed. Through mandatory and proper supervision, unsafe work practices can be corrected. The nature of food production requires that many items of equipment be sharp or hot. The most common types of kitchen accident injuries are directly related to these two areas as well as to the presence of wet or greasy floors and the element of human error. The most common type of injuries and their causes in the kitchen include the following.

1. *Lacerations.*   These are caused by improper use of chef's knives, slicers, choppers, broken ware, or glass.
2. *Power-driven equipment.*   When used improperly, blenders, mixers, slicers, grinders, or buffalo choppers can cause accidents. The chef supervisor is responsible for ensuring that each kitchen team member is fully trained in the safe use of all power-driven equipment.
3. *Glass and dishware.*   Glasses, bowls, cups, and plates are sources of injury. Broken glass in dishwashers or sinks causes accidents. Glasses and dishes should be stored separately to avoid crushing.
4. *Burns.*   Common injuries in the kitchen, burns and scalds of varying degree can result from contact with the hot surfaces of grills, ovens, stove burners, steam tables, fryers, and any other heating equipment that might be in use.[6]
5. *Slips and falls.*   Falls in the kitchen are typically caused by wet or greasy floors left unattended. The danger from greasy or wet floors is compounded by team members rushing about during busy periods. The kitchen team should be made aware by the supervisor of the necessity to keep floor surfaces safe. Kitchen team members should wear shoes with rubber or neoprene soles to prevent slipping. Leather-soled shoes should never be worn in the kitchen. Safety shoes that have strong uppers without openings should be worn since these help prevent cuts or crushing injuries.
6. *Fires.*   Because most kitchens usually have open flames of some type, potential fire hazards are obvious. More fires occur in foodservice establishments than in any other type of business operation. Chef supervisors should check these potential fire hazards regularly. Special fire-protection equipment should be provided in all areas where fires are likely to occur. These include hoods, grills, deep fryers, ovens, and stove tops. Direction in the use of fire extinguishers and evacuation procedures for guests and employees should be part of every new kitchen member's induction and orientation training.

Since training alone will not assure continual adherence to safety, chef supervisors should observe team members at work and show approval for safe work practices. When unsafe actions are observed, immediate corrective action should be taken.

Figure 11-3
Methods for Promoting
Safety.

- Publishing safety statistics. Monthly accident reports should be posted. Ideas and suggestions should be solicited as to how these accidents can be avoided.
- Using bulletin boards and menu wall display areas throughout the kitchen to display posters, pictures, sketches, and cartoons depicting safety situations.
- Setting high expectations for safety. Encourage the kitchen team to recognize positive safety actions and acknowledge those who contribute to safety improvements.

Make work interesting. Fatigue and stress can contribute to the cause of accidents. Simple changes can often be made in the kitchen to make tasks more meaningful.

Establish a **safety committee** composed of kitchen team members and other dependent department supervisors and managers. The safety committee provides a means of getting team members directly involved in the operation of the safety program. The duties of the committee include inspecting, observing work practices, investigating accidents, and making recommendations. The committee should meet regularly, at least once a month, and attendance should be mandatory. Additional ways to promote safety are shown in Figure 11-3.

HEALTH AND WELLNESS

Physical Health

Until the last two decades, safety and accident prevention received far more attention than did employee health. However, this has changed. Statistics show that occupational diseases may cost industry as much as or more than occupational accidents.[7] Many foodservice organizations now not only have attempted to remove health hazards from the workplace, but also have initiated programs to improve employee health. Some employers offer preventive health programs. These are programs that provide routine medical services, such as flu vaccinations, at a reduced charge or no charge.

Stress

Stress comes from two basic sources: physical activity, and mental or emotional activity. The physical reaction of the body to both is the same. The kitchen can be a stressful environment, particularly at busy service periods. However, not all stress is harmful. Positive stress is a feeling of exhilaration and achievement. This can be associated with a successful busy service period during which everything went well in the kitchen: Team members performed well as a group, record numbers were served, and 100 percent customer satisfaction was achieved. On the other hand, negative stress may cause people to become ill. Some of the causes of negative stress are shown in Figure 11-4.

Arguments with supervisors or fellow team members are a common cause of stress. Feeling trapped in a job to which a person is ill-suited can be equally painful. Other strains include lack of communication on the job and lack of recognition for a job well done. Stress has been linked to many things. It manifests itself in several ways: increased absenteeism, job turnover, lower productivity, and mistakes on the job. Stress-related disorders include tension, high blood pressure, muscle tightness in the chest, ulcers, and others requiring medical attention. **Burnout** is considered to be the most severe form of stress. Career burnout usually occurs when work is no longer meaningful to the individual team member. The factors that cause burnout are those that cause stress; in fact, burnout and stress have been viewed as interconnected issues.

- Conflicting expectations between chef supervisor and team member
- Uncertainty over team member's expected contribution to the team effort
- An unpleasant kitchen environment
- Poor preparation for the job
- Threats and hostility
- Performance evaluations
- Lack of social interaction
- High noise levels in the work environment
- Tasks that do not fully utilize team members' skills
- High temperature levels
- Long and irregular hours
- Personality conflicts
- Working during public holidays
- Group pressures
- Insensitive supervision

Figure 11-4
Causes of Negative Stress.

Counseling

Counseling is used by kitchen team builders to ensure good relations and to generate a team spirit. Team members may have problems of a personal nature that demand the chef supervisor's attention. These problems may or may not be job related. Changes in an individual's behavior, such as excessive absenteeism, tardiness, hostility, moodiness, withdrawal, and a decline in job performance, should be monitored. Good chef supervisors interact with their team on a constant basis and are usually in the best position to identify and observe these changes.

There are advantages and disadvantages to the chef supervisor assuming the role of counselor. The primary advantage is that the chef has the opportunity to become well acquainted with the individual. They can learn the team member's pattern of judging, valuing, thinking, and understanding and can predict an individual team member's behavior. However, the disadvantage to assuming the role of counselor within the team is that the chef supervisor may not be adequately trained to deal with complex human problems. It is then advisable to refer the team member to a specialist. Needless to say, the act of referring a team member for assistance requires considerable tact and skill.

As emotional and personal crises, alcoholism and drug abuse are considered to be personal matters. They also become the chef supervisor's problem when they affect the team member's ability to perform satisfactorily in the workplace.

Typically, in large organizations, employee assistance programs (EAPs) exist. These programs are in place to help employees overcome problems, and they provide guidance and referrals to outside professional help.

The most prevalent problems among individuals are personal crisis situations involving mental, family, financial, or legal matters. These are problems that can be brought to a chef supervisor's attention. Depending on the type or difficulty of the problem, in-house counseling or referral to an outside agency may be necessary.

Chef supervisors should be aware that the behavior of some team members might be adversely affected by some elements of the "physical" kitchen environment, which may necessitate reassigning, or rotating individuals to different sections of the kitchen.

It is estimated that 1 out of every 16 workers in the United States is affected by alcohol.[8] This results in lost work time, declining productivity, and increased absenteeism. Alcohol abuse has been a problem for the hospitality industry in general, and the kitchen employee in particular. Many theories for its prevalence have been put forward, from the notion that its accessibility contributes to the problem to the idea that the hot kitchen environment encourages the use of alcohol.

The approach to handling alcoholism is to monitor all kitchen team members regularly and systematically. Evidence of declining performance on the job should be carefully documented, so that the individual can be confronted with unequivocal proof that his or her work is suffering. Offers of help should be made available without any penalty to the individual. Mention of alcoholism should be avoided. As with any other health problem, the team member should be allowed to seek aid.

Drug abuse among employees is one of the wider societal issues confronting industry. While alcohol is the most abused substance, marijuana, cocaine, heroin, crack, and varieties of abused prescription drugs are found to be in use in the foodservice industry. Various approaches are used to assist individuals with a dependency. They range from out-patient treatment for an extended period to in-patient treatment. "Nearly 75 percent of all adult illicit drug users are employed, as are most binge and heavy alcohol users. Studies show that when compared with non–substance abusers, substance-abusing employees are more likely to

- change jobs frequently
- be late to or absent from work
- be less-productive employees
- be involved in a workplace accident
- file a workers' compensation claim."[9]

In recent years few workplace issues have received as much attention as acquired immune deficiency syndrome (AIDS). This is particularly important for the foodservice industry from the standpoint of transmission of the virus. There is no evidence that AIDS can be transmitted through casual contact or through food preparation. However, one of the major problems employers face is educating team members and customers on this issue. Since no cure or vaccine for AIDS presently exists, many foodservice organizations are turning to education as the most viable means of combating both the medical and social dilemmas posed by AIDS. Figure 11-5 shows the potential benefits of an AIDS education program for kitchen team members.

Employees who test HIV positive are protected under the Americans with Disabilities Act (ADA). This act provides comprehensive civil rights protection to individuals with AIDS. It bans discrimination against people on the basis of their disability. Employers are prohibited from dismissing or transferring infected team members from food-handling duties simply because they have AIDS or have tested HIV positive. In *EEOC v. Marsh's Sun Fresh* (2001), the court awarded $80,000 to the plaintiff. This suit was based on the unlawful termination of an HIV-positive employee.[10]

Figure 11-5
Benefits of an AIDS
Education Program.

- Prevention of new infections among individuals by helping everyone understand how human immunodeficiency virus (HIV) is and is not transmitted. (HIV is the first stage of AIDS.)
- Alerting managers and chef supervisors to the legal issues raised by HIV infection in the workplace.
- Helping to prevent discrimination by fearful or misinformed employees, which can decimate productivity. Through education, the same employees are equally capable of creating a humane, supportive, and therefore healthy working environment.
- "Raising morale through AIDS education training."

Management has a responsibility to maintain confidentiality of any employees who report that they have AIDS or any other illness.

Unfortunately, all indicators are that the AIDS epidemic will continue to spread. It is important for chef supervisors to understand that these issues are present among the kitchen team. It is also important for chef supervisors to recognize their limitations as counselors. However, through their roles as coaches and educators, chef supervisors can do much to make it known that help is available.

Wellness Programs

These are becoming a common feature in food-service organizations. Although these types of programs have been in existence for many years in other industries, they are relatively new to the foodservice sector. Essentially, wellness programs are designed to prevent illness and enhance the well-being of each individual. They include periodic medical exams, stop-smoking clinics, improved dietary practices, weight control, exercise and fitness, stress management, immunizations, and cardiopulmonary resuscitation (CPR) training. Documented results from these types of programs have shown a reduction in employee sick days and lower major medical costs. It is expected that as health care costs continue to increase, wellness programs will grow.

CONCLUSIONS

Supervising people in what, at times, can be an unpleasant environment at a busy service time (hot, noisy, steamy, and stressful) requires a great deal of skill. In addition to knowing how to cook and understanding the principles of heat transfer, the chef who can also build a team and tap into its collective culinary resources will succeed. There are no good reasons why kitchens should be unpleasant places, even during busy service. Poor physical working conditions can be overcome.

Considering the team member in a holistic way, with all that entails, is now considered to be a worthwhile investment. Needless to say, when frustration on the job is dealt with effectively and a safe and healthy work environment exists in the kitchen, job satisfaction is possible. What is more difficult to overcome is the breaking of the stereotypical animated image of temperamental chefs. The modern chef is, as the literal translation of the word means, a leader as well as a first-class culinarian.

SUMMARY

Most conflicts in the foodservice industry are interpersonal, between kitchen team members and other departments.

Frustration is a common contributor to conflicts, complaints, and grievances. Most frustration is caused by hostility, unpleasant working conditions, lack of training, insecurity, and being ignored on the job.

Complaints within the kitchen should be dealt with as soon as possible after they are made. The longer the complaint remains unresolved, the more other people get involved. Work quality suffers immediately, which impacts on customer satisfaction. The ideal resolution of complaints is a situation in which all feel they have won.

Job satisfaction has been shown to be linked to turnover and absenteeism. The greater the individual's job satisfaction level, the more productive he or she becomes.

Job satisfaction revolves around the creation of a team environment where each person is valued and respected.

Chef supervisors have a responsibility to ensure that a safe work environment exists, a place free from physical hazards, unhealthy conditions, and unsafe or dangerous practices. Effective health and safety practices promote a positive work climate.

Chef supervisors should be aware of the counseling role they may be asked to play with regard to team members' personal problems. They should know their limitations in this area and know how and when to seek professional help.

As with all other considerations for a safe kitchen environment, stress and stressful situations must be recognized and avoided.

DISCUSSION QUESTIONS

1. Define the following chapter key terms:
   a. Positive work environment
   b. Physical work environment
   c. Employee wellness
   d. Job satisfaction
   e. Wants
   f. Needs
   g. Replacement costs
   h. Aggression
   i. Anxiety
   j. Complaints
   k. One loses and one wins
   l. Win-win
   m. Safety hazard
   n. Occupational Safety and Health Act
   o. Hazard Communication Standard
   p. Material Safety Data Sheets
   q. Safety committee
   r. Stress
   s. Burnout
   t. Counseling

2. How does team member frustration affect the work of the chef supervisor?
3. How can elements of frustration be removed from the kitchen?
4. What are the steps that a chef supervisor should follow in dealing with team member complaints?
5. What are the differences between "needs" and "wants" in the area of job satisfaction?
6. What, if any, are the links between job satisfaction and team member turnover?
7. What propelled the passing of the Occupational Safety and Health Act in 1970?
8. What are the advantages and disadvantages of chef supervisors' engaging in counseling?
9. What are the elements that contribute to stress in the kitchen?
10. Wellness programs within the kitchen can contribute to reducing costs. How is this achieved?
11. What can be done to reduce interpersonal conflicts within the kitchen?

NOTES

1. Dina Berta, *Nation's Restaurant News—HR & Services.* "People Report: Worker Turnover Rate Continues to Climb." November 2006. http://findarticles.com/p/articles/mi_m3190/is_47_40/ai_n26710112/

2. Arthur Sherman, George Bohlander, and Herbert Crudden, *Managing Human Resources,* 8th ed. (Cincinnati: South-Western, 1988), 576.

3. Jack E. Miller, Mary Porter, and Karen Eich Drummond, *Supervision in the Hospitality Industry,* 2nd ed. (New York: John Wiley, 1992), 98.

4. http://www.osha.gov/pls/oshaweb/owadisp.show_document?p_table=OSHACT&p_id=3371, 2011, United States Department of Labor, Occupational Safety and Health Administration.

5. Ibid., p. 259.

6. Lloyd L. Bryars and Leslie W. Rue, *Human Resources Management,* 4th ed. (Boston: Irwin, 1994), 499.

7. Arthur Sherman, George Bohlander, and Herbert Crudden, *Managing Human Resources,* 8th ed. (Cincinnati: South-Western, 1988), 592.

8. Joseph L. Picogna, *Total Quality Leadership: A Training Approach* (Morrisville, PA: International Information Associates Inc., 1993), 312.

9. http://www.drugabuse.gov/infofacts/workplace.html, 2011, Nation Institutes of Health, National Institute on Drug Abuse.

10. National Restaurant Association, 2001, *Legal Monitor: Grocer Settles HIV-Discrimination Lawsuit with EEOC for $80,000.* www.restaurant.org/legal/lm/lm2001_06.cfm.

part three
The World of Management

Chapter 12
Management

OBJECTIVES

When you complete this chapter, you should be able to:

1. Define the customer within the wider context of the foodservice industry
2. Identify the principles and philosophies of scientific management, management by objective, reengineering, the elements of the excellence movement, and total quality management
3. Discuss contingency, systems, and chaos management theories
4. Discuss the development, strengths, and weaknesses of different concepts of management
5. Identify major trends and developments in the workplace that affect chef supervisors
6. Discuss quality in relation to the foodservice industry
7. Apply Deming's fourteen quality principles to the kitchen and the chef supervisor
8. Discuss the nature and importance of change and why people resist change
9. Indicate the guidelines for overcoming resistance to change

Case Study: Amber Light Steakhouse

The general manager of the Amber Light Steakhouse has received increasing numbers of guest complaints in the past twelve months. The restaurant has been in business for ten years in the same location. There has been very little change in the traditional chophouse-type menu offerings that have been the corner stone of their success. The staff of the restaurant, both front and back-of-the-house, has been relatively stable during that time. The customer base for the restaurant has not changed, since they still seem to be drawing their regular crowd. The customers are complaining about both the quality of the food and the service. The general manager is concerned that if the level and severity of complaints continue, the business will be affected.

The general manager has brought her concern to the attention of the chef and the dining room manager. She has directed them to motivate the staff to reduce the number of complaints. The response of both department heads has been to increase supervision of production and service. Additionally, each has met privately with the general manager to explain that the poor performance in the other department head's area is undermining their individual efforts to reduce the number of complaints.

The kitchen and service staff is comprised primarily of individuals with five or more years with the restaurant in the same positions. They were well trained when originally hired and have been doing the same job for a number of years. They are generally unconcerned about the guest complaints because when a guest complains they respond quickly to correct the problem.

Based on what you have learned from the previous chapters and the content of this chapter, answer the following questions.

- What is the overall reason for the challenges occurring in the Amber Light Steakhouse?
- What are the primary causal agents for the challenges occurring in the Amber Light Steakhouse?
- What role did supervision/management play in the decline in the Amber Light Steakhouse?
- What specific steps could have been taken to avoid the current situation occurring in the Amber Light Steakhouse?
- What, specifically, can be done to overcome the challenges and generate motion in a positive direction for the Amber Light Steakhouse?

INTRODUCTION

The act of **management** is defined as (1) the conducting or supervising of something and (2) the judicious use of means to accomplish an end.[1] In many ways supervision and management are the same. They also differ in many ways. The difference is in the level of responsibility for planning, expenditure of resources, and hiring and firing. Supervision can be limited to just that, supervising—watching to make certain that the job is done correctly and on time. The term *management* carries an assumption of responsibility beyond just supervising. The chef is indeed a "supervisor." But the "chef" today is also "management." The last two sections of this text are dedicated to areas of knowledge that go beyond simply supervising. This chapter specifically addresses theories of management and change. Future chapters will explore motivation, morale, team building, diversity, and discipline. Also discussed will be leadership, communication skills, management, and problem solving. Today's chef must be prepared both to supervise and to manage.

Traditionally, the foodservice industry has been a follower rather than a leader in the area of management theories. Most management models were developed with the manufacturing industry in mind. The hospitality and foodservice industries are strongly people oriented and sell services to, and make a profit from people. It has been said that

---

WHAT IS THIS BUSINESS?
ONE-ON-ONE DEVELOPMENT

Supervision in the hospitality industry today is more dynamic than it has ever been. With a culture of instant gratification and more access than ever before, employees and supervisors alike have adjusted styles, methods, and systems to be more effective. It is this ever-changing environment that makes managing in this field so exciting.

People in our industry come from diverse backgrounds, have various levels of skill sets, and are all motivated by something different. The traditional driving factor of more money is not always at the top of the list now. Many people are looking for a better quality of life, more opportunity for personal growth, or just simply to be recognized among their peers. A key with successful managing for me has been finding out what drives an individual and creating personal goals for that person that align with my vision. It creates a shared sense of direction and accomplishment. Constant and on-the-spot feedback has become a vital tool in allowing individuals and teams alike to grow. Direct coaching shows a sense of awareness and care, and forces people to be at their best. Delegating tasks that align with an individual's personal goals frees up more time to accomplish long-term and strategic goals.

Creating structure and guidelines allows people to understand expectations from the start of a project, which in turn creates an environment of consistency. Being tough on standards, and not on people, allows the task or goal to be completed while still maintaining excellence and nurturing individuals. This idea of fostering a firm, fair, and consistent environment has allowed me to be more successful and to build teams that want to work with and for each other.

Starting my training in the kitchen and moving quickly to a more involved managerial role made it an easier transition due to the understanding I gained while on the line. Working in the kitchen revolves around food, time, and people. All of these factors can change immediately and often do. Learning how to manage these limited resources and understanding what their driving forces are that will allow you to manage any situation. Working in the kitchen and learning to multitask has allowed me to be very responsive to any issues that might arise within the restaurant.

With an ever-changing environment and a constant drive toward differentiation, I see the managerial role becoming increasingly more involved with "one-on-one" development. Directly managing individuals with a hands-on approach and leading by example will separate the good managers from the great managers.

—Jacob League
General Manager
Hillstone Restaurant Group

---

a restaurant is a manufacturing plant directly attached to a distribution center and a retail outlet. Foodservice professionals must manage the production at the same time they are managing the distribution and the retail sale. There is an additional twist for the foodservice professional in restaurant, quick service, catering/banquet, club, and other settings where the consumer is directly served food. In all of these settings, consumers react immediately to the quality of the product, the service, and all other factors impacting their experience. The consumer's reaction is communicated through the chain of production and delivery requiring analysis and possibly changes. At each point in that chain, the human factor has an impact on the analysis and change. Bearing this in mind, it is understandable that foodservice professionals—the owners, operators, managers, and chefs—have been less inclined to embrace theories of management that focus on manufacturing (production) without considering distribution and interaction with the consumer.

According to the National Restaurant Association, in 2011 the restaurant industry employed approximately 12.8 million people and will employ 14.1 million by 2021. The restaurant industry is the second largest employer in the United States, with the United States government being the largest.[2] In 1955 the restaurant industry captured 25 percent of the consumer's money spent on food. In 2011 that share is expected to reach 49 percent. The restaurant industry had 322.6 billion in sales in 1997. It is projected to have $604 billion in sales in 2011.[3] The growth of the foodservice industry shows no signs of slowing. The need for the chefs and all other management to be well prepared for future challenges is great. The successful company in the twenty-first century and beyond will require the highest-quality supervision, management, and leadership from its managers, and that includes the chef.

Figure 12-1
Who is the customer?

Any of these at any age:

Casual restaurant diner
Hotel/motel restaurant guest
Cafeteria diner
Room-service guest
Hospital patient
Senior living home guest
School or college diner
Catered party guest
Airline, train, or cruise passenger
Fast-food diner
Theme and recreation park diner
Banquet diner
Office/factory diner
Upscale white tablecloth restaurant diner
Delicatessen and supermarket customer

THE FOODSERVICE CUSTOMER DEFINED

A **foodservice customer** is any person of any demographic group frequenting any commercial hotel; restaurant; or institutional, industrial, or military dining establishment who is prepared to pay for wholesome, nutritious meals prepared by professionals utilizing first-class quality food products and outstanding culinary skills in a safe and sanitary kitchen and served by friendly, caring, efficient dining room staff. The customer is more clearly defined in Figure 12-1.

PHILOSOPHIES, CONCEPTS, AND THEORIES OF MANAGEMENT

In recent years, many theories, philosophies, strategies, and concepts have been developed and put forward to assist business organizations, managers, and supervisors to restructure, refocus, and plan for change. All of these contain within them the elements of change, customer focus, quality, and leadership. Many of these theories have their roots in the manufacturing industries. Foodservice organizations and chefs are not immune to the actions and effects of these business strategies and philosophies. The main thrust of this book is toward human resource management for chefs rather than business management; nevertheless, many of these philosophies, strategies, and theories contain elements that directly impact the chef's management of both the business of the kitchen and the human resources of the kitchen.

Scientific Management

Discussion of this topic revolves around time-and-motion studies. The principles of **scientific management** were put forward by industrial engineer Frederick Winslow Taylor around the turn of the twentieth century. Taylor held that human performance could be defined and controlled through work standards and rules. He advocated the use of time-and-motion studies to reduce jobs to simple, separate steps to be performed over and over again.

Scientific management evolved during an era of mass immigration. The workplace was being flooded with unskilled, uneducated workers, and it was efficient to employ them in large numbers. This was also a period of labor strife, and Taylor believed that his system would reduce conflict and eliminate the arbitrary use of power because so little discretion would be left to either workers or supervisors. The methods used included careful selection of workers deemed to be competent, conforming, and obedient, and a constant oversight of work. This system caused much bitterness between unions and management. It is from Taylor's period that the phrase a "fair day's work" came.

Scientific management gave to employers a system that increased productivity and reduced the number of workers. It was also rule bound, hierarchical, and top heavy with corporate structure. This began the era of standardization that many today believe contributed to the slow recognition of the changing nature of employees and the methods of managing them.

Management by Objectives

Management by objectives (MBO) is a philosophy of management first introduced by Peter Drucker in 1954. It seeks to judge the performance of employees on the basis of their success in the achievement of set objectives established through consultation with managers and supervisors. Performance improvement efforts under MBO are focused upon goals to be achieved by employees rather than upon the activities performed or the methods by which employees achieve these goals.

Management by objectives is part of a systemwide set of organizational goals that begins with setting the organization's common goals and objectives and returns to that point. The system acts as a goal-setting process whereby goals are set for the organization, individual departments, individual managers, supervisors, and employees. A feature of MBO is a broad statement of employee responsibilities prepared by the supervisor, reviewed, and jointly modified until both sides are satisfied with them. The goals are accompanied by a detailed account of the actions the employee proposes to take in order to reach the goals. Periodic review assesses the progress that the employee has made. At the end of the review period, the employee does a self-appraisal of whether the previously set goals have been achieved.

Management by objectives enabled managers and supervisors to plan and measure their own performance as well as that of the employees. It shifted the emphasis from appraisal to self-analysis. The major criticisms of MBO included the methods by which individuals achieved their goals. Factors such as cooperation, adaptability, and concern were not included as part of MBO rationale. Another criticism of MBO was that employee-rated success is tied to issues that ultimately are not directed toward customer satisfaction. Another problem with MBO is its link to employee evaluation and rewards, which causes conflict between the supervisor's roles as judge and leader.

Deming was particularly critical of MBO. He believed that MBO is management by fear[4] and does not have a place in the quality movement because of its reliance on performance evaluations. He also believed that MBO discourages risk taking, builds fear, and undermines team work. In a team, it is difficult to tell who does what. Under MBO, people work for themselves, not for the organization.

The Excellence Movement

If it ain't broke, fix it anyway.[5] About the same time that Deming's quality principles were being rediscovered, the **"excellence" movement** began with the books *In Search of Excellence* by Peters and Waterman in 1982; *Passion for Excellence* by Peters and Austin in 1985; and *Thriving on Chaos* by Peters in 1988. These books and their strategies blended perfectly into what was happening in the world of business as the pace of change gathered momentum. The basic business and management philosophies put forward by these authors were to make excellence in the management of product, people, and service a first priority. These works proposed many innovative

Requirements for an Organization's Survival and Growth

- A bias toward action
- A simple form and a lean staff
- Continued contact with customers
- Productivity improvement via people
- Operational autonomy to encourage entrepreneurship
- One key business value
- Emphasis on doing what they know best
- Simultaneous loose and tight controls

approaches to management. They focused attention on the customer revolution and the need to gain a competitive advantage, to become more effective: "We must end excuse making and look for new organizational models fit for the new world. New survivors will welcome change rather than resist it, and realize that people power, not robot power is our only choice."[6] Figure 12-2 shows the primary factors at work in the organization that bases its survival and growth on the "excellence" and "thriving on chaos" philosophies.

Organizations must also see people as a prime source of "value added" and realize that they can never be trained or involved too much. Additionally, in the excellence movement, the structure of organization is flattened, layers of middle management are reduced, and functional barriers are broken. Peters believes that "front-line supervisors as we know them give way to self-managed teams. Middle managers become facilitators rather than turf guardians. Leaders become levers of change and preachers of vision."[7] Peters also states that strategies, ideas, and concepts come from the bottom up. Staff functions support the line rather than the other way around. Each person has a valuable role in this management model.

Management by walking around is an outgrowth of the excellence movement. It is one of the management concepts that the chef puts into action. Chefs are active people, and food production is activity oriented. Good chefs walk around and visit each person's work station. Ed Carlson, upon taking over at United Airlines, realized it was a service business that had lost sight of the customer. He introduced MBWA and instilled a hands-on customer focus. He said, "In a service business, you can't have a rigid set of rules. You can have some guidelines, but you must allow people the freedom to make a different interpretation."[8]

Reengineering

If adopted across the board by foodservice organizations, reengineering will probably have the greatest impact on executive chefs of large multiunit hotels, casinos, or similar-sized operations. **Reengineering** essentially calls for a radical rethinking of the ways in which organizations do business. Business reengineering involves putting aside much of what has been taught about industrial management for the past 200 years.[9] It has been described as "an approach to planning and controlling change."[10]

In reengineering, work units change from functional departments to process teams. Jobs change from simple tasks to multidimensional work. The roles of people change from controlled to empowered. The focus of performance measures and compensation shifts from activity to results. Values change from protective to productive. Organizational structures change from hierarchical to flat. The role of executives changes from scorekeepers to leaders.[11]

Part of the reengineering process is also about positioning within different markets. This planned positioning determines what should be reengineered.

Reengineering involves integrating tasks into processes and reorganizing the company around them. Often, this reorganization results in collapsing or doing away with departments. The format becomes more collective with people united on a common focus, such as a project. One of the outcomes can be a reduction in the need for continuous checking and controls. Conceivably, in this scenario chefs could become restaurant or unit managers responsible not only for supervision and management of the kitchen but also for complete management of a foodservice operation. Additionally, titles and individual lines of demarcation can disappear.

Total Quality Management

The **theory of total quality control** first espoused by Armand Feigenbaum in his 1951 book *Quality Control: Principles, Practice, and Administration*, which was released in 1961 as *Total Quality Control* by Joseph Juran, Philip B. Crosby, and Kaoru Ishikawa, was a management theory that could be effectively applied to the foodservice operator in the service setting. At the heart of total quality control is the conviction that it is possible to achieve error-free quality product most of the time. This assertion is phrased in various ways as getting it right the first time, working smarter, or zero defects. When total quality control was introduced in the United States by the U.S. Navy in 1981, the word "control" had been changed to "management."

Total quality management is not only about external customers, it is also about internal customers. In his book, *The Essence of Total Quality Management,* John Bank[12] discusses the internal customer. He defines this person as the person in a company who receives the work of another and then adds his or her contribution to the product or service before passing it on to someone else. In a restaurant, the chef has levels of internal customers in the culinary brigade and the service staff, and the chef must meet their requirements if they are all to please the guest.

The overreliance in the past on the narrow technical skills of supervision produced a supervisor not overly endowed with leadership qualities. Control was more of an issue than coaching and team building; certainly the old-style chefs were big on control and power. The theory of quality management that came to be called TQM is about team building and investment in the development of people. The TQM movement peaked in the mid-1990s, and the use of the terms total quality management and TQM have become marginal in discussion of management theory. The concept of commitment by a company to total quality as defined by zero errors in all aspects of the operation through team building and investment in the development of people has not diminished in importance to the foodservice industry as a management design. The concept of developing a workplace culture that focuses on quality in every aspect of the operation continues to be central to a foodservice operation's success. We will further discuss the concept of quality later in this chapter.

CONTEMPORARY MANAGEMENT THEORIES

Contemporary theories of management[13] attempt to account for and interpret the rapidly changing nature of the business organization and business environment in today's world. **Contingency theory** might be called the "it depends" theory. Contingency theory calls on managers to take into account all aspects of the current situation and act on those aspects that are critical to the situation at hand when making decisions. Managers using this theory of management make decisions that "depend" on the current circumstances.

Systems theory proposes that a system is a collection of parts joined to accomplish a goal. Any action taken with one part of a system ultimately affects the total system. For example, removing a spark plug from an engine changes how the engine runs. In an organization, a change impacting one part of the organization affects the total organization. Systems theory requires supervisors and managers to have a broader perspective of the organization. Managers and supervisors are driven to address issues in relation to the total organization. This is an important change in management perspective. In the past, managers have generally taken one part of an organization and focused on it. The result was often actions that had a positive impact locally but a negative impact on the larger organization. Systems Theory is particularly applicable to the foodservice industry. The actions of the kitchen have a direct impact on the dining room, and the actions of the dining room directly affect the kitchen. The more changes in these areas take into account both areas, the greater the potential for changes to be positive for both team members and customers.

Chaos theory is more of a scientific theory for the world and life in general. But the concept of chaos theory may have some application to management as businesses continue to grow. Chaos theory says that events are rarely controlled. In fact, it says that the more complex a system is, the more volatile it becomes and the greater the energy required to maintain a semblance of stability. As more energy is expended, more structure is required to maintain the system. This pattern continues until the system splits, combines with another complex system, or falls apart entirely. Does this sound like a company that you are familiar with? Chaos theory may indeed be used most frequently in reference to biological systems, but its application to management does not seem unreasonable.

WHAT IS THIS BUSINESS?
THE CHEF AND THE "HOW" AND "WHY"

The word *reengineering* was certainly not found in any of my cook books or apprenticeship texts, and in order to understand the concept behind this word, I had to look elsewhere. My training as a chef over the past 25 years has been purely classical. Along the way I managed to learn not only new cooking methods but also how to manage and motivate people in the kitchen environment.

I now have a much clearer understanding of the vision of the future for our industry. Reengineering is a tool to make this vision come true, and in many cases we have no choice but to go forward, accepting the changes that come toward us no matter how big or small they may seem.

In my case, reengineering came as a surprise when I found out that many of my colleagues in the company were without a job and that executive chefs were no longer needed. After looking at this situation a little more closely, I found out that this reengineering concept was really not as bad as it seemed.

Reengineering gave me the opportunity to look at my organization with a totally different set of eyes, and it made me realize that things can be done differently and in the long run, these changes would be beneficial to the customer and the company.

Once I was able to let go of the past, I was willing to accept the challenges of the future. With this new attitude, I was able to move forward and develop the necessary plan to put reengineering to work in my culinary world. This meant dismantling the current organizational structures, putting new concepts into place such as individual business unit leaders, elimination of departments, and redesigning job descriptions. During each of these steps, new questions and answers came up and I changed or adapted to them as they came along.

Many already well-defined systems had to be changed, eliminated, or even completely redesigned in order to move forward. Throughout this process many roadblocks had to be removed, only to show up again around the corner. Many personal egos had to be eliminated, and in some cases the people had to go along with them.

We were told by our corporate leaders that only the best would survive, and this was a problem for some. Those who were not willing to change found themselves struggling more and more. They were either terminated or quit during the process. Those who stepped up to the plate and started swinging at the ball made more progress than they even imagined.

We as culinarians should understand that if we don't change the way we do business, we will lose sight of our primary goal, which is customer satisfaction. It is the customer who steers in the direction we must go, and that is into the future.

—Dr. Robert Harrington, CEC, CCE,
Department of Food, Human Nutrition and Hospitality,
University of Arkansas,
Fayetteville, AR

QUALITY

It is not possible to meaningfully discuss supervision, management, or training in the foodservice industry, and particularly in the kitchen, without discussing quality. Quality must be the focus of any foodservice business and every part of that business both internally and externally. In the foodservice industry, a quality service or product may be defined as one that fully meets the expectations and requirements of those who produce or use it. Continuous improvement in quality food production is fundamental for any success in the foodservice industry. Continuous improvement in all areas contributes directly to improvement in food quality.

W. Edward **Deming's fourteen quality principles**, upon which much of the quality movement is based, recommend that each company or organization work out its own interpretations and adapt them to the corporate culture. While Deming's quality principles were directed primarily toward the manufacturing industry, they have many applications in the foodservice industry as well. The following list demonstrates how Deming's fourteen quality points may be adapted for application to a quality kitchen operation.[14]

1. Create constancy of purpose toward the improvement of product and service.   Commit the kitchen staff to continuous improvement. Create a common purpose; get the kitchen team to embrace continuous improvement.

2. Management must take the leadership role in promoting change.   Create a climate for change in the kitchen. Embrace change; make it your friend. Change with purpose, not just for the sake of change. Chefs who embrace change will need to be supportive and train the kitchen team. They must be proactive rather than reactive. Create and live a vision for the kitchen department that will become a beacon for team building and effective supervision. Remember, the one constant is change, and change can be a frightening concept for individuals who are accustomed to living in a comfort zone.

3. Stop dependence on inspection to achieve quality. Build quality into the product in the beginning.   The chef must be dedicated to preparing meals and providing service in a way that provides high standards from the outset. Chefs should abandon the notion that they know more about what the customer wants than the customer; they must not be gastronomic snobs. Without foodservice customers, there would be no need for chefs.

This refocused direction applies equally to all foodservice establishments whether they are white-tablecloth, healthcare, student-dining, or fast-food establishments. Quality is perceived by the customer; *they* define quality, *not* the chef producing the meal. The customer is the boss. One customer who is dissatisfied leaving the restaurant will tell twelve friends, who will tell six others, who in turn will tell three of their friends; eventually hundreds of people may hear about the poor meal and dining experience. This happens quickly today with the Internet.

Involve the kitchen staff members in menu development; let them vote on new dishes before they are introduced onto the menu. Involve customers; have *them* taste the menu items. Allow customers to vote on which dishes should be included on the menu. Ask the customers what they want and then provide it. A meal may look fine and taste fine to the chef preparing it, but that does not necessarily mean that customers will also feel that way about it. Customers may not always be right, but they are always the customers. They are the ones we want to satisfy and retain so that the foodservice business can grow and prosper.

Building quality into food preparation through team members at all levels is perhaps the chef's single most important task. This can be achieved only through excellent coaching and team-building skills and instilling in the kitchen team a sense of pride and passion for quality food standards. It is upon the delivery of high quality at all levels, provided through a motivated and well-trained kitchen team, that the success or failure of the modern chef rests.

4. Move to a single supplier for any one item. Create long-term relationships with suppliers. Chefs should view suppliers and vendors as a vital part of the road to quality in the kitchen. This means trusting suppliers and asking for their input. It means closer contacts and relationships with farmers and growers. More and more foodservice operators and chefs are dealing directly with local farmers and fishermen. Buying locally can give access to fresher and organically grown products. Suppliers can customize their products to meet the specific needs of a foodservice operation. Using single suppliers versus using two or more challenges the old strategy of playing one supplier against the other, using price and delivery as leverage and bargaining chips. As Bill Eacho stated, "Foodservice operators can improve quality and consistency, while at the same time lower costs by forming strategic partnerships."[15] While issues of price, quality, delivery, units of purchase, and credit terms will remain important business issues, quality product and produce from suppliers based on your foodservice specifications are paramount. A quality end product begins with quality ingredients.

5. Improve constantly the system of production and service and thus decrease costs. Quality equals profit, and motivated kitchen team members can reduce costs. Communicate the importance of each person's role in the quest for high-quality standards. Support and explain decisions to help each kitchen team member apply quality standards. On a weekly basis, brief the team on progress, policy, and points of action. As food quality improves through continuous quality review, waste is reduced and costs decrease. Food cost reduction programs in and of themselves do not often lead to improved quality. On the other hand, effective quality applications by informed team members lead to not only improved quality but also lasting reduction in food and production costs. Quality and costs are not opposites or trade-offs, with one being improved at the expense of the other. Instead, both can be constantly improved. Improvement of quality is a never-ending journey. It is therefore essential for the chef supervisor to provide an atmosphere where total communication can exist in the kitchen and where it is possible to tap constantly the collective brainpower of the team.

6. Institute training on the job. Train all kitchen team members, including the support team. Practice equal training opportunities and gain support from management for the concept of on-the-job training. Set examples; coach employees to reach their potential. Diversity and multiculturalism are common to foodservice operations; therefore, a good deal of on-the-job training is necessary. This training should always be conducted in a sensitive and caring way.

7. Institute leadership. The aim of supervision should be to help people and machines do a better job. Chefs must become better leaders. This requires delegating authority, empowering kitchen team members to become independent decision makers, providing guidance, and creating a positive work environment. Chefs as role models, leaders, and trainers should provide the tools and coaching required for the rest of the team to operate a successful, high-quality kitchen. Use technology and machines to support the efforts of the kitchen team, not just to replace them. Learn from successes and mistakes. Regularly walk around each team member's place of work, observe, listen, and praise.

8. Drive out fear, so that everyone may work effectively. The greatest fears of a kitchen team member are of the unknown and of rejection or failure: What am I expected to do? How do I know if I am doing a good job? Create an environment in which team members feel comfortable in offering suggestions and ideas. Just because members of a group do not say anything does not necessarily mean they have nothing to say. They may be shy or simply afraid to advance their ideas. Give constant feedback on team member performance. Feedback should be given only on issues of performance, not on the type of person the team member is.

9. Break down barriers between departments. Promote team building as people from different departments work together to solve problems and improve quality. Customers react holistically to quality and service. The dining experience involves other people besides the kitchen team. Quality food must be complemented by friendly, courteous service by staff dedicated to meeting and exceeding customer expectations. The service staff is the chef's internal customer and an integral part of the foodservice quality drive. Customers recall the negative aspects of the dining experience before they remember the more positive ones; therefore, negative and positive experiences don't go together. The animosity that has traditionally existed between dining room staff and kitchen staff has absolutely no place in a quality operation: Chefs must realize that the waiter is also a customer.

10. Eliminate slogans, exhortations, and targets for the workforce, asking for zero defects and new levels of productivity. Slogans containing production numbers only—numbers of meals served and degree of difficulty associated with the production of certain menu items—should be avoided as tools of measurement. Food cost percentage targets are important but should not be the major measurement tool for chefs in foodservice. Develop the kitchen team—emphasize people, not profit, and hire kitchen staff with hospitality attitudes: Technical skills are important, but good attitudes and a desire to please the customer by cooking the best meal possible are more important. Remember, a chef's reputation rests on the last meal served to a customer, not on any previous accolades or gold medals won at food shows.

11. Eliminate work quotas: substitute leadership. Practical experience has shown that quality in the kitchen is at its lowest during service time. To improve the kitchen work environment, rotate team members instead of assigning them to labor-intensive, boring work sequences. Ensure that no one is a prisoner of a particular station, area, or job. Design jobs and arrange work to encourage the commitment of individuals to the team. Communicate clearly so as to ensure quality performance standards; be understood and understand; be a good listener. Serve the team; care for their well-being and safety; work alongside team members and deal with grievances promptly.

Leadership within the kitchen must replace the old heavy-handed style of traditional chefs. There must be recognition that team members have initiative and creativity and that they can and will make valuable contributions to quality if provided a motivated work environment. Chefs increasingly will be required to lead a culturally diverse kitchen team. This necessitates skills in understanding the special values of diversity so as to turn diversity into a strength. Deming continuously honed these principles. He states: "For years point seven was a mandate to institute supervision, of late I believe leadership is a better word."[16]

12. Remove barriers that rob managers, engineers, and the hourly paid worker of their right to pride of workmanship. Change the emphasis from numbers to quality. Almost all kitchen team members want to give their best. Chefs should remove barriers in order to create a motivational environment. However, removing barriers alone will not create motivation; motivation comes from within each individual. Without motivational conditions in the kitchen, team members will operate at minimal performance levels. Figure 12-3 shows the most common barriers to motivation.

In kitchen operation, chef supervisors must realize that elements that motivate them probably will hold true for each kitchen team member. The example that the chef supervisor sets greatly influences the productivity and motivation of the team. Most kitchen team members take considerable pride in their work performance and the meals they serve. Simply blaming kitchen team members for poor business numbers

- Erratic mood swings by the chef supervisor
- Poor physical kitchen facilities
- High temperatures in the work environment
- Poor equipment
- Insufficient small wares
- Inappropriate floor surfaces
- Inconsistent treatment of individuals and no communication or feedback on job performance

Figure 12-3 Demotivating barriers to quality performance.

and lack of revenues makes no contribution to operational success. Quality equals profit in the promotion of pride, and a sense of self-worth will enhance profits.

13. Institute a vigorous program of education and self-improvement. Training and instructor skills are just as important to the chef as culinary technical skills. Invest in training; it will prove to be the greatest impetus toward the goals of continuous improvement. Chefs who arm themselves with instructor training skills and techniques and who use them in different planned training situations will win big. Training is not something done once; it has to be on-going, a way of life in the kitchen. At times, learning can proceed irregularly. Expect periods with no perceptible progress in some individuals, but with changes taking place in the culture of the kitchen team and in other individuals. The single most unifying force in developing people and creating conditions for quality product and a motivated kitchen team is the planned implementation of sequential and progressive training programs.

14. Put everyone in the company to work to accomplish the transformation. Make it an all-pervasive common goal and support it. Chefs investing in and applying Deming's quality principles will not only produce satisfied customers and practically eliminate their complaints but also will transform the role of the chef supervisor, the team, and the work environment in the kitchen. However, quality performance cannot be maintained unless the entire organization and the various supporting departments along with management adopt it universally. Continuous improvement must become the norm; supervising or managing the status quo is no longer an option in an increasingly competitive and uncertain foodservice industry.

Figure 12-4 shows some of the areas that should the focus of continuous improvement in the kitchen. Quality within the kitchen is not a procedure; it is a process and as such is never finished.

The main aim of the Deming philosophy is empowerment of the individual. The lesson is that we have to empower all our people with dignity, knowledge, and skills so that they may contribute. They have to feel secure, be trained so that they can do the work properly, and be encouraged so that the organization can develop and grow.[17]

- Improving external customer satisfaction
- Improving and developing closer supplier partnerships
- Improving communications within the kitchen
- Reducing waste
- Preventing special causes of food preparation variation
- Quantifying quality costs
- Improving food production and service methods
- Improving internal systems
- Providing flexibility and adaptability

Figure 12-4 Areas for continuous improvement.

CHANGE

Change is a key component of management for continuous improvement. Studies have shown that people do not basically resist change; they resist being changed, and participation empowers change.[18] A major factor that chefs should consider when changing the foodservice operation is the people affected by the change. Resistance to change within any organization is as common as the need for change. After management decides on making changes, they typically encounter employee resistance, usually aimed at preventing the change from occurring. This resistance generally exists because kitchen team members fear some personal loss, such as a reduction in personal prestige, a disturbance of established social and working relationships, and personal failure due to an inability to carry out new job responsibilities resulting from the proposed change.

Since resistance accompanies proposed change, chefs must be able to reduce the effects of this resistance so as to ensure the success of needed quality improvements. People need time to evaluate the proposed change before implementation. Eliminating time to evaluate how proposed changes may affect individual situations usually results in automatic opposition to the changes. The kitchen team members who will be affected by a change must be kept informed of the type of change being considered and the probability that the change will be adopted. When fear of personal loss related to a proposed change is reduced, opposition to the change is reduced. Individuals should receive information that will help them answer the following change-related questions shown in Figure 12-5.

If the chef follows some simple guidelines, then implementing change need not be too stressful. The following steps will assist in getting the kitchen team members to "buy into" the change:

- Inform those concerned in advance so that they can think about the implications of the change and its effect on their position within the kitchen team.
- Explain the overall objectives of the change, the reasons for it, and the sequence in which it will occur.
- Show people how the change will benefit them. Be honest with the team. If they are not to be part of the future plans of the kitchen objectives, tell them and provide them support and ample time to secure new positions.
- Invite those affected by the change to participate at all stages of the process.
- Allow time and demonstrate patience as the team adapts to new work or quality-driven changes.
- Provide for constant communication and feedback during the changes.
- Demonstrate constant commitment and loyalty to the change. Show confidence in the team and each individual's ability to implement the change.

The most powerful tool for reducing resistance to change is open display by the chef of a positive attitude toward the change and the anticipated outcome of the change. As with all change, time should be taken for evaluation, to examine what needs to be modified and what can be added to increase the effectiveness of kitchen operations.

Figure 12-5
Change: questions team members will ask.

- Will I lose my job?
- Will my old skills become obsolete?
- Will I be capable of being effective under the new system?
- Will my power and prestige decline?
- Will I receive more responsibility than I want?
- Will I have to work longer hours?

Figure 12-6
Statements that kill change.

- Don't be ridiculous.
- We tried that before.
- It costs too much.
- You must be crazy.
- That's beyond our responsibility.
- It's too radical a change.
- We don't have the time.
- We've never done it before.
- Let's get back to reality.
- We're not ready for that.
- We'd be laughed at.
- We did all right without it.
- Let's shelve it for the time being.
- Let's form a committee.
- It's not practical for an organization like ours.
- It's too hard to get accepted.
- It won't work in our kitchen.

Evaluation of change often involves watching for symptoms that further change is necessary, particularly if team members are oriented more toward the past than the future or if they are more concerned with their own "pecking order" than with meeting the challenges of quality. One challenge for the chef is the immediate and constant negative responders. These are the individuals who react negatively to change of any type. Some of the statements that "kill off" creative ideas and change are shown in Figure 12-6.

Chefs should listen carefully for these types of remarks and monitor the dissent within the group. This dissent should be met with a positive approach, and the benefits of the new ideas pointed out.

CONCLUSIONS

This brief overview of management theory is intended only to give a glimpse of what has shaped different directions in supervision and management. Each theory has had its own champions at various times. A noteworthy change is the subtle yet vitally important shift of designation from "personnel managers" to "human resources managers" and the greater emphasis placed on the development of people. This shift clearly reflects the philosophy that people must be led, not managed. This overview provides insight and understanding of change. It also shows that workers have changed; they *can* be more than mindless, uninterested employees who need constant control and supervision. Supervision, management, and leadership in the kitchen is evolving and changing. Chefs must shift from being old traditional "autocratic" rulers to being coaches. Chefs who come to realize that not all change is bad will succeed in the future foodservice industry.

SUMMARY

The theories of management have evolved from scientific management, total quality management, and management by objective to the contemporary systems theory. W. E. Deming provided strategies and philosophies directed toward continuous improvement in all aspects of production. These strategies may be applied in the foodservice industry. Deming's fourteen quality principles can be applied in a culinary operation by trained and knowledgeable chefs.

Change is a constant. Chef supervisors must reduce the effects of resistance to change within the kitchen. Understanding the elements of change and the fear with which people approach change is critical to moving toward continuous improvement and quality.

DISCUSSION QUESTIONS

1. Define the following chapter key terms:

   a. Management
   b. Foodservice customer
   c. Scientific management
   d. Management by objectives
   e. Excellence movement
   f. Management by walking around
   g. Reengineering
   h. Theory of total quality control
   i. Total quality management
   j. Contingency theory
   k. Systems theory
   l. Chaos theory
   m. Deming's fourteen quality principles
   n. Change

2. Quality in terms of the kitchen operation may be considered in relation to what areas?
3. What were the main contributions of Frederick Taylor's scientific management?
4. How can Deming's fourteen quality principles be applied to the kitchen and the chef supervisor?
5. Discuss the importance and role of continuous improvement in quality food and service.
6. What are the main differences between management by objective, the excellence movement, and reengineering?
7. What are the elements that contribute to people's resistance to change?
8. Who sets the pace for most change in the foodservice industry?

NOTES

1. http://www.merriam-webster.com/dictionary/management, 2011, Merriam-Webster.

2. http://www.restaurant.org/research/facts/, Research and Insights—Facts at a Glance, 2011, National Restaurant Association.

3. Ibid.

4. Rafael Aguayo, Dr. Deming, (New York: Carol, 1991), p. 243.

5. Tom Peters, *Thriving on Chaos: Handbook for a Management Revolution* (New York: Harper & Row, 1988), 3.

6. Ibid., p. 357.

7. Ibid., p. 358.

8. Tom Peters, "Putting Excellence into Management," *Managing Behavior in Organizations* (New York: McGraw-Hill, 1983), 603.

9. Michael Hammer and James Champy, *Reengineering the Corporation: A Manifesto for Business Revolution* (New York: HarperCollins, 1993), 2.

10. Daniel Morris and Joel Brandon, *Re-engineering Your Business* (New York: McGraw-Hill, 1993), 13.

11. Michael Hammer and James Champy, *Reengineering the Corporation: A Manifesto for Business Revolution* (New York: HarperCollins, 1993), 79.

12. Mary Walton, *The Deming Management Method* (New York: Putnam, 1986), 34.

13. Carter McNamara, *Historical and Contemporary Theories of Management*, http://managementhelp.org/management/theories.htm, 2007.

14. Deming's fourteen points are from *Out of Crisis*, by Dr. Edwards Deming (Cambridge, MA: MIT Center for Advanced Engineering Study, 1989), 111.

15. Bill Eacho, "Quality Service Through Strategic Foodservice Partnerships," *Hosteur*, Vol. 3, No. 1, Spring 1993, 22.

16. Deming's fourteen points are from *Out of Crisis*, by Dr. Edwards Deming (Cambridge, MA: MIT Center for Advanced Engineering Study, 1989), 111.

17. Mary Walton, *The Deming Management Method* (New York: Putnam, 1986), 34.

18. James A. Belasco, *Teaching the Elephant to Dance* (New York: Crown, 1990), 49.

Chapter 13
Motivation

OBJECTIVES

When you complete this chapter, you should be able to:

1. Define motivation within the context of the chef supervisor's job
2. List the major theories and philosophies of motivation
3. Explain the elements that contribute to a motivated kitchen team
4. Describe factors that are the ingredients of morale within the kitchen
5. Understand the elements of positive stimulus
6. Explain why feedback is an important element of morale
7. Describe the elements and effects of negative stimulus

Case Study: Appleton Cafeteria

Perry had been the dishwasher for the Appleton Cafeteria since before it had been the Appleton Cafeteria. The Appleton had originally had been a "Mom and Dad's Café." Perry was the first dishwasher hired at the "Mom and Dad's Café." When the Appleton Company bought the property, he was asked to stay on.

No one seemed to know exactly how old Perry was, but he was thought to be about 60. (His original application was lost in the buy-out, and a new one had never been completed since his payroll records were in good order.) If he had any family, the management or staff did not know them. Perry could barely read and write. He could, however, wash pots and pans at an amazing rate.

Perry had always been a minimum wage hourly employee. The only raises that Perry had received in his long history with Appleton and Mom and Dad's were the increases in minimum wage. Perry's schedule had always been to work a split shift from 11:00 A.M. to 2:00 P.M. and 6:00 P.M. to 9:00 P.M. Monday through Saturday, 36 hours per week.

Part-time Appleton employees received no benefits. A full-time employee was someone that worked 38 or more hours per week. Appleton had no full-time employees other than managers. Only full-time employees were provided with a meal. All other employees paid half-price for all food. Water, coffee, and tea were free to all employees. Employees paid half-price for any other beverages. The level of pilferage and theft at the Appleton Cafeteria was a constant challenge for managers (there had been four general managers in the property in the past 12 months).

When the district manager caught Perry eating a piece of fried chicken in the pot and pan room, he informed the general manager that Perry had stolen the food and that he was to be fired. The general manager stated that Perry had not stolen the chicken. He stated that he had given Perry the piece of chicken, and a soft drink the district manager had not noticed, as a reward for his hard work. The district manager expressed concern about the precedent that would be set by giving free food to employees. He told the general manager he would have to pay for the items himself. The general manager paid for the items as instructed.

The general manager submitted his notice the following week.

Based on what you have learned from previous chapters and the content of this chapter, answer the following questions.

- What is the overall reason for the challenges occurring in the Appleton Cafeteria?
- What are the primary causal agents for the challenges occurring in the Appleton Cafeteria?
- What role did supervision/management play in the decline in the Appleton Cafeteria?
- What specific steps could have been taken to avoid the current situation occurring in the Appleton Cafeteria?
- What, specifically, can be done to overcome the challenges and generate motion in a positive direction for the Appleton Cafeteria?

INTRODUCTION

A foundational aspect of the chef's role in the kitchen and total operation is that of motivator. It is through motivating the kitchen team that the chef achieves the goals of the operation. Motivating people is both a simple and a complex task. It is achieved by directing, praising, rewarding, and even correcting and disciplining. The critical factor in motivating anyone, including kitchen team members, is using the right method of motivation at the right time. The goal must always be to create an environment that encourages and supports while continuing to move always in the direction of the goals to be accomplished.

DEFINING MOTIVATION

A **motive** is something that causes a person to act. A **motivator** is someone who provides the motive for others to act. The chef is the motivator of the kitchen. The chef must move forward the process of motivating the kitchen team members. This action by the chef is defined as motivation. **Motivation** is the process of motivating and also the condition of being motivated.[1] The term *motivation* was originally derived from the Latin word *movere*, which literally means "to move."[2]

Motivation is concerned with three factors: what energizes behavior, what channels such behavior, and the conditions under which this behavior is maintained. The triggers and drivers of motivation are the same for all individuals. It is clear that the characteristics of the work environment, in this instance the kitchen, and the characteristics of the chef (the particular disposition and leadership style) affect the elements of motivation. The more the chef understands the kitchen team member's behavior, the better he or she should be able to influence that behavior and make it more consistent with the goals of the foodservice organization. Since quality and productivity are central to the success of the chef, the creation of the appropriate motivational environment in the kitchen is critical to this success.

Each person sees the world from an individual viewpoint. An individual's perception of the world is determined by his or her background and personal experiences, among other variables. The kitchen and the world generally are viewed through this personal and individual lens. The chef needs to work to learn how each team member is likely to respond to different events. He or she must strive to understand the diverse cultural issues that occur in the food service department. Each kitchen team member perceives and interprets instructions, actions, and communications in a unique way.

A team member's values and culture are a strong determinant of behavior. A value is any object, activity, or orientation that individuals consider very important to their way of life. Culture, on the other hand, refers to the team member's beliefs, practices, traditions, ideologies, and lifestyles. Values and culture have been shown to be related to decision making, motivation, communication, and supervisory success. Values are influenced largely by the culture in which we live and work.

The makeup of today's workforce in the United States is very diverse. According to the National Restaurant Association, in 2004, 56 percent of individuals in foodservice occupations were women.[3] Hispanics, a rapidly growing minority presence in foodservice, have grown by 5 percent since 1992 to 18 percent, and African Americans comprised 11 percent of the industry workforce in 2004.[4] The diverse nature of the industry workforce is changing the culture of the workplace in the foodservice industry. This diversity will continue to grow in the next decade.

Humans function in an integrated manner, not in individual parts. It is the total kitchen team member we are interacting with. While sometimes it is useful to focus our attention on certain segments of the personality in order to have a better understanding of the person, in the final analysis the team member should be viewed as a complete package.

Chefs must recognize that they cannot know the nature of many of the forces influencing the behavior of individual team members. Team members often do not reveal what they are currently experiencing in their lives away from the job. What happens to team members at home or through other activities will affect how they feel about their work and other aspects of their lives. What happens away from work also influences how well they perform at work and the degree to which they want their feelings known to others.

Remember, it is impossible to have the highest-quality team without a respect for people, their differences, and the strengths this diversity brings to the kitchen motivational environment.

THEORIES AND MOTIVATIONAL PHILOSOPHIES

Probably the most widely accepted description of human needs is the **hierarchy of needs** concept put forward by Abraham Maslow. Maslow states that we as humans possess five basic needs and that these needs can be arranged in a hierarchy of importance

---

CHEF TALK
"BUILDING MORALE"

To build morale at our club, we initiated several strategies that worked in creating a sense of family. One of these was the creation of an in-club newsletter through which all of the kitchen team could share their knowledge and different training experiences. The newsletter also acknowledged special awards employees had received as a result of their culinary skills. Special events such as birthdays, new babies, and marriages were included to add a personal touch. This type of employee recognition worked wonders for morale and team spirit.

I began to cross-train all employees for all positions in the kitchen. Rather than having one person on a station for years, cross training provided an opportunity for employees to learn new skills and develop a better understanding of problems in areas with which they had previously been unfamiliar. Switching positions exposed both sides of "the fence" and helped to develop problem-solving skills. These programs served as a catalyst for a strong commitment to

excellence. They demonstrated a willingness to develop new traditions and not to simply blindly imitate the past.

By providing these opportunities, we were able to attract enthusiastic young culinarians with great potential. This provided the shot in the arm we needed, and it inspired others to seek professional development and certification and to improve performance. The combination of all these changes helped to create improved conditions and build a terrific team spirit in the kitchen. It proved to us that a chain is only as strong as its weakest link. This experience also taught me that without people behind you, bonded by a common thread, nothing can be accomplished. This type of morale results in a strong team spirit and a staff that is dedicated and committed to culinary excellence.

—Tom Peer, CMC, CCE, AAC,
The Culinary Institute of America,
Hyde Park, NY

---

that relates to the order in which individuals generally strive to satisfy them. The needs (see Figure 13-1) listed in Maslow's hierarchical order are: 1. physiological, 2. security, 3. social, 4. esteem, and 5. self-actualization needs.[5]

Physiological needs. These relate to the normal functioning of the body and include the need for food, water, air, rest, and sex. Until these needs are met, a significant portion of an individual's behavior is aimed at satisfying them. If these needs are satisfied, behavior is aimed at the next level, the security needs.

Security or safety needs. These are the needs individuals require to keep themselves free from bodily and economic disaster. The foodservice organization can best help employees to satisfy their security needs through good and fair salaries, since it is with these salaries that employees can buy items such as food and housing. When security needs are satisfied, behavior tends to be aimed at satisfying social needs.

Social needs. These include an individual's desire for love, companionship, and friendship. Overall, these needs reflect a person's desire to be accepted by others. As these needs are satisfied, behavior shifts to satisfying esteem needs.

Figure 13-1
Maslow's hierarchy.

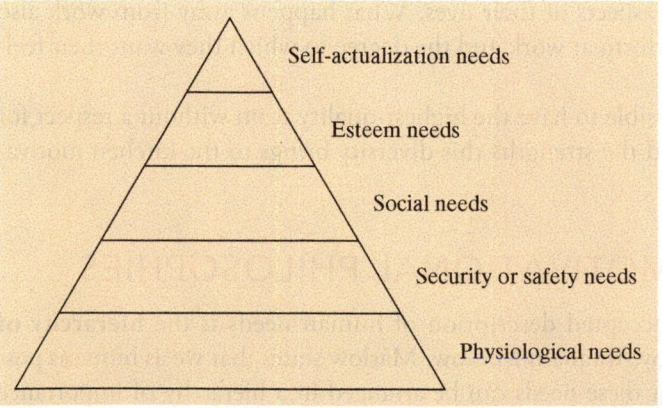

Esteem needs. These consist of an individual's desire for respect and are generally divided into two categories: self-respect and respect for others. Once esteem needs are satisfied, an individual emphasizes satisfying self-actualization needs.

Self-actualization needs. These needs are the desire to maximize whatever potential an individual possesses. For example, a motivated kitchen team member who seeks to satisfy self-actualization or self-realization needs might strive to become the leader or supervisor of the kitchen team. Self-actualization needs are at the highest level of Maslow's hierarchy.

These needs are the same for everyone. They apply when team members are at work, at which time there may be problems with *how well* they work. Maslow's need hierarchy theory is consistent with the reasons people work. However, individuals move from one level to another and do *not* remain at any one level in life. The motivational and self-realization environment in the kitchen is present only when these basic needs are met.

Herzberg's Two-Factor Theory

Frederick Herzberg put forward the **motivator-hygiene theory**. Proposed in 1959, this theory emphasizes the roles of motivator factors and hygiene factors (also known as maintenance factors). It is also known as the *two-factor theory* of work motivation. The factors that produce job satisfaction are called **motivator factors** because they satisfy a team member's need for self-realization. According to the theory, **hygiene factors** are important, but they are *not* motivators.

Herzberg's Hygiene Factors and Motivators

Dissatisfaction: hygiene factors

- Company policy and administration
- Supervision
- Relationship with supervisor
- Relationship with peers
- Working conditions
- Salary
- Relationship with subordinates

Satisfaction: motivation factors

- Opportunity for achievement
- Opportunity for recognition
- Work itself
- Responsibility
- Advancement
- Personal growth

When hygiene factors deteriorate to a level below what a team member considers acceptable, then dissatisfaction is present. However, removing the causes of dissatisfaction does not create satisfaction and will not motivate performance. If kitchen team members are required to work in an environment that is unpleasant, unsafe, and hostile, then a motivational climate cannot be created until such time as the hygiene or maintenance factors are at an acceptable level. When the hygiene factors of policy, supervision, kitchen-working conditions, relationships, and pay are good and adequate, the stage is then set for the motivating factors.[6] These motivational factors help create job satisfaction, which in and of itself is the primary motivating factor. In Herzberg's theory, the opportunity for kitchen team members to advance will require them to seek recognition, assume responsibility, and achieve success through the job. Recognition is the most important factor, more important than pay or any other element of the hygiene factors. If the job or position of a kitchen team member can be enriched to include more motivators, then the opportunity exists to have a motivated, participative member fully committed to the principles of success.

Herzberg is the person associated with the notions of job enrichment. In 1968 he stressed that "the only way to motivate employees is through challenging work in which they can assume responsibility."[7] This he proposed as a reaction to what he called the KITA (kick-in-the-ass) methods used widely by most managers and supervisors. Central to these proposals is the idea that strategies that modify jobs can offer a more meaningful role for employees and can give them the opportunity for recognition and ultimately greater responsibility.

Theory X—Theory Y

Another motivational theory involves the chef's assumptions about employees and the nature of people. Douglas McGregor, a Massachusetts Institute of Technology professor, identified two contradicting sets of these assumptions. Theory X involves assumptions that McGregor feels managers often use as the basis for dealing with people, while Theory Y represents the assumptions that McGregor feels managers should strive to use.[8]

Theory X, according to McGregor, assumes that the average person has an inherent dislike of work and will avoid it if possible. Because of this natural human dislike of work, most people must be coerced, controlled, directed, and threatened with punishment to get them to put forth adequate effort toward the achievement of organizational objectives.

The Theory X chef assumes that the average person prefers to be directed, wishes to avoid responsibility, has relatively little ambition, and wants security above all. The Theory X chef motivates staff primarily through fear. This type of chef closely controls the staff. The Theory X chef believes that he or she must protect the employees from their own shortcomings. This type of chef does this with heavy-handed control and coercion.

Theory Y assumes that the expenditure of physical and mental effort in work is as natural as play or rest. People will exercise self-direction and self-control in the service of objectives to which they are committed. Commitment to objectives is a function of the rewards associated with achievement.

The Theory Y chef assumes that under proper conditions the average person learns not only to accept but to seek responsibility. The capacity to exercise a relatively high degree of imagination, ingenuity, and creativity in the solution of organizational problems is widely and normally distributed in the population.[9] The Theory Y chef believes that he or she should lead by including the staff in planning. This type of chef encourages staff to experience personal satisfaction as they contribute to the achievement of objectives.

Theory X has a part to play in situations that require a firm but necessary position of authority. But it has no part to play in team building, or the creation of a kitchen team where each member is expected to contribute to the overall success of the team. The empowering of team members to take an active part in all aspects of the team is certainly not a part of Theory X. Rather, the successful kitchen team will fall into McGregor's category of Theory Y that relies on the assumption that people are naturally primed and ready to contribute; the only missing pieces are great leadership and a motivated environment.

Theory Z

Theory Z is a motivational philosophy that emerged in the 1970s. It was first fully presented in a book by William Ouchi in 1981.[10] Theory Z is a humanistic approach more similar to Theory Y than to Theory X. The difference between Theory Z and

Theory Y is the perspective. Theory Y looks at management from a view of employer to employee. Theory Z looks at management from an organizational view. Theory Z is based on long-term employment and slow, but continuous growth and progression. Employees are included in decision making for the organization but are still responsible for their own performance and development.

The Theory Z chef believes in encouragement and development of the individual. This chef also constantly considers the future of the total organization when working with staff. The welfare of the individual is directly connected with that of the organization.

Expectancy Model

Victor Vroom's expectancy model is based on the premise that felt needs cause human behavior. The model addresses the issue of motivation strength. Motivation strength is an individual's degree of desire to perform a behavior. As this desire increases or decreases, motivation strength is said to fluctuate correspondingly.[11]

$$\text{Motivation strength} = \text{perceived value of result} \times \text{perceived probability of successful completion}$$

According to this model, motivation strength is determined by (1) the perceived value of the result of performing a behavior and (2) the perceived probability that the behavior performed will cause the result to materialize. As both of these factors increase, an individual's motivation strength and desire to perform also increase. In general, individuals tend to perform those behaviors that maximize personal rewards over the long run.

An illustration of expectancy theory applied to kitchen operations might be as follows: A team member believes that if he or she produces meals that satisfy the foodservice establishment's standards and meet the needs of the customer consistently, then the perceived value of utilizing quality standards will produce for the individual a perceived probability of further reward and success.

Pygmalion Effect

The Pygmalion Effect states that the expectations the kitchen team members have of themselves will determine how well they perform. If you expect great things, great things will happen. If you expect mediocre performance, mediocre performance is what you will get. This is also known as the self-fulfilling prophecy. If you emphasize the positive and what your team can do, team members will begin to believe strongly in themselves. The more the chef supervisor tells the team how successful they can become, the more competent the team will be. When high performance and quality standards are set and team members are told they can rise to the occasion, the self-fulfilling prophecy determines that they will. Positive expectations equal positive results.[12]

MORALE

Morale is defined as the mental and emotional condition of an individual with regard to the function or task at hand.[13] So far in this chapter, we have examined some of the theories pertaining to motivating people in the workplace. These are important; they provide insight into why some individuals perform well while others do not. Motivation contributes to morale. There can be no great "kitchen morale" without the application of motivation by the chef. The kitchen is often a pressure-filled place of work during busy meal periods. Good team morale can reduce this pressure, increasing the confidence, ability, and harmony of the team and helping to deal with busy service periods.

The first and most important element of morale is the leadership style of the chef. The focus should be a leadership style that continuously demonstrates respect and a caring attitude toward the team. The chef who will make the greatest impact on morale is the one who believes in people. This belief is demonstrated by being approachable and sensitive to the individual's difficulties in achieving the kitchen team's goals.

There are elements that contribute to morale within the kitchen team. These elements include leadership attributes and a chef who can:

Create

- a happy relaxed atmosphere in which everyone is clear on *what* to do, *when* to do it, and *how* to do it.
- a climate that challenges each team member to contribute the best.
- healthy competition.
- individual passion and a pride in being the best.
- a team morale that provides a sense of belonging.
- an atmosphere in which individuals are encouraged to share opinions and ideas.

Show

- a caring awareness of individuals' problems.
- sensitivity and understanding of ethnic diversity and the special problems of integration that may exist within the team.
- respect for individual team members' dignity.
- a sense of humor.
- consistency of behavior in dealing with each member of the team.
- fairness at all times.
- displeasure for poor performance when appropriate.

Give

- praise when it is merited.
- reasons for uncompromising high quality standards.

Be

- an active listener.
- a coach.
- a team builder.

Morale is also about empowering and trusting team members to make the right decisions. A key element to positive morale is giving a sense of real involvement to individuals. Figure 13-2 shows what the chef should do when empowerment and trust are in place in the kitchen.

The chef must scrupulously avoid the appearance of favoring one person over another. This may be the most difficult challenge, as no human being is totally objective in dealing with another. We all have biases. Since we cannot be totally objective,

Figure 13-2
Empowerment and trust.

Activators
- Give the team members important work to do.
- Allow individual team members to do their work in their own way.
- Give them the resources to do the work.
- Make them feel their decisions are part of the overall plan.
- Actively encourage teamwork.
- Be tolerant with failure.
- Celebrate successes.

we must recognize our subjectivities and compensate for them. To build morale, each individual team member must be treated fairly.

Empowerment contributes to the esprit de corps of the kitchen team. **Esprit de corps** is the spirit of the group. It is the common enthusiasm and sense of honor that drive the team to success. This is a critical concept when building a team. When the team loses its spirit, performance quickly diminishes in quality.

Trust is also critical to the morale of both the individual and the team. Trust is the foundation for respect. Respect is the foundation for conforming to standards. Standards are the foundation for quality. To achieve quality, trust must exist. When trust does not exist, morale will turn to the negative side.

Communication is also critical to morale. Team members need to know what is expected of them. Without good, constant dialogue, standards of quality, goals, and objectives for the team and the individual cannot be communicated. Be honest with the team; they want to have confidence in your leadership. They will be more inclined to feel confident when a participative involvement is demonstrated. Be available for discussion, walk around the kitchen, and be visible. Make each team member's job more interesting and challenging, get to know each individual, have a sense of their social needs, and set a good example.

Another important element of morale consistent with Maslow's needs hierarchy theory is the team member's security. Therefore, a stable, nonthreatening environment must be created, one in which unpredictable supervisor mood swings are not present.

As we have observed from different approaches to motivation, employees generally perform at their best when they feel useful and needed, in an environment where they are contributing and valuable team players, enjoy a sense of belonging, are involved in decision making, and are trusted and not oversupervised. These elements make up individual and team morale. The creation and maintenance of this morale is part of the chef's job. It is easy to determine when poor team morale or no morale at all is present in the kitchen; it is difficult to tell if morale is just average; but it is obvious when good morale is present. It is reflected in low employee turnover and a kitchen that is well led and productive, where team members show pride in producing high-quality customer-focused meals.

STIMULUS AND MOTIVATION

Stimulus is something that causes action. Motivation and demotivation are the result of stimulus. **Demotivation** can be defined as something that reduces or removes the desire to complete a task or continue to carry out a function. Motivation is the result of positive stimulus such as praise or rewards. Demotivation is the result of negative stimulus such as put-downs, failure to make good on promises, or favoritism. Stimulus can be physical, verbal, nonverbal, or combinations of all three. Most of the stimuli we get as adults are verbal and nonverbal as opposed to the physical ones we received as children. Normal stimuli are different aspects and factors that, when applied to individual kitchen team members, are motivators and builders of morale. Negative stimuli in the form of put-downs, insensitivity, insults, sarcasm, poor working conditions, and poor leadership can damage relationships and destroy morale.

Positive Stimuli

Positive stimuli are necessary in the kitchen to satisfy the esteem and ego needs of individuals. At its simplest, a positive stimulus may be a smile from the chef or a nod of recognition. Figure 13-3 provides examples of nonverbal and verbal stimuli.

Positive stimulus is also about catching team members doing a good job. The greatest example of the highest level of motivation is to receive praise in front of the team and other department employees.

Figure 13-3
Stimulus: nonverbal/verbal.

Nonverbal

Making eye contact
Giving listening signals
Shaking hands
Waving

Verbal

Using a person's name
Checking for understanding
Making reference to past experiences
Praising
Greeting
Thanking
Saying farewell

Figure 13-3
Stimulus: nonverbal/verbal.

The highest performance or overall quality is achieved when there is buy-in by the team members. This is achieved by involving team members in determining team direction and goals. When the team members feel that the organization's vision is "their" vision, they will achieve. Creating buy-in is part of motivating staff.

When a climate of cooperation and communication is established through organized, sensible motivational techniques, individuals become a team rather than just a work group. This is a challenge for the chef and the kitchen team, but the potential rewards for the foodservice establishment are great.

Benefits are important motivators, but not the most important. The prospect of earning more money does not motivate as much as recognition, responsibility, and the prospect of advancement. However, incentives and benefits can be used as methods of positive stimuli. Organizations that provide health care and insurance benefits usually are ones that invest in people, that care, and that have a low employee turnover. The costs of getting sick and staying healthy are high for most people, especially lower-paid employees. The benefits of group programs of health care, insurance, and wellness schemes include reduced stress and increased motivation and morale.

Incentives and awards are positive stimuli and team reinforcements. Small rewards may be more effective than large ones. The small rewards may become a cause for positive celebration. Awards, prizes, and ceremonies are important to kitchen team members. What Tom Peters refers to as "little things with high impact"[14] are shown in Figure 13-4. Whatever programs, awards, or rewards are instituted, it must be ensured that all team members are included and are eligible to participate.

Figure 13-4
Stimulus: little things with big impact.

- Keep a calendar of team members' birthdays and recognize them with a cake, flowers, or a card or by simply wishing them a happy birthday.
- Celebrate happy family events with team members.
- Have a special meal with the kitchen team to celebrate achieving a particular goal.
- Create a player of the week or month program.
- Dine with team members on a regular basis.
- Send out thank-you notes regularly.
- Create incentives to address gaps or needs in quality and production.
- Provide opportunities for team members to attend food shows or culinary arts–related seminars.

- Inconsistent behavior by the chef supervisor
- Abusive or abrasive behavior
- Poor working conditions
- Fear of supervisor, loss of job, or change
- No team atmosphere
- Lack of recognition
- Poor supervisory leadership
- Lack of incentives, ambitions, or goals for the kitchen team
- Use of ridicule or sarcasm
- Over supervision and lack of trust
- Unfair job allocations
- Decisions for the team made without consultation
- Lack of communication
- Lack of respect for persons of different age, ethnicity, gender, physical abilities and qualities, and sexual preference

Figure 13-5
Stimulus: negative—to be avoided.

Negative Stimuli

Examples of negative stimuli are reprimanding or putting down of a team member. These are also known as demotivators. If these are in widespread use in the kitchen, then morale is nonexistent and the leader is probably operating in a Theory X mode—the chef who leads through fear. If no positive stimuli are available to team members, then they will work for negative stimuli rather than suffer the least acceptable situation—no stimuli at all. Examples of common negative stimuli or demotivators that should be avoided are shown in Figure 13-5.

When people are unhappy at work, absenteeism increases, productivity goes down, the quality of the meals produced is lower, and employee turnover increases, all of which adds up to a failing business. Negative stimuli contribute to low morale.

Stimuli are part of morale building, which together make up the motivational climate. As has been pointed out, motivation comes from within each individual. Simply removing negative stimuli and demotivators does not really motivate kitchen team members; it simply brings them to average satisfaction. Therefore, a chef's leadership qualities and supervisory style will exert a great influence over the team and will determine whether individual team members motivate themselves.

FEEDBACK

Feedback is not only a useful method of providing information to the team member on performance but also an excellent method of giving reinforcement and positive motivation. Quality feedback is driven by a number of factors. The first and most important of these is that feedback must be intended to help the person. Additional characteristics of quality feedback are shown in Figure 13-6.

The purpose of giving feedback is to reinforce the team member's commitment and abilities. It should be given when requested by a team member. Feedback should be given on two positive levels: *needs improvement* or *is doing well.*

Excellent morale within the kitchen is instilled by a chef who believes that most team members want to do a good job and in most instances will do a good job. The achievement and success of the team are the results of each employee at all levels of the team.

As Daryl Hartley Leonard, CEO of Hyatt Hotel Corporation, states: "If there is anything I have learned in my 27 years in the service industry, it is this; 99 percent of all employees want to do a good job. How they perform is simply a reflection of the one for whom they work."[15]

Figure 13-6
Quality feedback
characteristics.

- It is intended to help the person.
- It is given directly to the person (face to face).
- It actually describes what the team member is doing and the effects the actions are having.
- It is a description of a person's actions, not a type of person.
- It is specific, rather than general, with good, clear, recent examples.
- It is given at a time when the team member appears ready to accept it and as soon after the event as possible.
- It is given in private where other team members cannot overhear.
- It includes only those things that the team member can reasonably be expected to do something about.
- It does not cover more than the team member can handle at any one time.
- It is always given when asked for.

CONCLUSIONS

What motivates? As we have learned, each person requires different things. The expression "different stimulus for different folks" is perhaps the best way of summing up motivation, morale, and stimuli. In the kitchen, people want to join a team or pursue quality objectives that will enable them to realize their value and potential. They need to see that what they're doing is not wasted effort but is making a contribution to the kitchen team's goals. They must see value in what they are doing. Motivation comes not only from activity but also from the desire to become active members of the team.

As the positive work environment of the kitchen develops and gains momentum, team members will support what they create. Being part of the quality objective setting process is motivating; it allows people to feel needed and that their contributions *are* making a difference. When kitchen employees are given the opportunity to provide input, they have a stake in the issue. Seeing objectives reached and becoming a reality along with helping to shape the future is fulfilling. Participating in setting objectives and being empowered to make decisions builds team spirit; it enhances morale and allows each team member to feel important.

Recognizing kitchen staff for the accomplishment of particular tasks also contributes to team morale. Team members want credit for personal achievements and appreciation for their participation in the overall kitchen team objectives. Often, giving team members recognition is another way of saying thanks. Kitchen employees are motivated when they know exactly what is expected of them, and they will then have the confidence to do it successfully. No one wants to assume a task that is vague. Give clear instructions; make the unknown known.

Motivation rises in the kitchen when the objective goals and individual responsibilities are made clear by the chef. Don't discourage individual team members' growth. Encourage the team to stretch; give them opportunities to try new things and acquire new skills. Chefs should not feel threatened by the achievements and successes of individuals but should be supportive of their success.

Allow the team members to fail as well as succeed. Build the team's *esprit de corps,* which says to each member of the team, "If you grow, we all benefit." Chefs can establish morale through trust, direction, high standards of conduct, encouraging innovation, providing adequate training, treating each member with dignity, and being a servant of the team.

SUMMARY

Chefs cannot motivate individuals, but they can create a kitchen environment in which individuals can motivate themselves. Each person sees the world from a different and individual viewpoint. Chefs therefore should learn how each kitchen team member is likely to respond to different events.

Motivational theories have demonstrated that most individuals are highly motivated when they can see their value to the goals of the foodservice organization. Among these theories are Maslow's needs hierarchy theory, Herzberg's two-factor theory, Douglas McGregor's Theory X and Theory Y, Ouchi's Theory Z, Victor Vroom's expectancy theory, and the Pygmalion effect.

Morale within the kitchen is closely related to the leadership ability of the chef, who can create a happy atmosphere, show respect for individuals, seek their opinions, and build a team environment.

Stimuli contribute to motivation and morale. Negative stimuli such as put-downs, insensitivity, insults, sarcasm, and poor working conditions are considered demotivators, which damage relationships and destroy morale within the kitchen. Positive stimuli are necessary to satisfy the esteem needs of individual kitchen team members. Feedback is an important element of creating an environment where positive stimuli encourage team members to motivate themselves and the team.

DISCUSSION QUESTIONS

1. Define the following chapter key terms:
   a. Motive
   b. Motivator
   c. Motivation
   d. Hierarchy of needs
   e. Physiological needs
   f. Security needs
   g. Social needs
   h. Esteem needs
   i. Self-actualization needs
   j. Motivator-hygiene theory
   k. Motivator factors
   l. Hygiene factors
   m. Victor Vroom's expectancy model
   n. Morale
   o. Esprit de corps
   p. Trust
   q. Communication
   r. Stimulus
   s. Demotivation
   t. Feedback

2. What is the definition of motivation and how can the chef create the motivational environment within the kitchen?
3. What are the elements of Maslow's hierarchy of needs theory?
4. What methods can a chef implement to motivate the kitchen team?
5. What are the differences between intrinsic and extrinsic motivators?
6. What are the elements of Herzberg's two-factor theory?
7. What are Theory X and Theory Y as motivational concepts?
8. What is Theory Z?
9. What factors contribute to developing morale within the kitchen?
10. What are the effects of the use of positive stimuli?
11. Why is feedback important to morale within the kitchen work environment?
12. What effects do negative stimuli have on motivation and morale?

NOTES

1. http://www.merriam-webster.com/dictionary/motivation, 2011, Merriam-Webster.

2. Arthur Sherman, George Bohlander, and Herbert Crudden, *Managing Human Resources,* 8th ed. (Cincinnati, OH: South-Western, 1988), 290.

3. National Restaurant Association, *State of the Restaurant Industry Workforce: An Overview* (Chicago: National Restaurant Association, 2006), 9. http://www.restaurant.org/research/.

4. Ibid, pp. 10–11.

5. Abraham Maslow, *Motivation and Personality,* 2nd ed. (New York: Harper & Row, 1970).

6. Frederick Herzberg, *Work and the Nature of Man* (Cleveland: World, 1966).

7. Frederick Herzberg, "One More Time: How Do You Motivate Employees," *Harvard Business Review,* Vol. 46, No. 1 (1968), 55.

8. Douglas McGregor, *The Human Side of Enterprise* (New York: McGraw-Hill, 1960).

9. Ibid.

10. W. G. Ouchi, *Theory Z: How American Business Can Meet the Japanese Challenge* (Reading, MA: Addison-Wesley, 1981).

11. http://www.enotes.com/management-encyclopedia/theory-z, E Notes, Encyclopedia of Management, 2011.

12. Victor H. Vroom, *Work and Motivation* (New York: John Wiley, 1964).

13. Mary L. Tanke, *Human Resources Management for the Hospitality Industry* (Albany, NY: Delmar Publishing, 1990), 204.

14. http://www.merriam-webster.com/dictionary/morale, Merriam Webster, 2011.

15. Tom Peters, *Thriving On Chaos* (New York: Harper & Row, 1988), 371.

16. Daryl Hartley Leonard, "Perspectives," *Newsweek,* August 24, 1987, 19.

Chapter 14
Team Building

OBJECTIVES

When you complete this chapter, you should be able to:

1. Identify and describe the rationale for a kitchen team approach
2. Know and understand the principles of building a kitchen team
3. Identify the crucial elements of developing a kitchen team commitment
4. Define the elements of establishing goals and objectives for kitchen team building
5. Describe the key aspects of facilitating kitchen teamwork
6. List the major criteria associated with effective kitchen teams
7. Define empowerment
8. Explain the requirements of understanding and trust in relation to team building
9. List the steps essential to improving kitchen teamwork
10. Explain the requirements of inter-team dependence in the foodservice industry
11. Identify and describe the elements that contribute to the creation of an organizational "vision"

Case Study: Southerton Country Club

Bob Larson, the general manager of the Southerton Country Club, was excited about the inauguration of the Club's first annual Epicurean Experience. The Epicurean Experience was three days of food and fun for which club members paid a flat fee. The general manager consulted extensively with event planning specialists and chefs specializing in the various types of foods to be served, such as the roasting of a whole steer over an open fire. When the planning was complete and the menus determined, the general manager met with the chef and provided him with all the details and what would be required of his kitchen staff. To assist the chef with the specialty items, he hired a consulting chef to oversee the preparation of the major items for each of the nine primary meals.

The quantity and complexity of the foods being prepared required that the kitchen crew work overtime for five days before the event and every day during the event. The event was a major success. The consulting chef received tremendous praise from Bob and the club members for the outstanding food, service, and overall experience. Bob personally thanked the chef for the hard work of his staff.

Immediately following the conclusion of the event, Bob contracted with the consulting chef for a repeat performance the following year and began working with the consulting chef to develop menus and the event planners to create the theme. When Bob mentioned the planning that was taking place to the chef and other staff members, they showed little enthusiasm for the next year's event. Bob actually felt that they did not support a repeat of the event. Many of the staff indicated that they probably would not be available to put in the overtime required and that Mr. Larson might need to consider arranging for an outside crew to handle the event.

Based on what you have learned from previous chapters and the content of this chapter, answer the following questions.

- What is the overall reason for the challenges occurring in the Southerton Country Club?
- What are the primary causal agents for the challenges occurring in the Southerton Country Club?
- What role did supervision/management play in the decline in the Southerton Country Club?
- What specific steps could have been taken to avoid the current situation occurring in the Southerton Country Club?
- What, specifically, can be done to overcome the challenges and generate motion in a positive direction for the Southerton Country Club?

INTRODUCTION

No individual is more important than the others. People on the team share varying degrees of responsibility, but the success of the kitchen team is really determined by the performance of each individual, and the contribution of the individual makes the team effort.

> *Never tell people how to do things. Tell them what you want to achieve and they will surprise you with their ingenuity.*
>
> General George S. Patton, 1944

Teamwork is the fuel that allows common people to produce uncommon results:

Together

Everyone

Achieves

More

More and more management theories are being influenced by people who advocate teamwork, vision, trust, openness, flexibility, and participation. These concepts, ideas, and values form the core of team building.

An important reason why foodservice organizations seek to develop teams is because teams are more effective at improving work methods and providing high-quality food and service.

Part of the approach to quality management is to ensure that everyone has a clear understanding of what is required of them and how their methods relate to the foodservice business as a whole. The more people understand the total business and what is going on around them, the greater the role each kitchen team member can play in continuous improvement.

Teamwork, which is vital to successful management programs, has become the dominant form of organizational design. Critical to effective teamwork is the need to become an effective team player and, indeed, become a team leader. Chefs achieve better, more-inclusive communication with all staff in a team environment. This means that people skills have become extremely important, and even chefs will have to learn how to follow. The team approach to culinary supervision and management is also about chefs becoming coaches, facilitators, and teachers, rather than administrators, inspectors, bureaucrats, directors, and control agents. Chefs are builders of teams and developers of strategies of commitment from employees. They maximize the value of employees by improving the organizational resources, by fostering teamwork, and by rewarding contributions by individual team members.

According to Marshall J. Cook:

> "You don't want compliant subordinates. You want committed co-workers who identify their self-interest with yours and want excellent job performance. They'll work just as hard and just as well when you're not watching—because they're not working for you, they're working with you."[1]

A mature, well-trained kitchen/foodservice team is capable of making better-quality decisions than are individuals. The use of a team approach improves the overall quality of decision making, and the level of commitment becomes much higher. When kitchen team members share the process of problem solving, they are more likely to "buy-in" to the company's plans and to do everything possible to transform the plans into reality. Collective wisdom is virtually always superior to individual wisdom.

This team approach, therefore, offers to progressive forward-thinking chefs a positive management philosophy that gets results while at the same time respects each kitchen team member—his or her needs and capabilities.

Today, in many successful foodservice organizations, the most widespread form of employee involvement is through teamwork. Simply defined, **teamwork** is a group of people organized into teams—doing similar or related work who meet regularly to identify, analyze, and solve product, to process quality and operational problems, and to improve general guest satisfaction. There is a difference between a group and a team. A **group** is simply people who have been brought or gathered together. People in a group do not necessarily share common values or goals. A **team** is a group of people who have common values and goals. A team has a common purpose. The modern-day parable "Lessons from Geese," shown in Figure 14-1, speaks directly to what a team is and its effectiveness.

GROUPS AND TEAMS

What is it that most of us want from work? "We would like to find the most effective, most rewarding, and most productive way of working together."[2] Team building involves getting each employee to feel a sense of belonging and ownership in what they are doing as a kitchen team. It has been said that there is no other business that requires more teamwork than the restaurant business. However, with a team effort, and with

Figure 14-1
Lessons from geese.

When you see a flock of geese heading south for the winter and flying in a "V" formation, you might consider what science has discovered as to why they fly that way.

As each bird flaps its wings, it creates an uplift for the bird immediately following.

By flying in a "V" formation, the whole flock adds at least 71 percent more flying range than possible if each bird flew on its own.

People who share a common direction and sense of purpose can get where they are going more quickly and easily because they are travelling on the thrust of one another.

Each member of the flock is responsible for getting itself to wherever the flock is going: Each member of the flock looks to itself—not the leader—to determine what to do.

Every member knows the direction of the flock. Sharing the common direction makes assuming the leadership role easier. Every member is willing to assume leadership when the flock needs it. When the lead goose gets tired, a fresher goose from the back of the pack assumes the leadership position. This allows the flock to maintain the fastest pace possible.

Followers encourage leaders. Flock members honk from the rear to encourage leaders to maintain a fast pace.

Members of the flock look after each other, helping all members to achieve the goal. If a wounded goose goes down, two geese follow to protect and feed it until it either recovers or dies.

"If we had the sense of a goose, we will stand by each other."

When the nature of the work changes, the geese reorganize themselves for best results. They fly in a "V," land in waves, and feed in fours.

. . . Source Unknown

everyone helping each other, the job is so remarkably easy that few could imagine how it could be done any other way.

Dealing with a group of individuals is not quite the same as dealing with an individual. More is required when a person has to lead a team.

"Teamwork can be seen and felt—it is a tangible thing. The real problem is very often people are organized into groups; they are called teams but don't act like a team."[3] The words "group" and "team" tend to be used interchangeably, but one expression is central to both concepts and that is "common identity."

When is a group a team? If it is either, does it need leadership? If so, are there any special reasons that make the role of the leader more crucial in some circumstances than others? This is the central core of leadership and kitchen teamwork. What is clear, however, is that managers should at least appreciate their role as leaders and be able to see when the label "team" might be appropriate.

It is quite easy to spot sets of individuals who are not yet a team. They meet, and someone says "What do we do now?" or "Who is going to start first?" or "Who is going to do what?" ". . . Teamwork is one of the key features of involvement and without it, difficulty will be found in gaining the commitment and participation of people throughout the organization."[4]

When the concept of kitchen team building is adopted, it becomes easier to generate a continuous drive for quality. It also provides encouragement for each team member to work together to develop a kitchen team spirit. It helps people get to know each other so that they in turn can learn to trust, respect, and appreciate individual talent and abilities.

About Teams

Many leading foodservice executives see the formation of teams as a solution to the problems of continual quality guest–foodservice interactions. This means facilitating

Sometimes I think I'm spoiled because I work in a very controlled atmosphere. The Balsams Grand Resort Hotel is the only structure of any significance in Dixville Notch, New Hampshire. One-third of my kitchen staff are chef apprentices. They work, eat, and live there, and many of them play there. It's not surprising, therefore, that there is a sense of family, and what makes it so is a strong team spirit.

Teamwork is very important at the Balsams. For me, it's vital for professionalism in the foodservice industry. I coach our apprentices on the importance of team spirit and the value of helping and supporting one another within the kitchen team. Team building is part of developing our young chefs. In addition to cooking skills, they also learn how to interact with each other. They learn to respect each member of the hotel team and the contribution each makes toward ensuring that our guests have a wonderful experience at the Balsams. They appreciate the standards our team sets, particularly in the area of sanitation and professional courtesy, and most importantly, they learn to respect themselves.

The nature of our work at the Balsams is both physically and mentally demanding. We work most weekends and public holidays; we are here early in the morning and late at night. Therefore, constant ongoing coaching is necessary to keep our kitchen team inspired and motivated. Team building, I find, requires a conscious effort. I ask the team for their input every day. We have a five-minute meeting each night, at which time we discuss and assess the events of the day. Our apprentices are inspired by the different distinguished visiting chefs who visit the Balsams as part of our visiting chefs lecture series. We also encourage our apprentices to enter food shows. This is a great tool for developing teamwork. All the apprentices support the competition entry, which produces a great team spirit.

At the beginning of each "season," we come together as a group and brainstorm. We discuss ways to improve menus and production methods and we try to identify new food trends. I seek the opinions of our chefs on new dishes and have them critique these dishes. Together we establish goals for the forthcoming year. This involves the apprentices identifying what they see as priorities in their professional development.

Building a team is not an easy task, but without teamwork we would not be successful. We have a warm caring environment at the Balsams; each day we sit down together and eat as a group. Consequently, our kitchen employees are a team—they have a sense of pride in their profession with respect for firm, fair, and friendly leadership, and they have a strong loyalty to our hotel.

—Charles Carroll, CEC, AAC,
previously Executive Chef,
The Balsams Grand Resort Hotel;
currently Executive Chef,
River Oaks Country Club,
Houston, Texas

people working together, instilling a sense of teamwork, and recognizing the interdependence of all departments. The guest responds to the total crew and facility, not just the actions of one department. Plain and simple, a kitchen team is a group of individuals working together to achieve a common goal. A group of individuals performing their jobs to the best of their ability while supporting each other is successful teamwork. Members of the kitchen team recognize their interdependence and understand both personal and kitchen team goals. "Teams bring together skills and experience that collectively exceed those of any individual. . . . Consequently teams can respond to a variety of challenges, for example, process improvement, product development, or customer service, more readily and more effectively."[5]

When one person is unable to perform at 100 percent, the difference must be made up by the other team members. This places additional stress on teammates because they will have to work harder to meet the same goal. When this happens, it is clearly noticeable. It is extremely gratifying at the end of a successful day to know that all kitchen team members have pulled together and reached the goals.

DEVELOPING A KITCHEN TEAM

The development of a kitchen team requires the chef to think about a number of factors. One of these factors is why people become committed to a team. Figure 14-2 lists the primary reasons an individual commits to a team. The level at which each team member

- **Self-interest.** The person believes he or she will gain a personal advantage by being a member of the kitchen team.
- **Belief in a vision.** The person believes he or she is helping a greater vision come to fruition.
- **Belief in the leader.** The person feels loyalty to the leader of the team.
- **Common values.** The person shares the team's set of basic beliefs about what is said and what is not important.
- **Mutual support.** The person feels a sense of comradeship with his or her kitchen teammates.
- **Sense of duty.** The person is committed because he or she believes that this is part of the price to be paid for being on the team.
- **Demanding tasks.** The person is committed because he or she wants to achieve goals or a standard of accomplishment that requires the assistance of others.
- **Feeling of accomplishment.** The person is committed to the team because by working together, the members participate in a shared celebration of success.
- **Structured socialization.** New people are welcomed and are made to feel that they are part of the team.

is affected by these primary reasons will ultimately determine the level of that member's commitment to the team. The more that team members feel that it is in their best interest to be a member of the team, the greater commitment they will have to the team.

In the late 1970s a "new" philosophy of service was introduced to the dinner house segment of the restaurant industry. This philosophy of service, which is very common today, was a team service system. The server was no longer assigned a specific set of tables and held responsible for that set. The server was expected to work as part of a total property service team with the common focus of providing the highest possible level of service to all guests. This service system required a commitment by all team members to the success of the whole rather than just their portion. This service system was readily adopted. It was a good fit to the dinner house, where efficiency of service was considered by the guest to be as important as the personalization of the service.

While the service of the table by multiple servers diminished the personal aspect of the service to some degree, it made up for that in the efficiency of the service. Food came to the table hotter, beverages were refilled with greater regularity, and in general more of the guest's needs were met. This service system made the concepts of self-interest, mutual support, sense of duty, and common values real and very connected to the individual's and team's success.

The chef has the ability to build this same team model in the kitchen. Building the kitchen team begins with the chef communicating the connection between the team members' self-interest and the vision of both the company and the chef.

ORGANIZATIONAL AND OPERATIONAL TEAM STANDARDS

Ensuring that action follows insight requires the chef to establish the organizational and operational standards of the team. The more the team is involved in this process, the greater the "buy-in." The term **buy-in** is defined as the commitment of an individual to an idea or course of action. The standards include team composition, scope of team and individual responsibilities, performance expectations, performance appraisal, timelines, and resources. Determination of all of these characteristics will be based on the anticipated work to be assigned to the team.

Team Composition is the combination of the skills, knowledge, and physical and mental capability of the individuals and the number of individuals needed to accomplish the work assigned to the team in an effective and efficient manner. For example, composition of the scullery team will include individuals with the physical capacity to lift heavy items with a high degree of regularity. The team members will need to have been trained or willing to be trained in the proper operation of the dishwashing and pot washing equipment and janitorial equipment. The members of the scullery team may not need to have the required level of knowledge to determine and maintain the china, flatware, and glassware inventory.

Scope of Team and Individual Responsibility is both the amount of work and complexity of work assigned to the team and ultimately to the individual. For example, the banquet prep team may be responsible for the preparation of food for catering in the hotel, but they are not responsible for determining the supplies needed and making certain they are available. The scope of responsibility of the scullery will probably include, but not be limited to the ongoing cleaning, sanitizing, and returning to stock of all china, flatware, and glassware used in the operation. The determination of appropriate inventory levels of china, glassware, or flatware would probably not be part of their scope of responsibilities. An individual member's responsibilities will be based on his or her assigned work. The scullery team member assigned to dishwashing during a particular meal period would be responsible for the cleaning, sanitizing, and returning to stock of all china, flatware, and glassware used during that time as well as keeping the dishwashing area in an orderly, safe and sanitary condition.

Performance Expectations are the clear definition of what the expected outcomes are to be from the work assigned. For example, suppose that a banquet prep team is assigned the preparation of canapés for 500 guests. Performance expectations will include:

- ensuring the quality (taste, appearance, accuracy of recipe duplication) of the finished canapés
- finishing the canapés on time; completing the correct amount of canapés
- providing the canapés ordered
- presenting the canapés in an attractive and appetizing manner
- protecting the safety of the canapés during preparation and storage

Performance Appraisal is the evaluation of the completed work, which must be based on clear communication of how the performance will be measured. For example, measuring the team's attainment of the communicated performance expectations may include the following actions by the chef: random product tasting; inspection of finished products; regular inspection of preparation and storage areas, and guest satisfaction surveys. The effectiveness of performance appraisal is directly tied to the immediacy of the feedback. Once the appraisal is complete, feedback should be provided to the team and individuals with direction for correction and improvement.

Time is both the specific time requirements that come with assigned work and the general time requirements for the team and individuals. For example, a general requirement is that team members report on time for work and that they produce an acceptable amount of product during a shift. A time requirement tied to assigned work is an order for 500 canapés by 5:30 P.M. today.

Resources consist of the number of team members, equipment, and facilities needed for the team to perform its assigned work as well as the food cost and overall expense expectations for the team and its work. For example, the team has limited members, equipment, and space to use in the preparation of the 500 canapés that have been ordered, and this order is not the only one the team has for the day. Prioritizing

Figure 14-3
Team Objectives—SMART.

- **Specific.** Express objectives in terms of the specific results to be achieved, not in terms of the activities needed to achieve them, i.e., outputs, not inputs. Avoid ambiguity.
- **Measurable.** Identify what measures will be used to judge success. Make them as quantifiable and specific as possible, e.g., time/quantity/quality/cost. Use customer-related measures as well as internal measures.
- **Agreed.** The team should have the opportunity to discuss and buy into the objective rather than simply have it imposed.
- **Realistic.** The objectives are to be neither too easy so that talents are underused, nor too difficult so that the team may burn out. Take past performance into account in assessing realism. Be sure the objective is achievable given the resource available and the demands of other priorities.
- **Timebound.** The objectives should include a date by which they should be achieved. Also include interim milestones and review points if the overall timescale is long. Choose an appropriate time frame relative to the complexity of the task.

Build That Team Steve Smith

and using the available resources in an efficient manner will be necessary to deliver on all orders not only in a quality manner but within the team's food-cost target.

ESTABLISHING GOALS AND OBJECTIVES

Goals give a kitchen team something at which to aim. They may be broad, and they can be achieved in a variety of ways. An example of a goal might be: "*To improve food quality levels substantially.*" They are short, general statements of purpose and direction. On the other hand, objectives are very clear statements of what output you need to achieve. "*To reduce complaints in the dining room by 75 percent by year's end.*" Effective objectives are more comprehensive and, as shown in Figure 14-3, should be, according to Steve Smith, "**SMART**."[6]

The buy-in of team members is critical to the achievement of the team's goals and objectives. Shared kitchen team goals are present when all members have participated in a process that clarifies the kitchen team's collective goals. Effective kitchen team members know and understand the team's purpose, objectives, and performance measures. All members need to believe that the kitchen team's goals are both achievable and important. If the team's expressed goals seem to be impossible to achieve, team members will become cynical and demotivated. Frustration and discouragement are the consequences of a kitchen team's failing to ensure that action follows insight.

FACILITATING KITCHEN TEAMWORK

A team of foodservice individuals—kitchen team members, servers, stewards, storeroom, supervisors, management—requires much more coordination and integration of its efforts than does a "group."

Just because a group is called a team doesn't mean its members will automatically function as a team. Teams may appear to be easy to form and operate, but hard work is needed from everyone involved for a kitchen team to be successful.

The role of a "**team facilitator**" or "leader" consists of leading team discussions and group processes so that individuals learn, and kitchen team members feel that the experience is positive and worthwhile. "A **team leader** is the person responsible for assuring that people will want to work together to achieve a common goal or objective. The important idea here is to want to *work together,* so a leader does not need to coerce, but rather facilitates the elements necessary for the team to perform well."[7]

CHEF TALK
"TRANSFORMING A GROUP INTO A TEAM"

I began my mentorship with Dorsey High School (Los Angeles, California) in 2009 with innocent eyes and a passionate spirit, and with full enthusiasm I jumped right into the thick of its preparations for the Statewide ProStart Cooking Competition. My aims were to provide a comfortable, accepting, and open environment for the students to brainstorm, and to develop proper team building by allowing them to consult with one another and work alongside each other for this common goal, the ProStart Competition. I assured them that in every situation in life, they would be working in some sort of team, and the only way to determine the success of the team is to build it properly from the start.

During the first few months of preparation, the students had not grasped the sense of urgency and motivation needed for engagement in the competition. For example, when each student was asked to watch the pertinent videos and bring recipe books for our idea sessions, none of the students had followed through. In addition, none of the students had any previous culinary experience, which forced me to start from scratch. Another issue that I was forced to overcome was the fact that my socio-economic background differed from theirs and there was a gap between the two "worlds" that I needed to bridge. Thankfully, I was able to relate my culinary experience to theirs after learning examples of places where they enjoy eating out. One student gave IHOP as an example of a fine dining restaurant. After hearing some of the other students' responses, I needed to rethink my strategy of getting them to work together well with me as their guide and mentor. It took a lot of coercion plus positive reinforcement on my part for the students to accept me as their mentor and to see the importance of being a unified team.

The students' first task was to create a three-course menu together. Each team member was required to speak to the others about ideas, likes and dislikes, and culinary knowledge and experience. To initiate the team building process, I just casually conversed with the students about food in general. One student in particular spoke incessantly about grilling steak and how the only way he would participate was if steak was the entrée for the menu. While I admired his assertive nature and passion for the art, I explained to him that we must have consensus on having grilled steak as the team entrée. With that in mind, I explained to the group that each member must equally put forth their ideas. As expected, conflict arose since some wanted salmon while others wanted chicken. After much deliberation, however, the team did decide on grilled steak for the main course. The decision was worth the effort of getting the whole team to voice all their individual ideas and then as a group to discuss all the pros and cons of each idea, and finally to come to total agreement, thereby establishing the goal of the whole team, not of just one individual. It was very gratifying and inspiring to watch team members while I guided them through the recipes, as the group began to gel and develop cohesiveness, and I could tell that they felt as if they were part of something important and were proud of their team. When competition time arrived, the team was ready and confident with their menu. They cooked with and from their hearts and proudly participated as the Dorsey High School ProStart Team.

—Colleen Sabrina Wong—Chef Instructor,
Art Institute of California, Hollywood, CA

Typical activities for a chef include team activities in which quality improvements are assessed. In group discussions where all team members feel committed to the quality improvement actions, awareness of kitchen team efforts usually is enhanced. Participation by all is facilitated, and kitchen team members are invited to present their viewpoints, levels of expertise, and attitudes regarding topics of quality. Team activities stimulate thinking, create enthusiasm, and assist in analyzing different approaches to quality service.

DECISION MAKING AND THE KITCHEN TEAM

Often, in the past, chefs failed to invite comments or feedback on initiatives from kitchen team members. While our kitchen team members expect leaders to "take charge," leadership is also about service; therefore, the team that the leader represents must reflect the views of that team. The leader and team must share values and goals to succeed.

When people work closely together, what one person does usually affects the others. Yet chefs, without consulting kitchen team members or even notifying them in advance, often make decisions or take actions that affect them. Doing so, unfortunately, usually upsets the kitchen team members, who are kept in the dark, and destroys good working relationships.

Why do chefs sometimes neglect to consult those affected by their actions? Usually, the idea simply doesn't occur to them, or they assume there is no need. Perhaps the chef thinks he or she already knows what the kitchen team members will say, or are sure the right decision has been made. Because the supervisor believes he or she has the authority to do so, the supervisor just "tells" the other person what has been done and expects that person to accept it. But people do not like being controlled by others, even if what is decided is in their own interests. Kitchen team members like to participate in the decision-making process, even if they would have made the same decision anyway. The chef should always consult team members who would be affected by any of the new decisions.

WORKING TOGETHER

As everyone knows, it is possible to win at one level and lose at another: in other words, to get what is wanted, yet make an enemy; or to not obtain what is wanted, but strengthen a working relationship. That means thinking, "I will treat this person well whether or not I like what he or she thinks or does."

"Many believe that we should deal with difficult people in the same way those people treat them, by reciprocating what they receive. This may be called an 'eye for an eye' policy. If the other person yells at them, they yell back. If the other person insults them, they insult that person right back."[8] The "eye for an eye" policy is based on a traditional approach to justice. Unfortunately in a modern organization, it is largely ineffectual and even dangerous, because the "victim" is often harmed as much as the perpetrator. Reciprocation sets off a negative spiral and does not resolve anything.

Each of us sees the events in our own lives and other people's behavior from our own vantage point. Even though we each see only "part" of the whole, we tend to think that only our personal perspectives accurately represent what is occurring. Nevertheless, there are usually at least two sides to every story and many ways to view every incident.

Reason and emotion must be balanced. It is a fact that, in some instances, too much emotion can diminish performance. On the other hand, an organization with little or no emotion is dull and lifeless. Some experts say that the most effective leaders are extremely emotional—and even act as cheerleaders—about the goals they are trying to achieve.

Responding impulsively and emotionally to a difficult person usually only worsens the relationship, especially if one person is making the other person angry. A good working relationship with a difficult person requires a reasonable approach.

Sometimes, a kitchen team member is blamed for something that goes wrong rather than looking at how the whole kitchen team was working together. This undermines the individual kitchen team member along with his or her sense of belonging to the team. It also sends a message to the kitchen team that individual performance is more important than the entire kitchen team's performance.

UNDERSTANDING AND TRUST

Chefs cannot deal effectively with difficult team members or difficult situations unless they understand them. Most people assume that what other people say is absurd or untrue, so they try to imagine what could be wrong with them to make them say something so ridiculous.

Therefore, working relationships are better among trusting people. People who can be counted on to keep their word are trustworthy.

If I believe you will do what you say, then I perceive you as trustworthy. If I suspect you will not, your credibility with me is low.

Faith in people is fragile. Once broken, it is difficult to restore. Being trustworthy most of the time does not earn trust. Every breach of trust diminishes one person's confidence in another. Even if someone keeps his or her word nine out of ten times, others will remember the one time he or she did not and wonder when they will be disappointed next.

Within any foodservice organization, persons with authority are tempted to force or coerce people who are being difficult to make them comply. However, compliance through coercion (such as threatening harm) provides only short-term gains and long-term losses. All team members resent being coerced and eventually express that resentment in angry outbursts or acts of revenge. Coercion creates competition to see who will win, as methods to create win/win solutions are overlooked. Rather than solve difficulties, coercion usually just perpetuates or escalates them.

A difficulty should be seen as a problem that both parties wish to solve through cooperation. Both should be on the same side of the line, attacking the problem instead of each other. Managing difficult behavior is not a contest. It is a challenge to invent a solution that all team members support and feel committed to implementing.

It is tempting to scorn and reject people who do not fulfill our expectations. When disappointed, a person becomes critical and disdainful, slamming the door on communication and giving up on problem solving.

CHEF TALK
"TRUSTING YOUR KITCHEN TEAM"

I learned some valuable lessons with regard to my co-workers during my time with the U.S. Culinary Olympic Team. When someone is trying out for the team, it is initially an individual effort. Later, when the team is formed, it becomes necessary to retrain oneself for the team effort. A good chef supervisor in this case is one who can balance the many commitments. The demands from the U.S. Culinary Team may easily take more time than any other item such as your job or personal life. In my case, when the time arrived for tryouts, I had to make sure that my employer was willing and able to get me the time off and to help financially.

Fortunately, I was able to build a strong team of chefs at the club. This assured consistency in the quality of the foodservice operation while I was away. This required the employer's placing a great deal of trust in the kitchen team as well as in the chef supervisor.

Later, when I started my own restaurant, I used my time away from the restaurant in a positive way. Each time I had to go to a team practice, I made sure my guests knew about it, and when I returned, I cooked special Olympic meals and made the guests aware of what I was doing. I had my own local support group cheering me on every step of the way. My kitchen team also benefited from the experience by seeing the new items prepared and the projects I was working on. Being involved with the U.S. Culinary Team provided me with the publicity I needed to find qualified professionals who wished to work with me at the restaurant.

The important lesson I learned was that I could trust my team and leave my sous chef in charge. While that was a hectic time professionally, it also proved to be a very rewarding time when I, as captain, led our team to a gold medal. I could not have had any of this success without my kitchen team behind me. It also proved that by treating people with respect and demonstrating trust, they will always rise to the occasion.

—Klaus Friedenreich, CMC, AAC,
Chef Instructor,
Le Cordon Bleu College,
Orlando, Florida

Figure 14-4
Elements of inter-kitchen team dependence.

1. Foodservice organizations can be likened to living organisms.
2. The whole organism or system consists of a series of parts. Each part plays an important and vital role in the provision of a complete and high-quality foodservice experience.
3. If any part of the system is defective, it will damage the entire organization.
4. If kitchen teams are not sympathetic to one another and do not work together in a complementary fashion, the foodservice organization may break up. If the discord is serious, it could become irreparable.
5. A key function in maintaining a healthy foodservice organization is for the boundaries that exist among its parts to remain open, allowing for the exchange of ideas and information. If boundaries are closed, the organism itself (the foodservice organization) will be seriously damaged and possibly disappear.

INTER-KITCHEN TEAM DEPENDENCE

Often foodservice kitchen teams may regard one another as neutral but still fail to communicate or recognize their interdependence. In the foodservice industry, kitchen teams must constantly interact, because guests view a property as a total entity, not pieces, whether in the foodservice or hotel sector of the industry. They don't separate segments or portions of their foodservice experience; they react and evaluate the entire product or service. Elements of inter-kitchen team dependence are shown in Figure 14-4.

The process of improving inter-kitchen team dependence requires a conscious effort at cross-kitchen team communications. Also, if members get to know one another on a more personal basis, they may be more inclined to work together and to consider one another when making decisions. The need for personal contact becomes greater when the possibility of conflict exists.

Kitchen teams that work well together strengthen the entire foodservice organization. Each kitchen team has both internal suppliers and internal customers. As kitchen teams learn to collaborate, they overcome narrow thinking. Inter-kitchen team development also serves to strengthen individual kitchen teams.

> *Southwest Airlines has two customer types—external and internal. Passengers pay our way—they are our external customers. Employees are our internal customers. As CEO, I must endeavor to satisfy both. Dissatisfied internal customers generally care little if they provide satisfactory service. Therefore, all customers eventually become unhappy.*
>
> Herb D. Kelleher, CEO, Southwest Airlines

VISION AND TEAM DEVELOPMENT

A **vision** is defined as the ability to perceive something not actually visible, or to see the future, or what could be. A vision also describes the way things should be. If everything were just exactly as it ought to be, what would it look like? That's your vision. It is a product of the heart as well as the hand and head. The vision is values based. The vision is a statement that contains clear, inspiring, and empowering criteria.

Mission statements are very often referred to as vision statements, but a vision is not a mission statement. **Mission statements** are usually short, simple statements outlining what is unique about your establishment, items that positively distinguish it in the minds of everybody—guests and kitchen team members.

A vision describes not just where the chef wants to be and what he or she wants to be like, but why he or she wants to be there, making what contribution, and serving what purpose (beyond making a profit). The vision should inspire; if it doesn't, it is not much of a vision. If it doesn't, then the chef certainly can't expect it to excite or motivate the kitchen team.

The single thread that runs through all success stories is the involvement of team members in drafting a vision statement and empowering people to support this vision. Kitchen team members, managers, owners, and chefs who effectively communicate their organization's vision note significantly higher levels of job satisfaction, commitment, pride, loyalty, and clarity about the organization's values.

Involving kitchen team members in developing a vision produces powerful results. Kitchen team members can only be empowered by a vision they have contributed to and understand. Understanding is enhanced by participation.

Attributes of Effective Kitchen Teams

Often, successful kitchen teams share several attributes and demonstrate achievement in many areas. Leadership is shown by the chef who has the skills and the desire to develop a team approach and allocates time to team-building activities. Management of the foodservice team is seen as a shared function, as illustrated in Figure 14-5. Team members other than the leader are given the opportunity to exercise leadership when their skills are appropriate to the needs of the kitchen team.

Kitchen team members are committed to the aims and purposes of the team. They are willing to devote personal energy to building the team and supporting their fellow members. Even when they work outside the team boundaries (e.g., chefs may have worthwhile suggestions on elements of the dining experience outside their control), the members feel that they belong and represent the kitchen team.

The kitchen team climate encourages people to feel relaxed. The members feel they can be direct and open and are prepared to take risks. The kitchen team is clear about its objectives. It sets targets of performance that require members to "stretch" mentally.

Effective team structures allow for the lively and energetic solving of problems. Roles are clarified, communication is open, and administrative procedures support the team's approach. The kitchen team generates creative strength and new ideas from its members; innovative risk is rewarded and good ideas are put into action.

Team and individual errors and weaknesses are examined without personal spite to enable the members to learn from experience. Latent individual potential is often fulfilled through team membership. These members grow and become more outgoing and capable, and their professional competence is enhanced as they meet new challenges with one another's support.

Relationships with other kitchen teams are developed systematically. It is obvious in the foodservice industry that effective and cohesive interrelationships are vital. The guest thinks of the property as a total unit and evaluates the complete foodservice experience—not sections of it.

The effective team is one that is in the improvement mode continuously and whose improvement effort is supported by the actions of the chef and the organization. The type of support that the chef and the organization must provide is shown in Figure 14-6.

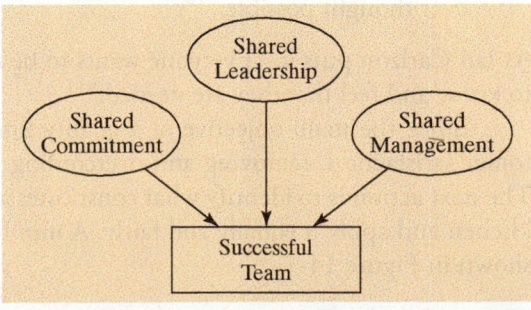

Figure 14-5
Management as a shared function.

Figure 14-6
Improving kitchen
teamwork.

Figure 14-6
Improving kitchen
teamwork.

Chef Supervisor and Organizational Support

- Support the kitchen team effort through the corporate culture of the foodservice organization.
- Sustain the kitchen team activities through the expected plateaus.
- Provide retraining or bring in an outsider to observe and report the findings to the kitchen team.
- Allow the kitchen team to work on problem solving, sorting through not just operational issues but also interpersonal and technical skills issues.
- Provide career paths and opportunities for some kitchen team members to transfer out of the kitchen team, if necessary, so that unresolved personality clashes between key people do not persist and drag everyone else down.
- Expand kitchen teams to all parts of the foodservice organization or work on removing external barriers that may be hampering team operations.
- Provide members with the full picture by providing information to give them more context.
- Make sure that personal and kitchen team growth is an objective.
- Refine and improve kitchen team development.
- Recognize team successes and make sure that the team receives a great deal of acclaim, approval, and visibility.
- Have a job rotation program where members learn all the jobs as well as gain a better appreciation of the interdependence of the job. This can help the nonperformer see the light and improve.

BREAKING DOWN BARRIERS

Every organization has a certain climate or culture. "That climate can be one that is positive, warm, and supportive . . . believe it or not, it can even be a climate in which people have fun and a desire to come to work."[9] To create the best possible kitchen work environment, a number of barriers need to be defined, addressed, and overcome. Many of the issues that create barriers are often not even noticed. Some chefs fail to anticipate or recognize potential barriers because of a lack of training, or perhaps even due to insensitivity and their thinking that their management style is okay because "I treat my team members in a much better way than I was treated." This type of thinking is irrelevant. The chef who adopts this type of thinking usually is one who fails to recognize the changing nature of the workplace and kitchen employees. Ted Balestreri and Bert Cutino, founders of the award-winning "The Sardine Factory" in Monterey, California, state:

> "We thought we had to do everything ourselves in the beginning. We realize, however, that there are people who can do things as well, if not better than we can . . . By bringing talent to the kitchen, giving them the tools, the authority, and the incentive, we found we have moved a lot quicker than we ever thought possible."[10]

As Jan Carlzon puts it, "Everyone wants to be treated as an individual; everyone needs to know and feel that they are needed."[11]

Since the main objective of a quality kitchen team is internal and external customer satisfaction, removing and overcoming barriers is the first step in that process. The next action is to identify what constitutes a positive team work environment in the kitchen and apply it equally and fairly. A number of the barriers to building a team are shown in Figure 14-7.

Figure 14-7
Barriers to team building.

- **Inappropriate leadership.** The chef supervisor is unable or unwilling to use a kitchen team approach and does not encourage the use of kitchen team building activities. He or she often uses a "command" decision style rather than a "consensus" decision style. The leader does not share his or her power or leadership responsibilities.
- **Unqualified membership.** Kitchen team members are not qualified (professionally or socially) to contribute to the kitchen team and as a result are unable to contribute to the successful completion of its goals.
- **Insufficient kitchen team commitment.** Kitchen team members are not committed to the aims and purposes of the kitchen team and are reluctant to expend personal energy on meeting the kitchen team's goals.
- **A non–kitchen team building climate.** The kitchen team's climate and culture discourage members from feeling comfortable, being direct and open, and taking risks.
- **Poor perception of possibility of achievement.** The kitchen team may not understand its objectives; or even if it does, it may not believe that they are worthwhile. It may set targets that are either uninspiring or unachievable.
- **Poor upper management support.** The kitchen team may be excluded from corporate planning. It may not understand or envision its role in the wider context of the foodservice organization.
- **Ineffective work methods.** Problems are not solved in an efficient, timely, and effective manner.
- **Lack of role clarity—who does what, when, where, and how?** Members' roles are not clearly defined; efficient communication procedures have not been developed; and administration are not supportive of the kitchen team's efforts.
- **Weak critiquing program.** Kitchen team weaknesses are not addressed adequately so as not to upset members.
- **Member maturity.** Members may not have developed the maturity and confidence needed to be assertive or to deal with other members' strong personalities.
- **A lack of creativity.** Members do not generate new ideas and are unwilling to take risks that may be discouraged by the organization's corporate culture.
- **Negative relations with other teams.** Kitchen teams that are not interdependent compete rather than collaborate. If kitchen teams do not meet to compare their plans and agendas, priorities may conflict.

EMPOWERMENT AND KITCHEN TEAMS

"Customer satisfaction means something different to every guest who walks into any of our 73 hotels and resorts worldwide. It's what a particular guest says it is on any given day. That's why it is so important that associates are truly empowered to meet our guests' expectations on the terms the guests use to define customer satisfaction. A guest satisfied with the accommodations and services we provide day in and day out is the one who will come back and contribute to our continued success."

Jim Treadway, President, Westin Hotel Company.

A customer is usually defined in commercial terms; for example, as a person paying for services or products provided. On the other hand, the term "guest" means something of a higher and more personal nature—a guest is someone we entertain in our home, someone we desire to please. This has an entirely different framework than that of a customer. Therefore, pleasing a guest is much different than satisfying a customer. Probably the only way to do this in a foodservice establishment is through the concept of empowerment.

What Then Is Empowerment?

According to Ken Blanchard, **empowerment** is the process of enabling people to do what they have been trained for and are qualified to do. People already have power through their knowledge and motivation—empowerment is letting this power out.[12] Therefore, empowerment means increasing the amount of control and discretion each kitchen team member has over his or her job. Empowerment provides involvement in decision making that supports the guests' level of quality and satisfaction. Empowering kitchen team members to take more initiative is viewed as essential to quality guest service.

Empowerment is also a key element in team building. There is no better way to have a shared vision and to generate commitment and loyalty than through empowerment. This results from pushing down the decision-making process to give greater latitude to each employee and then providing training that facilitates its inception.

Empowerment also seeks to improve the foodservice organization's performance by successfully solving problems that cause dissatisfaction for internal or external customers. Daryl Hartley Leonard of Hyatt Hotels stated:

> "We know we've got atriums and fancy-schmancy resorts, but if you ask people what makes them stay here, the answer always come back, the employees. A large portion of guest problems are not foreseen, so every employee has to feel empowered to correct a problem on the spot. Our guests should expect an above-and-beyond effort to fix any detail that goes wrong. In a service business, you can't have a rigid set of rules. You can have some guidelines, but you must allow people the freedom to make different interpretations."

Open and ongoing communications with and in the team are critical to the formation and maintenance of high-performing teams. Empowerment plays a critical part in those communications. Part of being empowered is the freedom to comment on and discuss, without fear of reprisal, the policies, procedures, and decisions affecting the team. Quality standards must be established and communicated, but their execution is ultimately in the hands of the team members. The chef cannot be everywhere at the same time, so relying on team members to perform is essential.

Empowerment does not occur in a micro-management environment. The chef who recognizes team members' need for the freedom and responsibility to make decisions about the methods for accomplishing assignments creates an environment of trust that drives quality performance. Part of establishing empowerment in a team is communicating the message that freedom to fail also exists. Team members who fear failure for whatever reason will not take the risks that are often necessary to find solutions.

Empowerment means actively seeking ideas from kitchen team members on how to improve. Empowerment comes from teaching others ways in which they can become less dependent on you. Therefore, empowered kitchen teams can do more than empowered individuals. Empowerment means encouraging innovation and allowing kitchen team members to implement their ideas. If the entire kitchen team is empowered and comes to realize that their opinions, views, and ideas are important, they will quickly take ownership of an innovation they have contributed and will seek to continuously improve it. Empowerment is not a substitute for leadership or a reduction of authority. The more the kitchen team is empowered, the greater the need for leaders who can set goals and define a vision.

The paradox of power: In order to gain power, you must give some of it away.

The outcome of empowerment linked with training includes operational improvements in areas such as problem solving, safety and sanitation, cost, production, and guest satisfaction; in other words improvement of overall quality. These improvements are accompanied by or generated from a positive work environment where individuals and beliefs are respected and the success of the team and satisfaction of the internal and external guests are the focus.

A GREAT PLACE TO WORK

Why would kitchen team members want to say this? Is it because the atmosphere is so relaxed, nobody bothers you, people come and go as they please, the chef is a "push-over," there is no harsh discipline, and the pay isn't too bad either? No, it has nothing in common with this scenario. Some reasons why kitchen team members believe a certain kitchen is a great place to work is because it is well led by a caring, sharing chef who believes in challenging the other team members to participate in the running of the kitchen, who delegates responsibility and empowers the team, and is sensitive to the team's attitudes and feelings. This chef believes in building morale and a team spirit, and his or her kitchen is a place where people are treated with dignity.

A great place to work is characterized by loyal employees who are proud of their work and organization and who produce high-quality meals that meet and satisfy customer needs. It is a place where the *kitchen team* encourages the chef, where high ethical standards are practiced, and where a shared purpose and appreciation exists among all team members. These items come first. Pay and working conditions, although they are part of "a great place to work," are not the most important factors.

As John Maxwell puts it, "I know that no amount of money, attention, privileges, and promises will motivate a staff member who really does not want to be on the team."[13] If a positive work environment where no intimidation or anxiety exists is created in the kitchen, then the motivational, training, and communication environment is also created.

CONCLUSIONS

The use of teams has become standard in the foodservice industry. The terminology of teamwork is used constantly, such as in a title like "Banquet Team." The question that must be asked is whether this is just a title or it is a description. Merely calling a group a team does not make it a team. When a team has been developed, its power is greater than the sum of its parts. In a team, the individual knows that his or her personal power is amplified by that of the team. The chef who builds a successful team has created a major resource for customer satisfaction both internally and externally.

DISCUSSION QUESTIONS

1. Define the following chapter key terms:
   a. Teamwork
   b. Group
   c. Team
   d. Buy-in
   e. SMART
   f. Team facilitator
   g. Team leader
   h. Vision
   i. Mission statements
   j. Empowerment

2. When the concept of kitchen team building is adopted, it becomes easier to create an atmosphere that continuously works to achieve quality. Explain.
3. Discuss the principles of building a kitchen team.
4. List the elements of kitchen team commitment.
5. What are the attributes of successful kitchen teams?
6. Describe the elements of a kitchen team environment that is conducive to great guest service.
7. What are the main advantages of empowerment programs in the foodservice industry?

8. Why is empowerment so important relative to dealing with guest problems and complaints?

9. List and describe the barriers to kitchen team building.

10. Why is it so important for the company to support the kitchen team effort?

11. Explain why inter-kitchen team dependence is critical to guest satisfaction in the foodservice industry.

NOTES

1. Marshall J. Cook, *Motivating People* (New York: Macmillan/Spectrum, 1997).

2. Ken Blanchard, John Carlos, and Alan Randolph. *Empowerment Takes More Than a Minute* (San Francisco: Berrett-Koehler Publishers, 1996), 23.

3. John A. Woods, *Teams and Teamwork* (New York: Macmillan, 1998), 56.

4. Dale G. Barrie, Cary L. Cooper, and Adrian Wilkinson, *Managing Quality & Human Resources: A Guide to Continuous Improvement* (Oxford, England: Blackwell Publishers, 1997), 31.

5. Steve Smith, *Build That Team* (London: Kogan Page Ltd., 1997), 6.

6. Ibid. p. 45.

7. John A. Woods, *Teams and Teamwork* (New York: Macmillan, 1998), 123.

8. Ken Blanchard, John Carlos, and Alan Randolph, *Empowerment Takes More Than a Minute* (San Francisco: Berrett-Koehler Publishers, 1996), 78.

9. Wolf J. Rinke, *The Winning Foodservice Manager: Strategies for Doing More With Less,* 2nd ed. (Rockville, MD: Achievement Pub., 1992), 206.

10. Ted Balestreri, *Nobody's Perfect: Lessons in Leadership* (New York: Van Nostrand Reinhold, 1991), 18.

11. Jan Carlzon, *Moments of Truth* (Cambridge, MA: Ballinger Pub., 1987), 5.

12. Ken Blanchard, John Carlos, and Alan Randolph, *Empowerment Takes More Than a Minute* (San Francisco: Berrett-Koehler Publishers, 1996).

13. John C. Maxwell, *Developing the Leader Within You* (Nashville: Thomas Nelson, 1993), 165.

Chapter 15
Respect

OBJECTIVES

When you complete this chapter, you should be able to:

1. Describe issues and elements that create fear within the kitchen work environment
2. List the steps that contribute to encouraging team members to give feedback
3. Describe the changing nature of the kitchen work environment relative to a diversified workforce
4. Define the elements of diversity and capitalize on diversity as an advantage
5. Reduce potential conflict among kitchen members resulting from cultural misunderstandings
6. State the elements that make up sexual harassment and describe the legal responsibilities of the chef in this area
7. State and describe the primary laws regarding equal opportunity in the workplace

Case Study: Alta Linda Regional Medical Center

John Kirby, the chef of the Alta Linda Regional Medical Center, was an excellent administrator. He had to be in order to ensure total quality for the patients in the 1,000-bed hospital. John had started working in kitchens when he was 16 years old. He had risen to be executive chef of the largest hospital in the state. He was responsible for an extensive kitchen staff that included line cooks, prep cooks, bakers, purchasing staff, stewards, and scullery personnel.

John worked very hard to maintain a team atmosphere among his staff. He had seen many changes in the individuals who made up the kitchen staff in his 40 years in the kitchen. He had learned to accept the changes in racial mix, the use of languages other than English, and the open acceptance of different sexual orientation. John considered himself to be open-minded and unbiased. He expected individuals to do their jobs and become part of the team. If they did that, then they got along with John. John's team members considered him to be good leader, manager, and chef.

John even tried to get along with the people that worked in the dietetics department. He did not feel they knew anything about how to cook. In fact, he did not think they really had true food knowledge. They were, however, responsible for assisting in developing the menus and providing the guidelines for individual patients' meals. John respected the importance of meeting patients' dietary requirements. John generally met dietitians' suggestions that moved beyond just dietary requirements with lack of interest or derision. John often made derogatory comments about the dietitians to the kitchen staff. He was quick to point out when a dietitian was large and appeared overweight. He always suggested that the individual pay more attention to his or her own diet rather than telling him how to do his job.

John suggested to the head dietitian that she should follow John's example in team building since the dietitians were not good team players. The head dietitian submitted a report to the hospital administration charging John with sexual harassment, discrimination, and abusive behavior to her staff.

Based on what you have learned from previous chapters and the content of this chapter, answer the following questions.

- What is the overall reason for the challenges occurring in the Alta Linda Regional Medical Center?
- What are the primary causal agents for the challenges occurring in the Alta Linda Regional Medical Center?
- What role did supervision/management play in the decline in the Alta Linda Regional Medical Center?
- What specific steps could have been taken to avoid the current situation occurring in the Alta Linda Regional Medical Center?
- What, specifically, can be done to overcome the challenges and generate motion in a positive direction for the Alta Linda Regional Medical Center?

INTRODUCTION

Do unto others as you would have them do unto you. This is a phrase that is often heard but also often forgotten when we deal with other people. It is the **Golden Rule**. Respect in the workplace encompasses many things, but first and foremost it must result in a comfortable work environment. A comfortable work environment is one where team members feel they are evaluated and judged by their performance and not their race, gender, or personal beliefs. It is a work environment that develops all team members to their fullest potential. Team members in a *Golden Rule Environment* don't do things because they fear the consequences of not doing them. Rather, team members do things because they want success for everyone, including themselves and the operation. Point 8 of Deming's fourteen points addressed driving out fear so that everyone may work effectively. According to Dina Berta, "Restaurants that can successfully brand themselves as a desirable place to work stand to have an edge in attracting

- Sensitive to issues and interests of team members
- Respectful of differences in people
- Open and participative in problem solving
- Anxious to use the power of their position to serve the team well
- Fair and equitable in the distribution of work
- Constant in their efforts to find solutions that are both technically and politically sound
- Constant in seeking individual team member input on decisions
- Willing to put the welfare of the team before private interests
- Never "better" than other team members
- Honest and willing to consider retaliation a sign of serious weakness

Figure 15-1
Characteristics of a Golden Rule Chef.

talent in an ever-shrinking labor pool, according to operators and personnel experts."[1] The *Golden Rule Environment* is key in branding an operation as a desirable place to work.

In the foodservice industry, and the kitchen in particular, the use of fear as a tool of control was not uncommon in the past. The myths and legends of chefs that berated, threatened, and verbally abused the kitchen staff contain all too much fact. The industry and the chef have changed in recent decades. Effective chefs, and management at all levels, recognize that fear is harmful to the foodservice organization and to the individual kitchen team member. The use of fear as a tool of control prevents people from thinking: "It robs them of pride and joy in their work and kills all forms of intrinsic motivation. The thinking and creative potential of the workers are stopped cold."[2] Most chefs who rely on fear believe that those working under them are incapable of thinking, and this concept becomes a self-fulfilling prophecy.

Chefs may not be able to eliminate *all* fear from the minds of all the kitchen team members, but they can eliminate *the sources of* fear built into the management structures.[3] Figure 15-1 shows characteristics of the chef that generate a *Golden Rule Environment*, an environment free of management-generated fear.

According to Ryan and Oestreich,[4] chefs who use threatening and abusive behavior ". . . immediately destroy trust and end communication. They create a thick wall of antagonism and resentment." No one respects a chef who repeatedly puts others down or loses control of his or her temper. Elements of threatening or abusive actions or behaviors that demean, humiliate, isolate, insult, and threaten team members are shown in Figure 15-2.

- Silence and glaring eye contact
- Snubbing or ignoring people
- Insults or put-downs
- Blaming, discrediting
- Aggressive, controlling manner
- Threats about the job
- Yelling and shouting
- Angry outburst or loss of control
- Physical threats
- Racial, ethnic, or gender slurs
- Blatant or discriminatory comments

Figure 15-2
Elements of Threatening or Abusive Action.

RESPECT AND CRITICISM

A primary responsibility of any chef is the quality of the team's work. Achieving quality outcomes requires evaluation of team member performance. Performance evaluation is fully effective only when the findings are reported to the individual being evaluated. The findings are not always positive, but the goal must be to use the knowledge of both positive and negative performance as a vehicle for improvement of performance. This can be accomplished only when "respect" is part of the workplace. Criticism is never easy for an individual to accept, but when it comes from someone that an individual respects and knows respects him or her, it is easier to accept. It is the accepting of, and ultimately acting on the criticism that brings about improved performance.

A chef who gives the team member negative feedback in a positive manner is demonstrating respect for the individual. The following are guidelines to giving negative feedback in a positive manner:

Limit the comments to the team member's behavior. Don't label the person as always stubborn, difficult, or easy-going. Do not criticize the *person;* focus on the *activity,* not on the type of individual he or she is. Be specific and don't generalize about a particular behavior.

Criticize as quickly as possible following the problem. The problem is fresh in the mind of the team member, so you will probably get a more accurate response.

Listen carefully to what individual team members have to say. Get their opinion; let them tell you what went wrong. Ask what they think the problem is. Do not prejudge an answer. Keep an open mind to what you hear.

Be considerate. Get your point across without being loud, rude, or abrupt. Losing control will put the other person on the defensive and probably won't help you solve the problem or determine its cause.

Don't present criticism with praise. This sends a confusing message. Often there is a tendency to want to say something nice to soften the blow. It rarely works; it may blunt the criticism, but the praise means nothing. The team member hears only the bad news.

Don't trap or humiliate kitchen team members. If a complaint is received from a customer, the chef should be straightforward in talking with the team member about the complaint.

Don't blame the entire kitchen department for a problem. Mistakes happen. It may be someone's fault, but as a chef, you should not generalize and accuse the entire kitchen team of acting poorly.

Verbal criticism is usually less severe than written criticism. Unintended results may occur as a consequence of written criticism. It can be far more severe than verbal criticism, and it becomes part of the individual's record, which could affect promotions and layoffs. The kitchen team member may not have had an opportunity to respond or explain what occurred. Written criticism remains an issue for an extended period of time, and comments made may lack clear meaning because the tone of voice or any further explanation is not available to the reader. Criticism should also be communicated in private. Choose a time that will facilitate solving the problem. Generally, the best time to criticize is early in the day so that the team member can get on with the job.

Encourage the kitchen team to give you feedback. Encouragement communicates trust, respect, and a belief in someone else. Discouragement results in lowered self-esteem and alienation from others. A discouraging chef is one who constantly criticizes and points out mistakes and has unrealistic expectations of others and does

Figure 15-3
Phrases of Encouragement.

"You did a good job."
"What did you learn from that mistake?"
"Keep trying; you will succeed."
"Great improvement."
"If you need any help, let me know."

Figure 15-3
Phrases of Encouragement.

not allow for mistakes. Examples of phrases used by an encouraging chef are shown in Figure 15-3.

The difference between the best kitchen team members and the average ones often depends on the leadership style and ability of the chef. A good chef can turn some average team members into outstanding performers. It is what the chef does that influences performance. Sincerity is of the utmost importance. If team members are treated with respect, then they are their own best source of motivation. Ferdinand Metz, Executive Dean and Chair of Le Cordon Bleu's National Advisory Board, recommends: "Build a team that will work towards a common objective. Lead by example. Always be willing to do what you ask others to do. They will respect you for this."[5] The Chef Talk by Dr. Silkes discusses what it was like for a woman in the kitchen in the 1980s. The Chef Talk by Jennifer Shen describes what it is like for a woman in the kitchen in 2011. As you will see, respect is still an issue in the kitchen today.

CHEF TALK
"PERMISSION TO SUCCEED"

When I went to culinary school, my class makeup was 50% female. I remember thinking, "This can't be so bad; there are a lot of people just like me who desire to cook." When I went to work in a hotel kitchen, I was the only female. I never really gave it much thought, though. I just figured if you worked hard, showed up on time, and possessed a strong interest in your job and the company, you would get promoted.

I started as a prep cook and worked in banquets, then graduated to line cook but was placed in garde manger making salads and desserts. I wasn't allowed to move over to the hot line. I was never given a chance. Male cooks were hired and moved to the hot line with less experience and no formal training.

One day, I asked the chef to move me to the hot line. I told him I was ready for a chance. His response was, "The hot line isn't what you were cut out to do. Let the guys handle the hot line. You do such a great job with the salads and desserts. We really need you there."

About a week later, I got my big break on the hot line when a line cook called in sick. I stepped up to grill spot and just started prepping the station for service. When the replacement guy came up from the back to fill in for the no-show, I sent him to the salad and dessert station. He didn't question where he was working because he was a fill-in and I had been in the kitchen for a year. I was busy prepping the grill station and looked like I knew what I was doing.

I worked the grill for the first time, working 200 covers with no returns. It was one of my greatest days in the kitchen. I remember thinking that I know what I want to do for the rest of my life now. I felt like I could do anything after that!

The next day, the chef called me into his office. I remember thinking that I was going to get fired for the stunt I pulled, telling a guy to work my dessert station. The chef asked me who taught me to work a grill so effectively. I told him, no one really; I had been watching the grill cook for months and was just waiting for the day he called in sick. He laughed and told me to get back to work at my new station on the hot line.

Looking back, that was probably a turning point for my career, a defining moment. I was waiting for an opportunity to prove myself, to say that I was just as good as the guy standing next to me. I figured out that I wasn't just as good, I was better. I kept waiting for someone to give me permission to succeed. In the end, I just took it. I don't regret my time at that hotel. The lesson that I learned was priceless, and it changed me. It made me a better chef, really, and a better person. When I became executive chef and had to make the promotion decision, I watched and listened to my employees. I gave everyone permission to succeed.

—Dr. Carol Silkes, CEC, CCE,
Assistant Professor, Kemmons Wilson School at the
University of Memphis,
Memphis, TN

CHEF TALK
"NO EXCUSES"

As a woman working as a professional chef in this industry, I recognized early on that my biggest disadvantage in a kitchen would be to surrender to the fact that I am at a disadvantage simply because I am a woman.

My parents were very skeptical when I first showed interest in cooking professionally. My mother argued that it would be too hard for me physically. She thought that I would face too many challenges. She grew up in a different time.

I pursued . . .

In the first restaurant kitchen I worked in, the hotline was comprised of 25% women. Thinking of it now, as uncommon as an all-female hotline would be, today it is almost as unusual to see an all-male hotline as well.

Times have certainly changed . . .

The female cooks were tough. They were what you would imagine a person who has been judged and risen above expectations over and over again to be like. They were forces of nature and somewhat maternal, which helped to balance an otherwise testosterone-filled kitchen. On the surface, they were like every other cook: incredibly passionate, full of desire to please, and with the same drive to compete and be better than the person standing next to them.

Learning to fight . . .

Of course, there is still judgment and challenge for women in a modern kitchen. As I grew acclimated to kitchen life, I soon recognized that people would not just hand you respect, you have to fight for it. I noticed that the male cooks did not take me as seriously. When I needed to be heard, I would find myself screaming. It seemed to be the only thing that worked, but it made me appear emotional and out of control. I learned to find strength from the women who surrounded me and it helped me to accept the adversity and make it my greatest ally. Others' doubting me became my reason for succeeding, and gave me an opportunity to prove them wrong. As I began to progress as a cook, my confidence grew. It was not about being a woman or a man anymore; it was about who could do the job—who would do it well, who could complete it the fastest, and so on.

As I continue to pursue my career, the function of my job has evolved from focusing solely on developing technical skill; it has become more about teaching, coaching, inspiring, and motivating others. My mentors have embodied all of these things and have shown me how to hold myself to the highest standards of personal integrity. The best teachers I have had have taught me that I should make no excuses for myself, which includes never pretending that I am at any disadvantage, and that respect is a privilege that will be earned along the way.

—Jennifer Shen-Seto
Pastry Chef, Wolfgang Puck CUT,
Singapore

DIVERSITY

"According to the Census Bureau, the ethnic population of the United States will continue to rise. Projections show that by 2050, Hispanics will account for more than 24% of the population, Blacks will make up over 13% and Asians will account for almost 9%."[6]

The foodservice industry has always had higher numbers of minorities and women than most other industries in the United States. The diversity in the restaurant workforce is not diminishing. "Results show a 3% increase in the number of corporate executives from an ethnic/racial minority group from 2004 to 2005. The most diverse groups of employees work at the hourly level, where 50% of workers represent an ethnic/racial minority group a 2% increase from the previous year's findings. In addition, the ethnic diversity of unit level management increased 3% from 2005."[7] According to the National Restaurant Association, in 2006, 72% of the restaurant industry workers were women and minorities.[8]

As we move further into the twenty-first century, the foodservice industry is faced with issues of supervising not only greater numbers of people, but also a more diverse workforce. Supervision within the kitchen requires a greater respect for the values and cultures of all kitchen team members. An establishment that values diversity is one in which kitchen team members learn to appreciate individuality and avoid prejudging people. Encouraging an awareness of diversity will facilitate the discussion of assumptions each team member may hold regarding certain groups of people. "Understanding and accepting diversity enables us to see that each of us is needed: recognizing diversity helps us to understand the need we have for opportunity, equity, and identity in the workplace."[9]

"Now, companies are embracing diversity as a business focus and corporate value. Embracing diversity isn't just the right thing to do; there's a strong business case for it."[10] Acceptance of diversity by chefs can mean getting used to different accents or languages or people who dress differently. It means feeling comfortable with team members whose skin is a different color. Diversity in a team refers to the following physical and cultural dimensions that separate and distinguish us as individuals and groups: age, gender, physical abilities, ethnicity, race, and sexual preference. Miller et al. state: "Failure to understand and to respect the diversity of your employees can result in misunderstandings, tension, poor performance, poor employee morale, and higher rates of absenteeism and turnover . . . when diversity is respected, the working environment is richer."[11]

The first step in improving respect for diversity is communication. Establish a climate that encourages a free exchange of ideas. Explore how all team members come to the kitchen with a unique combination of backgrounds and influences. Start with yourself and your own background. Get to know your team members. Don't make ethnic- or gender-oriented jokes, and don't tolerate even good-natured jokes in this area. Encourage diversity and an awareness of different cultures through events such as special days in the cafeteria devoted to ethnic foods.

If individuals are having difficulty with English, be patient and encouraging. Ask them for their input. The fact that some people may not say anything does not mean they have nothing to say. Persons changing from one culture to another may experience culture shock, which may be manifested as fear. Encourage the rest of the team to understand and respect differences in people. The chef is the model. If the chef shows respect for team members who come from different backgrounds, the team will follow the example. The self-esteem of diverse team members remains intact if they believe their backgrounds are accepted and respected.

The following is abstracted from a job notice that appeared in an advertisement in the *Boston Globe*, October 7, 1990. It demonstrates a comprehensive understanding of "valuing differences":

> In every aspect of life there is diversity. Accept this and you open yourself to endless possibilities. Close your mind to diversity and you are confined in isolation. Where one may see a problem, two may find a solution.
>
> We value and encourage the contributions of all. We recognize that while each one of us sees our own level of achievement, acceptance, and recognition, together we can attain higher goals. We can contribute to the well-being of our community by building strong bonds and implementing new ideas. This is our team—a group of people working together for the common good, while accepting the views, support, and uniqueness of each individual.

A kitchen work environment filled with ethnic diversity has the potential for conflict based on differences. This conflict may be based on misconceptions or stereotyping by the chef and other kitchen team members about different ethnic groups, languages, or cultures. Each side can misinterpret or dismiss the viewpoint of the other by failing to understand the framework in which the other operates.

DISCRIMINATION

Harassment

In recent times, harassment in the workplace has become mostly synonymous with sexual harassment. There are many forms of **harassment** in the foodservice industry of people who are different; of gay people, minorities, and physically or mentally impaired people. Federal laws, executive orders, court cases, and state and local statutes provide a broad legal framework that protects these categories of employees.

The Equal Employment Opportunity Commission (EEOC) issued guidelines on sexual harassment in 1980, indicating that it is a form of discrimination under Title VII of the 1964 Civil Rights Act. The EEOC states that sexual harassment consists of "unwelcome advances, requests for sexual favors, and other verbal or physical conduct of a sexual nature." The conduct is illegal when it interferes with an employee's work performance or creates an "intimidating, hostile, or offensive working environment." The *Uniform Guidelines* holds employers strictly accountable for preventing the sexual harassment of female or male employees. The EEOC also considers an employer guilty of sexual harassment when the employer knew about or should have known about the unlawful conduct and failed to remedy it. Employers are also guilty of sexual harassment when they allow nonemployees (guests or salespersons) to sexually harass employees. Where sexual complaints or charges have been proved, the EEOC has imposed severe penalties that include back pay, reinstatement, payment of lost benefits, interest charges, and attorney's fees. Sexual harassment can result in criminal charges if it involves physical contact. Damages are assessed against both the offender and the employer. The number of charges of sexual harassment received by the EEOC has declined from 15,889 in 1997 to 12,025 in 2006.[12] The percent of charges of sexual harassment received by the EEOC from males has increased from 11.6% in 1997 to 15.4% in 2006.[13]

Increasingly, foodservice organizations are becoming more proactive in the area of sexual harassment. There is a fine line between harassment, teamwork, and camaraderie. While certain working conditions in the foodservice industry may contribute to sexual harassment, it is people who commit the offenses. The majority of sexual harassment situations involve harassing women; but the occurrence of women harassing men is also on the increase. In both instances, not acting to prevent sexual harassment is the same as condoning it.

CHEF TALK
"PIONEER APPRENTICE"

In 1978 Elizabeth Tobin became the first female apprentice in my kitchen. Up until that time, options for female chefs were confined to working as "cooks," usually in hospitals or other institutions or as assistants in the pastry shop. The title "chef" was reserved for males only. From the first day, I insisted that Elizabeth break from the traditional mold set for women in the kitchen. At that time women did not even wear the traditional chef's uniform. It was difficult for Elizabeth; she was battling 100 years of male dominance in the culinary world of the Gresham Hotel. She encountered many difficulties, not least among them the idea that women could not handle the stress and tension of service time in a busy kitchen or the often "rich" language used in kitchens.

Elizabeth was a pioneer female apprentice back then. Not only was she an excellent chef, but she turned out to be a great role model for aspiring young female chefs. She rotated through all the departments and graduated with flying colors.

The purpose of this insight into the first female apprentice in my kitchen (which was also the first time the trade union recognized female chefs) is to outline the progression in thinking from 1978 to the present time. As I reflect back on that time, it seems almost inconceivable that culinary arts or the kitchen in general were male-only preserves.

—Noel C. Cullen, Ed.D., CMC, AAC

Chefs have a responsibility to recognize and prevent sexual harassment in the kitchen. Every organization must have a clearly defined policy on sexual harassment. It should be clearly communicated to every team member. The best cure for workplace sexual harassment is a policy and an educational program designed to prevent it. Policy statements should be in writing and should stress that harassment will not be tolerated. Figure 15-4 shows the fundamental elements of an effective sexual harassment policy.

Equal Opportunity Employment

The **Equal Pay Act of 1963** is considered by many to be the starting point of the Equal Employment Opportunity movement in the United States. This law was passed as an amendment to the 1938 Fair Labor Standards Act. The amendment requires that men and women in an organization who perform basically equal work receive equal pay. Although this law was passed in 1963, equal pay is still the subject of numerous lawsuits today.

Title VII of the Civil Rights Act of 1964 continued to emphasize equality in personnel policies. The law applies to all employers with 15 or more employees. Title VII prohibits employment discrimination based on race, color, sex, religion, and national origin. Employers that have fewer than 15 employees may be subject to state regulations. There are two exemptions to Title VII. The first one is when a business owner can prove that the discriminatory qualification is a **bona fide occupational qualification (BFOQ)**. Common examples of a BFOQ are women working in a women's

- A systemwide comprehensive policy on sexual harassment should be developed. Experts in the area of sexual harassment should be involved in its preparation. This policy should be part of all new employee induction and orientation training programs. Current employees should be made aware what the policy is, and a strong organizational statement condemning sexual harassment should be issued by management.
- Chef supervisors should receive training in how to prevent sexual harassment in the kitchen.
- Procedures for dealing with complaints in this area should be established.
- Action should be taken immediately to investigate complaints of harassment.
- Offenders should be disciplined and, in serious cases, dismissed instantly. The policy should be equally and fairly applied to all team members.

Figure 15-4
Effective Sexual Harassment Policy.

locker room and specific ethnic performers for ethnic performances. The other exemption is discrimination based on a **business necessity**. This is very narrowly defined and the employer must show that the practice is essential to its business. An example of a business necessity exemption would be the reassigning of pregnant female security guards to a desk position during pregnancy. The role of the guard position is to provide protection, and the pregnant guard's ability to carry out that duty is diminished. Note that in the case of both BFOQs and business necessity justifications for discrimination, the burden of proof rests with the employer.

Discrimination may be direct and indirect. The terms currently used are disparate treatment and disparate impact. **Disparate treatment** is when individuals who are being considered for employment or are employed by a company are treated differently based on race, color, sex, religion, national origin, or some other protected characteristic. **Disparate impact** is when a policy has greater impact on one group than on another.

In the restaurant industry, policies that have the potential to create disparate impact include uniform requirements, education requirements, and grooming requirements. The question that must be asked whenever a policy is being considered is: "Is the action the policy requires actually necessary for a team member to do the job? Does a head covering required by a woman's religion actually prevent her from doing her job or reduce the restaurant's business by ruining the perceived ambience? Today's chef, and all of management, must address this type of issue with an open mind.

The **Age Discrimination in Employment Act** was passed in 1967. This law prohibits employers from discriminating against applicants 40 years old or older on the basis of age. This law impacts all employers of 20 or more employees and all unions with 25 or more members. Common abuses of this law are firing older workers to hire younger replacements or promoting young workers over older workers.

The **Vocational Rehabilitation Act** was enacted in 1973 and bars discrimination against otherwise qualified people with disabilities. The **Pregnancy Discrimination Act** was enacted in 1978 and prohibits discrimination against pregnant women. The **Immigration Reform and Control Act** was enacted in 1983 and prohibits the recruiting and hiring of aliens who are not eligible to work in the United States.

The **Americans with Disabilities Act** was enacted in 1990. Although this Act was similar to the Vocational Rehabilitation Act of 1963, the terminology used is somewhat different. The Americans with Disabilities Act (ADA) also has broader application. The ADA applies to most employers, and the Vocational Rehabilitation Act applied only to federal contractors and subcontractors. Specifically, the ADA prohibits workplace discrimination against people with disabilities. The ADA also requires the workplace to make reasonable accommodation to create an accessible workplace for all qualified employees.

The **Family and Medical Leave Act** was passed in 1993. This act provides opportunity for employees to take up to 12 weeks unpaid leave for birth or adoption. Additionally, the act allows the use of the leave for care of an elderly or ill parent, spouse, or child, or to undergo treatment.

CONCLUSIONS

The chef is a critical element in any operation's success in creating and maintaining an atmosphere of respect in the workplace. The chef who models respect and makes it clear that all employees are valued will achieve that atmosphere of respect. The result will be a culture that encourages growth, embraces risk taking, and supports advancement. The outcome of that culture will be success for both the operation and the employees with pride in achievement spanning all.

DISCUSSION QUESTIONS

1. Define the following chapter key terms:
   a. Golden Rule
   b. Harassment
   c. Equal Pay Act of 1963
   d. Title VII of the Civil Rights Act of 1964
   e. Bona fide occupational qualification (BFOQ)
   f. Business necessity
   g. Disparate treatment
   h. Disparate impact
   i. Age Discrimination in Employment Act
   j. Vocational Rehabilitation Act
   k. Pregnancy Discrimination Act
   l. Immigration Reform and Control Act
   m. Americans with Disabilities Act
   n. Family and Medical Leave Act

2. Describe a Golden Rule environment.

3. What are the steps that can contribute to creating fear within the kitchen work environment?

4. What factors contribute to alienating team members within the kitchen?

5. What are the phrases a chef uses to encourage the kitchen team?

6. Women and minorities are often lumped together as a single class. What do these two groups have in common? What are the major differences between them?

7. How could a foodservice operation use diversity as a competitive advantage?

8. Why is management of diversity vital? Is this a temporary or long-term phenomenon?

9. When is sexual harassment illegal? What are the consequences of these illegal actions?

10. Why do chefs have a responsibility to prevent sexual harassment?

11. List and describe the primary laws affecting equal opportunity in the workplace.

NOTES

1. Dina Berta. "Building an Employment 'Brand,'" http://www.enewsbuilder.net/peoplereport/e_article 000733022.cfm?x=b11,0,w. Nation's Restaurant News.

2. Ibid.

3. Rafael Aruayo, Dr. Deming (New York: Carol, 1991), 184.

4. Kathleen Ryan and Daniel K. Oestreich, Driving Fear Out of the Workplace (San Francisco: Jossey-Bass, 1991), 75.

5. Ferdinand Metz, "Success Has a Future Perspective," Lessons in Leadership (New York: Van Nostrand Reinhold, 1991), 36.

6. Paul Frumkin, "At Your Service: Dining and Diversity: Catering to a Multicultural Clientele: As the U. S. Population Becomes Increasingly Diverse, Training Servers to be Sensitive to the Distinct Desires of Different Groups Becomes More Important than Ever." Nation's Restaurant News, September 2005, Vol. 39, Issue 38, 110.

7. Shyam Patel, Sr. Research Analyst. "Just Published People Report Survey of Unit Level Employment Practices Highlights Rapid Shifts in the Workforce." January 2007. www.peoplereport.com. http://www. enewsbuilder.net/peoplereport/e_article000733019. cfm?x=b8Rr58S,b520tHgk

8. Dina Berta, "Diversity at the Top: Quick-Service Outshines Other Segments with the Highest Percentage of Women and Minorities in Management Positions: Segment Study: QSR & Diversity." Nation's Restaurant News. February 6, 2006, Vol. 40, Issue 6, 33.

9. Max De Pree, Leadership Is an Art (New York: Dell, 1989), 9.

10. Richard Koonce, "Redefining Diversity: It's not just the right thing to do. It also makes good business sense." Training & Development, December, 2001, www.findarticles.com/cf_ntrstnws/m4467/12_55/83045836/print.jhtml, p. 1.

11. Jack E. Miller, Mary Porter, and Karen E. Drummond, Supervision in the Hospitality Industry, 2nd ed. (New York: John Wiley, 1992), 92.

12. The U.S. Equal Employment Opportunity Commission. Sexual Harassment Charges EEOC & FEPAs Combined: FY 1997—FY 2010. http://www.eeoc.gov/eeoc/statistics/enforcement/sexual_harassment.cfm

13. Ibid.

Chapter 16
Discipline

Outline

- Introduction
- Chef's role
- Approaches to discipline
- Administering discipline
- Approaches to positive discipline
- Exit interviews
- Summary
- Discussion questions

OBJECTIVES

When you complete this chapter, you should be able to:

1. Define discipline in its broader sense as it applies to the role of the chef
2. Describe the discipline parameters in which the chef operates relative to unions and the EEOC
3. Outline the steps in the progressive approach to discipline
4. State the guidelines for administering discipline in a fair and equitable way
5. Distinguish between positive and negative approaches to discipline
6. Define the strategies and rationale for conducting exit interviews

Case Study: Stone Lion Hotel and Conference Center

Bruce Connors joined the management team at the Stone Lion Hotel and Conference Center three months ago as executive chef. Jesse Atwood is the executive sous chef. Jesse has been working at Stone Lion for six years, working his way up from dishwasher. Chef Connors believes in empowering his staff. He believes in delegating duties and authority. He does not believe in micromanaging his staff once he has delegated responsibilities to them. One of Chef Connors's first actions as executive chef was to delegate the authority to hire and fire personnel to the executive sous chef, Jesse. His belief was that as executive sous chef, Jesse had a better understanding of the staff's performance and could make more considered judgments regarding their performance.

Today the Stone Lion Human Resource Officer (HRO) informed Chef Connors that the number of dismissals and new hires in the kitchen has been consistently increasing over the past two months. Additionally, one of the employees recently dismissed has filed a wrongful dismissal charge with the Labor Board. While preparing to respond to the charge, the HRO met with Jesse. The HRO asked Jesse why he had fired the individual in question. Jesse stated, "The guy's work was sloppy, and he was slow." The HRO asked to see the documentation of the employee's performance, and Jesse stated, "The guy was not in the new position long enough to document anything. I needed to get rid of him, so I got rid of him."

The HRO informed Chef Connors that the employee had been with the Stone Lion for 3 years with a previous history of performance problems. The employee had been placed in the new position by the executive sous chef two weeks before he was dismissed. The HRO stated that it was clear that the Stone Lion could not defend the dismissal. Either the former employee would be reinstated or a settlement amount would be negotiated to avoid further "fallout." The HRO also indicated that after speaking with the executive sous chef it was clear this was not the only incidence of improper dismissal. Chef Connors assured the HRO that he would meet immediately with Jesse and "straighten things out."

Based on what you have learned from previous chapters and the content of this chapter, answer the following questions.

- What is the overall reason for the situation that has arisen at the Stone Lion Hotel and Conference Center?
- What are the primary causal agents for the situation that has arisen at the Stone Lion Hotel and Conference Center?
- What role did leadership and supervision/management play in the situation that has arisen at the Stone Lion Hotel and Conference Center?
- What specific steps could have been taken to avoid the situation that has arisen at the Stone Lion Hotel and Conference Center?
- What, specifically, can be done to avoid a repeat of the situation that has arisen at the Stone Lion Hotel and Conference Center?

INTRODUCTION

Occasionally, a team member does something that requires disciplinary action by the chef. It may be an issue of job performance; too many absences; outright violation of an order, rule, or procedure; or some illegal act such as stealing, fighting, gambling, or involvement with illegal drugs.

The words *discipline* and *disciple* share the same root, which means to "mold" or "teach." True **discipline** should teach a correct action. Yet, many chefs think of discipline merely as punishment or reprimanding a team member for a mistake. The word disciple literally means "follower." Therefore, good discipline is based on leadership, which includes the ability to guide, coach, correct, and affirm the actions of others. Discipline is an inner force that develops within each team member and causes him or her to want to follow high standards in life and the workplace. Effective discipline is not just about reprimanding or inflicting penalties. True discipline involves an entire program that teaches and guides individuals to become loyal, motivated, responsible team players.

Discipline in a broader sense concerns the process of socialization. Team members are given the quality values and rules necessary for survival and growth of the foodservice organization. This process is complete when the team member comes to accept those values and rules as legitimate. Within the kitchen team, the rules serve a purpose and each member benefits by obeying.

Application of discipline has come to be split into two distinct areas. On the one hand, there is the traditional notion of discipline as punishment, and on the other hand, there is the positive discipline approach. **Positive discipline** is about exploring other ways for compliance with the rules. It is about reversing the concept of discipline as punishment only and emphasizes development along with encouraging responsibility and self-directed behavior. It is an extension of the training and coaching process.

CHEF'S ROLE

No chef enjoys the act of disciplining a team member, but this is an unavoidable part of the job. The kitchen may be running smoothly, with each team member doing his or her job well. Then a team member is careless, an accident occurs, and the chef must take corrective action. Good leadership ability minimizes the need to be punitive. If the team members respect the chef, then there likely is a good team atmosphere and it is easier to head off problems. Kitchen team members who feel that the chef is interested in their welfare will not be disruptive.

In general, team members accept rules and directions as a condition of employment and do not set out to break rules. These same team members will observe how the chef reacts with members who get out of line. Each individual is concerned with getting fair treatment. Team morale is lowered when members observe some individuals getting away with violating rules or witness unduly harsh discipline.

Before any disciplinary actions are contemplated, the ground rules for performance and conduct should be clearly communicated to the team. These policies and procedures are part of orientation and training programs. However, it is unwise to assume that they have been read and are understood just because they were included. Some rules need constant reiteration. These concern issues of safety and sanitation should be policed constantly. Team members must know from the outset what the penalties are for any rule infraction in this area. This information should not be in the form of threats and warnings. The rules should be stated clearly and succinctly: "Knowing the consequences has its own security: people know where the boss stands, and they know what will happen if they go beyond the limits."[1] The reasons for a particular rule should always be explained. Acceptance of a rule is heightened when team members understand the reasons for it. Rules and procedures should always be written, and the language used should be clear and unambiguous. If a rule has had lax enforcement, then the rule must be restated along with the consequences of its violation before disciplinary action can begin. While an individual must be advised in advance of all rules and their violation, some conduct can be reasonably expected to be generally known as unacceptable.

APPROACHES TO DISCIPLINE

Discipline should not only be fair and consistent but also conform to legal requirements. Despite worker protection laws, the EEOC reports that a high percentage of all charges filed are for discriminatory dismissals.[2]

Chefs who operate in a union environment have to take extra care when disciplining team members. Binding labor contracts set forth rules and procedures that must be followed, and they set penalties on management and workers for failing to abide by the rules. Even minor deviations from labor contract procedure can overturn an otherwise justified disciplinary action. These contracts usually contain a provision for impartial review or an arbitration process. Additionally, in union-organized establishments workers often have an increased awareness of their rights that may cause

The Hot Stove Rule Principles

- An unpleasant experience
- Immediate action
- Consistent punishment
- Impartiality

Figure 16-1
The hot stove rule.

some of them to challenge the chef's disciplinary decisions. This does not mean that no form of discipline is possible under union contracts. On the contrary, it may be easier. The nature of collective bargaining requires both union and management to be rigid and specific regarding rules and procedures.

Discipline and the Hot Stove Rule

A hot stove with its radiating heat gives a *warning* that it should not be touched. Like those who violate a rule, team members who ignore the warning and touch the hot stove are assured of being burnt. The hot stove immediately burns each person who touches it in the same manner. Therefore, disciplinary policies should be administered quickly and impartially. Team members should be disciplined for what they have done, not because of who they are. The four principles of the hot stove rule are shown in Figure 16-1.

Generally, discipline is imposed in a progressive manner. By definition, **progressive discipline** is the application of corrective measures by increasing degrees. It should motivate team members to take corrective action on misconduct voluntarily. This progressive approach is aimed at nipping the problem in the bud by utilizing only enough corrective action to remedy the problem. The sequence and severity of the disciplinary action varies with the type of offense and the circumstances surrounding the misconduct. Following is a typical sequence of progressive discipline:

Step 1: Oral reprimand: When a team member makes an immediate change in the way something is done or breaks a minor rule, an oral reprimand may be appropriate. In general these reprimands should be made in private, away from other team members. The rule is to "discipline in private, praise in public." The chef should ensure that he or she makes clear and specific what should be stopped (or started). Remember, most people fear public embarrassment more than the discipline action itself. In the course of the reprimand, be firm and fair. Do not argue or debate side issues, but treat the individual with respect. Sometimes, however, it is necessary to reprimand instantly without first considering an individual team member's sensitivity. This concerns misconduct in the critical area of food sanitation and safety. Because of potential hazardous risks to public health, the chef should react immediately. When this happens, it is best to soften the reprimand as much as possible. The important point is to stop the team member from continuing the harmful action. As with all elements of discipline, actions requiring reprimands should always be documented. A record of the oral reprimand is made and placed in the individual's personnel file with a note that it is not a "written reprimand."

Step 2: Written reprimand: For the second offense, the team member receives a written reprimand. Typically, this informs the team member that his or her conduct is in violation of rules or procedures and that further violations will result in suspension or loss of pay. The written reprimand must be signed by the chef and the team member. The team member's signature is an acknowledgement, not of agreement with the reprimand, but that they have seen the notice. Normally, the team member has the right to place a written response to the reprimand in the personnel file. Copies of this reprimand are also given to the union steward, if this is applicable. If the team member

CHEF TALK
"USING THE CORRECT LANGUAGE"

Working as an executive chef in a highly unionized hotel requires careful disciplinary strategies. Not least among them is knowledge of all the elements of the union/hotel contract and using appropriate language in the disciplinary process. I learned an important lesson on this subject when I dismissed a dishwasher.

Following a late-night banquet, I was summoned to the pot washing area in the kitchen. There I met "Joe," a dishwasher who was employed as a night porter. His job was to wash and sanitize the kitchen pots, pans, and utensils and prepare the kitchen for the breakfast chef. When I came upon Joe he was staggering around the dish room, dripping wet. (He had fallen into the large pot sink and had been rescued by the manager, who had summoned me.) There was a strong smell of alcohol from him. I asked him what had happened. How had he fallen into the sink? In his response he was barely coherent, his eyes rolling; he could hardly stand upright. He clearly was in no condition to work. I informed him that the best thing was for him to go home and come to see me the following day. Joe arrived the next day, and I informed him that I was recommending his discharge. I felt comfortable with my decision. He had exhausted all previous disciplinary steps and had been warned verbally and in writing, with each warning appropriately documented.

However, I was not prepared for what was to follow. Within a week I was summoned to the general manager's office. There I found not only the manager but also Joe and his union representative. Following preliminary discussion to establish the sequence of events leading up to the disciplinary action, I was asked by the union official why I had dismissed Joe. At this stage I was feeling rather agitated by what I considered to be a waste of time, going over what I felt was an obvious open-and-shut termination action. I responded, "Because Joe was drunk on duty."

The union official turned to me and asked me what credentials I possessed that enabled me to make such a judgment, "Was I a qualified medical doctor?" I was taken aback. Looking at the union official, I said, "You know what my credentials are!"

The end result of that meeting was that Joe had to be reinstated with full pay because I had accused him of being "drunk." What I should have said was, "His condition would lead any reasonable person to believe he was under the influence of alcohol." Joe's excuse to the union was that on that particular night he had taken medication for an ear infection, which gave him the appearance of being under the influence of alcohol.

Within six weeks, Joe was again discovered on duty in a similar condition. This time I made sure I had a colleague with me to witness the situation. Joe was dismissed, but this time I used the correct language.

—Noel C. Cullen, Ed.D., CMC, AAC

is probationary, the letter will usually indicate that improved performance is necessary. Probation should be handled in writing so that a written record exists in the event that termination is necessary if the required improvement does not occur.

Step 3: Suspension: Violations of rules and minor illegal acts often are treated with a temporary layoff or suspension. This suspension is without pay and consistent with the seriousness of the offense. The details are written and handled the same as the written reprimand. This written communication indicates also that another violation will call for discharge.

Step 4: Termination: If, after the third offense, it appears that there is little chance of bringing the individual's performance up to an acceptable level, termination may be the best course of action. It is presumed that the team member has been given every opportunity to conform. It is at this point that the documentation of each previous step becomes critical.

Some infractions are so serious that discharge is permitted with the first violation. Cases involving instant dismissal are rare. They usually involve illegal acts or serious misconduct that threatens the safety and security of other individuals or the foodservice organization. Team members must be given an opportunity to improve, and specific reasons for discharge must be documented. This category also includes requested resignations. When it appears that the foodservice organization is not meeting a team member's interests, it may be appropriate to request him or her to seek employment elsewhere: "The decision to discharge an employee must be based on quality and quantity of evidence, not hearsay, personal prejudices, speculation, or rumors."[3] Some of the

Figure 16-2
Major violations leading to immediate dismissal.

- Possession of, drinking, smoking, or being under the influence of intoxicants or narcotics on the foodservice establishment's property
- False statements or misrepresentation of facts on employment application forms
- Sleeping on the job
- Stealing company or personal property
- Fighting on company property
- Issues that threaten the well-being of team members or guests
- Gross discourtesy to guests
- Gross negligence involving sanitation/safety
- Excessive absenteeism without prior notification
- Sexual harassment
- Refusing to follow reasonable job-related directives from the chef

(These violations are basic and are not intended to be all-inclusive or cover every situation that may arise.)

Figure 16-2
Major violations leading to immediate dismissal.

major violations that frequently require dismissal are shown in Figure 16-2. Some of the violations requiring progressive discipline are shown in Figure 16-3.

ADMINISTERING DISCIPLINE

Discipline should be administered as soon as possible after the infraction has taken place or has been noticed. For the discipline to be most effective, it must be taken immediately without involving emotional or irrational decisions. Notation of rule infractions in a team member's record does not constitute advance warning and is not sufficient to support disciplinary action. A team member must be advised of the infraction for it to be considered a warning. Noting that the team member was warned about the infraction and having him or her sign a form acknowledging the warning are both good practices. Failure to warn a team member of the consequences of continuous rule violation is one reason often cited for overturning a disciplinary action.

The chef must recognize that each act of discipline is different and that each team member must be handled differently. The better the chef knows all team members and how they react, the better he or she can handle disciplinary actions. Sometimes, negative reactions are experienced. For example, rather than being motivated to improve performance, a team member may be motivated to retaliate or "get even." The following guidelines will help ensure a positive reaction.

- Tardiness
- Absence for one day without notifying supervisor
- Leaving the kitchen without permission
- Use of abusive language
- Not performing to set quality standards
- Disorderly conduct during working time
- Racial slurs
- Obscene or immoral conduct

(These violations are basic and are not intended to be all-inclusive or cover every situation that may arise.)

Figure 16-3
Violations leading to progressive discipline.

Discipline and the Offense

Match the discipline to the offense. A trivial rule infraction does not require harsh or unreasonable discipline. A team member's previous record must be considered. Determining the appropriateness of the discipline action involves serious consideration of:

- The circumstances surrounding the incident
- The seriousness of the incident
- The previous record of the team member
- The disciplinary action taken in similar situations
- The existing rules and disciplinary policies
- The provisions in the labor contract (if applicable)

The chef must take the correct steps and stay calm to effectively match the discipline with the offense.

Know the facts: Investigate thoroughly. Determine who was involved in the incident, what happened, where it happened, and what the team member's involvement was.

Interview: Discuss the discipline problem with the team member in private. Keep it as informal as possible to allow the discussion to proceed calmly.

Listen: First, the chef should ask the team member to tell his or her side of the story. Ask questions to get further details; try not to interrupt until the individual has finished. Listen with an open mind. Do not prejudge the situation.

Stay calm: Control feelings and emotions. Do not argue. Do not engage in any type of name-calling. The chef may win the argument, but will lose the loyalty and contribution of an important team member.

Avoid entrapment: Do not set out to "get" a team member. Do not get involved unless something is wrong.

Be firm but fair: Being firm does not suggest getting tough. Being firm but fair involves explaining to a team member why behavior is unacceptable. Do not humiliate the team member in any way.

Document: Make notes on what happened and what the resulting action was. Records of disciplinary action are important for the purpose of demonstrating later on that there was a fair and equitable resolution of the incident.

Inform others: Be sure to inform the team member of the intended course of action. Remember, the chef is not the final voice in matters of discipline. The foodservice organization and the union (if applicable) should be informed. Matters of serious discipline are much too important for one person to decide.

It is always a good idea for the chef to discuss intended disciplinary actions with other members of the foodservice establishment's management or with members of the human resources department. These are the people who have to support the chef's actions. It is also wise and prudent to discuss intended disciplinary action with a trusted colleague. This will help to establish a better perspective for the action.

Terminating a Team Member

Before a decision is reached to terminate a team member, the following questions should be answered:

- Was the team member forewarned of the possible disciplinary consequences of his or her actions?
- Were the work requirements required of the individual reasonable in relation to the safe, orderly, and efficient conduct of the foodservice organization?

Figure 16-4
Reducing trauma associated
with dismissal.

- Make the discussion private, brief, and businesslike.
- Be tactful, honest, and straightforward.
- Give any information regarding severance pay or other benefits information.
- Outline the period the team member has before he or she must leave the organization.
- Avoid any personality differences between the chef supervisor and the team member.

- Were all reasonable efforts expended to fully and fairly determine the facts?
- Was the team member given ample opportunity for improvement?
- Were all other options of disciplinary action considered?
- Was the team member afforded "due process" and a fair hearing?
- Are there any unusual or mitigating circumstances surrounding the case?
- Is this action discriminatory?

For most managers, dismissing a team member can be a painful experience. Often, it gives managers a feeling that they have failed the individual in some way. The best way to think of termination of a team member is to consider it an act of "unhiring." Regardless of the reasons for dismissal, it should be accomplished with consideration of the individual. Every effort should be made to ease the trauma that a dismissal can create. Figure 16-4 shows guidelines that can help reduce the trauma associated with dismissal. Being dismissed can be a terrible blow to a team member. It is important to allow the team member to leave with self-esteem intact.

APPROACHES TO POSITIVE DISCIPLINE

One approach to disciplinary action is positive discipline, or discipline without punishment, an idea originally developed by John Huberman, a Canadian psychologist. Punitive and positive disciplines differ in both attitude and procedure.[4] Most of the time, individuals are unaware that they are doing something they are not supposed to do. In spite of good induction and orientation training and rules and procedures clearly posted or contained in employee manuals, there are still things that team members don't know. They may observe some other team member doing something and believe it's all right for them to do it. A positive approach to discipline, therefore, is continuous education. Discipline that is applied positively is used to teach and mold. Team members will see that it is for their welfare. Positive discipline shows team members that obeying the rules and safety or sanitation regulations benefits them as well as the organization.

What, then, is "positive discipline"? The philosophy behind positive discipline is that most people come to work wishing to do a good job. They appreciate being treated as adults. They want to learn, welcome responsibility, can be self-directed, and are capable of self-discipline. The dynamics of positive discipline are a team effort where the team members and the chef engage in joint discussion and problem solving to resolve incidents of rule infractions.

Positive discipline focuses on the early correction of team member misconduct. While positive discipline seems similar to progressive discipline, its emphasis is on giving team members reminders rather than reprimands.

Steps in Positive Discipline

Step 1: This is an oral reminder. In a private discussion with the chef, the team member is encouraged to explain the reason for the misconduct. In a friendly way, the rules and procedures are restated along with the reasons for having them. The chef refrains from reprimanding or threatening the team member with further disciplinary action. This meeting may be documented, but a written record is not placed in the team member's file unless the misconduct occurs again. During this meeting the team member agrees not to repeat the misconduct.

Step 2: If improvement is not made following step 1, a second meeting takes place with the offending team member. During this private meeting, the chef adopts the role of counselor. At this stage, however, a written reminder is given to the team member that summarizes the discussion and the concluding agreement. Both the team member and chef then sign it.

Step 3: When steps 1 and 2 fail to produce the desired results, the team member is placed on "decision-making" leave with pay. The purpose of this paid leave is to allow the offending team member time to decide whether to remain part of the team; whether to return and abide by the rules and conditions, or to leave. If the team member returns, it is on the basis of an agreement to conform to the organization's rules and that further infractions will be followed by termination. The foodservice organization pays for this specified leave in order to demonstrate its desire to retain the team member. Paying for the leave eliminates any negative effects that suspension without pay has on individuals.

Step 4: If the agreed improvements do not take place, then the team member has broken the agreement. There is then a clear reason for termination.

Positive discipline works. Organizations that have used it report success:[5]

> Many people who use it report that about 75 percent of the time employees decide to come back and follow the rules. They may not maintain their turnaround indefinitely but three months or even three weeks of productive behavior is preferable to finding and breaking in somebody new. And it is infinitely better than the hostile employee you are likely to end up with after an unpaid layoff.

EXIT INTERVIEWS

Team members who leave voluntarily often provide feedback on their experience with the organization that can be useful in averting further employee turnover. Exit interviews enable chefs to compile data about the kitchen work environment as well as establish the effectiveness of induction and orientation training programs. They are used to establish the primary reasons people leave.[6]

Exit interview data can help determine whether there is a trend for voluntary departures. To get the most accurate data from departing employees, the interview is best conducted by a supervisor other than the chef. Another approach is to turn the whole procedure over to the human resources department. Some of the questions appropriate for this interview are:

- "What did you like most about working here? What did you like least?"
- "If you were a consultant to our organization, what changes/improvement would you recommend?"
- "What was it like working for Chef John Doe?" If the answer is vague or answered weakly "on the grounds that nobody is perfect," the chef may want to ask: "What would have made Chef John Doe a better supervisor, in your opinion?"
- "Where are you going to be working?" This question is an attempt to gather information about competitors and find out whether professional recruiters are poaching from the kitchen.

To get as much information as possible from the interview, the interviewer needs to probe for specific details from each answer. No team member should leave the food-service organization without being interviewed. Team members who leave voluntarily have to be replaced. This process is expensive not only in terms of dollars and time, but also often in terms of team morale.

SUMMARY

Discipline should not be interpreted only as punishment. It is also about molding and teaching team members to become loyal, motivated, responsible workers.

Discipline is an inner force that develops within team members and causes them to want to follow high standards in life and the workplace. Effective discipline is not just reprimanding or inflicting penalties. Discipline is split into two distinct areas: discipline as punishment, and the positive discipline approach. The leadership abilities of the chef may minimize the need to be punitive.

Chefs should ensure that each member of the kitchen team understands the policies and procedures of the foodservice organization. Disciplinary actions must be in accordance with EEOC legislation and other discriminatory laws. Chefs should know and understand all union labor contract procedures and agreements relative to employee discipline.

Discipline should be administered in a consistent, fair, and equitable way. Progressive discipline involves the steps of oral reprimand, written reprimand, suspension, and termination. Administering discipline requires the chef supervisor to gather the facts, treat the offender with all "due process," and know the advance steps before termination.

Positive discipline approaches require the chef to act in a way that invests in the team member by shifting responsibility to the individual. Its philosophy is that most people are self-disciplined, and with counseling and guidance, team members who break rules can become productive. An important element of the process is the third step, which provides offending team members with a paid period to decide their future with the organization, thus placing the responsibility on them for the next steps.

Exit interviews with team members who voluntarily leave provide the organization with information that can assist in profiling the kitchen as a workplace and the chef as a supervisor.

DISCUSSION QUESTIONS

1. Define the following chapter key terms:
   a. Discipline
   b. Positive discipline
   c. Progressive discipline
2. Why does true discipline involve more than punishing or reprimanding?
3. What are the two distinct application areas of discipline?
4. What is the effect of selective application of discipline on the kitchen team's morale?
5. What are the rules within the kitchen that require constant reiteration?
6. Why do minor deviations from labor contract procedures overturn otherwise justified disciplinary actions?
7. What is meant by the hot stove rule as it pertains to discipline?
8. What are the steps of progressive discipline?
9. What are the five major rule violations that frequently require team member dismissal?
10. What are the consequences of failing to warn a team member of continued rule violations?
11. What are the guidelines for administering discipline in a fair and equitable way?
12. What are the fundamental differences between positive and negative discipline?
13. What benefits can accrue to the chef and the foodservice organization as a result of exit interviews?

NOTES

1. Jack E. Miller, Mary Porter, and Karen E. Drummond, *Supervision in the Hospitality Industry,* 2nd ed. (New York: John Wiley, 1992), 257.

2. E. R. Worthington and Anita E. Worthington, *People Investment* (Grant's Pass, OR: Oasis Press, 1993), 56.

3. Vincent H. Eade, *Human Resources Management in the Hospitality Industry* (Scottsdale, AZ: Garsuch Sciarisbrick Pub., 1993), 204.

4. George L. Frunzi and Jack Halloran, *Supervision: The Art of Management,* 3rd ed. (Englewood Cliffs, NJ: Prentice-Hall, 1991), 380.

5. Jack E. Miller, Mary Porter, and Karen E. Drummond, *Supervision in the Hospitality Industry,* 2nd ed. (New York: John Wiley, 1992), 259.

6. Barbara A. Pope, *Workforce Management* (Chicago, IL: Business One Review, 1992), 89.

part four
The World of Leadership

Chapter 17
Leadership

OBJECTIVES

When you complete this chapter, you should be able to:

1. Distinguish between supervision, management, and leadership
2. Describe the elements of directive behavior and supportive behavior
3. Describe desirable leadership behavioral qualities
4. Explain directing, coaching, supporting, and delegating as they pertain to situational leadership
5. Outline actions that contribute to leadership self-confidence
6. Apply steps that are particular to culinary leadership

Case Study: Crown Hotel

Chef Mark Macklin, after thirty-six years as executive chef of the Crown Hotel, has retired. Chef Macklin, affectionately known as Chef Mac, was held in high esteem by the hotel staff. Chef Mac hired the hotel's thirty-five chefs and cooks and twenty-nine kitchen support staff, and many of them have worked at the hotel for over twenty years. It was widely known by the hotel staff that Chef Mac's decision to retire was encouraged by the hotel owners.

The chef selected to replace Chef Mac as executive chef is Chef Wayne Bryson. Chef Bryson is twenty-six years old. He is the youngest chef ever to earn the prestigious certification of "Master Chef." Chef Bryson has won multiple gold medals in state, national, and international competition. He has even been mentioned in culinary circles as the possible future manager of the American Culinary Olympic Team. Chef Bryson was executive sous chef of the renowned Windsor Hotel for three years before coming to the Crown Hotel as executive chef.

The owners of the Crown Hotel have widely publicized that Chef Bryson will be leading the culinary team at "the Crown." The owners have been quoted in the newspapers as saying, "Chef Bryson is a tremendous addition to the Crown family. An addition we anticipate will bring the Crown to new levels of culinary excellence." The grapevine in the hotel says that the owners have instructed Chef Bryson to bring the Crown's food into the twenty-first century.

Chef Bryson has been at the Crown for three months. He meets at least once a week with the kitchen management team to present new initiatives that they are to carry out. He regularly notifies the other kitchen staff by memo of the initiatives and their role in the initiatives. Chef Bryson has developed new menus and all of the recipes and other information to support the menus for all areas of the hotel. Development of the recipes for the menus has required that Chef Bryson spend a great deal of time in the small catering and banquet kitchen, working closely with the small team of cooks that he brought with him from the Windsor. He has also spent a great deal of time working with the office staff, technology consultant, and print designer to finalize the menus and support material. Chef Bryson introduced the new menu and recipes to the kitchen management two weeks in advance of the rollout of the new menus with instructions for them to train their teams.

The new menus have been in place for one month with extremely poor results. Food and labor costs have increased, customer complaints have increased, and absenteeism is at an all-time high. The nonguest count in the hotel's restaurants has declined by 10 percent. The hotel's white table cloth restaurant, the only two-star restaurant in the city, is due for review in two months, and currently the possibility is strong that it will be down-rated to one star. The owners of the Crown had anticipated that it would become the only *three-star* restaurant in the city with Chef Bryson on the team.

Based on what you have learned from previous chapters and the content of this chapter, answer the following questions.

- What is the overall reason for the challenges occurring in the Crown's foodservice department?
- What are the primary causal agents for the challenges occurring in the Crown's foodservice department?
- What role did leadership and supervision/management play in the decline of the Crown's foodservice department?
- What specific steps could have been taken to avoid the current situation occurring in the Crown's foodservice department?
- What, specifically, can be done to overcome the challenges and generate motion in a positive direction for the Crown's foodservice department?

INTRODUCTION

Authority, supervision, management, and leadership are generally interrelated, but they are not synonymous. Carefully consider the following definitions.

- **Authority** is the right and power to command.
- **Supervision** can be limited to just that, supervising. Watching to make certain the job is done correctly and on time.

Figure 17-1
Hierarchy of positions and
levels of authority.

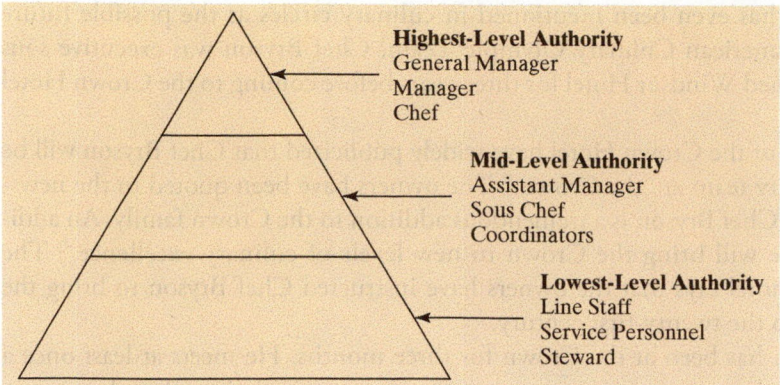

Highest-Level Authority
General Manager
Manager
Chef

Mid-Level Authority
Assistant Manager
Sous Chef
Coordinators

Lowest-Level Authority
Line Staff
Service Personnel
Steward

- **Management** is both the act of controlling something, such as a business, and the group invested with the authority to control something.
- **Leadership** is influencing, guiding, and leading people to follow a course of action or line of thought.

Authority, the right and power to command, in business and in the kitchen is linked to the various positions. Simply put, incumbent in the position of chef is the right and power to command the staff in the kitchen. The level or extent of authority incumbent in a position is linked to the hierarchy of the positions in the establishment. Generally, positions and therefore authority can be viewed as a pyramid. The greatest, broadest authority is at the top of the pyramid and resides in very few positions, as shown in Figure 17-1. The chef is generally close to the top or at the top of the pyramid.

Authority and power are derived in two ways:

- Authority is invested in the position.
- Delegation of authority: Specific activities in the kitchen require a manager. This is often the chef with the most skill or experience. Skill or experience is frequently a factor in the promotion to the position of chef.

The **authority of position** exists by virtue of the position, not the individual. The chef uses the authority of the position to manage the kitchen. The power of the authority invested in the chef's position provides the means for controlling and directing the kitchen team. How the authority is used determines the working environment for the kitchen team and ultimately the success or failure of the team. If the chef's authority is by virtue of the title alone, there likely will be a lack of team commitment, poor morale, low productivity, and high turnover in the kitchen workforce.

Leadership does not rest with a position. Leadership is rooted in the individual and empowered by the group. Leadership is not the sole domain of those in positions of authority. A leader is invested with power by the individuals they lead. People follow a leader for a variety of reasons including common beliefs, their belief in the leader's vision, respect for the leader, and their belief that, through the leadership, their goals will be achieved. There can be no leader without followers. Leaders exist at all levels of an organization, and appreciation of this fact increases the chef's ability to manage the kitchen team.

Leadership in the kitchen does not depend on team member incentives or pleasant working conditions. The chef's ability to motivate people to perform is independent of these factors. Leaders are *made,* not born. Leadership can be learned the way chefs learn culinary skills. Myth associates leadership with superior position. It assumes that when you are on top you are automatically a leader. But leadership is not a place; it is a process. It involves skills and abilities that are useful whether one is in the executive suite or on the front line.[1] The one who influences others to follow only is a leader with limitations. The one who influences others to lead is a leader without limitation.[2]

WHAT IS THIS BUSINESS?
"THE MANAGER IN THE CHEF AND THE CHEF IN THE MANAGER"

The foodservice industry is constantly growing and changing. This is especially true in the past decade with food television becoming so widely enjoyed as both entertainment and education. Chefs are more than creators of the masterpieces on the canvas of the plate; they are sensory rock stars of the palate and the maestros of the food industry!

So what does it take to be a chef in this evolving industry? In the past the kitchen was off limits to front-of-the-house managers. Chefs ran the kitchen by different rules—their rules. The chef did not consider the rest of the operations their concern as long as the servers were there for pick-up and ran the food when it was hot, stacked their dishes correctly, and listened up. Creations were king, purveyors were the adversary, and the guests—well, depending on the chef—were not king, but unknowing and troublesome. Those days are long gone.

Today's professional chefs, in many ways, are more well-rounded than any other member of the management team. They have to be since they carry the biggest responsibility for costs: labor and food. As the captain of the "engine" or the conductor of the train, the chefs are the ones that can make or break the show. Sequence of service; food and beverage pairing; selection of service ware, the canvas of the food presentation; and descriptions of creations—all these points and more are critical to chefs and their desired goal of menu mix, labor control, and food cost.

So, is the art of creating the incredible dish that the guests will come begging for lost? The leaders, the chefs who inspire through inspiration and intimidation—are they gone? The chef that knows it all and the guests that are left wondering, "How did they do that?"—is this gone? The answer to these questions is a resounding yes and no. What is certain is that knowledge is power, and the knowledge is out there in buckets! The availability of culinary education has exploded in the past few decades. The chef's knowledge of food and techniques must be solid because guests aren't as easily impressed with dishes, methods, or tricks of the trade. The guests are also pursuing food knowledge through books and food TV. They themselves are becoming great home chefs.

Food is not enough in today's market. The "new" chef must be able to do more than make a good burre blanc sauce. Today's chef must be a professional manager with a specialization in food. The quest for more knowledge must run through the chef's veins like that of a doctor studying medicine. This quest for knowledge must be their "co-inspiration," so to speak, in the preparation and creation of delectable dishes. A passion for knowledge and a passion for food are the twin motivators for today's chef.

Computers and technology are a chef's best friends. Today's professional chef uses technology as a tool for managing the kitchen. Costing out recipes, studying menu mixes, order guides, training programs, product check lists—all these processes and many more are managed through technology.

While those of Generation X desire more, better, and faster, they are not as likely as people of past generations to study under a chef for 3 to 5 years to gain the experience. Training practices, evaluation methods, managing, leading, and inspiring need to be sharp. The team members are smart, and desire more explanation, which means that teachers must be on top of their game. Concerns with team members used to be handled by human resources, but to keep the operation out of hot water, the chef needs to be very well versed in laws, regulations, and professional industry practices; the walls between the front of the house and the back of the house are disappearing.

The guests of the restaurant are expecting more. Food is being evaluated critically by much more educated consumers. They are aware of foodborne illness, of the difference between select and choice, of heirloom vegetables and organics. They question the methods, temperatures, and pairing of foods and beverages. Today's chef has to have knowledge of food and nutrition trends on a par with or ahead of that of the guests.

Purveyors are not to be viewed as pushy salesmen, but rather as allies in the quest to make great, profitable food. The products and services that they offer a chef provide a support structure that can improve food cost and help control labor costs. The timeliness of deliveries, pack sizes of products, and product availability can keep an operation ahead of the curve and help make a chef and his operation successful.

The industry is alive and well and is being developed by those who see the future of the professional chef. The manager is in the chef, and the chef is a manager, one who utilizes skills, talents, information—in other words, all the resources available.

—Guy Fieri, Food Network Star

The chef can have the authority of the position and manage the kitchen without being a leader. Adding leadership to the mix of authority and management can bring another level of power. This power moves beyond that of directing and controlling to influencing, guiding, and leading the team. Leadership moves the chef from the authority to the leader of the team. The central theme of leadership is getting things accomplished through people. Leadership in the kitchen confers on the chef the privilege and responsibility of directing the actions of the kitchen team in carrying out the pursuits of the organization. As team leader, the chef can bring the

CHEF TALK
"LEADERSHIP IS A PRIVILEGE"

Like a good recipe, there are many ingredients that make up a good leader, and like a good recipe it takes quality components, just the right seasoning, and preparation to create a dish worthy to be called delicious. Leadership is tough, but so rewarding! As a female culinary professional, I've experienced the highs and lows of developing my own leadership style. When I get overwhelmed at times with my personal and professional responsibilities, I try to put it into perspective, thinking about it as I do preparing a good recipe: choosing quality and continually working to polish myself into a well-seasoned individual.

The bottom line is this: Leadership is a privilege. Others put their faith, hope, and trust in you as an individual who can demonstrate competency from a technical as well as a conceptual perspective. As a leader, you have the dedicated responsibility of providing the right climate in which the goals of the organization can be met as well as those of whom you are leading. What a challenge, and more than that—it's the most extraordinary juggling act!

In October of 2000, I was challenged with the opportunity to serve as captain for the Team 2000 U.S. Culinary Olympic Team. My charge was to coordinate a team of chefs so tightly that we could anticipate each other's needs, polish our skills, and achieve the goal of winning a gold medal at the 2000 Culinary Olympics in Erfurt, Germany. Not only did we win one of five gold medals in our category, we placed third in the overall championship out of 44 teams worldwide. It was one of the greatest highlights of my professional career. But as the saying goes, it's not the destination but the journey in getting there. It was not an easy path, since we definitely had our share of obstacles. We experienced flurries of emotions and faced logistical challenges such as working in a foreign country, shipping food ingredients overseas, and praying they got through customs! We had sleepless nights, we had laughs, and we had moments of frustration. As the leader of this group, I had the duty of providing the atmosphere that would serve as the platform for us to realize our individual and team goals. When the officials placed that gold medal around my neck and we shot our team photo, it was such a moment of accomplishment. As the one who was responsible for the team, even if we hadn't won, I can say with confidence that we prevailed as we did because we were prepared.

As a leader, you must be prepared. It's a matter of taking the philosophies we practice in the kitchen as chefs and allowing those to trickle into other areas of our lives. *Mise en place* isn't just in the kitchen. It's important to have our professional and personal *mise en place* just as organized to be a successful leader! I believe it is paramount to choose to be a good example and demonstrate proper confidence. Almost anyone can manage a system if they are trained, but it takes an extraordinary individual to demonstrate oneself as a good example for others to follow as well as to project oneself as a dedicated leader while managing what is going on in the environment. We desperately need better leaders in this field. There are too many crummy managers out there; we have all worked with them and have had to tolerate them. It's a challenge to make a conscious choice to be the example, to promote others through good management, and to project ourselves as the outstanding leaders we can be. *Mise en place*—surround yourself in it because it is the foundation to success.

—Chef Jill K. Bosich, CEC, CCE
(Regional Team Captain, Team USA 2007),
Chef Instructor, Orange Coast College,
Costa Mesa, CA

team to a higher level of cooperation and teamwork. The successful chef will effectively use the authority that comes with the position and will earn the power that can be derived from leadership.

LEADERSHIP DEVELOPMENT

Leaders play a crucial role in quality. They have to be primary agents for improvement. They work to create an environment where the kitchen team can experience pride. Their efforts are directed toward allowing all kitchen team members to perform their jobs to the utmost. Leaders take risks based on the self-knowledge that mistakes are opportunities, not failures. They have the ability to let go of concepts that block new ideas of learning. Leaders balance action against inaction and praise against correction. Competent leaders have sufficient expertise to make good judgments and get things done. President Eisenhower summarized leadership as follows: "The one quality that can be developed by studious reflection and practice is the leadership of men."[3]

Bennus and Nanus observed the following myths:[4]

Myth 1: "Leadership is a rare skill." Nothing could be further from the truth. While great leaders may be as rare as great runners, great actors, or great painters, everyone has leadership potential. The truth is that leadership opportunities are plentiful and within the reach of most people.

Myth 2: "Leaders are born, not made." Biographies of great leaders sometimes read as if these individuals entered the world with an extraordinary genetic endowment, that somehow their future leadership role was preordained. Don't believe it. Whatever natural endowments we bring to the role of leader can be enhanced.

Myth 3: "Leaders are charismatic." Some are, most aren't. Charisma is the result of effective leadership, not the other way around.

Myth 4: "Leadership exists only at the top of an organization." In fact, the larger the organization, the more leadership roles it is likely to have.

Myth 5: "The leader controls, directs, prods, and manipulates." This is perhaps the most damning myth of all. Leadership is not so much the exercise of power as the empowerment of others. Leaders are able to translate intentions into reality by aligning the energies of the organization behind an attractive goal. Once these myths are cleared away, the question becomes one not of how to become a leader but rather of how to improve one's effectiveness at leadership.

Traits that are the basic elements of leadership can be taught. When the desire to be a good leader is present in the chef, nothing can stop the process. Ninety percent of the leadership traits can be taught through development. The 10 percent who are gifted will succeed only if the development and growth of leadership are pursued. As John Maxwell states in his book, *The 21 Irrefutable Laws of Leadership*, "Leadership Develops Daily, Not in a Day."[5]

The terms management and leadership often are used interchangeably. They can be synonymous, but usually they mean different things. In the past, terms such as people management were used to indicate authoritarian control. This people management philosophy has been shown to be folly. As H. Ross Perot states, "People cannot be managed. Inventories can be managed, but people must be led."[6] The piece from the *Wall Street Journal* shown in Figure 17-2 subtly attempts to demonstrate the difference between management and leadership:

Figure 17-2
Let's get rid of management.

People don't want to be managed.
They want to be led.
Whoever heard of a world manager?
World leader, yes.
Educational leader.
Political leader.
Scout leader.
Community leader.
Business leader.
They lead.
They don't manage.
If you want to manage somebody, manage yourself.
Do that well and you'll be ready to stop managing and start leading.

Figure 17-3
Persistence—Calvin
Coolidge.

Nothing in the world can take the place of persistence.
Talent will not; nothing is more common than unsuccessful men with great talent.
Genius will not; unrewarded genius is almost a proverb.
Education will not; the world is full of educated derelicts.
Persistence, determination alone are omnipotent.
The slogan "press on" has solved and always will solve the problems of the human race.

According to Patrick L. O'Malley, chairman emeritus of the Canteen Company, leadership in the foodservice industry is about the following:[7]

> Doing the job at hand with the energy required with all your resources being used efficiently. It means getting the right people in the right place for the job they will be committed to do. It means motivating your colleagues and employees, directing them skillfully, providing adequate training, getting to understand them and communicating with them.

In order to skillfully lead the kitchen team, chefs must master the skills of leadership and have a passion to succeed. They must show the way and lead by example. They must have a clear idea of what they want to do and the strength of purpose to persist in the face of setbacks, even failures. They know where they are going and why.

Calvin Coolidge astutely pointed out that persistence in any endeavor will equal success as shown in Figure 17-3. Developing leadership skills requires a great deal of persistence.

Leadership style is something that each chef will develop individually. Essentially, style is based on two behaviors, known as directive behavior and supportive behavior.[8] Directive behavior is authoritarian behavior, which concentrates on control, structure, and strict supervision. The supportive chef leadership behavior style is about enabling, coaching, facilitating, and praising. Solid chef leadership is established through a combination of these. A true leader is a person that people want to follow because they trust and respect that individual.

Leadership development is first a process of self-development. It is facilitated by education, training, mentoring, and experience. Success for the chef as a manager is dependent upon more than the source of authority or having a title thrust upon him or her. The better the chef's leadership skills, the greater the level of satisfaction and productivity achieved by the kitchen team. These kitchen leadership qualities and skill sets are shown in Figure 17-4.

These elements of leadership are necessary so that the team members may have confidence in the chef as a manager and in the knowledge that there is direction and purpose for what they do. Trusting the chef's leadership is vital to having a productive kitchen team environment. Leadership includes open and honest communication and helps to promote the loyalty and commitment of the team.[9]

TRAIT THEORIES

The **trait approach** to leadership is based on early research that seemed to assume that a good leader is born and not made. The reasoning was that if a complete profile of the characteristics (traits) of a successful leader could be summarized, it would be fairly easy to pinpoint the individuals who should (and should not) be placed in leadership positions. This was known as the **"Great Man" theory**.[10] The theory has been

WHAT IS THIS BUSINESS?
"CO-WORKERS"

My company, Lawry's Restaurants, Inc., is an "institution" nearly 92 years old. I use the word "institution" because, in so many ways, that is what we have become.

It was founded by my father and maternal uncle, and is still owned and operated by two families, the Franks and the Van de Kamps. The enterprise started in 1915 as a tiny retail potato chip shop in downtown Los Angeles. It evolved over two years into a successful bakery chain (Van de Kamp's), and later a food products manufacturer (Lawry's Foods) and the restaurant group that we still control.

Very few family businesses spanning three generations of management have managed to survive and prosper. In our instance there were several good reasons for the accomplishment. For one, we had an entrepreneurial vent that led to the development of two famous brands; for another, we were in the right place (Southern California) at the right point in time. But, by far, the most important reason was the business culture that has engendered the continuous enthusiasm and loyalty of our employees. We call this our co-worker culture.

It began early on and was based upon a set of business principles and ethics in which the company founders embodied and believed. My father never acknowledged that an "employee" worked for him. Instead they were co-workers—beginning with him and including every other person on the payroll. The key to the culture is that our co-workers have always considered themselves as an important part of an important venture, regardless of the position they hold. Without that belief, the work would fall flat and be meaningless.

Remarkably, we have been able to instill this sense of self-importance in the co-workers of very different types of business, in many geographical locations and over nine decades. This came about, in part, because the owners and executives have lived it, believed in it, and preached and promoted it. Co-workers follow suit and become ambassadors and salespeople to those newly employed, as well as to the other company constituents they meet, i.e., customers, purveyors and the public at large. This engenders a sense that there is something unique and important about being a member of the organization. The co-worker "spirit" leads to a feeling of pride and loyalty as well as a team attitude, all of which builds upon itself. If newcomers don't "get it" in a reasonable time, they don't fit in and they leave.

Some 25 years ago, I put the unwritten set of principles in writing. Called *Lawry's Code of Business Principles and Ethics*, a copy is given to every new co-worker as he or she joins the company, and plaques of the Code are prominently displayed in all places where our business is conducted. We want our customers, as well as our co-workers, to be aware of what we stand for. And many times the question is asked, "Are we following our code of ethics if we do or say that?" It actually forces a discipline of doing the right thing.

One very important positive that has endured from our company culture is the far lower co-worker turnover than is found in most competitive restaurant businesses and, in fact, in business firms in general. This phenomenon has occurred throughout the long period of family ownership, with the average of all co-workers' tenures being 5 to 10 years, and this is in kinds of businesses in which a large segment of the payroll is in low wage categories. Twenty-five, 30, 40, and even 50 years of service has not been unusual. We give out numerous long-term service awards each year and sponsor an annual Heritage Club luncheon for those who have given the company 15 and more years of service. It's a much-anticipated and appreciated event.

This loyalty obviously is strongly evident in our company kitchens. Our executive chefs and their sous chefs, for the most part, have worked for us for years, and many started at the very bottom jobs. They are proud to be a part of the team, and we are even prouder of them. These are the people who, with their co-workers, have made the business prosper, and while those of us in the "executive suite" may point the way, it's our co-workers who deserve the credit.

—Richard N. Frank,
Chairman, Lawry's Restaurants, Inc.
Pasadena, CA

- Creativity
- Confidence in one's abilities
- Good communication skills
- Ability to make decisions
- Trust in the kitchen team to do the job
- Desire to develop skills in others
- Comfort level in giving directions
- Ability to motivate the people
- Ability to take measured risks

Figure 17-4
Kitchen leadership qualities and skills.

abandoned over the years because an evaluation of these trait studies proved inconclusive. Over 80 years of study have failed to produce one single personality trait or set of qualities that can be used consistently to separate those who are leaders and those who are not. Chefs of diverse backgrounds, ethnic origins, gender, and personality have been effective leaders. All they needed was the desire to lead. However, studies also have shown that there are some personal characteristics that distinguish effective leaders from ineffective ones.

Research has shown that there are two distinct **dimensions of leadership**: (1) employee centered and (2) production centered. Therefore, a leader's personal characteristics and behavior by themselves do not guarantee leadership effectiveness. Perception of the kitchen team, the nature of the tasks, the relationship with the team members, and the organizational climate in the kitchen all must come together to provide effective supervisory leadership.

BEHAVIORAL THEORIES

Behavioral theories were directed toward the study of leaders, supervisors, and work groups rather than just the characteristics of successful leaders. In the past, emphasis was placed on studying the behaviors that provided effective interaction between work-group members. Studies have shown that two characteristics, arrived at independently of one another, were important elements of supervisory behavior.[11] Elements of **consideration** include behaviors indicating mutual trust, respect, and a certain warmth and rapport between the supervisor and the group. **Structure** includes behavior in which supervisors organize and define group activities and their relations to the group.

In their book, *The Leadership Challenge*, Kouzes and Posner similarly reported that the behaviors followers expect from their leaders include honesty, competence, vision, and inspiration.[12] A study by Cichy, Sciarini, and Patton discovered fourteen desirable leadership behaviors and qualities,[13] shown in Figure 17-5.

Denis Kinlaw, in studies outlined in *Coaching for Commitment*, uncovered similar behaviors of superior leaders, which he summarizes under six sets of common practices:[14]

1. *Establishing a vision.* Superior leaders create expectations for significant and lasting achievement. They give meaning to work by associating even menial tasks with valued goals.
2. *Stimulating people to gain new competencies.* Superior leaders stimulate people to stretch their minds and their wills. They freely share their own expertise and keep people in touch with new resources.

Figure 17-5
Desirable leadership behaviors and qualities.

- Provide a compelling message or vision
- Have a strong personal value or belief system
- Recognize that the ability to adjust is a necessity
- Make desired outcomes tangible
- Encourage and reward risk taking
- Listen as well as, if not better than, they speak
- Provide appropriate information, resources, and support to empower employees
- Are inquisitive
- Emphasize quality continuously
- Know personal strengths and nurture them
- Place a high value on learning
- Maintain precise desired outcomes
- Change their minds seldom
- Have strong family values

3. ***Helping people to overcome obstacles.*** Superior leaders help others to overcome obstacles. They help others to find the courage and strength to persevere in the face of even the greatest difficulties.

4. ***Helping people to overcome failure.*** Superior leaders help people to cope with failure and disappointment. They are quick to offer new opportunities to people who fail.

5. ***Leading by example.*** Superior leaders are models of integrity and hard work. They set the highest expectations for themselves and others.

6. ***Including others in their success.*** Superior leaders are quick to share the limelight with others. People associated with superior leaders feel as successful as the leaders.

LEADERSHIP STYLES

The emphasis of leadership study has shifted from the trait and behavioral approach to the situational approach. This modern **situational approach** to leadership is based on the assumption that all instances of successful leadership are different and require a unique combination of leaders, followers, and leadership situations. According to Blanchard, Zigarni, and Zigarni, the four basic styles of situational leadership are:[15]

Style 1: Directing. The leader provides specific instructions and closely supervises task accomplishment.

Style 2: Coaching. The leader continues to direct and closely supervise task accomplishment but also explains decisions, solicits suggestions, and supports progress.

Style 3: Supporting. The leader facilitates and supports subordinates' efforts at task accomplishment and shares responsibility for decision making with them.

Style 4: Delegating. The leader turns over responsibility for decision making and problem solving to subordinates.

These leadership styles have also been summarized as "different strokes for different folks." There is no one best or appropriate style suited to all situations. A leadership style often described as made up of the three F's—firm, fair, and friendly—is a combination of many elements, but at times this style does not work. The three F's presuppose there is a homogeneous kitchen team who will readily react and perform favorably in response to this chef leadership style.

As a situational leader, the chef will need to analyze the team. Within the group there will be individuals who have high commitment to the team and its goals but without the necessary array of skills. In this situation the chef uses a detailed set of instructions to lead the team member—a directing style. Other team members may have some culinary skill competence but a low commitment to the team's vision and goals. Here, a coaching and correcting style highly supportive of the team member would be appropriate. A team member who is sometimes committed and has a lot of skills will require a supporting leadership style. Such a team member is capable of working alone with little direction, while team members with well-developed skills and a great deal of team commitment require that tasks be delegated to them in order to feel fulfilled.

Leadership ability is inextricably linked to motivation. As we observed earlier, what motivates one person may not motivate another. Motivation comes from within the individual. The leadership style provides the basis for a motivational environment.

One extreme in leadership style is the strict authoritarian, the aloof chef who rules the kitchen with a rod of iron. The advantage of this style is good control and

CHEF TALK
"LEADERSHIP AXIOM"

When I was in college there was a group of us that gathered in the basement of the dorm on Saturday morning to watch old movies on the TV if we were not working or studying. One Saturday morning the movie was about young Thomas Edison and it starred Mickey Rooney as the young Thomas Edison. At one point in the movie, young Thomas Edison's mother is extremely ill and will die before morning if the doctor does not operate on her. The doctor, however, cannot operate because this was before Thomas invented the electric light and there is no light bright enough for the doctor to do the operation. Young Thomas proceeds to place a large number of kerosene lanterns in front of a large mirror on one side of the room, directing the mirror toward a mirror on the opposite side of the room, reflecting the light of the lanterns from mirror to mirror. (This procedure, I later learned, is called refraction.) The result was light far brighter than lamplight that was not reflected from mirror to mirror. This concept of the increased intensity of refracted light has stayed with me over the years and has become the basis for my own personal leadership axiom.

Many opportunities arise when an individual in a position of authority allows those working with him or her to showcase their expertise, abilities, and knowledge. The leader who not only allows, but encourages co-workers, teammates, and subordinates to develop and showcase their capabilities and, when possible, to move into the spotlight and to advance themselves will find that the light refracted back on him or her by the success of those individuals is far greater than the spotlight itself.

My Leadership Axiom:

Provide opportunities for the growth, development, and advancement of others. Be a role model and provide leadership directed toward the best interest of those you lead. Concentrate on the promotion of others and the promotion of you will take care of itself.

—Jerald W. Chesser,
Ed.D, CEC, CCE, FMP, AAC, Professor,
The Collins College of Hospitality Management,
California State Polytechnic University Pomona,
Pomona, California

discipline over the team. The disadvantages are resentment, no cooperation, and poor communication with subordinates. These are certainly not the ingredients of a coaching leadership style in a quality environment.

The other extreme is the chef who tries to be democratic to be accepted by other team members as a complete equal. The democratic style promotes a good atmosphere, good communication, and cooperation. However, the disadvantages can outweigh the advantages because the democrat is taken for granted, has no authority, and will eventually lose control of the team. Somewhere between these two extremes is the ideal leadership style.

The old-fashioned authoritarian, dictatorial chef has no place in the complex modern culinary world. Kitchen team members need to be led, not controlled or managed. The best leadership style in the kitchen is one that works for the individual chef and is based on the make-up of the team, the personal characteristics of the chef, and the ever-changing daily situations facing the chef. Situational leadership provides the chef with a flexible approach to each situation as it arises.

THE NATURE OF CULINARY LEADERSHIP

Few concepts are as difficult to analyze as leadership. Why do some individuals seem to effortlessly succeed and others fail so miserably? Within the culinary world, there exist tremendous opportunities for leadership. As Jerry Hill, former chairman of the Michigan Restaurant Association, observed:[16]

> If you are interested in developing leadership skills and tackling leadership responsibility, you'd be hard pressed to find another field that offers more opportunity than the foodservice industry. Not only are many leadership positions available, but those positions are likely to be true leadership roles. We fortunately have a wealth of culinary leaders to draw analysis from.

But what is the nature of leadership? A good place to start is the principles of leadership listed in the U.S. Army's manual of leadership. The following ten principles have been adapted from this manual and may be applied to culinary leadership:[17]

1. ***Know yourself and seek self-improvement.*** Identify your strengths and weaknesses. Set goals for each weakness or desired improvement. Develop plans to achieve goals. Evaluate progress toward goals.

2. ***Be technically and tactfully proficient.*** Be knowledgeable in all aspects of your job. Be able to pass this knowledge on to your fellow kitchen team members.

3. ***Seek responsibility and take responsibility for your actions.*** When you see a problem, initiate actions to solve it; do not wait for others to tell you what to do, or say "it's not my job." If you have made a mistake, admit your errors, accept your criticism, and promptly correct the matter.

4. ***Make sound and timely decisions.*** Use problem-solving, decision-making, and planning methods to rapidly assess the situation and make the most appropriate decision. Indecisiveness causes confusion and a lack of confidence.

5. ***Set an example.*** As a role model, this is the chef's most important leadership skill. You should not ask your fellow team members to do anything you would not do yourself. As a leader, you should earn the respect of the team, not demand it.

6. ***Know your subordinates and look out for their well-being.*** Take the time to learn about your team by listening to them. Know what it takes to motivate each member individually. It is important to recognize the team's need to be needed. If you take care of your kitchen team, they will take care of you.

7. ***Keep your subordinates informed.*** Don't just give orders; explain the rationale for the request. Informed persons consider themselves part of the team effort. Your kitchen team cannot grow and perform well if you keep them in the dark.

8. ***Develop a sense of responsibility in your subordinates.*** Delegation of responsibilities will enhance the team's development. It will reflect your confidence in them and cause them to seek additional responsibilities. Acknowledging their accomplishments fosters their initiatives.

9. ***Ensure that the task is understood, supervised, and accomplished.*** Orders and directives should be clearly understood and all team members should know what is expected of them. There is a fine line between undersupervision and oversupervision. Giving the order is 10 percent; the other 90 percent is ensuring it gets done.

10. ***Train your personnel as a team.*** Team work occurs when all members of the team are proficient in their individual assignments and mutually respect and trust one another. A team must have its own spirit and confidence in its ability to accomplish the culinary and customer satisfaction objectives. Cohesion builds confidence and morale.

These fundamental elements of leadership are common sense. Each one has its own merits, and they all complement each other. People leadership, unlike "thing management," has a connection with the heart. When chefs resort to logic alone, they not only risk treating their team members like machines, but also are often unable to motivate and inspire. In addition to being sensitive to the team's emotional needs, the chef should encourage and reward risk taking to accomplish the organization's goals. Culinary leadership is demonstrated by the chef who:

- Can sacrifice personal glory for the good of the team, has strength of purpose to achieve the goals, cannot be easily discouraged, and does not compromise but adapts

- Understands that working through hardship is an experience that builds courage, can deal with adversity and overcome mistakes, and can achieve anything for which he or she is willing to pay the price
- Does not allow team members' weaknesses to prevail over their strengths and will always set realistic goals for each team member based on his or her abilities
- Has an open style and believes in a win-win relationship with the team and uses diplomacy based on respect of, trust in, and courtesy to the team
- Has a clear vision of the possibilities of the team's potential and inspires them through motivation by aiming high and going after things that will make a difference, rather than seeking the safe path of mediocrity
- Has stamina, high energy levels, tenacity, and a positive attitude; helps the team reach the foodservice organization's goals and objectives, communicates openly with the team, shares the risk taking, and leads by example
- Has a sense of humor, shuns publicity that may be at the expense of the team or the organization, and accepts failure in some things in order to excel in more important ones
- Focuses on problems as opportunities, is tolerant, and never confuses power with leadership
- Invests himself or herself in adequate training of the team, adopts a coaching and correcting style, and understands that training the team is the vital ingredient for quality supervision and leadership

BUILDING LEADERSHIP SELF-CONFIDENCE

Confidence is a matter of style. Chefs should be assertive, not overbearing. Leadership self-confidence can be developed in four action steps. All have to do with one fact— self-confidence—which will increase as leadership tasks are accomplished successfully. In his book, *The Art of the Leader,* William Cohen suggests the following action steps to increase leadership self-confidence:[18]

- Become a leader by seeking out situations and volunteering to be a leader whenever you can.
- Be an unselfish teacher and helper to others. Others will come to you for leadership. Always treat those you lead with respect.
- Develop your expertise. Expertise is a source of leadership power.
- Use positive mental energy. Simulations in the mind are rehearsals for success. They are interpreted by the mind as real experiences. Consequently, they will boost leadership self-confidence just like the actual experiences.

The kitchen team will readily follow a chef who displays confidence. It demonstrates the right to authority. It also makes the team members feel comfortable that there is direction and purpose for what they do.

The way the chef dresses is also part of developing leadership self-confidence. The chef's professional attire and grooming must always be outstanding. This obviously includes a clean, well-groomed, white chef uniform with safe, polished shoes. Personal grooming should be immaculate and reflect the highest standards. The chef is the role model. Professional practices and high personal standards in the kitchen set the chef apart as a leader. Involved in this is the practice of a code of professional ethics for culinary art. Great leaders throughout the ages have understood that their number-one responsibility was their own discipline and personal growth. If chefs cannot lead themselves and manage their lives, they surely will be unable to lead others. Leaders can never take other people further than they have gone themselves. Dwight Eisenhower once said, "In order to be a leader, a man must have followers, a man must have their confidence; hence, the supreme quality for a leader is unquestionably integrity."[19] Training and experience develop a personal assurance with which chefs can meet the challenges of leadership. Those who portray a lack of self-confidence in their ability to carry out leadership assignments give signs to the team that these duties are beyond their capabilities. They therefore become weak leaders.

William Cohen stated, "The first way to develop self-confidence while you develop your leadership skills is to become an uncrowned leader."[20] Individual chefs have many opportunities to become leaders. In the kitchen there may be team members who need help. Seizing the opportunity to lead can help these people build the chef's confidence as a leader. Waiting for management to give direction on team building, however, may stunt a chef's leadership potential. A thinking proactive chef will not wait for direction from above. Instead, he or she will begin immediately to take charge and lead the rest of the team to greater culinary heights.

According to Bennus and Nanus, "Being a manager has to do with doing things right. Being a leader has to do with doing the right things."[21] It is therefore unnecessary to have an official sounding title to be a leader. Leadership development is first and foremost a process of self-development.

DEVELOPING CULINARY LEADERSHIP

What is culinary leadership? Is it about winning gold medals at food shows? Is it about being a celebrated TV chef or being highly rated by some agency? Is it about being an executive chef in a large, prestigious hotel or restaurant? Well, the answer is that it could be all of these things, but not necessarily. The best rating you can have as a culinary leader is from the customers who come back to your restaurant and a loyal kitchen team that follows the chef leader and is concerned for the success of the foodservice operation. Culinary leadership is all about high standards of culinary practices that satisfy restaurant guests and for which the kitchen team has been motivated and trained. Remember, quality is quality no matter the size or type of foodservice operation.

There are several areas in which leadership within the kitchen may be developed. The following are some suggestions that work and will assist in developing a great team atmosphere and will contribute enormously to culinary leadership.

- Develop a particular food philosophy and style. Get each team member involved. Set up food tasting/critique sessions. Involve your customers and dining room staff in these sessions. Formulate your menu items based on the results of these critiques. Aggressively put forward innovative culinary philosophies. Become known for a particular style of food.
- Educate yourself. Take development courses. Join a professional chef's organization. Become certified within your profession. Read trade magazines. Study the latest culinary trends. Network with other chefs.
- Involve the team in entering food shows. This is an excellent method of building team morale and esprit de corps. Train your team. Invest continuously in training. Training a kitchen team is a never-ending task.
- Allocate days during the week for each team member to have his or her own signature menu item.
- Provide the team with distinctive uniforms.
- Insist on the highest culinary standards. At all levels, give the team the authority and responsibility to solve problems and prepare exceptional menu items.
- Build partnerships with your purveyors. Set specifications on quality with them.
- Seek out ways to constantly develop your team. Enroll them in development courses. Arrange for them to attend chef seminars and conferences.

- Involve the support team in all the chef and food philosophies.
- Maintain scrupulous standards of personal hygiene. Insist on high standards of safety and sanitation within the kitchen area.
- Show concern for the welfare of the kitchen team. Treat each member with respect, and trust them to carry out the assigned tasks. Be approachable and sympathetic in the kitchen.
- Visit the dining room. Meet your customers. Encourage feedback from them. Build a strong relationship with the dining room staff. They are vital to achieving culinary success.
- Recognize that empowerment is not a substitute for leadership or a reduction of authority. The more the kitchen team is empowered, the greater the need for culinary leaders who can set goals and define a vision. The paradox of empowerment is that in order to gain power, you must give some of it away.
- Implement the solution through the kitchen team. Solving a problem in the kitchen is not worth much unless you can do this.
- Celebrate your kitchen team and their success, including their promotions, awards, birthdays, marriages, reunions, anniversaries, and holidays, along with the organization's anniversary, the introduction of new menus, and the articulation of the food service organization's vision. Celebration within the kitchen can build individual self-esteem. Each team member will feel important and empowered. Celebration also enhances communication, promotes teamwork, and makes members feel bonded. It makes work fun and creates a positive outlook.

Developing culinary leadership is concerned with encouraging the kitchen team to succeed. To encourage is to inspire others with courage and spirit. Encouragement will help kitchen team members change behaviors and attitudes. It will develop in each individual self-confidence and positive feelings about his or her own capabilities. Encouragement should be given during times of stress, particularly when failure is looming. It should be given equally and fairly to all team members, emphasizing the positive and not the negative in others. Encouragement will give the kitchen team a sense of belonging, provide positive self-image, and encourage positive attitudes toward the chef.

When the team is placed first, the highest possible productivity will result in the kitchen as well as total quality relative to culinary practices and customer satisfaction. Profits for the foodservice organization will follow.

HUMOR AS A LEADERSHIP TOOL

"Always leave them laughing." This old phrase is one of the chef leader's best guides. A kitchen that is highly emotionally negative inhibits the development of a "Golden Rule" environment in the kitchen. As stated in a previous chapter, "Team members in a *Golden Rule Environment* do not do things because they fear the consequences. Rather team members do things because they want success for everyone, including themselves and the operation." A golden rule environment thrives on positivity. **Positivity** is the state of being emotionally positive. There is no better vehicle for achieving positivity in the kitchen than humor. Fun relieves tension and improves concentration. It counteracts boredom and reduces the potential for conflict within the kitchen. The bottom line? A kitchen team whose members enjoy and support one another is more productive.

Clarification is called for here. Inappropriate humor, such as jokes made at the expense of others or in a manner that demeans people, does not contribute to a positive environment. More importantly, it is wrong and should never be tolerated. Also, humor that distracts the team from its focus and its goals is destructive, not constructive. The humor that is being talked about here is humorous to everyone and promotes a positive environment.

Figure 17-6
Suggestions for using humor in the kitchen.

- Maintain a humor file.
- Include appropriate humor in your team meetings.
- Tailor your humor to the taste and preferences of the kitchen team.
- Look for humor in those little interruptions that occur during meetings or during the service period.
- Keep your humor brief.
- Recognize when humor is not appropriate.
- Don't joke about people's gender, ethnicity, and personal or physical characteristics.

While humor comes easier to some people than others, we all have the ability to introduce humor into the mix. Remember, however, that humor works best when it is natural and not forced. Humor is a powerful tool for enhancing self-confidence and building empathy. Humor can promote positive attitudes within the team, making it easier to hear feedback and new information. Humor also distracts from worry; lightens stress, anxiety, depression, and pain; increases creativity; and offers perspective and balance. It can help express the truth when the truth is feared and repressed. The use of humor decreases discipline problems and pressure on team members to be perfect. It also improves listening and employee retention and creates a comfort level in the kitchen. Studies have shown that employees who have fun at work are less likely to be late or absent.[22] Figure 17-6 shows some suggestions to consider for using humor in the kitchen. As a team member, and eventually as a chef, work to cultivate a sense of humor and then use it to motivate and create a positive work environment.

CHEF TALK
"CHEF LEADERSHIP"

During the 30 years of my career, I have experienced many forms of leadership, from the very simple and basic in the beginning to the complex and brilliant later. I had the privilege to learn from some of the best not only in a working environment, but also during culinary team practices and association activities. While developing my own style, I was able to listen to good advice as well as experience some less-desirable forms of leadership. For some reason, it seems easier to recall the horrors than the positive situations. This may be due to the fact that good leaders seldom resort to extremes to get the job done.

During the early part of my apprenticeship, when I was very young—15 in fact—a transformation of power was going on that I found interesting to reflect upon later. Due to my youth, my father was reluctant to give up his control over me. This was apparent from his overly protective interest in what I was doing. I spent most of the day working a split shift. I started at 8:00 A.M. and returned home at 10:00 P.M., with a 3-hour break in the afternoon. My father wanted me to be at home to work during my break. My chef, on the other hand, wanted us to use this time to study and rest because the workload from school was heavy and we worked 6-day weeks. I was not doing well in school, and my chef realized that he needed to intervene. He suggested to my father that I should stay with other apprentices in the room at work and go home on my day off. My father agreed

reluctantly. My chef spent some time studying with me, and I made a remarkable turnaround in school.

Since my chef took an interest in me, I became more confident in my work. Soon I was helping him with his work on shows, and during my last year, in 1960, he took me to the IKA (Culinary Olympics) in Frankfurt for my first exposure to this remarkable show. My chef's leadership style was not very polished. He could have been described as rough and abrasive. He would say, "Let them do hard and dirty work for one year and if they are still there, I might remember their name." If you made it, however, it got better in the third year. The kitchen was run by the apprentices on Mondays, two from each year, when the chef and cooks were off. This was our turn to practice leadership by getting the job done. Since we had a daily menu, the third-year apprentices could write it and direct the kitchen. Looking back, I noticed that every Monday the crew elected me to be the chef. What made it happen was that I was willing to do the research necessary to write the menu, order the food, make the production charts, and, most importantly, take the heat if something went wrong. Not much went wrong on my Mondays because I made sure everything was well planned.

—Klaus Friedenreich, CMC, AAC,
Chef Instructor,
Le Cordon Bleu College,
Orlando, Florida

CONCLUSIONS

There is no single best style of leadership. The best leadership pattern is the one that works best for *you*. Excellent personal qualities and characteristics help in being a good leader. However, leadership skill sets are learned and are not something that you are born with. The team is the greatest resource the foodservice operation has. How the team is led will ultimately determine the success or failure of a restaurant.

A very old leadership tenet states that you should be willing to do everything you ask those you lead to do. Therefore, personal example is very important. Most people do not like to follow leaders who cannot make up their minds and have trouble coming to a decision. Therefore, be a decisive leader. The leader sets the tone. A large component of this tone is a leader's ego. If the leader sets a positive example—one of service, dedication, support, and concern—others will strive toward the same goal. The leader's role is one of service. His or her job is to create structures that allow each team member to achieve the desired quality result. Good chef leaders actively create structures and symbols that remind team members of their concern for the human side of the culinary operation. Items that support this effort are:

- Periodic social get-togethers
- Recognition of individual and team accomplishments; ensuring that everybody in the organization (not just the kitchen) knows what the kitchen team does
- Creating an internal kitchen team slogan
- Encouraging mild competitiveness among team members and between department groups
- On a rotating basis, putting up photos of various people in the team

Though such things may seem frivolous, they are important since they help keep a human feeling in the kitchen.

There are only two ways to get others to do what you want. You can compel them to do it, or you can persuade them. Persuading requires an understanding of what makes people tick and what motivates them, that is, a knowledge of human nature. Great leaders possess this knowledge. Max DePree sums up what he feels are the traits and behaviors most people resent in leaders:[23]

- Superficiality
- Lack of dignity
- Injustice, the flaw that prevents equity
- Arrogance
- Betrayal of principles of quality
- Overuse of jargon, because it confuses rather than clarifies
- Viewing customers as interruptions
- Watching bottom lines without watching behavior
- Never saying thank you to others
- Failure to permit team members to do their best
- Dependence on policies and hierarchy rather than on trust and competence

Many leaders note that the most efficient way to get good performance from others is to treat them like heroes. Giving public credit to someone who has earned it is a great leadership technique. Successful leaders often say that if you trust others to do well, they will. If, on the other hand, you believe your team will fail, they will. Good leaders learn to sound and look like winners. Competence will galvanize the team. They will look to you for guidance and direction. When team members get excited about their work, all the team's energy is channeled into the tasks. The best way for the chef to generate excitement is to be enthusiastic. It is contagious. Good leaders cannot do it alone. They should delegate. Make the team look good, and the team will make the chef look good.

SUMMARY

Leadership in the kitchen confers on the chef the privilege and responsibility to direct the actions of the kitchen team in carrying out the goals and objectives of the food-service organization.

Leadership can be learned in the same way chefs learn culinary skills. Leadership development is a process of self-development. It is facilitated by education, training, mentoring, and experience and is dependent on the chef's ability to lead people in such a way that team members will want to follow.

The trait approach to leadership was based on early research that assumed that good leaders were born,

not made. Behavioral theories are directed to the study of work groups, leaders, and supervisors rather than the characteristics of successful leaders.

Situational leadership is based on the premise that different situations will require different leadership styles. The four basic situational leadership styles are directing, supporting, coaching, and delegating.

Culinary leadership is as much about respecting and valuing kitchen team members as it is about great culinary creations.

Humor is a valuable leadership tool. Laugh with your kitchen team, not at them.

DISCUSSION QUESTIONS

1. Define the following chapter key terms:
   a. Authority
   b. Supervision
   c. Management
   d. Leadership
   e. Authority of position
   f. Trait approach
   g. "Great Man" theory
   h. Dimensions of leadership
   i. Behavioral theories
   j. Consideration
   k. Structure
   l. Situational approach
   m. Positivity
2. In what way is leadership different from supervision?
3. What are the more significant factors that affect chefs' leadership styles?
4. What are the differences between autocratic and democratic leadership styles?
5. Is there one best leadership style? Explain.
6. What are situations appropriate for the four styles of situational leadership?
7. What are some of the myths associated with leadership?
8. What are the essential differences between "directive" and "supportive" leadership behaviors? When and why are they used?
9. The "Great Man" theory relied on profiling a certain set of characteristics. It was believed it would be easy to pinpoint leaders when these traits were summarized. Do you agree with this theory? Give reasons for your answers.
10. What are eight characteristics of chef leaders?
11. The paradox of empowerment states that in order to gain power, you must give some of it away. How does this affect the chef as a leader?
12. What are the benefits of using humor as a leadership tool?

NOTES

1. Peggy Anderson, ed., *Great Quotes from Great Leaders* (Lombard, IL: 1989), 53.

2. James M. Kouzes and Barry Z. Posner, *Credibility: How Leaders Gain and Lose It, Why People Demand It* (San Francisco: Jossey-Bass, 1993).

3. John C. Maxwell, *Developing the Leader Within You* (Nashville, TN: Nelson, 1993), 103.

4. Warren Bennus and Burt Nanus, *Leaders: The Strategies for Taking Charge* (New York: Harper-Collins, 1985), 222.

5. John C. Maxwell, *The 21 Irrefutable Laws of Leadership* (Nashville, TN, Thomas Nelson Publishers, 1998), 21.

6. James M. Kouzes and Barry Z. Posner, *The Leadership Challenge* (San Francisco: Jossey-Bass, 1988), xv.

7. Patrick L. O'Malley, "Make Excellence a Habit," *Lessons in Leadership* (New York: Van Nostrand Reinhold, 1991), 40.

8. Kenneth Blanchard, Patricia Zigarni, and Drea Zigarni, *Leadership and the One Minute Manager* (New York: Morrow & Co., 1985), 31.

9. *Sky Magazine,* Delta Airlines, July 1993.

10. Warren Bennus and Burt Nanus, *Leaders: The Strategies for Taking Charge* (New York: Harper-Collins, 1985), 5.

11. Arthur Sherman, George Bohlander, and Herbert Crudden, *Managing Human Resources,* 8th ed. (Cincinnati, OH: South-Western, 1988), 355.

12. James M. Kouzes and Barry Z. Posner, *The Leadership Challenge* (San Francisco: Jossey-Bass, 1988), 16.

13. Ronald Cichy, Martin P. Sciarini, and Mark E. Patton, "Food-Service Leadership: Could Attila Run a Restaurant," *The Cornell Hotel and Restaurant Administration Quarterly,* February 1992.

14. Denis C. Kinlaw, *Coaching for Commitment* (San Diego, CA: Pfeiffer, 1993), 122.

15. Kenneth Blanchard, Patricia Zigarni, and Drea Zigarni, *Leadership and the One Minute Manager* (New York: Morrow & Co., 1985).

16. Jerry L. Hill, "Steer Clear of the Minefields," *Lessons in Leadership* (New York: Van Nostrand Reinhold, 1991), 135.

17. *Sky Magazine,* Delta Airlines, July 1993, 24–28.

18. William A. Cohen, *The Art of the Leader* (Englewood Cliffs, NJ: Prentice-Hall, 1990), 97.

19. Peggy Anderson, ed., *Great Quotes From Great Leaders* (Lombard, IL: Great Quotations, 1989), p. 52.

20. William A. Cohen, *The Art of the Leader* (Englewood Cliffs, NJ: Prentice-Hall, 1990), 85.

21. Warren Bennus and Burt Nanus, *Leaders: The Strategies for Taking Charge* (New York: Harper-Collins, 1985), 23.

22. Joseph L. Picogna, *Total Quality Leadership: A Training Approach* (Morrisville, PA: International Information Associates Inc., 1993), 348.

23. Max DePree, *Leadership Is an Art* (New York: Dell, 1989), 138.

Chapter 18
Communication

OBJECTIVES

When you complete this chapter, you should be able to:

1. Describe the elements of effective communication
2. Identify barriers to good communication
3. Describe aspects of nonverbal communication
4. Define the elements of effective listening and describe ways to improve listening
5. Outline the steps for leading and managing kitchen team meetings
6. Identify methods of giving directions to kitchen team members so as to ensure satisfactory and timely completion of tasks
7. Communicate effectively in written form
8. Identify the positive and negative aspects of communication via the grapevine

Case Study: La Maison Blanc

Chef Herve is executive chef of La Maison Blanc, one of the city's finest restaurants and its premier banquet facility. Chef Herve has been with La Maison Blanc for two weeks. Chef Herve is extremely frustrated because he does not understand why the food for the event in the second-floor ballroom is not ready. The function was scheduled to start at 5 P.M. and it was 4:30 P.M. Additionally, the food that was ready was either improperly prepared or presented, or in many cases both.

The function was assigned to Sous Chef Heinz, who has been with La Maison Blanc for 3 years and should know how to handle a function of this type and size. Chef Herve had discussed the event with Heinz for almost an hour the day before to ensure that everything would be taken care of properly. He had a clear recollection of the meeting.

At the meeting, Chef Herve had read the work order to Heinz. This had taken longer than he anticipated because he had to answer the phone several times. He had then asked Heinz if he had any questions. Heinz had asked some questions, and Chef Herve had answered his questions as rapidly as possible between phone calls. Chef Herve also remembered that he had not finished answering Heinz's last question because the phone rang and Heinz had excused himself, returning to the kitchen.

Chef Herve does not understand why Heinz did not follow instructions. He has found Heinz to be a very conscientious worker and a skilled culinarian. Heinz has a reputation for being proud of his culinary team and the work they produce. When Chef Herve asked Heinz why the food was not ready, Heinz said that the function did not start until 7 P.M., the normal start time for a function of this type. When asked why the food was not prepared and presented as it was supposed to be, Heinz said that he and his team had done the best they could with the information they had.

Chef Herve instructed Heinz to immediately complete the preparation of the food and take care of the guests. He also told Heinz that they would discuss his failure to perform the next day, when time allowed. Heinz responded that he would be there when the Chef found the time.

Based on what you have learned from previous chapters and the content of this chapter, answer the following questions.

- What is the overall reason for the challenges occurring in the La Maison Blanc?
- What are the primary causal agents for the challenges occurring in the La Maison Blanc?
- What role did supervision/management play in the decline at the La Maison Blanc?
- What specific steps could have been taken to avoid the current situation occurring in the La Maison Blanc?
- What, specifically, can be done to overcome the challenges and generate motion in a positive direction for the La Maison Blanc?

INTRODUCTION

A chef uses communication to gather, process, and transmit information essential to the well-being of the organization. Since this communication moves in many directions, the needs of peers, superiors, and fellow team members need to be given careful consideration. Communication is a crucial element of the supervision, management, and leadership process. Chefs often run into problems because of their inability to communicate effectively. As much as 85 percent of a chef's day is spent in some form of communication, most of it speaking and listening to others.[1]

Communication involves a sender, a receiver, and the transfer of information from a source to a destination. Effective supervision, management, and leadership—delegating, coaching, team building, and information transfer—depend on understanding all the elements of communication. It is the most exacting of all the skills and the one the chef is called upon most frequently to use. Communication is the basis for understanding, cooperation, and action within the kitchen. An open, well-developed communication system will result in a higher standard of quality food production and service through a two-way flow of ideas, opinions, and decisions.

Communication grows and develops in a positive kitchen work environment in which the elements of trust and understanding are adopted. The purpose of communication in the foodservice establishment, and particularly the kitchen, is to ensure that all individuals understand the vision, goals, objectives, policies, and procedures of the organization. Kitchen team members who are confused, unhappy, and *uninformed* may become discontented. Communication is much more than talking, speaking, and reading. If successful, the sender will direct or communicate a message that is clear and accurately understood by the receiver in the way that the sender intends. Most problems with effective communication occur in the middle portion of communication. These are known as the "**noise**" or the elements that cause misunderstanding.

Communication between sender and receiver passes through filters of culture, age, gender, education, and different fields of past experiences, which cause noise in the understanding of messages.[2] This often leads to misperceptions, misinterpretations, and misevaluations. It is therefore necessary to recognize these differences and develop a communication style that helps each individual to understand. Words and gestures often mean different things to different people. Understanding these differences is an important skill for a chef.

Communication must flow in many directions—upward from supervisors to higher management, downward to subordinates, and laterally to team members. Effective upward communication can help team members contribute to the organization and can provide an opportunity for the chef to get to know and understand each team member better. The more avenues created to facilitate communication within the kitchen, the better the work environment.

The chef should set an example of being open and honest. The more feedback and ideas provided to the kitchen team, the more comfortable members will feel about sharing their ideas and feelings. To encourage open communication, the chef should reward rather than punish open expressions of feelings, opinions, or problems. Openness should be rewarded by showing appreciation for team members who share negative or sensitive messages.

Some chefs may feel threatened by ideas from creative individuals within the kitchen. This need not be so. In some cases supervisors may talk down to individuals, thus causing feelings of anger and hurt. Only when messages are understood as intended can effective coaching be a reality. Misinterpretations can cause many problems in the kitchen among team members and between different departments. For example, if a customer's meal order is misunderstood, not only is this costly in terms of wasted food and time, but also it contributes to customer annoyance and delays and exasperation on the part of the wait-person.

Since foodservice employees sometimes do not speak English, it is important to understand the barriers to communication that arise from different cultural attitudes, values, and beliefs. In some cultural groups, people say "yes" when they do not mean "yes."[3] In addition to difficulty in understanding English, nonnative speakers may have difficulty interpreting body language. These signals may have different meanings for different groups and thus cause communication problems. Good communication within the kitchen is essential for successful implementation of goals and objectives. It also ensures a safe work environment. Communication consists of many parts and has different elements. These are discussed in the following sections.

ELEMENTS OF COMMUNICATION

The communication activities of a chef involve interpersonal communication. To be complete, the interpersonal communication process must contain the three basic elements shown in Figure 18-1.

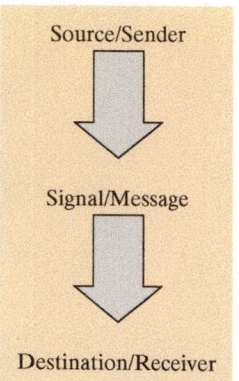

Figure 18-1
Basic elements of the interpersonal communication process.

The **source/sender** is the person who originates and encodes the message he or she wishes to share with other members in the foodservice operation. Encoding is the process of putting information in a form that can be received, decoded, and understood by others. Using menus to convey ideas and thoughts is a form of encoding.

In the **signal/message**, information that the source (sender) intends to share is a message. A message that has been transferred from one team member to another is called a signal.

The **destination/receiver** is the person who receives the message and with whom the sender is attempting to share information. The team member receives this information and decodes or interprets the message to determine its meaning. Communication, therefore, is an interpretive transaction between individuals. The sender of the message encodes it according to his or her knowledge (field of experience), and the receiver decodes it according to his or her field of experience.

What is important to effective, clear, and accurate understanding of information in the kitchen is the chef's skill in encoding messages so that the message means the same thing to those receiving it. Kitchen team members come from many different backgrounds. Each will interpret a message differently based on his or her background (field of experience).

Often, jargon (French culinary technical terms) is used to describe skills and culinary principles. Assuming that each individual has a clear understanding of these terms may frequently cause communication gaps. It should not be assumed that information has been transferred and interpreted in the way intended, as demonstrated in Figure 18-2.

Assuming that each team member understood what was communicated can cause confusion and frustration for both parties. Check for understanding; not doing so may cause operational problems. The aim of good communication is to ensure that the sender and the receiver both have the same picture of the message in their minds. To increase the probability that communication will be successful, the sender (chef) must encode the message to ensure that the way in which the signal is decoded is equivalent to the receiver's experience of the way in which it should be decoded. Simply put, the message should be said in a manner that makes it both clear and understood the same by both the sender and the receiver.

BARRIERS TO COMMUNICATION

The interpretation of what the chef says is directly affected by each team member's knowledge, experience, and culture, to name just a few factors. The factors and issues that decrease effective communication within the foodservice operation and in all

> This is the story of four people: Everybody, Somebody, Anybody, and Nobody.
> There was an important job to be done, and Everybody was sure that Somebody would do it.
> Anybody could have done it, but Nobody did it.
> Somebody got angry because it was Everybody's job.
> Everybody thought that Somebody would do it.
> But Nobody asked Anybody.
> It ended up that the job wasn't done, and Everybody blamed Somebody, when actually Nobody asked Anybody.
>
> —Anonymous

Figure 18-2
What went wrong?

Figure 18-3
Subconscious barriers to communication.

Age
Appearance
Eye contact
Facial expressions
Gender
Movement
Personal space
Skin color
Touch

communication are called communication barriers. One of these barriers is language. Many foodservice workers do not speak English, and this can pose many problems that need to be overcome. When dealing with team members whose native tongue is not English, it is important to be familiar with not only their language but also their culture. There are also other factors that receivers subconsciously apply to messages they receive. These subconscious factors, shown in Figure 18-3, affect how the team member both interprets the message and assesses the source of the message.

Barriers to effective communication become obvious during the first few minutes of inter-action when attention span is at its highest, the eye and ear focus on the sender, and the brain receives what it sees and hears. People tend to focus on what they see first. It takes only two to four minutes to create a positive or negative impression.[4] Success as a communicator is measured by the impressions created in the kitchen. Four key questions need to be addressed to overcome perception barriers:

- How am I perceived by others?
- How do I "sound" to others?
- What do I say to others?
- How well do I listen to others?

Depending on the field of experience of the receiver, significance may be applied to a part of you that has little to do with your skills as the chef, for example, the nonverbal messages sent by your body language, how quickly you speak, your handshake, and how well you maintain eye contact.

Guidelines for Effective Communication

The effectiveness of communication is the responsibility of both the sender and the receiver. The sender can communicate more effectively with the receiver by observing the following guidelines:

- Keep the message focused on its original purpose. This makes communication clearer and easier to follow for all team members.
- Check for understanding by asking questions and requesting feedback.
- Demonstrate interest and encourage clarity of interpretation by asking open-ended questions that begin with *who, what, when, where,* and *how.*
- Ideas should be communicated at the proper time and place. Try to catch team members at a time when their frame of mind is receptive to information. Use nonverbal signals. This shows that you are interested in what is being said.
- Enhance the receiver's (team member's) self-confidence and encourage communication by complimenting the receiver.
- Use the receiver's name whenever possible. This demonstrates respect and acknowledgment.

- Communicate by your tone of voice, facial expressions, words, body language, and appearance that you care about the receiver and the message. All of these factors affect the reception of the message.
- Have the message clear in your mind before communicating. The more systematically the chef analyzes the problem or idea to be communicated, the clearer it becomes. Planning is essential to good communication. Consideration of the attitudes and emotions of the receiver who will be affected must be factored into the communication plan.

The receiver can be a more effective receiver by doing the following:

- Summarize by paraphrasing or restating the core of the message.
- Ask questions when unsure. A lot of confusion may be avoided by asking the sender to repeat or rephrase the message.
- Respond to nonverbal cues. This clarifies the meaning of a bodily reaction. It will ensure that behaviors and words convey the same message and also demonstrate understanding.
- Sincerity and *insincerity* in communicating will become apparent if careful thought is not part of the reception of ideas and opinions. In any communication there must be feedback from the receiver to the sender. The receiver should feel free to respond fully.
- Seek not only to be understood, but also to understand.
- Be a good listener. When we are talking, we often are not listening. Listen for the full meaning of the sender's message.
- Analyzing body language, eye contact, and the verbal message assists in reaching meaningful conclusions about the information.

Trust and success are built on consistency and balance of interpersonal communications. What you sound like reveals a lot about your personality, attitude, and anxiety level. Being aware of how you sound can help you correct and improve your communication skills. It is possible to learn to recognize signs of tension and stress in your voice and the voices of others. What you say is reflected by how you say it. Balance between language and delivery is critical in removing barriers. Verbal skills should support and balance the nonverbal and verbal messages sent.

Since the kitchen team often is diverse, agreement on meanings will vary. There will be variations on what a "pinch" of salt, a "dash" of pepper, or a "big" steak is, or what "seasoned to taste" means. Assumptions and expectations distort the intended communication. Clarify and explain each piece of the message. Clearly, a skillful chef does more than just relay the message. The problem is that many barriers muddle the process and hinder clear communication.

It should not be assumed that just because the chef "gave the message" the receivers "got it." One of the biggest problems of communicating in a tension-laden kitchen environment is the emotions of people who are sending and receiving messages. If something is said in anger, then it is the anger that comes across and not the message. Tempers flare, the receiver is likely to hear things that were not said, and the sender is likely to say things that were not intended. When we are criticized, we often become emotional and excited. Defensive reactions to feedback on job performances are common.

The fundamental communication barrier between people stems from differences in backgrounds, personalities, beliefs, education, religion, life experiences, and professional outlook. Our ability to receive messages is limited by our tendency to hear only what we want or expect to hear. It is a normal human phenomenon that the mind resists what it does not expect or want to perceive. We have a natural tendency to judge

WHAT IS THIS BUSINESS?
THIS IS NOT ROCKET SCIENCE

What we do in the restaurant business is not rocket science. The recipe for success is basic: hire the right person, train them to do the job, and follow up on their performance, praising often and correcting as needed. As simple as the recipe may seem, I was in this business for many years before I discovered this critical truth. I would describe my early management style as grounded in the 1950s and 1960s. If I did not like what a staff member was doing, I asked them to leave. I did not discuss what they were doing wrong or try to correct their actions. I was afraid that I would lose the opportunity to get rid of them if I tried to discuss the situation or correct their actions. But even then I believed that it is all a team effort. I believe that we all work together. So the individuals that make up Grill Concepts and its restaurants do not work for me; we work together. Yet in those early years I fired in a summary fashion: "Here is your check; leave because you do not work here anymore."

In the early days of The Grill on the Alley, Chef Fausto was part of the team. The operation was running at an unanticipated pace with a minimum of 200 covers per night, and often as many as 300. I was not satisfied with Chef Fausto's performance, so I prepared his final check, called him into my office, and told him that he was fired and gave him his final check. When I did this, the look on his face was one of complete surprise. As he left, I realized that he had no idea that he was not doing exactly what I wanted him to do. That was a critical turning point for me as a manager: the realization and acknowledgement to myself that the problem was not Chef Fausto; the problem was my failure to communicate.

The philosophy of Grill Concepts and its restaurants is the acronym PEOPLE: Pride-Excellence-Opportunity-Profit-Leadership-Enjoyment. PEOPLE is a philosophy that must be applied internally and externally. It must be imbedded in the Grill's culture. This philosophy must be constantly communicated through the actions of those in a position to lead.

When I was in my twenties, my father closed his restaurant and I was unemployed with a family to support. I took a job at a paint store. It was a temporary position because the store was closing and going out of business, but it helped me stay afloat until I could get another job. The first thing that we did when I went to work at the paint store was organize the inventory and the store for the sale. In a very short period of time everyone was coming to me to find out how to organize and where stock was located. I began to realize that people trusted me and would listen to me.

When I went to work later for a company called FEDCO, Mr. George Cohn told me that "Follow-Me" was one of the most effective management styles. Today this is called modeling. One of the keys to my success has been my "Follow-Me" style. I do not just lead or manage; I work to literally take everyone forward with me. I let them know that this is a company founded by someone who used to wash dishes and has experienced setbacks and losses.

Communication is critical to the success of any operation and any company. Hiring the right person must be followed by training. Training is the communication of expectations for performance. In the training process, the values and the culture also are communicated. Training must be followed by positive action. What is being done correctly must be praised, and what is not correct must be recognized and assistance provided to bring about change.

The goal of Grill Concepts is to hire, train, and follow through in a manner that makes being part of the Grill the last restaurant job the individual needs to find. The communication of a path to a career is critical to retaining high performers. I am particularly proud of the number of team members that have been with the Grill for 15, 20, and 25 years. These individuals take pride in their work, and that pride is critical. These team members do not produce outstanding food because they are told to; they do it because that gives them a feeling of satisfaction and fulfillment, a feeling of a job well done.

What we do in the restaurant industry is feed people. Follow me and we will execute this basic task with excellence. We give our customers pleasure and enjoyment. We help them understand that you eat to survive, but that does not mean it cannot be enjoyable.

—Bob Spivak,
Founder, Grill Concepts,
Woodland Hills, CA

or evaluate statements and to reach hasty conclusions. We evaluate messages from our own frame of reference instead of understanding the sender's point of view. This does not add up to effective communication. Instead, two ideas are being advanced without an exchange of information. A closed mind hinders communication.

Limits on time impede communication. Chefs are busy people and tend to give hurried instructions and then move on to the next task. The receiver can be confused or frustrated by these incomplete messages. Additionally, chefs should pay particular attention to the problem of stereotyping. Stereotypes are attitudes favoring or rejecting certain groups without examining individual circumstances or traits. The need to understand numerous tasks forces the mind to arrange things into easily identifiable groups. Another barrier that often surfaces in the kitchen is the tendency to see everything in black and white, which distorts reality and oversimplifies situations.

In the kitchen a great deal of jargon is used. This jargon is familiar to those within the chef profession but is usually unintelligible to outsiders. Care should be taken when using French culinary terms such as *mise-en-place, sauté, garde manger, sous chef, chinois, rechaud,* and *a la carte* and the names of various dishes in different languages. Using these terms not only tends to alienate team members, but also adds to confusion. Because many words have several definitions, their meanings can easily become confused in conversation. They often convey a message to a receiver quite different from that intended by the sender. Nonverbal signals, such as tone of voice, gestures, and appearance, are the most important factors in determining how a message is received and understood.

NONVERBAL COMMUNICATION

In general, senders are consciously attentive only to the spoken word. But individuals often communicate without using words. This is referred to as **nonverbal communication** or **body language**. Elements of nonverbal communication include gestures such as nodding of the head, use of hands, and facial expressions. All of these send messages. Smiling and frowning convey emotion, as does voice intonation or loudness. Ideally, the right nonverbal cues accompany the verbal communication. Nonverbal communication may influence the impact of a message more than verbal communication alone.

The meanings of gestures and movements vary from culture to culture. Communication scholars agree that nonverbal communication is most successful between people of similar cultural characteristics. When these characteristics differ, communication barriers occur.[5] Nonverbal gestures that would not be considered offensive in some cultures may be insulting to team members from other cultures. Some common gestures and what they mean are shown in Figure 18-4.

The chef should be aware of the gestures and body language used as well as the signals sent with such gestures. Nonverbal body language provides many cues that indicate when communication will be most effective. These aspects of nonverbal communication are expressed through facial gestures, posture, orientation, gestures, eye contact, and appearance.

Figure 18-4
Nonverbal gestures.

- Leaning forward is a positive gesture. The person is listening and wishes to hear what is said. This also suggests acceptance and willingness to take action.
- Direct eye contact is a positive gesture in Euro-American cultures. Lack of eye contact despite sincere words is interpreted as untrustworthiness. However, many Oriental societies find direct eye contact rude.
- Open hands may be a sign of agreement and careful listening, while crossed arms and legs or leaning backward may be considered defensive, resisting, and rejecting.
- Arms folded over the chest with fists clenched is usually a sign that the person is not listening. This is indicative of a person who is nervous, anxious, uptight, and holding in emotions.
- Leaning away from you in a chair may indicate disinterest in what you are saying.
- Leaning far forward with defiant expression, hands spread on table, is indicative of a person with a volatile personality who may be frustrated, angry, and explosive.
- Backing away or avoidance is generally a sign of disagreement with what you say.
- Shaking a closed fist is a threatening gesture.
- Shoulders hunched forward and down with arms extended and hands overlapped in front of the body usually indicates shyness.

LISTENING

Communication is always a two-way process. One person says something, and another person hears what was said. Since each person comes to the listening situation with different fields of experience, there is often a gap between the speaker's intention and the listener's interpretation. **Listening** is the complex and selective process of receiving, focusing, deciphering, accepting, and storing what we hear. Listening does not occur without these five interrelated, yet distinct, processes.[6] Hearing is the absorption of sound. Listening is something quite different. Ineffective listening can be a major communication problem. Chefs who listen carefully to their team will have fewer problems and greater success in quality management.

Poor listening habits may result in conflicts, costly errors, and inefficiency. Becoming an active and effective listener in the kitchen has important benefits:

- The chef can gain information from sources that he or she may previously have missed through poor listening.
- Even though the chef may not always agree with team members, at least the chef will be perceived as open and fair-minded.

This is achieved by being open and listening to team members' work problems without jumping to conclusions. Maintaining eye contact, an interested facial expression, and a calm voice reflects a posture of good listening. If the chef is narrow-minded, then active listening is impossible. Understanding the active listening process allows the chef to target deficiencies in his or her own listening skills and to better receive messages. In addition, active listening is one of the most powerful means of creating warmth and sensitivity, which contributes to the overall motivational environment in the kitchen.

Types of Listening

Critical listening involves analyzing a message and judging the message for facts, documentation, logic, relationships, inferences, and personal biases. We use this form of listening whenever people try to persuade us to their point of view.

Discriminative listening involves comprehension and recall. It requires listening for details, sequences, and then developing questions and answers, summarizing main points, evaluating ideas, and giving feedback. This is an essential listening skill for a chef.

Therapeutic listening involves listening with an understanding of another person's feelings, beliefs, and values. It requires supportive and sympathetic verbal and nonverbal feedback. It is appropriate when kitchen team members have work-related or personal problems they want to talk out. Nonverbal feedback includes sympathetic gestures—smiling, nodding, and leaning toward the speaker. This type of listening creates an atmosphere that lowers the speaker's defenses, allowing him or her to verbalize the problem.

Appreciative listening is generally reserved for relaxation, satisfaction, or gratification. It is for personal enjoyment and can range from listening to music or enjoying the sound of the speaker's accent—the tone, rhythm, or brogue.

Courteous listening is conversational and social listening. We use courteous listening to keep interpersonal relationships intact. Courteous listening is used mainly to keep lines of communication open.

Ways to Improve Listening Skills

- *Avoid distractions.* When communicating with someone, avoid distractions. Focus, concentrate your attention. Don't let your mind wander. Most people think at a rate of 500 words per minute. People talk at a rate of 150 words per minute. Stay focused on what is being said, or you will risk missing key points.

- *Listen for main ideas.* People sometimes formulate ideas as the conversation develops. These ideas and comments may be vague. Individuals may have trouble coming to the point, particularly if it concerns sensitive issues. Restate the other person's main ideas in your own words and ask whether you have understood correctly.

- *Ask questions.* Ask questions during the discussion or conversation. If something is unclear or seems to contradict your personal sense of logic, seek clarity. This encourages the talker and shows that you are listening and are interested in what he or she has to say.

- *Suppress your biases.* We all have biases, opinions, and prejudices. While listening we often allow certain words, ideas, or statements to trigger emotional responses. Give the speaker a chance to make the point. We may not like what is being said, but we should listen.

- *Indicate to the sender your feelings about the communication.* This shows empathy and clarifies the sender's position. However, refrain from interrupting the person speaking until he or she has had a chance to complete the sentence or thought.

- *Give your full attention.* Refrain from fidgeting, squirming, scribbling, twiddling your thumbs, sorting papers, and writing menus. Give the speaker your undivided attention. Most of us can do only one thing well at a time. Looking away during conversation communicates indifference to what the other person is saying. Show the other person the interest and attention that you yourself would like to receive.

- *Be sensitive and seek understanding.* Listen for the rationale behind what the other person is saying. This is important if what he or she is saying does not make sense to you. A kitchen team member may be making a request on the basis of erroneous information about the organization. Be sensitive and make sure you understand why people say what they do.

- *Respond to nonverbal cues.* This clarifies the meaning of a reaction. It ensures that behavior and words convey the same message and shows understanding.

- *Don't stop the flow.* Listen to all messages, not just the interesting ones. If we are poor listeners, our inclination is to stop listening. Too often we allow external or internal distractions to divert us from the speaker's message. Active listening skills are key. Seldom is a message so boring that we can't find reasons to listen.

- *Listen to their point of view.* Consider the other person's emotions and background. Some people's background and motivations are so different from ours that we tend to ignore their perceptions. You may learn something new.

Listening will help the chef get in touch with the feelings of the kitchen team. Chefs who actively listen demonstrate respect, sensitivity, and patience toward the kitchen team. In addition, team members may have ideas on ways to speed up production and may suggest new menu items and recipes. But unless the chef is willing to listen, the ideas are lost, and so are additional team-building opportunities. The "Ten Commandments" for good listening shown in Figure 18-5 give solid suggestions for being an effective listener.

People generally like to hear what is consistent with their own belief structures; they usually resist contrary ideas.[7] It takes an open mind to be able to listen to criticism. Feedback as an element of communication is closely linked with good listening abilities. Unfortunately, most people do not learn feedback skills and therefore give critical feedback poorly.

1. Stop talking! You cannot listen if you are talking.
2. Put the talker at ease. Help the talker feel free to talk. This is often called a permissive environment.
3. Show the talker that you want to listen. Look and act interested. Do not read your mail while he or she talks. Listen to understand rather than to oppose.
4. Remove distractions. Don't doodle, tap, or shuffle papers. Wouldn't it be quieter if you shut the door?
5. Empathize with the talker. Try to put yourself in the talker's place so that you can see his or her point of view.
6. Be patient. Allow plenty of time. Do not interrupt the talker. Don't start for the door or walk away.
7. Hold your temper. An angry person gets the wrong meaning from words.
8. Go easy on argument and criticism. This puts the talker on the defensive. He or she may "clam up" or get angry. Do not argue: Even if you win, you lose.
9. Ask questions. This encourages the talker and shows you are listening. It helps to develop points further.
10. Stop talking! This is the first and last commandment, because all others depend on it. You can't listen well while you are talking. Nature gave us two ears but only one tongue, which is a gentle hint that we should listen more than talk.

Figure 18-5
Ten commandments for good listening.

GIVING DIRECTIONS

Giving directions to other team members in the kitchen is what gets every task started. The communication flow for effective directions is illustrated in the model in Figure 18-6. The manner used to give directions is as important as the information given. The clarity of directions given, along with tone of voice and facial expressions, will determine how well the direction is received.[8]

Timing is very important. Try to catch team members in a frame of mind to listen. Present one idea at a time. For example, if you are training team members in the preparation of a new dish, break the process into its most basic steps. Present each step separately and ensure that each step is understood before proceeding. Keep to the topic. Try to speak clearly. Avoid ambiguities. Moderate the volume and speed of your speech. Maintain eye contact and leave time for questions and answers. Give team members any background information they may need to fully understand the directions. Keep it simple by using basic language with commonly used words. Explain any technical terms and take special care to explain culinary terms. Make it brief. Don't use more words or time than needed. Too much information is as bad as too little. Without making it too obvious, repeat anything that is important for the listener to remember.

Personalize what you are saying and present it to the team member. Avoid generalizing or sounding vague. Eye contact is important. It will enable you to gauge reactions. We cannot respond to one another without it. Sounding bored or looking

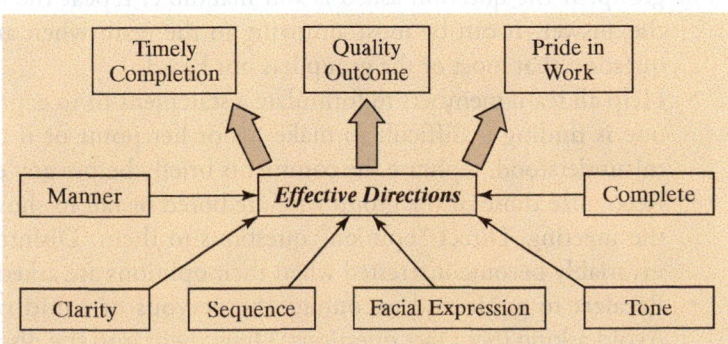

Figure 18-6
Effective directions.

disinterested tells the team member that what you are saying is unimportant. Speak clearly and loudly enough to be heard. Do not mumble or talk fast; a short, sharp growl will ensure that the team member will not accept the direction. Explain carefully; do not assume that the team member knows what you are thinking. Make sure you're understood. If they look confused or don't question your ideas, chances are they have not understood. Encourage the team member to give thoughtful answers. Ask questions about what you have said. This will allow you to check for understanding.

An atmosphere conducive to open communication, cooperation, and trust will bring about a collaborative team that will accept directions as a natural extension of coaching.[9] Bringing team members together on issues of mutual interest to generate suggestions is one way to do this. When kitchen team members recognize the benefits of helping one another and realize it is expected, they will work together to achieve common goals. The chef's ability to give directions to the kitchen team is directly related to the team's ability to carry out the workload to the required total quality standard.

LEADING A MEETING

Effective supervision, management, and leadership all require you to conduct meetings on an on-going basis. The chef who can skillfully lead these meetings will provide the basis for improvements through getting the entire kitchen team involved. These meetings should proceed on the basis of what is known to the unknown information. Meetings can be time consuming. Leading a successful meeting requires quality operation, facilitation, and management of the meeting. The following are some guidelines for each of these facets of leading a productive meeting.

Meeting Operation

- Start and end the meeting on time.
- Keep the meeting to a maximum of 12 people whenever possible.
- Be informal. Put the team at ease.
- Respect the contribution of every team member. Never belittle or ignore any statement made; every individual has the desire to be recognized. In their minds, whatever they say is worthwhile.
- Avoid arguments.
- Avoid personally disagreeing with a team member in the group. Instead, call on others for their opinions and convey your thinking through their answers.
- Be tactful when correcting statements or opinions.
- Avoid giving too many personal opinions and experiences.

Meeting Facilitation

- Help each person in the team share in the discussion. Ask people in the team to speak up. Be sure that any question an individual asks is heard by the entire group. If the question asked is still inaudible, repeat the question before giving the answer. It can be most annoying to the team when an answer is given to a question that most of the group has not heard.
- Help all team members to formulate a statement or to express themselves. If anyone is finding it difficult to make his or her point or if the statement is being misunderstood, rephrase the comments briefly before any discussion begins.
- Recognize those in the group who are bored or fail to show sufficient interest in the meeting. Direct "opinion" questions to them. Disinterested team members invariably become interested when their opinions are asked.
- Be alert to guide and encourage the nervous or timid members of the team. Avoid asking them fact questions. Draw them into the discussion by asking their

opinions, directing "do you agree" questions to them, and complimenting them when they volunteer correct answers, saying, "That's exactly right" or "That's a good point."

Meeting Management

- Direct a question to a specific person in the team or interrupt and summarize the key points under discussion when the meeting gets out of control. Conclude with the correct information and begin discussion on another topic.
- Direct rapid-fire questions as a review, calling on specific individuals to arouse discussion if the team appears disinterested or is slow to offer opinions. Make a negative remark to arouse a defensive response from the team, or ask debatable questions (such as "Which is a better method . . ." or "Which is more practical . . .").
- Compliment the team before you close the meeting if you have had a particularly good session.
- Develop interest in the next meeting before closing a meeting. Briefly give highlights of the next session.

Meetings with productive outcomes are greatly influenced by how well the chef leads the meeting. Keep the discussion focused and don't let the team go off on tangents or other issues. Save other issues for future meetings. The goals of a good meeting are action and results. Summarize the meeting and assign key result areas to individual team members with agreed benchmarks for future areas of improvement.

WRITTEN COMMUNICATION

Principles of Written Communication

Audiences   The first thing to do is to establish exactly who the audience is with regard to the written communication. Doing this will help you communicate to that audience in a more unambiguous and effective way. It will also help limit the task of getting the message across. Decisions regarding the interpretation of the message will become clearer. How much time is available to your audience to determine their attitude toward the topic and writer? What do they know already? How much do they need to know? How will they use the information?

Use of Language   Generally, simplicity is preferred in written communication. Avoid ambiguity, long words, and above all, culinary jargon. Simplify the subject for the reader and be brief. It is best to use action verbs rather than passive verbs.

Be direct and to the point at all times. This is essential, particularly when giving written instructions. Sentences should contain one idea and should normally average 20 words. The correct use of punctuation in sentences is important in order to highlight certain items and not to confuse the reader.

Paragraphs are used to signal the reader and contain a theme. They should be six to seven lines in length. The first sentence of the first paragraph sets the tone of the communication.

Short words (or phrases) are easier to read. Shorter words, such as "so," are easier to understand than longer ones meaning the same thing, such as "accordingly" and "consequently." Some examples of suggested word usage are shown in Figure 18-7.

General Guidelines

In today's business world, between letters, memos, phone fax, e-mail, and text messaging, not to mention visiting social networking sites, individuals can be overwhelmed just trying to "keep up" with incoming communications. Before sending any communication, ask

Figure 18-7
Examples of word choice.

Don't Write	Instead, Write
activate	start, begin
approximately	about
demonstrate	show
dispatch	send
discontinue	stop
endeavor	try
facilitate	make easier
implement	carry out
optimum	best
requirement	need
terminate	end

yourself, "Is the content worthwhile?" Figure 18-8 provides some baseline standards for worthwhile communication.

Effective business communication must be well organized. The writer must ensure that the document's organization is sensible by answering the following questions:

- Have you stated the major point or idea in the first sentence?
- Have you considered a plan for an audience that could be angered, resentful, or disappointed about the content? (explanation given before refusal)
- When presenting bad news, have you opened with a neutral statement that your reader will find agreeable?
- Have you provided enough transitions and connectors to signal relationships?
- Is the material organized for best emphasis?
- Have you used a topic (orienting) sentence to begin each supporting paragraph?
- Are your paragraphs short enough to be readable?
- Does the document have a distinct introduction, body, and conclusion?
- Have you closed positively?

The writer must also determine whether the style is readable and appropriate:

- Is each sentence clear? (understandable on first reading)
- Is your message concise? (the most information expressed in the fewest words)
- Are your sentences fluent? (sentences varied in construction and length)
- Is the document written in plain English? (words that the audience will understand)
- Is the language precise? (conveys your exact meaning)
- Have you replaced abstractions and generalizations with concrete, specific, and exact language?
- Is the tone unbiased and appropriate for your purpose and audience?
- Have you focused on the audience's needs and interests? (their perspective)

Figure 18-8
Worthwhile communication.

- Relevant
- Informative
- Of significance
- Credible
- Complete
- Of interest
- Clearly beneficial
- At appropriate knowledge level
- Clear and understandable
- Easy to read

- Have you addressed your readers directly?
- Have you eliminated sexist language?
- Is your tone informal and conversational?

Menu and Recipe

In the kitchen many instructions are transmitted to the team via written menus. How these menus are written by the chef determines how well individual team members perform the skills required for high-quality culinary art. Menus that are "posted" may be forthcoming banquets, special functions, or seasonal offerings. While the menu is primarily designed to convey descriptive meaning to customers, it can also be the basis for a more technical, annotated written document through which the team receives instructions.

The annotated, expanded menu will convey not only all the essential dish ingredients but also other information such as portion size and various accompaniments. A menu used as a written form of communication and job instruction to kitchen team members should contain the following:

- Full descriptions and recipes for each dish
- How the dish should be prepared: breaded, cutlet, etc.
- Method of cooking: roasted, braised, sautéed, etc.
- Cut of meat: shoulder, loin, rib steak
- Quality of grade: USDA choice, prime, etc.
- Method of serving: casserole, skewer, etc.
- Explanation of culinary terms
- Cooking time instructions
- Garnishing information
- Number of portions to be cooked
- Who is to perform tasks

Providing complete information that is easily understood, including the where, when, what, and how, will allow your culinary team to achieve consistently high quality. Team members will be better able to make efficient use of resources and team member skills to save time and simplify their tasks. Effective written communication to the team makes the unknown known, allowing team members to plan and better integrate their knowledge to improve efficiency and quality.

A critical part of effective culinary communication is the recipe. A common fault in recipe writing is assuming that those reading and preparing the recipe understand culinary terms. The following lists the essentials of writing a clear recipe (including a photograph of the finished dish).

- Menu classification: dinner, lunch, breakfast, brunch, banquet, room service, or take-out
- Name of dish
- Yield, number of servings, portions
- Equipment and smallware needed
- Ingredients in order of use
- Quantity of ingredients (allow for cooking shrinkage)
- Complete detailed instructions
- Timing and temperatures to be used, other information for each phase of the preparation, and an outline of any special instructions
- Descriptive passages (avoid long ones; use simple instructions)
- Equipment needed for service
- Setting times and temperature for reconstituting prepared items
- Template to assist layout

Figure 18-9
Before writing, ask yourself.

- Why am I writing this? Is there a better way of getting my message across?
- What do I want the reader to do?
- How will I approach my subject?
- Who are my readers?
- Why will they be reading what I write?
- What does the reader already know about the subject?
- How will the reader use this document?
- What should I include?
- What should I leave out?
- What should I say first?
- How will I know when I've said enough?
- If the reader forgets everything else, what key point do I want remembered?
- Should I be writing this at this time?
- Should I send this at all? Am I too late?
- Is someone else communicating the same information? Should I check with that person?
- Should I include deadlines?
- Is my method of transmission the best? For example, should I be using e-mail, traditional mail, or fax?

Business Writing

In addition to menu writing, the chef is involved in other types of business writing, such as memos to team members, superiors, and other department heads; the preparation of job descriptions, policies, and procedures; and notices to, and general business communication with suppliers and vendors. Before writing a communication, you should answer a number of questions such as "What am I trying to say?" Figure 18-9 shows additional questions you should address before writing a memo, letter, or other business communication.

Memos   Memos are frequently used by chefs to convey information to the kitchen team. These memos may vary in length, although they tend to be short notes. They often serve as permanent records of decisions and plans made during telephone conversations or meetings. The memo might be a reminder, a request, an acknowledgment, or a complaint. It might also convey good or bad news, information, or speculations. Memos may be sent to one team member or to other individuals within the foodservice organization. With this broad range of purpose and audience, memos vary considerably in formality.

Letters   Like memos, business letters vary in length and formality. Some are brief notes, while others extend over multiple pages. Letters allow chefs to present themselves to outsiders, so they can serve as an important public relations tool. The businesslike format of a letter is as important as its clear prose style and coherent organization. The purpose of most letters is to inform, request, or persuade. Unlike a telephone conversation or other oral communication, letters provide written records and often serve as contracts. As in all written communication, revision, and rewriting are essential. Write simply; use concrete words and short sentences. Unify paragraphs on a single topic. The first sentence should set the tone and give the reason for the communication. Finally, never sign a letter until you are sure it is perfect. Regardless of who processes the letter, if you sign it, you are responsible for its appearance and content.

E-mail   The primary form of interoffice/interproperty communication is e-mail. E-mail provides an inexpensive, efficient means of communication within the business. Often, however, e-mail is viewed as a less-formal form of communication and therefore one not adhering to the same principles as written communication. This perspective is faulty. While an e-mail "stream" can generate actual dialogue between parties, all the parties should remember that the e-mail is written communication.

Figure 18-10
E-mail clarity.

Guidelines for E-mail Clarity

- Be careful about assuming the reader has the background knowledge and experience necessary to understand the message.
- Remember that the reader cannot hear the inflection in your voice or see the expression on your face. This can be extremely important in the use of humor or when responding to an emotional issue.
- Use correct spelling and punctuation.
- Avoid slang and idioms.
- Proofread your message.

Misunderstanding can arise from e-mail. Users often respond to e-mail as if they were talking to the person in person or on the phone. But the recipient does not always interpret an e-mail's content as intended by the sender because the reader does not have the benefit of voice inflection to help guide them to the correct interpretation. Remember the concepts of sender and receiver discussed earlier in this chapter. When communicating by e-mail, make absolutely sure not only that the words are correct but that they will be interpreted as intended when read without voice inflection or nonverbal communication clues.

To ensure effective e-mail communications, you should apply the principles of communication as you would to a letter or memo. While speed of communication is a benefit of e-mail, adhering to some simple guidelines will help make your e-mail communication effective as well. Some basic guidelines for e-mail communication are shown in Figure 18-10.

Remember also that what you put in an e-mail is a written record. Do not write something in an e-mail that you will regret if it is made part of a document later. The key to effective e-mail communication in the workplace is to apply the same principles to it that you do to memos and letters.

COMMUNICATION VIA THE GRAPEVINE

The "grapevine" is informal communication, and it typically follows the pattern of personal relationships among kitchen team members. Informal communication networks generally exist because team members have a desire to know information that is not formally communicated. The informal communication, grapevine, or gossip element can be a useful way for the chef to test a new idea or some proposed change. The grapevine has some distinct characteristics. It springs up and is not controlled by the chef. It is used largely to serve the self-interests of the members within it.

Chefs should be aware of the potential advantages and disadvantages of the information conveyed via the grapevine. It may be used to test team members' reactions before the official information is "handed down." Informal feedback from the team can be used to gauge acceptance or compliance with new ideas or change. It is important that information relayed through the grapevine not harm or frighten team members. Rumors of change can cause team members to feel insecure and create fear. False or damaging information from the grapevine can be harmful to the whole foodservice organization. The degree of harm that inaccurate information causes depends largely on the work climate prevailing in the kitchen. If morale is low and poor chef supervision exists, harmful rumors can easily find acceptance.

Some rumors should be dispelled immediately. To do this, the source of the rumor needs to be established. Ask the team members about the rumor and offer to share the facts. Rumors flourish where there is limited communication. By supplying the facts and adequate information in an open, honest, and free atmosphere, rumors can be quashed and the uncertainty on which they grow removed. Gossip regarding team members' personal lives should not be tolerated.

CONCLUSIONS

Communication is a vital element of the chef's job. Without open, honest, and continuous communication, quality diminishes and can be lost. It is not unusual, however, to encounter chefs who believe that they are effective leaders if they are "removed" and aloof from the rest of the kitchen staff. In the past, this type of chef was acceptable. This is no longer true. Team building, coaching, and continuous improvement of the foodservice operation require communication, which is fundamental to supervision, management, and leadership. A good chef communicator will be rewarded with a motivated team prepared to give their best and go beyond the norms. Communication, of which listening is such an important element, will also convey sincerity and develop trust among the team. Communication is important. It is the bedrock of quality management. Information is power. When transferred to the team, it *empowers* them to develop, grow in confidence, and make valuable contributions to the growth of the business and the reputation of the foodservice organization.

SUMMARY

As much as 85 percent of the chef's working day is spent in some form of communication. Effective supervision, management, and leadership rely on the ability of the supervisor to transfer information in such a way that it is understood by the receiver as the chef intended. Open and honest communication is critical to this process.

Interpersonal communication contains three basic elements: the source/sender, the message, and the destination/receiver. Understanding these elements ensures successful communication. Barriers may exist that prohibit effective communication. Communication barriers between people stem from differences in background, personalities, and life experiences.

Nonverbal communication is important. The chef should be aware of gestures and body language used. Many cues may be picked up from body language.

Listening is an important aspect of good communication. Chefs who listen carefully to their team have fewer problems and greater success in implementing qual-

ity management. Poor listening skills often result in conflicts, errors, and inefficiency. Ways to improve listening skills should be understood and practiced.

Giving directions is what gets the job done. The manner and methods used to give these directions are as important as the directions given.

Managing meetings effectively requires skill. Carefully managed and controlled meetings can make major contributions to continuous improvement and quality management. Productive outcomes are greatly influenced by how well the chef manages the meeting.

Written communications via e-mail, memos, letters, and menus are important methods of transferring information. The language used should be clear and jargon free. The principles of written communication should be applied to all forms of written communication.

The "grapevine" is also a method of transferring information. Therefore, the chef should have an awareness of the potential advantages and disadvantages of this informal communication method.

DISCUSSION QUESTIONS

1. Define the following chapter key terms:

   a. Communication
   b. Noise
   c. Source/sender

   d. Signal/message
   e. Destination/receiver
   f. Nonverbal communication
   g. Body language

h. Listening

i. Critical listening

j. Discriminative listening

k. Therapeutic listening

l. Appreciative listening

m. Courteous listening

2. Communication between sender and receiver passes through filters of culture, age, gender, education, and fields of experience. What are the effects of this process?

3. How do overlapping fields of experience often lead to effective communication?

4. What are the elements of nonverbal communication? How do these differ within various ethnic groups?

5. What are the different types of listening? Give a brief explanation of each.

6. In what five ways can chefs improve their listening skills?

7. Giving directions to other team members is what gets every job started. What are the five steps essential to getting the job done?

8. Meetings can be time consuming! What steps can be taken to decrease meeting time consumption and increase meeting effectiveness?

9. What strategies should be adopted with regard to written communication?

10. What are the guidelines for writing e-mails that clearly communicate the intended message?

11. How can communication via the grapevine be used to serve the interests of those within it?

12. What is meant by the phrase "information is power" with reference to the kitchen team?

NOTES

1. Donna Fantetti, *Career Directions* (Providence, RI: P.A.R. Inc., 1987), 34.

2. Robert Heinich, Michael Molenda, and James D. Russel, *Instructional Media and the New Technologies of Instruction,* 3rd. ed. (New York: Macmillan, 1989), 6.

3. Anna Katherine Jernigan, *The Effective Foodservice Supervisor* (Rockville, MD: Aspen, 1989), 31.

4. Franklin B. Krohn and Zafur U. Ahmed, "Teaching International Cross-Cultural Diversity to Hospitality and Tourism Students," *Hospitality & Tourism Educator,* November 1991.

5. Raymond Dumont and John M. Lannon, *Business Communications,* 2nd ed. (Boston: Brown & Co., 1987), 526.

6. Bruce B. Tepper, *The New Supervisor: Skills for Success* (New York: Irwin, 1994), 48.

7. Robert B. Maddux, *Team Building: An Exercise in Leadership* (London: Crisp, 1992), 48.

8. Ibid., p. 49.

9. Adapted from Raymond A. Dumont and John M. Lannon, *Business Communications,* 2nd ed. (Boston: Brown & Co., 1987).

Chapter 19
Time Management

OBJECTIVES

When you complete this chapter, you should be able to:

1. Identify issues associated with unproductive time use
2. Develop a plan for effective use of time
3. Recognize the pitfalls of procrastination
4. List the steps that cause time leaks
5. Distinguish between being busy and productive

Case Study: Ms. Bee's Restaurant

Ms. Bee's Restaurant has become a landmark in a city known around the world for its food and hospitality. As executive chef of Ms. Bee's, Lee Derby is expected to ensure that the restaurant retains its stature and profitability in a fiercely competitive restaurant market and to represent the restaurant as a shining example of culinary knowledge and professionalism. Chef Derby has found the balancing of these two roles to be increasingly difficult. The economy as a whole has taken a downturn in the past three years. The restaurant is still pulling its share of the city's restaurant traffic, both local and tourist, but the number of overall guests, particularly tourists, has decreased. Additionally, the guests who do dine at Ms. Bee's are spending less. They are ordering less-expensive dishes and fewer add-ons such as appetizers and deserts.

Chef Derby is concerned about his ability to "get the job done." Maintaining the profit levels of the restaurant is requiring intense management of all profit and cost centers. Maintaining the restaurant's visibility to local guests and tourists requires that Chef Derby respond to numerous requests for interviews and guest chef appearances. He is working more hours every week and yet feels that he is accomplishing less each week. Chef Derby knows that he has a great kitchen team, but he also realizes that he is spending less and less time interacting with them. He is giving less attention to the preparation of the food and day-to-day operation of the kitchen. He is feeling more and more like an absentee chef and supervisor. Chef Derby considers an incident that occurred at the restaurant last night to be evidence that he needs to be giving more attention to the operation of the kitchen.

Yesterday, Saturday, the restaurant was fully booked for dinner. Between 6 P.M. and 9 P.M. they would completely turn the dining room. Ms. Bee's has a reputation for its constantly changing menu and regional specialty dishes. One of the restaurant's most popular items is its Ribeye au Poivre. At 8 P.M. a large group of guests was seated. They were trade-show attendees from out-of-town and had made their reservations two months in advance. The host of the group, as an appreciation dinner for his clients, had called on Friday to find out what kind of beef would be on the menu on Saturday evening. One of his clients, who ate only beef and particularly liked ribeye steak, could be an extremely difficult customer. The host was extremely pleased when he heard that Ms. Bee's would be offering their Ribeye au Poivre, an item he had greatly enjoyed on previous visits. The host told his guest about the Ribeye au Poivre and how great it was before arriving at the restaurant.

The waiter came to take the group's order and immediately told them that he regretted that they were out of the Ribeye au Poivre. The group's beef-lover began to make a scene about the restaurant's being out of the item at 8 P.M. on Saturday night. He asked to speak to the chef and was told that the chef was unavailable. After thirty minutes of intense, unpleasant dialogue between the guest and various service staff and kitchen staff, the manager-on-duty and the sous chef resolved the situation when they sent a staff member to a neighboring restaurant to get a ribeye. They told the guest they had found one last ribeye and were preparing it for him. The incident left both the restaurant staff and all the guests in the restaurant with bad feelings.

Chef Derby was told about the incident on Sunday and was very disturbed by the failure of his staff to have sufficient product on hand when they knew a major trade-show and conference was in town. He was also disturbed that it took 30 minutes before the manager-on-duty and sous chef thought to go across the street to get a steak from a steakhouse owned by the owner's brother. The general manager spoke to Chef Derby about the incident on Monday and told him that he felt Chef Derby had to get better control of his kitchen staff and ensure that the restaurant's reputation was protected from this kind of incident.

Chef Derby resolved that if he had to work 100 hours per week, he would get things under control.

Based on what you have learned from previous chapters and the content of this chapter, answer the following questions.

- Do you believe that the action planned by Chef Derby will allow him to achieve his goal and meet his commitment to Ms. Bee's Restaurant? Explain your answer including the following:
  - Overall reason
  - Primary causal agents
  - Role of leadership and supervision/management
  - Specific steps that could have been taken to avoid the current challenges
  - Specific steps that should be taken in the future

INTRODUCTION

Lack of time is perhaps the excuse most often used in kitchens for not doing certain things: "It's a great idea, but we don't have time to do that here." How often have chefs been overheard to say: "If we only had more time," or "We do not have time here to get too heavily involved with fancy dishes and presentation"? The result is that things that impact overall quality and customer satisfaction, such as quality culinary practices and motivating the kitchen team, often are not done because of "lack of time." The fact is that failure to implement agreed-upon quality standards of cooking and presentation of menu items is a question not of time, but rather of poor planning and a failure to execute good *mise en place*. Planning and *mise en place* are fundamental to quality management and leadership.

Timing is a fundamental element of all chefs' training, and it is ingrained in every aspect of cooking, preparation, and presentation of food items. Lack of sufficient time to implement quality foodservice often results from selecting complex recipes inappropriate for the skill level of those preparing them. Failure to use a team approach to menu development and to anticipate the constraints of busy meal service periods along with the absence of training plans all contribute to a sense of lack of time. Therefore, lack of time is not the culprit of shoddy culinary practice; rather, it is the result of poor supervision, training, and management.

Time management means better organization to get as much as possible from the time allowed. The aim is not to fill up life with activity, but to identify what is wanted out of life and plan how to go about getting it.[1]

If you had a bank that credited your account each morning with $86,400, that carried over no balance from day to day, allowed you to keep no cash in the account, and every evening cancelled whatever part of the amount you failed to use during the day, just what would you do? Draw out every cent, of course!

Well, you have such a bank and its name is *Time*. Every morning it credits you with 86,400 seconds. Every night it rules off as lost, whatever part of this sum you failed to invest in good purposes. It allows no overdrafts. Each day it opens a new account for you, each night it burns the record of the day. If you fail to use the day's deposits, the loss is yours. There's no going back; there's no drawing against tomorrow.

You must live in the present . . . on today's deposits. Invest it so as to get from it the utmost in health, happiness, and success.

In agreeing with this message, there is a logical question each chef should ask himself or herself: How am I using my time in relation to personal goals and the goals of my foodservice organization?

The chef who manages work time effectively can prioritize so as to organize all of the elements crucial to the quality operation of the kitchen operation. The fact is, most people waste time, but productive chefs waste less of it. The principles and techniques of time management are no secret. However, they can work only if they are adhered to.

Time management on an individual level is not concerned solely with the amount of time spent on certain issues in terms of minutes, hours, days, or months. It is, of course, wise and prudent to track how time is spent every day. This helps to determine where it might be wasted. But the real goal is to free up time to get more done. The first step is to examine often-held assumptions about time and how these assumptions may prevent time from being used productively in the kitchen.

WHAT IS THIS BUSINESS?
"CHEF AS ENTREPRENEUR"

I thank God for Food Fetish, Inc. It was truly divine intervention that helped bring my business into reality.

To become a business owner was never something that I consciously went after, at least, not at first. I did not go into my culinary apprenticeship thinking that, one day, I would want to own a distributing company. I was raised with the idea and spirit of making things happen for myself. If it is to be, it is up to me.

I remember telling my Chef once during my evaluation that I would rather have more time off than a raise. He didn't understand my preference then. For me, it was always about my personal time. The freedom to do what I wanted, when I needed to do it was more important than the additional tax burden from the raise.

For years a group of us would get together to brainstorm on business opportunities that best utilized our individual expertise. We had great concepts, but no real intent. Eventually, we would see our ideas become someone else's reality.

I took additional classes and seminars on writing business plans, how to become a business owner, and other related topics. I accepted adjunct teaching positions at the two local culinary schools, and became a regular chef on a local television cooking show. Those opportunities gave me great insights on different career paths. I did not want to be the chef who stayed too long in the kitchen, the dinosaur who couldn't keep up or be on that ever-changing cutting edge. Working in a hot kitchen 5 or 6 days a week, 8 to 12 or more hours a day, on a concrete floor will take its toll on anyone. Working weekends, nights, and holidays was not how I wanted to spend the rest of my career. So owning a restaurant, bakery, and catering business was not an option for me. My health and my family had already sacrificed enough. Our daughter was raised with me working the long days, and holidays that didn't really start until I got home. Her brother, 11 years younger, has a much different reality.

A serious conversation over wine and dinner with my specialty foods sales rep shifted my focus, and changed my course. We decided to combine our expertise and form our own distribution company. We focused primarily on baking and pastry items because that was our strength, and there was a void locally for such a business in what became our niche. Over the next 7 months, Charlton Douglas and I wrote and rewrote our business plan, secured financing, signed a lease on a warehouse facility, and started to buy supplies and equipment needed to run operations. We also quit our jobs!

As co-owner and Corporate Pastry Chef of Food Fetish, Inc., I get to utilize my 20+ years as a culinarian. I teach and train our customers on product usage, and keep them aware of our ever-changing inventory because new ideas and techniques are always evolving. I do cooking demonstrations and competitions to keep my skills sharp, and to gain first-hand knowledge of new products and equipment that is now more readily available. I feel that I have learned many invaluable lessons and honed in on some strengths and weaknesses I didn't necessarily know that I possessed. I was technologically challenged and ignorant of accounting procedures needed to run a business. I never wanted to sell anything. I always ran the other way whenever I was approached to sell wares. I did not like, and still don't like rejection or the word "no."

It's amazing what you will do when you have to. When it's your bottom line, there is not an acceptable excuse. The word "no" becomes another opportunity. You learn to hire someone who is trained and capable of either helping or doing whatever it is that you cannot.

I believe that my past executive pastry chef experiences have helped shape my Food Fetish experience. The training of personnel, ordering supplies and equipment, scheduling, handling and storage of inventory, and dealing with chefs and suppliers are the same, just on different scales. I now get the opportunity to see and talk to the chefs instead of just hearing about "Chef Mary Jane" up the street. There are no blinders on; I am not pigeon-holed in my own little pastry world, unaware of and too busy to see what is happening in my own backyard.

I love working for the Fetish. I have always been a hard worker, so why not work hard for something that I helped create and own? For me, starting my company was a great culmination of my skills, time, and energy. Who could ask for anything more?

—Kimberly Brock Brown, CEPC, CCA, AAC, Kimberly Brock Brown, LLC

TIME MANAGEMENT MISCONCEPTIONS

There is never enough time to accomplish what is important in the kitchen—wrong! There is always enough time to accomplish what is important, and what can be postponed should be. It is this decision that determines whether time is being used wisely.

Some chefs use the following as an excuse for poor time management practices: "Other people make too many demands on my time." Others do not control how a chef spends his or her time. If other people have that much control over a chef's time, the chef is letting himself or herself be intimidated and is not behaving as a leader. Learning to say no can be one of the most effective time savers. When saying no, be courteous; give a brief explanation of why the request cannot be granted and avoid a prolonged discussion about the reasons.

Busy schedules are used as reasons for not being able to prioritize work: "To control your time and your life, it is not only possible to prioritize, it is essential. Set priorities and stick to them."[2] **Prioritization** is the determination of what must be done in what order. Prioritization works hand-in-hand with delegation. **Delegation** is the act of giving someone else the responsibility for and power to complete assigned tasks. Learning to delegate frees up time to tackle other matters that require attention.

Other erroneous misconceptions of time management frequently cited by chefs are:

- "I'm much too busy to plan any activities."
- "If only there were more hours in the day."
- "I can't devote that much time every day to one project."
- "I've so much to do I don't know where to start."
- "I prefer to do the simple tasks first and save the big ones for later in the day."

These statements usually are covers for lack of self-discipline and poor individual planning ability. Working more hours every day produces mental and physical fatigue and devours personal time. Success is achieved by learning to work smarter, not longer. The busier the chef, the more important it is to take time out to plan. Planning is critical to effective time management. Without a plan, chefs are unlikely to be in control of their workday. They will react to events as they happen rather than being the ones who set the agenda.

Procrastination is the thief of time. Procrastination is when we put things off rather than finishing the work. Sometimes procrastination kicks in as a way to avoid tasks that are unpleasant or uninteresting. Resolve to deal with these areas head-on; steady progress is a great motivator. The most misleading of all assumptions about time is that something can be done "later"; this is because "later" seldom arrives. Time cannot be lengthened or shortened, only used, and it cannot be saved and used later. A chef cannot choose to not use time. Either use the moment, or lose it forever.

"Never put off until tomorrow what you can do today."[3] This familiar adage was written by the Earl of Chesterfield in 1749 and is clearly a warning against procrastination. However, just because a job can be done now does not necessarily mean that it should be done now. Sometimes priorities need to be chosen.

CHOOSING PRIORITIES

Obviously, not all tasks and projects have the same importance. Chefs often feel as if they are under pressure to respond to the situations or persons exerting the greatest pressure. This situation is called "**firefighting**." This causes some chefs to solve problems in the order in which they arise, do the easy work first, or take care of the hard work first, on the assumption that doing so is the fastest way to get rid of it. Dealing with matters in this way should be avoided at all costs. "Lining up your ducks . . . its origins are obscure, but its meaning is transparent: if you're dealing with things in a logical, orderly sequence, you're sure to bring efficiency and results to your efforts."[4] Dealing with matters in the order they occur in the kitchen is fine in some circumstances, for example, expediting table orders; but in most other situations, it is an unproductive use of time: "Important does not necessarily mean urgent, nor does urgent necessarily mean important."[5] The goal should be long-term solutions, not just firefighting. The flow for both quality time management and effective response to challenges is shown in Figure 19-1.

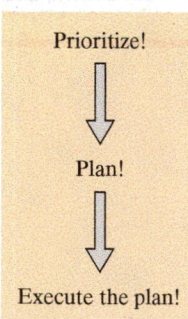

Prioritize!

↓

Plan!

↓

Execute the plan!

Figure 19-1
Flow for quality time management and response to challenges.

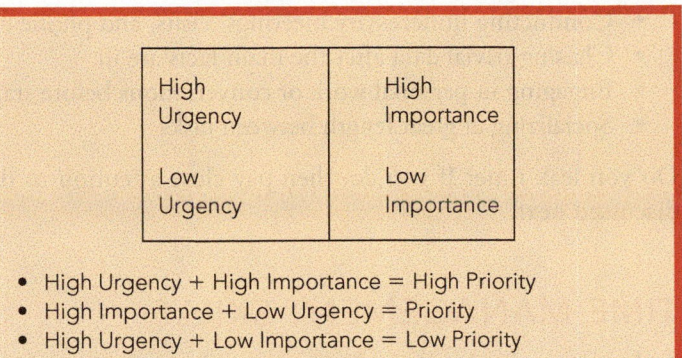

Figure 19-2
Priority matrix.

- High Urgency + High Importance = High Priority
- High Importance + Low Urgency = Priority
- High Urgency + Low Importance = Low Priority
- Low Urgency + Low Importance = Low Priority

Tasks should be analyzed based on urgency and importance. The priority matrix shown in Figure 19-2 can be used to conduct a quick task.

The simplest and most effective way to prioritize time is to analyze how time is spent in an average day and week. Since everyone has the same amount of time, the key question is, is the chef using the time effectively? Or is he or she doing things that are unnecessary? If the chef is satisfied that only the necessary work is being done, the next step is to set priorities: "Make a list of things to do. Compare what you want to do with what you are already doing or planning to do. The result will be a priority list that tells you what to do first, what to do next, and what to do last."[6] It is also helpful to keep a time log of a typical week to see how you actually spend your time. Disorganized priorities are common ground for procrastination. Of all management procedures, none is more relevant to time management than prioritizing issues of quality.

TIME LEAKS

Time leaks are working habits and practices that eat up time unproductively. Review the list of potential time leaks below and see if any apply to you.

- Spending too much time on problems brought by a team member
- Oversupervising the kitchen team
- Undersupervising with consequent crises
- Scheduling less-important work before more-important work
- Starting a job before thinking it through
- Leaving jobs before completion
- Doing things that can be delegated to a team member
- Doing things that can be done by modern equipment
- Doing things that aren't part of the job
- Spending too much time on previous areas of interest or competence
- Doing unproductive things from sheer habit
- Keeping too many, too complicated, or overlapping records
- Pursuing projects that are probably unachievable
- Paying too much attention to low-yield projects
- Failing to anticipate crises
- Handling too wide a variety of duties
- Shrinking from unfamiliar duties
- Failing to build barriers against interruptions
- Allowing conferences and discussions to wander
- Allowing conferences and discussions to continue after their purpose is fulfilled

- Conducting unnecessary meetings, visits, and phone calls
- Chasing trivial data after the main facts are in
- Engaging in personal work or conversations before starting business work
- Socializing at great length between tasks

Do you leak time? If you do, then pay close attention to the time management skills discussed next.

TIME MANAGEMENT SKILLS

A chef can make the most effective use of his or her time by planning and getting organized. The reason for managing time is to be sure that the chef has enough of it to meet specific goals at some point in the future. Most people are familiar with personal planners or calendars. Today, these are generally kept electronically in an iPhone, Black-Berry, or other device. They can provide a convenient place to keep daily lists, plus extra space to keep records and charts that are essential for planning, and are simple, yet powerful time management aids. It is important to remember that calendars and personal planner diaries are useful only if they are used. Reserve blocks of time to get the job done and develop the habit of managing time effectively. Planning activities that can assist you in managing your time better include:

- Make weekly and daily to-do lists in order of priority. Check off each task as it is completed. This will provide a feeling of accomplishment at the end of the day.
- Plan what needs to be done at least one day in advance. If a chef knows what tasks await tomorrow, he or she can organize tomorrow's to-do list today. Schedules serve as a disciplining tool, helping to do what is planned.
- Plan telephone calls in advance to ensure an agenda is covered and to reduce time spent on the phone.
- Plan meetings (one-on-one or with the entire kitchen team) in advance. If calling the meeting, take control of the agenda and stay on the subject.
- Evaluate your time management several times during the day. Take a look at the schedule about one-third of the way through the workday and again two-thirds of the way through. Are the objectives met for the day? If not, what got in the way? Should it take priority over what was planned?

Planning is critical, but planning alone will not make the chef the "time manager" instead of the one being "managed by time." The chef must learn to handle common distractions because they are part of the reality of life. Controlling the time taken by drop-in visitors requires both courtesy and good judgment on the chef's part. Limiting the number of people invited to the kitchen will decrease commotion and distractions for both the chef and the culinary team. A chef who needs to meet with someone should go to that person's work area. It is much more difficult to get people to leave the chef's work area than it is for the supervisor to leave theirs.

Communicate efficiently. In today's technological world, communication takes place in so many forms that the communication itself can become a barrier to good communication. The chef must be a model of the efficient use of communication. Keep memos, e-mails, phone conversations, conference calls, Skype calls, or Web-based meetings short. It will save time thinking, speaking, and writing and team members' time listening, reading, and understanding. Sorting unsolicited e-mail and regular business mail is time intensive. The chef may need to have someone sort both e-mail and regular mail, using guidelines on what needs to be seen and what should be routed to other team members.

CHEF TALK
"PLAN THE WORK AND WORK THE PLAN"

It has been said that time can't be managed. But what can be managed are activities and how we "spend" time! And all the experts agree. Managing our activities begins with good planning. So, by knowing what's important for us—planning our work and working our plan—we become wise chef managers.

We have to make time for getting big tasks done every day. Plan your daily workload in advance, single out relatively small tasks that must be done immediately, then tackle the large tasks to completeness. In all, planning is the power tool for achievement!

In the foodservice industry today, there are greater demands and challenges than ever before. We chefs especially don't always believe we have enough time to meet our responsibilities to our company, our employees, and our families. That's a negative belief, not a positive belief.

My day starts with an exercise program at 6:30 A.M. After this is completed, I am ready to face number 2 on my list of priorities: networking with my staff regarding their needs for the day. So, as each item on the list is completed, I move to the next task.

In addition, there are other ventures or affiliations that I am involved with, and thus, I need to balance my time, concentrating on accomplishing the greatest results with the least effort expended. Thus, making decisions and acting on these decisions will reflect leadership and a positive image to my staff.

Through dedication, planning, and goal-oriented thinking, I believe any chef can achieve great success in his or her future endeavors.

—Bert Cutino, CEC, AAC, HBOT, HOF
Co-Owner, The Sardine Factory,
Monterey, CA

Time management also includes making timely decisions. The chef who fails to make a decision because of unwillingness to face unpleasant decisions and being over-cautious hampers the performance of the total team. The chef should also complete one job at a time. Important tasks need plenty of uninterrupted time and cannot be completed between other activities. This wastes time. Each time a project is restarted, there is a need to get familiar with the project again.

The chef should delegate tasks to other team members. To delegate (not dump) tasks is a key time management skill. Sometimes, a chef does not have time to delegate—the unexpected happens, and he or she must deal with it. In that case there is only one protection, and that is anticipating the unexpected before it occurs. The chef should keep a flexible schedule because emergencies do occur and meetings do run overtime.

Two of the simplest but most valuable time management skills the chef can exercise is learning to say no and organizing the work area. In some cases, demands placed on a chef's time will exceed his or her ability to accommodate all of them. When taking on more than can be handled, quality begins to suffer. Saying no does not have to offend someone. When an alternative is offered, things can be worked out to everyone's satisfaction. Is valuable time spent looking for things? Consider how often each item is needed in the kitchen. The kitchen should be organized so it is easy to complete normal tasks.

Bruce Tepper states: "Being busy has nothing to do with productivity. Maximizing how [to] use your time means a great deal more. It will open either more free time, or more time for creating new ideas."[7] Get an accurate indication of how time is actually used and decide where improvements can be made. An important part of being a good chef is knowing what tasks should and should not be delegated to other team members. A chef's job is not just to do things, it is also to organize and coordinate the kitchen team. The following are some ways to save time:

- Use waiting time. When waiting for an appointment, don't think of it as a waste of time, but as a gift of time. Use it constructively: to relax, to ponder a decision, to review the daily checklist, or to read a food book or foodservice industry magazine article. Always carry a pen and notebook to write down ideas.

- Combine activities, such as discussing related matters over lunch.
- Have a place for everything and keep everything in its place. If something is worth having, it's worth knowing where it is when it is needed.
- Master the technology that will improve your productivity and that of your team.
- Schedule some "togetherness time." Time management should not segregate the chef from the rest of the kitchen team.
- Spend time as if you had to buy it. Before spending an hour reading a report or going to a meeting, ask, "Would I spend my own money to do this?" If time is looked at as a financial investment and how it is spent is monitored, less will be wasted.
- Maintain a regular physical exercise program. Exercising can help reduce stress. It also helps to maintain a sense of balance, discipline, order, and control in life. An exercise program results in feeling better, looking better, and having greater self-confidence. Personal time is not a luxury or something to postpone until it can be fitted into the schedule. It is a requirement for maintaining a proper sense of balance and control in life.
- Constantly ask, "Is this the best use of my time right now?" Time management aims for relaxation and gives more time in which to relax.

PERSONAL TIME MANAGEMENT

Life balance is one of the greatest challenges faced by the chef. Life balance refers to the need to balance work and personal life such as family. While no one likes to think they have to "schedule" time for their family and for themselves, in the reality of today's fast-paced business world, this may well be the case. Scheduling time does not necessarily mean that the chef schedules an appointment for his or her children to visit. It does mean that planning must include time off. The fact that everyone needs time to recharge their batteries is all too often forgotten in the rush.

The chef must remember that they work smarter and more productively when they are rested and do not feel the guilt of not being at work or not being at home. It also needs to be remembered that the same is true for all team members. While work may be the total focus of some team members, it cannot be expected to be the total focus of all team members. The chef who manages everybody's time in a manner that allows everyone to enjoy the fruits of their labor is a chef that will have a loyal and highly productive team.

SUMMARY

Everyone can use their time better, particularly busy chefs. Look at how time is currently being used. Schedule necessary work and work that only the chef can do rather than busy work. Do not confuse lack of time to complete tasks with lack of self-discipline or poor supervisory skills. Maintain a balance between controlling time and other people controlling it. Learn to prioritize tasks and say no to low-priority demands that may overload. In particular, trade off low-priority commitments for high-priority ones that come up unexpectedly in the kitchen. Learn to plan time. The busier a chef is, the more important it is to take time out to plan. Planning is critical to effective time management.

Time leaks are working practices that eat up time unproductively. The reason for managing time is to ensure that there is enough of it to meet specific goals at some point in the future. Develop time management skills and become disciplined in their application in terms of personal planners, diaries, and calendars. Provide time in schedules for the unexpected. A chef cannot anticipate everything that will happen, so time must be left each day to handle crises. Consider investment time. This is the careful investment of time that not only is useful but also has the benefit of further payoff in terms of new skills. Time management is not a matter of dealing only with isolated activities. It is a process that goes on and on over a lifetime, involving thousands of activities.

DISCUSSION QUESTIONS

1. Define the following chapter key terms:
   a. Time management
   b. Prioritization
   c. Delegation
   d. Procrastination
   e. Firefighting
   f. Time leaks
   g. Life balance
2. Why is effective use of time critical to the success of total quality management?
3. Why is the real goal of time management to free up time?
4. What are the elementary techniques that may be used to free up time?
5. How can the use of a time log assist the chef in prioritizing work?
6. What are time leaks?
7. How does the use of calendars or personal planners aid in time management?
8. What is the meaning of the statement "Being busy has nothing to do with productivity"?
9. What is investment time and how might chefs use it?

NOTES

1. Barrie Hobson and Mike Scally, *Time Management: Conquering the Clock* (San Diego, CA: Pfeiffer & Co., 1993), 84.

2. Thomas J. Quick, "The Art of Time Management," *Training*, January 1989, 60.

3. Robert Hochheiser, *Time Management* (New York: Barron's), 1992.

4. Marc Mancini, *Time Management* (New York: Irwin Inc., 1994), 73.

5. Alfred W. Travers, *Supervision Techniques and New Dimensions* (Englewood Cliffs, NJ: Regents/Prentice-Hall, 1993), 111.

6. Robert Hochheiser, *Time Management* (New York: Irwin Inc., 1992), 15.

7. Bruce B. Tepper, *The New Supervisor Skills for Success* (New York: Irwin Inc., 1994), 43.

Chapter 20
Problem Solving and Decision Making

OBJECTIVES

When you complete this chapter, you should be able to:

1. Describe the primary elements of sound decision making and problem solving
2. Outline the elements in the decision-making process
3. Evaluate the links between decision making, empowerment, and quality management
4. State reasons why problems recur within the kitchen
5. Define the steps used to identify problems relating to issues of quality and customer satisfaction
6. Use the strategies of the Pareto principle to chart cause and effect of problems
7. Describe elements of open and closed problems

Case Study: JL Beach Club

The Fourth of July was always an extremely busy day at the JL. The sunrise breakfast, the pool and beachside lunch buffet, and the extravagant evening BBQ for all club members, combined with the private parties in the JL's private beach cabanas pushed the limits of JL's kitchen staff. Jed Murray, general manager of JL, was beginning to think that this year the kitchen staff would not be able to meet the challenge. There is only one week left before the big day, and the menu and staffing plan had not been finalized for any of the events except the private parties, and the guests booking the events determined the menus for these.

Jed had begun meeting with Chef Loman in May to plan the menus, staffing needs, and logistics. Chef Loman joined JL in April. Jed discussed with Chef Loman at the first meeting how important the Fourth of July events were to the JL's members. Chef Loman assured him that he would create appropriate menus and plan for sufficient staff to meet the challenges of the day.

Jed and Chef Loman met again in late May to review the chef's menus and staffing plan. Jed told Chef Loman that the menus were too ambitious and that his staffing plan grossly exceeded what they normally spent on staff. Chef Loman met with Jed again in early June to review his revised menus and staffing plan. Jed was very disappointed with what the chef presented. He told Chef Loman that the menus and staffing he proposed were not up to "JL standards." Jed told Chef Loman to again revise his menus and staffing plans and they would meet two weeks before the Fourth for a final review.

Jed met with Chef Loman again two weeks before the Fourth and reviewed the menus and staffing plan. Jed still did not feel that the menu and staffing plan were acceptable. Chef Loman pointed out that they were quickly running out of time to arrange for supplies and staff. Jed suggested that they just use the original menu and staffing plan the chef had presented in May. The chef agreed, but pointed out that the cost would be higher. Jed told Chef Loman to revise the menus and staffing plan one more time to get the cost down.

Jed asked Chef Loman today, one week before the Fourth, to see the revised menu and staffing plan. Chef Loman responded, "I will get them to you when I can. Currently I am arranging for staff, ordering supplies, and developing the work orders to ensure that we are ready for the Fourth."

Based on what you have learned from previous chapters and the content of this chapter, answer the following questions.

- What has taken place at the JL Beach Club?
- What is the overall reason for the situation that has arisen at the JL Beach Club?
- What are the primary causal agents for the situation that has arisen at the JL Beach Club?
- What role did leadership and supervision/management play in the situation that has arisen at JL Beach Club?
- What specific steps could have been taken to avoid the situation that has arisen at the JL Beach Club?
- What, specifically, can be done to avoid a repeat of the situation that has arisen at the JL Beach Club?

INTRODUCTION

To succeed and become a more effective manager, the chef must learn to make sound decisions and solve problems. This is much easier said than done. There is an old business adage that says, "A manager has only challenges, not problems." There is a more recent adage that says, "Four hundred challenges in one day are a lot of problems!" The potential for challenges in the kitchen is endless. Nothing is concrete, and new challenges confront the chef every day. The only constant is change. The problems may be customer satisfaction, motivating the kitchen team, time usage, competition, money, personal relationships, or health. These problems recur periodically, and their solutions involve decisions. How well and creatively those problems are solved and what the basis of the decision-making process is determine the chef's effectiveness.

CHEF TALK
"CHEF: RESEARCHER, PROBLEM SOLVER, DECISION MAKER"

The chef is a master in the art of food preparation. His practical knowledge and experience in creating exciting and appealing foods for customers shows the chef's importance in the food industry. Within the industry lie different opportunities for an inspired chef. The relatively new field of culinology blends the culinary and food science fields into one arena, and from this combination comes the position of "research chef," a new breed of chef who is highly desired by the corporate world. The research chef applies the science of food and the art of food preparation to create new and exciting food products. The role of the research chef is both exciting and challenging.

The research chef in the corporate world, due to his practical knowledge and experience creating exciting and appealing foods for consumers, considers the individual to be the focal point in food development. The chef has to think in a creative fashion while applying physical sciences to the projects at hand. Some of those sciences include chemistry, engineering, physics, microbiology, and rheology. The sciences are an integral part of the research chef's career, and his knowledge of these makes him a valuable asset to the company. The chef's experience in working with produce, different cooking methods, and the presentation of the food is a major part of the product development, a methodical but rewarding process that is an area of expertise for the research chef. Successful chefs are inspired through consumer marketing trends, which then challenge the chef to produce novel products that are cost effective and appealing. With the advancement of each product, the research chef has to understand how to be consistent between products. In order to keep products consistent, the research chef must understand how to measure and quantify certain features of the products. This drives the chef to approach the situation from the perspective of a scientist.

The research chef has to have the mindset of a scientist while working in a corporate environment. This means that the chef sometimes needs to step out of his comfort zone and work directly with scientists. The food scientist/chef should be comfortable working with laboratory equipment for analyzing products. While many companies have technicians to assist the scientist, there are times when the scientist needs to operate equipment to acquire data. This ability is important to understand the source of reliable data. The food scientist also needs to have a working knowledge of statistics to understand the analysis of data. By learning statistics, the chef is able to communicate with statisticians who can guide him through experimental design and analysis of data. This skill becomes important when presenting results. Statistical evidence can show significant differences in data that can be an important input for determining the course of development projects. With accurate results and use of statistics, culinary scientists can produce credible data that can influence the final product. The skill of a culinary scientist is another strength of the research chef that makes him an integral part of the company's success.

The research chef's unique abilities to understand both the physical sciences and the culinary world make him a major contributor to successful product development in the corporate world. His artistic mindset uses the building blocks of science to produce new products and solve problems. The research chef's ability to combine art and science makes him a valuable resource.

—Joshua Goldman, Associate Food Scientist,
Development and Quality
Cheese and Dairy Research
Kraft Foods
Glenview, IL

Problem solving does not come from divine inspiration (although that might be helpful); it is a skill that can be learned. Making decisions is a part of everyday life. Some are made by default: A decision is delayed to the point that some other event removes the opportunity for decision making. Others are made on the basis of feelings or emotions and often in haste. Good decisions, however, are made based on careful thought using facts and logic. There is no substitute for good decision making. **Decisions** are choices between two or more options. Before a choice can be made, the exact nature of the problem must be understood. The chef must know exactly what the problem is before attempting to correct the situation.

Chefs need to be decisive. When the time for action arrives, action must be taken. Decisions are not made in a vacuum. Each decision has an impact on the team and future decisions.

THE DECISION-MAKING PROCESS

To avoid jumping to conclusions, a rational procedure should be followed when making decisions. This procedure will enable the chef to make decisions based on facts and logic, not on emotion. In any decision there are three basic options:

1. To proceed.
2. To oppose.
3. To take no action (let the problem solve itself).

The starting point in the process is to analyze the situation. Ensure that the real problem has been analyzed. Break up the problem into small parts. The six-step model is an effective model for problem solving and decision making. The steps in the model are:

1. *Objective:* What is the desired result of the decision? This refers to the desired end result. It should not contain the method by which the chef arrives at the decision.
2. *Examine:* Determine the problem through careful investigation. This is the "why" portion of the decision. Once all potential causes of the problem have been located, the actual cause can be determined.
3. *Evaluate:* Gather the facts. Make a list of possible solutions to the problem. Narrow this list to a handful of best solutions. The initial step in the process is to make a broad list that can later be narrowed.
4. *Determine:* What are the alternatives and other options? What are the best alternatives? Evaluate the potential best solutions. The greater the number of alternatives, the more likely it is that the best choice will be among them.
5. *Choose:* What is the best option? Making a choice does not complete the decision-making process. Choosing involves writing a detailed plan outlining the action steps. This typically requires who is responsible, the start dates and end dates, what is involved, what changes will take place, and how these changes will take place.
6. *Implement:* What is the best choice? Implement the solution and evaluate its progress. Follow up using the plan developed in step 5. Monitor it at every stage. Evaluation provides the decision maker with information to judge the quality of the decision.

Using this six-step model is the starting point: "Often defining the problem is the important step. If the problem is not clearly defined, all the good intentions and committed efforts that follow will not guarantee that you will find the right solutions, let alone implement them."[1]

PROBLEMS

What is a problem? A **problem** is a situation that a person judges as bad or as something that needs to be corrected. A problem can be experienced in a number of ways but usually is looked upon as a shortfall, a deficit, a lack, a disharmony, a puzzle, an inconvenience, a discomfort, or a pain of some sort. A problem implies that a state of wholeness does not exist and "should" exist.[2]

The causes of many problems in the kitchen are linked with the quality of the food served. Associated with this are problems of timely service and production. Obviously, no two establishments have the same level or number of individual problems in these two areas. However, when all of these problems are analyzed, they almost certainly will be "people issues," such as level of training, attitudes, or skills. Often, the

CHEF TALK
"FINDING GILMAN"

There are so many challenges in the course of a business day! Many are small, some are big, some are with clients, and others are with employees. For some unknown reason, the restaurant industry seems to be a "hotbed" for such challenges, day in and day out. The solutions to these problems often surprise even the experienced manager.

Faced with heavy bookings during the holiday season, I was disappointed to learn that two of our key apprentices were leaving to join our competition. Disappointment turned to anger when I learned that they had left without giving formal notice. After a quick assessment of the situation, a frantic search began to fill these positions with at least one good cook and to "make do" for the rest of the season. We began the task of advertising and interviewing hopeful candidates in a hurried fashion.

I was in the midst of negotiating the terms of purchase on a new manufacturing facility for our soup and sauce production. A building had been located and architects had been summoned for the initial design work. Though the facility seemed perfect for our needs, the architects informed us that possibly a firm with food knowledge would be more appropriate for the design work. Yes, just one more challenge was added to my stack.

Upon returning to the restaurant, I learned that we still had not located a replacement for the apprentices. Entering the kitchen, I noticed a new face at the pot sink. Before I could

even say good morning, he extended his hand and introduced himself. "Gilman" thanked me for giving him the opportunity to be a part of our company. Seeing how excited he was about the pot washing position, I wanted to discuss his choice of our company. He stated without a thought, "Opportunity is why I'm here. I will begin a kitchen career in any position, pot sink, dishwasher, it doesn't matter. I won't stop, however, until I become a chef!" I discovered that he had come from a rich Cajun and Creole heritage and a long line of good cooks. But the shocker was that this was a career change for Gilman. He had graduated five years earlier from Louisiana State University in architecture. After working in his field at one of the most respected firms in Baton Rouge, he came to realize that his true love was cooking. A quick glance at the pot sink that morning turned out to be a golden opportunity not only for Gilman, but for our company as well. Gilman realized his dream of becoming a chef. As an added bonus, we discovered our own resident architect on staff. With Gilman's architectural background and our knowledge of food and food production, imagine the team. I will never walk past the pot sink again without stopping and shaking a hand or two. Who knows what gem lies in that stack of dirty pots.

—John D. Folse, CEC, AAC,
Executive Chef/Owner,
Chef John Folse & Co., Donaldsonville, LA

easiest problems to solve are ones that concern products or equipment. In spite of the best planning efforts, problems occur. Problems occur because circumstances change or the unexpected happens. Some problems could have been foreseen and prevented, and others are largely outside the control of the chef. When improperly handled, problems can contribute to increased costs and can lower the morale of the kitchen team.

The reasons that problems occur in the kitchen are generally centered on the following:

- *Team members may fail to do certain things.* They may forget to inform the chef that food materials have run out or that they have failed to arrive.
- *Team members may do some things but fail to complete the job.* They listen to complaints concerning food items from wait staff or customers but fail to follow through by solving the problem.
- *Team members may do the wrong things.* They get confused during service, prepare the wrong order, or overcook or undercook dishes.
- *Team members may do tasks poorly.* Food quality is reduced or there is indifference to food quality and/or customer service.
- *Team members may be poorly motivated.* Lack of leadership within the team affects motivational levels.

The following questions may be used to identify some problems relative to issues of quality and customer service:

- Has the quality level of each menu item been established with each team member?
- Has the customer profile for the menu items been clearly identified?

- Has the foodservice establishment confirmed its menu acceptance by customers?
- Were the customers involved in determining the menu?
- Is there a clear relationship between customer expectations and the kitchen team?
- Are the customer satisfaction levels measurable? If not, can they be made measurable?
- Have all team members been trained to fulfill their roles?
- Has team responsibility been identified in each quality step?
- Has the menu been evaluated to ensure consistent quality levels during busy periods?
- Is there a shortfall between "actual" and "target" quality levels?
- Is there an opportunity to achieve better than target at no additional cost?
- Does the target level reflect competitive best practices?
- Can everyone on the kitchen team contribute to solving the problem?

In a well-developed kitchen team, each member has the responsibility to watch for potential or existing problems and look for ways to resolve them. Each member should be encouraged by the chef to grow and develop and contribute to solving problems.

THE PARETO PRINCIPLE

Many aids and mechanical methods and procedures exist that allow for problem analysis. These range from what is known as "mind-mapping" to mathematical probability ratings. Perhaps the best-known problem analysis method is the Pareto principle. Use of the **Pareto principle** allows for collecting data, charting it, and grouping problems to determine cause and effects.

Vilfredo Pareto, an Italian economist who conducted extensive research on income distribution, discovered that in his native country 80 percent of the wealth was held by only 20 percent of the population. In international comparative research, he established the same ratio. He eventually realized that he had discovered a universal law: 80 percent of anything is attributed to 20 percent of its cause. For example, 80 percent of the important decisions are accomplished in 20 percent of the time. The 80-20 rule has come to be called the *Pareto principle.*

In problem solving this can also be determined as 80 percent of the effect can usually be attributed to 20 percent of the cause. Therefore, the Pareto principle may be used to chart the 20 percent of key causes that lead to 80 percent of the problems and cure them. An analysis of customer complaints, for example, can identify areas of concern that are directly related to the bulk of complaints. Diagrams and charts are used to present the frequency of occurrences of complaints so as to determine where the bulk of problems with customer service lie. Over a period of time, data can be accumulated from customer comment cards. Table 20-1 and Figure 20-1 are examples of using the Pareto principle.

From the data listed in the table and figure, it is possible to establish what areas are receiving the most complaints. From the total of 75 complaints, 59 are divided among three areas. This represents 78 percent of all the complaints. Therefore, corrective action can be taken to reduce almost 80 percent of the total complaints. Solutions to the three areas can be determined: (1) ways to speed up seating, (2) ways to speed up service, and (3) ways to ensure that the customer receives hot food.

RULES OF PROBLEM SOLVING AND DECISION MAKING

Solving problems is something that is done as part of regular daily activities in the kitchen or personal lives. Problem solving can be both challenging and frustrating. It has often been said that problems are opportunities to be creative. On the other hand,

TABLE 20-1
COMPLAINTS IN A RESTAURANT

Summary of Data	Number of Complaints	Rank	Percentage of Complaints
Food cold	13	3	17
Service unfriendly	2		
Food undercooked	1		
Food overcooked	4	4	—
Flatware dirty	1		
Dining room cold	3		
Long wait to be seated	27	1	36
Room crowded	2		
Portions too small	1		
Decor	1		
Service slow	19	2	25
Noise Level High	1		
Total	75		78

there are so many difficulties with problem solving that it is necessary to use a sequential process. Knowledge gained from experience is a valuable asset, and its importance should not be underestimated. Fear of failure also can be a powerful force in decision making. There is no such thing as a decision without risk or a set of personal traits that guarantee correct decision making. Most people make decisions on the basis of "risk avoidance." Sometimes, risk avoidance blocks a person from applying innovative solutions and ideas. Other elements that contribute to poor decision making in solving problems are shown in Figure 20-2.

What is the ideal best solution for a problem? The ideal "best" solution probably doesn't exist. There are many possible solutions for each problem, and some are better than others. The best solution is nothing more than the best compromise under the circumstances.

The essential elements of problem solving are:

1. Recognizing the problem.
2. Specifying the problem.
   - What is the problem, and what is *not* the problem?
   - Where is it, and where is it *not?*
   - Where did it happen?
   - How big is the problem?
   - Does it change with time and, if so, how?

Figure 20-1

Percentage of total complaints.

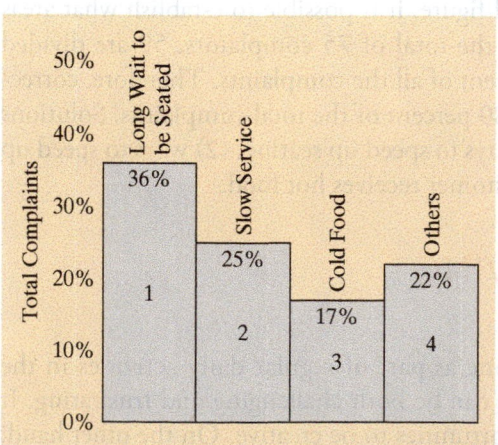

- Getting involved with problems beyond the scope or ability of the kitchen team
- Failing to involve others in the solution of the problem
- Relying only on previously used solutions
- Failing to adequately investigate the cause of the problem
- Failing to seek advice
- Not suspending judgment to generate solutions
- Not being open minded
- Allowing people to think the chef supervisor has the best answers

Figure 20-2
Elements leading to poor decision making.

3. Identifying possible causes.
   - What aspects stand out from the answers to the previous questions?
   - What aspects can be eliminated?
   - Using the experience of the chef and that of the team, what could have caused the problem?

4. Testing causes.
   - Could the cause or causes have accounted for the entire problem?
   - Are they within the control of the chef?

5. Alternative solutions.
   - What could the chef or the kitchen team do that would remove or reduce the cause?
   - What would the consequences of each action be?
   - Which is the best solution?

6. Implementing a plan.
   - What must the chef do to implement the solution?

7. Reviewing effects.
   - Is the problem solved?
   - Were there any unforeseen consequences to the actions?

Open and Closed Problems

Closed-ended problems are those in which the boundaries and constraints are fixed. They usually have one solution.

Examples

- "Where should we locate?"
- "What supplier should we use?"
- "How do we handle accounting problems?"

    Open-ended problems are those where boundaries and constraints can be questioned and may change during the solution.

Examples

- "What dishes should we feature on our new menu?"
- "How do we solve our quality problems?"
- "What are tangible rewards for outstanding performances?"

Potential Problems

The chef must also recognize and deal with "potential problems." The chef who deals with issues only when they become "problems" becomes a firefighter rather than a problem solver. The following guidelines assist in dealing with potential problems before they become real problems.

1. Recognize the potential problem.
   - What could go wrong?
2. Specify the potential problems.
   - What is likely to go wrong?
   - Where is it likely to go wrong?
   - When is it likely to happen?
   - How big a problem will it become?
   - How is it likely to happen?
3. Decide the action.
   - Can it be prevented from happening?
   - If so, what action can be taken to prevent it?
   - If not, what action can the chef take to reduce its effects if and when it happens?
4. Plan the action.
   - What steps can the chef take now to prevent it and reduce its effects?
   - What steps can be taken later to reduce its effects and prevent it from happening again?
5. Implement the action.
   - Often, defining the problem is key to successful problem-solving skills.
   - If the problem is not clearly defined, all the other steps and efforts will be rendered useless.

SUMMARY

One of the most important duties of the chef is to make decisions and solve problems. Good decisions help the foodservice organization, whereas poor ones weaken it.

Decisions should be made on the basis of careful thought using facts and logic. Decisions are choices between two or more options. The decision-making process includes three basic options:

Proceed
Oppose
Take no action (let the problem solve itself)

Decision making follows six steps:

1. Set the objective for the decision.
2. Examine the problem.
3. Evaluate the facts.
4. Determine alternatives.
5. Choose the best option.
6. Implement the choice.

The causes of many problems within the kitchen are generally linked to food quality, and most of these problems are "people" issues. These include:

- Failing to do things
- Failing to complete the job
- Doing the wrong things
- Doing tasks poorly
- Poor motivation

By taking a proactive stand to solving potential problems, the kitchen team may avoid many problems of quality.

The Pareto principle is an effective method for determining where problems lie. The Pareto principle is also known as the 80/20 rule. Using this system can help discover where most of the problems can be found in the kitchen program.

Using a structured and sequential set of steps allows for a more thorough decision-making and problem-solving procedure. These include:

- Recognizing problems
- Specifying problems
- Identifying possible causes
- Open and closed problems and other potential problems

DISCUSSION QUESTIONS

1. Define the following chapter key terms:
   a. Decision
   b. Problem
   c. Pareto principle
   d. Closed-ended problem
   e. Open-ended problem
2. What are the three basic options in decision making?
3. What are the elements of the six-step model used to define problems?
4. Why do most problems in the kitchen center around people issues?
5. What are the steps used to identify problems of quality and customer service?
6. What are the elements of the Pareto principle?
7. What are the uses of the Pareto principle relative to identifying and solving problems?
8. Why do most people make decisions on the basis of risk avoidance?
9. What is the difference between an open and a closed problem?

NOTES

1. Richard N. Chang and P. Keith Kelly, *Step by Step Problem Solving* (Irvine, CA: Richard Chang Associates, 1993), 83.

2. Adapted from Brian Thomas, *Total Quality Training* (London: McGraw-Hill, 1992), 121.

Appendix A
Transactional Analysis

INTRODUCTION

Transactional analysis is a wide-ranging set of theories and techniques that individuals and groups can use to grow and develop to their full potential. The framework of transactional analysis is based on the theory of personality and communication founded by Eric Berne, a Canadian psychotherapist who wrote the founding work of transactional analysis, *Games People Play*, in 1964.[1] This seminal work captured the interest of millions worldwide and has been reprinted many times. The book is well written, easy to understand, and uses ordinary language. Many people feel that the theories detailed in the book make sense of their experiences; help them to understand their feelings, thoughts, and actions; and offer them alternative behaviors to cope with difficulties in their personal and working lives.[2]

Essentially, transactional analysis is a tool for improving interpersonal relations. It is a method of analysis by which an individual can determine the basis from which another individual is communicating or interacting. Once this basis is established, it is then possible to decide how best to respond. Transactional analysis can be used easily in the kitchen and everyday work situations as well as during the training setting. As a chef, you can use it to better understand where each individual team member is "coming from" and what his or her true feelings and disposition are. This will contribute to better interaction with the team and fellow managers.

Over time, it becomes clear from observing a person's behavior that the individual's disposition changes. That is, an individual's modes of speech, body language, interest, and attitudes do not remain constant; they fluctuate over time. According to transactional theory, there are three aspects or roles within each of us: the ego states of *parent*, *adult*, and *child*. These different ego states determine the way in which we communicate.

Berne based his theory on three obvious assertions:

1. Everyone has had parents (or substitute parents or caregivers), and everyone will have internalized, consciously or unconsciously, some of the views of these parents or parent figures.
2. Everyone is capable of behaving in a rational way. This means that each of us can behave according to the realities of the situation rather than react irrationally or purely in terms of emotions or prior conditioning.
3. Everyone sometimes reacts to situations the way they reacted to similar situations in the past.

Outline

- Introduction
- Identifying ego states
- Crossed transactions
- Psychological games
- Summary

IDENTIFYING EGO STATES

The following guide provides the basis for some of the verbal and physical aspects of the parent, adult, and child ego states:

Parent

Physical: Severe or stern expression, folded arms, furrowed brow, pointing finger, the "horrified" look, eyes to heaven; aggressive tone of voice, talking down to others; gestures of concern and helpfulness, patronizing others.

Verbal: "Never, do, don't, ought, should, must, if I were you, the best thing for you to do . . . , don't worry, I'll take care of it." Examples of automatic responses are "disgusting, shocking, ridiculous, not again, stupid, typical, will they ever learn, what can you expect from them." These words MAY identify the parent, but the adult can also decide on the basis of reasoning that certain things are shocking, disgusting, stupid, etc.

Adult

Physical: The adult face is open and expressive. It shows interest and listening when appropriate. Active listening is one of the recognizable behaviors of the adult.

Verbal: The adult vocabulary includes such words as "what, where, why, when, who, how." Other words and phrases are those showing reflection and evaluation such as: how much; comparative; true; false; I think; in my opinion; probably; possibly; likely; apparently; it seems.

Adult-to-adult interaction provides the basis for both groups to be productively engaged in training, planning, decision making, and organizing. Crossed transactions between unparallel ego states will usually be counter-productive. Therefore, recognition of the ego state will direct the course of the interaction and determine its possible outcome.

Child

Physical: Teasing, carefree excitement, laughter, curiosity, giggling, pouting, tears, temper tantrums, sulking, downcast eyes, anxiety.

Verbal: "I wish; I want; I don't care; big; better; best; hey, that's fantastic; what am I going to do now." The tone of voice can be loud, energetic, compliant, whining, defiant, and demanding.

The three ego states are commonly represented as three circles arranged vertically as shown in Figure A-1.

The arrangement of these circles will have the parent on the top, the adult in the middle, and the child at the bottom. This does not imply that a hierarchy exists. This is the basic structure of personality as described by Berne. It is the basis upon which the chef as supervisor or trainer can determine the ego state in which each kitchen team member is transacting.

In most cases, the adult creates the most positive basis for communication by treating the receiver on an adult or an equal basis. However, the parent and child ego states also have their use: the child for humor and the parent for directive behavior.

The following are examples of how transactional analysis is related to the chef's role as trainer. They demonstrate situations in which the three ego states might be encountered in the kitchen:

- Parent ego state: "You have to learn this technique."
- Adult ego state: "You have been able to master all the other techniques up to now. I'm certain that with some coaching you will master this one too."
- Child ego state: "I'll never be able to do this."

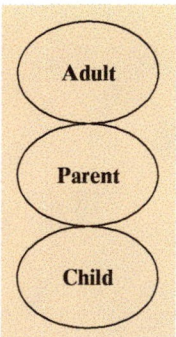

Figure A-1
Three Ego States.

> **Key Contributing Factors**
>
> - Natural child: friendliness, creativity
> - Adapted child: politeness, courtesy
> - Nurturing parent: nurturing, caring
> - Controlling parent: firmness, control
> - Adult: Problem solving, identifying compromises
>
> **Problems**
>
> - Controlling parent: Being righteous, their way is best
> - Nurturing parent: Desire to take care of everyone
> - Adult: Clinically dismissing every idea
> - Natural child: Being silly, horseplay
> - Adapted child: Not participating, waiting to be asked

Figure A-2
Key Contributing Qualities and Problems of Ego States.

Some individuals seem to be programmed to communicate in certain ways. Many times this is true. Chefs who adopt the parent ego state will automatically respond just as their parents did. The adult mode is somewhat more difficult to achieve and maintain. The three ego states identified by Berne—parent, adult, and child—can be further divided into different styles. Subdivisions of the parent ego state are *controlling parent, nurturing parent, natural child,* and *adapted child.* These different ego states are also sometimes referred to as the "tape recorder in your head." People function from the points of view of these remembered ego states.

Generally, parent and child ego states are replays from the past: for example, in the parent ego state, attitudes, values, thoughts, and behaviors are copied from parents, mainly during the first eight years of a child's life. Similarly, Berne's theory states that the child ego states are replays of thoughts and feelings from childhood. The adult ego state includes the ability to deal with situations in the "here and now" and involves being objective, logical, and rational. The key contributing qualities and the potential problems of each ego state are shown in Figure A-2.

The adult ego state is associated with the skills of problem solving and decision making: "Employing the concept of ego states gives us a method for checking our behavior and consciously selecting the most appropriate option for our current objective."[3]

CROSSED TRANSACTIONS

Communication is a two-way process, and in this process transactional analysis is most beneficial. Consider the following: If a team member speaking in the adult mode is responded to as an adult, the communication is likely to be successful; and if the responding team member is also speaking from the adult mode, so much the better. Communication problems arise, however, when an individual speaks as an adult and is responded to in the child or parent mode. This is called a crossed transaction. An example of an uncrossed (adult-to-adult) transaction is:

CHEF	"Tomorrow will be a busy day for the kitchen." (*adult*)
Kitchen team member	"Good, we'll be prepared." (*adult*)

An example of a crossed transaction is:

| Chef | "Tomorrow will be a busy day for the kitchen." (*adult*) |
| Kitchen team member | "Not again! I don't know how we are going to cope." (*child to parent*) |

Uncrossed transactions occur when the ego state addressed is the ego state that responds. If, for example, the controlling parent addresses the adapted child and the reply is from the adapted child, we have an uncrossed transaction. The rule for an uncrossed transaction is that communication can continue indefinitely. However, crossed transactions usually mean that a break in real communication will occur. This does not necessarily mean that all crossed transactions are bad and that all uncrossed transactions are good. If, for example, a team member is shouting at the chef from a controlling parent ego state about a mistake and the chef is in an adapted child ego state, the chef may respond with an uncrossed transaction by apologizing. If the apology is ignored, it is appropriate for the chef to break the communication and to shift to adult-to-adult communication for some problem solving.

Know your ego states. Use the adult to stimulate healthy discussion on the kitchen training sessions. Use the controlling parent to tell team members the rules concerning the sessions. Use the nurturing parent to reassure team members regarding their ability to learn the methods in which they are being trained. Use the natural child to bring fun and excitement into the training sessions. Use the adapted child to be polite and courteous to team participants. At the end of each training session, review what happened. Select some areas of the training session that require work. Analyze the transactional ego state used and consider what other ego states might have worked better. Determine what the likely effects of each ego state might have been, decide which offers the best results for future training sessions, and resolve to handle these areas more skillfully next time.

PSYCHOLOGICAL GAMES

In *Games People Play,* Eric Berne outlined a series of psychological games that people engage in. These repetitive and unsatisfactory interactions usually have negative effects.

People play psychological games, often unconsciously, and tend to choose as spouse and business associates people who play the role opposite to their own. This holds true for people in foodservice organizations as well. Although there are many different games, in each one there are three basic elements:

1. A series of complementary transactions that on the surface seem plausible.
2. An ulterior transaction that is the hidden agenda.
3. A negative payoff that concludes the game and is the real purpose for playing.

Games tend to be repetitious. People find themselves saying the same words in the same way, only the time and place may change. The replay often contributes to what often is described as déjà vu, or, "I feel as if I've done this before."

Some people have favorite ego states, as well as a favorite game role. Games may involve some or all of the dramatic roles of *victim, persecutor,* and *rescuer*—the manipulative roles learned in childhood. Games played in the persecutor or the rescuer role serve to reinforce a negative opinion of others.

Games prevent honest, intimate, open relationships between the players. Yet people play them because they fill up time and provoke attention.[4]

The Game of "Yes, But!"

In the game of "Yes, But," the chef in a meeting presents a problem and then shoots down all suggested solutions. A person who plays "Yes, But" does so to maintain positions such as "Nobody's going to tell me what to do" or "People are stupid." In childhood they may have had parents who either tried to give them all the answers or didn't give any answers, so they took a stand against them.

To initiate this game, one player presents a problem in the guise of soliciting advice from other players. If hooked, the other player advises, "Why don't you . . . ?" The initiator discounts all suggestions with "Yes, but . . . ," followed by reasons the advice won't work. Eventually the "Why don't you . . . ?" advice givers give up and fall silent. This is the payoff of the game to prove the position "Nobody can tell me anything" or "People are stupid."

In this game the child ego state "hooks" the nurturing parent in the other player. Although the transactions may appear to be adult to adult on the surface ("I've got a problem. Tell me the answer."), the ulterior transaction is child to parent ("I've got a problem. Just try to tell me the answer. I won't let you.").

The Game of "Kick Me"

In the game of "Kick Me," the player does something to provoke another player to put him or her down. For example, a team member states, "I stayed out late last night and didn't prepare the *mise en place* for this morning." Chef responds, "Sorry about that. This is the last day I can give you extra time off." (Ulterior transaction: "Yes, you are a bad boy, and here is your kick.")

Though he or she may deny it, a person who plays the game of "Kick Me" tends to attract others who can play the complementary role and are willing to "kick."

The Game of "Harried"

"Harried" is a common game acted out to justify an eventual collapse or depression. Chefs who play "Harried" say "yes" to everything, volunteer to come early and work late, take on additional assignments, and bring work home. For a period of time they are able to act like Superman, but eventually appearances begin to reflect this harried state. They are unable to finish work and their physical and mental health deteriorates. They collect and save so many feelings of depression that they finally collapse, too depressed to function. Variations of this game are "Harried Chef," "Harried Manager," "Harried Purveyor," "Harried Waitperson," "Harried Supervisor," and others.

The Game of "See What You Made Me Do"

In the kitchen, this game is played when a team member makes a mistake while the chef is watching from behind. Rather than taking responsibility for the error, the team member turns to the supervisor and angrily says, "See what you made me do!" thus blaming someone else for the mistake. If this happens often enough, the chef may feel guilty and leave the team member alone. In this way, the purpose of the game—isolation—is fulfilled. Sometimes, the "See What You Made Me Do" player may be collecting feelings of purity instead of anger: "After all, it's not *my* fault. It's *your* fault I made my mistake. I'm pure."

The Game of "Stupid"

An example of the "Stupid" game is when a secretary "accidentally" puts a letter in a bottom drawer and "forgets" about it. Later, when the letter is rediscovered, the secretary makes a fuss, complaining, "How could I have done such a stupid thing! This was the letter that you wanted in Washington, DC, last month."

> **Game Stoppers**
>
> - Give an unexpected response
> - Stop exaggerating your own weaknesses or strengths
> - Stop exaggerating the weaknesses and strengths of others
> - Structure more of their time with activities, intimacy, and fun
> - Stop playing the rescuer, helping those who don't need help
> - Stop playing the persecutor, criticizing those who don't need it
> - Stop playing the victim, acting helpless or dependent when you are really able to stand on your own two feet

Figure A-3
Game Stoppers.

Other Popular Games

Themes of other easily recognized games are the following:

I'm only trying to help you: "My advice is so good! Why do you want to think for yourself and reject my ideas when I'm only trying to help you?"

Wooden leg: "Surely you can't expect much from me when I have such a handicap," i.e., wrong race, wrong background, etc.

See how hard I tried: "Don't blame me if things turn out wrong. After all, see how hard I tried."

Uproar: "I'm stronger than you are. You stupid fool; you never do anything right."

Now I've got you: "I've caught you making a mistake and will now make you suffer."

Games may be foiled by a refusal to play the expected hand or to give a payoff. For example, refusing to give advice or suggestions to a "Yes, But" player usually stops the game. Some of the ways to stop a game are shown in Figure A-3.

Why do we play psychological games? One major reason is that most people are unaware that they are. According to Julie Hay, writing in *Transactional Analysis for Trainers*, because there are "apparent advantages that accrue from playing psychological games, we find it hard to stop the repetitive sequences, even when we become aware of them."[5] When team members' game preferences have been identified, it is possible to determine how games affect the culture of the training session or activity in the kitchen. The chef supervisor then can determine how to behave differently so as to avoid them in the future. Thomas Quick states: "Transactional Analysis doesn't provide a universal explanation for every aspect of human behavior, but it provides some realistic bases. In a very short time using the transactional model you could train employees, especially those who deal with the public, so as to effectively deal with the various kinds of behavior they encounter."[6]

SUMMARY

Transactional analysis is a tool that can help improve interpersonal relations. It is a method of analysis by which one person can determine the basis from which another individual is communicating or interacting. Understanding transactional analysis contributes to successful training and supervision.

Transactional analysis was developed by Eric Berne who noted that, over time, it becomes clear from observing a person's behavior that the individual's disposition changes. Transactional analysis posits the existence of three aspects in every person—the ego states of parent, adult, and child—and they determine the way in which each communicates.

These three ego states in turn may be subdivided into the natural child, the adapted child, the nurturing parent, and the controlling parent. Ego states are also referred to as the "tape recorder in your head." Generally, parent and child ego states are replays from our past. Each is indicative of a particular set of values, attitudes, thoughts, and behaviors from the past. The adult ego state deals with the "here and now." An understanding of crossed and uncrossed transactions from different ego states facilitates successful communication, supervision, and training.

People play psychological games, often in an unconscious way. Although there are many different games, each has three basic elements:

1. A series of complementary transactions that on the surface appear plausible.
2. An ulterior transaction that is the hidden agenda.
3. A negative payoff that concludes the game and is the real purpose for playing.

Chefs can assess the climate and culture that exist in the kitchen for training by spotting the various games that team members play.

NOTES

1. Eric Berne, *Games People Play* (London: Grove Press/Penguin, 1968).

2. Brian Thomas, *Total Quality Training: The Quality Culture and Quality Trainer* (Berkshire, England: McGraw-Hill, 1992), 122.

3. Julie Hay, *Transactional Analysis for Trainers* (Berkshire, England: McGraw-Hill, 1992), 83.

4. Adapted from Eric Berne, *Games People Play* (London: Grove Press/Penguin, 1968).

5. Julie Hay, *Transactional Analysis for Trainers* (Berkshire, England: McGraw-Hill, 1992), 136.

6. Thomas Quick, "Simple Is Hard, Complex Is Easy, Simplistic Is Impossible," *Training & Development Journal*, May 1990, 96.

Appendix B

Glossary of Terms

Active listening Encouraging the speaker to continue talking by giving interested responses that show that the listener understands the speaker's meaning and feelings.

Affirmative action Actions or programs designed to improve employment opportunities for members of protected groups, such as minorities, the aged, and the handicapped.

Androgogy Concept of adult education.

Apprentice A worker serving a special training period that combines formal schooling with job experience in preparation for entry into a skilled job.

Authority The rights and powers to make the necessary decisions and to take the necessary action to get the job done.

Autocratic leadership A leadership style characterized by a high concern for tasks (getting the job done) and a relatively low concern for people.

Body language Expression of attitudes and feelings through body movements and positions.

Brainstorming Generating ideas within a group without considering their drawbacks, limitations, or consequences.

Budget As a planning tool, it commits organizational resources to projects, programs, or activities, and results are measured in quantifiable terms over predetermined time periods. As a control device, it compares actual performance against expectations.

Case study A form of training that provides trainees with materials that describe particular situations for which the trainees are to analyze the case and make recommendations.

Closed-end questions Interview questions that require specific and usually restricted responses.

Coaching Individual, corrective on-the-job training for improving performance.

Collective bargaining The process of negotiating and administering a union contract.

Communication The process of passing along information and understanding from one person to another person or group.

Critical incident technique A form of performance appraisal in which supervisors observe and record outstanding employee behavior, good or bad.

Culinarian Person who works in a kitchen preparing food.

Cultural empathy Being sensitive to cultural differences and similarities by seeking to understand others' approach to life and their ways of thinking and living.

Decision Conscious choice among alternatives.

Delegation The process of distributing work to others and providing them with the appropriate resources and authority to do the task.

Democratic leadership A leadership style characterized by a high concern for both people and task accomplishment.

Demotivator An emotion, environmental factor, or incident that reduces motivation to perform well.

Discipline Punishment of employees for violating the rules or performance requirements of the organization. The process of socializing employees to accept and follow the rules and values of the organization.

Dissatisfiers Factors in the job environment that produce dissatisfaction, usually reducing motivation.

Diversity Physical and cultural dimensions that separate and distinguish individuals and groups: age, gender, physical abilities and qualities, ethnicity, race, and sexual preference.

Downward communication The process of passing along information and understanding from the higher levels of the organization to the lower levels.

Due process The means by which employees are given a chance for fair treatment by their employers. The process includes such protective measures as having reasonable work rules, a chance to defend against any accusations, and review by higher levels of management.

Employee rights The concept that employees are to be treated fairly and with dignity by their employers; and if there are violations of those rights, employees should have recourse against the employers.

Empowerment Giving employees permission to make decisions. In the foodservice industry, empowering employees to satisfy the customer.

Ethnocentrism A belief that one's own culture or way of doing things is best.

Exempt employee An employee who, under the provisions of the Fair Labor Standards Act, is exempt from the overtime pay requirements of the act; generally considered to be persons employed in a bona fide executive, administrative, or professional capacity.

Exit interview An interview of a terminating employee to learn the employee's honest reactions or his or her reasons for leaving the organization, usually conducted on the last day of employment.

Expectancy theory A motivation theory that holds that individuals are motivated to act when they believe their actions will bring about desirable results for themselves.

Facilitator A new dimension to the supervisor's job that gives emphasis to the supervisor's taking appropriate measures to make it easier for workers to do their jobs, as well as removing obstacles that hinder performance.

Foodservice organization   Any establishment that prepares and serves food by utilizing professionals.

Grievance procedure   A procedure set up either by management or by management and the union to resolve employee complaints fairly.

Grievances   Real or imagined complaints of workers against management or working conditions, often related to union–management relations.

Halo effect   The tendency to assume that because one or a few things are done well by a person, all things about that person are good.

Hazard Analysis Critical Control Point (HACCP)   A food preparation safety system that targets high-risk foods and preparation at critical points and seeks to maximize safe food handling.

Hierarchy of needs theory   Abraham Maslow's motivation theory that identifies and arranges in order of dominance the five levels of human needs.

Hot stove rule   A disciplinary technique designed to ensure fair treatment to all employees that compares the taking of disciplinary action to what happens when one touches a hot stove.

Human relations movement   A belief that the workplace is a social setting and, as such, more attention has to be given to human needs, motivation, and interpersonal relations.

Hygiene factors   Frederick Herzberg's concept that the job-related factors of working conditions, interpersonal relations, organizational policies and procedures, quality of supervision, and pay can cause worker dissatisfaction.

Induction training   The absorbing of new team members into the culture and philosophy of the organization.

Insubordination   Refusal by an employee to follow a direct order from a supervisor.

Job description   A written statement that sets forth in general terms the duties of a position and related responsibilities so people can understand what is done by the person holding that particular job.

Job interview   A purposeful conversation between an employer and a job applicant that deals with the exchange of relevant information about job-related matters.

Job rotation   Periodically moving team members to different jobs for such purposes as cross-training and relieving worker boredom.

Job satisfiers   Frederick Herzberg's concept that the job-related factors of achievement, recognition, responsibility, advancement, and opportunity for growth give employees satisfaction on the job and thus serve as motivators.

Job specifications   A written listing of the specific requirements to perform a job.

Job talk   A training technique of imparting information from the supervisor to the team member. Relies on an illustrated lecture.

Leadership   The ability to influence others to do something voluntarily rather than because it is required or because of a fear of the consequences of not doing it or an expectation of reward for doing it.

Learning objective   A training goal stated in measurable or observable terms.

Management by objectives (MBO)   A results-oriented management technique that seeks employee involvement, leading to supervisor and employee mutually setting goals and evaluation criteria, and that will serve as the basis for evaluating that person's contribution to the overall organizational goals.

Management by walking around (MBWA)   An active management technique in which the supervisor visits each workstation for hands-on management and supervision.

Mise en place   Preparation, everything ready; in kitchens, refers to preparation prior to food service. A collection of items necessary to prepare menu items.

Morale   Group spirit with respect to getting the job done.

Motivation   The stimulating or causing of purposeful activity that is directed to satisfying needs or wants.

Negative discipline   Maintaining discipline through fear and punishment.

Nonexempt employee   An employee who, under the provisions of the Fair Labor Standards Act, is entitled to overtime pay for hours worked in excess of the statutory requirements.

Nonverbal communication   Communication without words. Use of gestures, facial expressions, or body language.

On-the-job training   Training that is done in the workplace under regular working conditions.

Open-end questions   Interview questions that allow for a range of responses.

Organization   A collection of individuals who are working together to reach common goals.

Organizing   The prelude to action and the process of mentally and physically preparing and arranging the necessary resources to accomplish results.

Orientation   The programmed introduction of new employees into the organization, during which they learn what is important to the organization, to the supervisor, and to fellow employees.

Participative management   A style of management that seeks to give employees meaningful involvement in their job and conditions of employment.

Performance appraisal   Systematic evaluation of the employee's work performance and potential with the organization.

Personal space   The area within 2 to 3 feet of a person.

Persons with disabilities   People who have or are considered to have a physical or mental impairment that substantially limits one or more major life activities.

Planning   The process by which management determines expected outcomes and coordinates resources, personnel, and activities to reach these objectives.

Policies   Written statements of the goals and intentions of the top management of the organization.

Positive discipline   A punishment-free formula for disciplinary action that replaces punishment with reminders and features a decision-making leave of absence with pay.

Procedures   Written statements that spell out the details of what is to be done and how.

Productivity   A measure of the relationship that exists between outputs, such as so many pieces per hour, to inputs, such as hours worked to produce the items.

Pygmalion effect   J. Sterling Livingston's concept that the performance level of subordinates is affected by the supervisor's expectations and abilities.

Quality   The concept that the product or service meets the stated and implied specifications.

Rating scale   A form of performance appraisal that requires the evaluator to make a selection from several predetermined choices.

Reengineering   Redesign of work processes and implementation of the new design.

Role model   One who serves as an example for the behavior of others.

Role playing   A form of training that attempts to create common and realistic learning situations (such as performance reviews or disciplinary actions) by having employees act out assigned roles.

Rules   A form of control that spells out the code of conduct that is required by the organization, and, in many cases, states the penalties for violation.

Scientific management   The concept developed by Frederick Taylor that holds that work is most efficiently performed when management studies each job scientifically, determines the basic elements of each, standardizes the methods and tools used, selects workers suited to the specific jobs, provides for job specialization, and sees to strong supervisory support.

Sexual harassment   Unwelcome advances, requests for sexual favors, and other verbal or physical conduct of a sexual nature when compliance with any of these acts is a condition of employment, or when comments or physical contact create an intimidating, hostile, or offensive working environment.

Situational leadership   Adaptation of leadership style to the needs of the situation.

Socialization   The process by which people learn and come to accept the appropriate values and behaviors for various situations.

Supervisor   An employee who is in a management position and has authority to perform such management duties as assigning work, hiring, firing, and making promotions and transfers, or who can effectively recommend such actions.

Supportive leadership   A leadership style characterized by a high concern for people and a relatively low concern for task accomplishment.

Theory X   Douglas McGregor's concept that some supervisors assume a generally negative view of workers, believing that the typical employee is lazy, dislikes work, and must be closely supervised.

Theory Y   Douglas McGregor's concept that some supervisors assume a generally positive view of workers, believing that the typical employee is willing, personally responsible, and responds best to a minimum of supervision.

Total quality management (TQM)   A business and management philosophy/process in which all efforts are expended through concerted effort directed at servicing customers by continuous improvements, utilizing, and maximizing human resources.

Training   Planned and organized activity that seeks to provide employees with the necessary skills and attitudes to function effectively on the job.

Transactional analysis   Theories and techniques that can be used by individuals and groups to determine the basis from which another individual is communicating or interacting.

Unstructured interview   A form of interview in which the questions and sequence are accommodated to the applicant's unique background and responses to prior questions.

Upward communication   The process of passing along information and understanding from the lower levels of the organization to the higher levels.

Values   Strongly held beliefs that either define right or wrong or indicate preferences.

Win–win problem solving   A method of solving problems in the kitchen in which the chef supervisor and team member discuss the problem together and arrive at a mutually acceptable situation.

Work standards   The established time that a normally capable worker should take to do a specified task.

Workers' compensation   A form of no-fault insurance that entitles workers who are injured or who become ill because of job-related conditions to compensation in the form of money, medical treatment, and vocational rehabilitation, if necessary.

Aguayo, Rafeal. *Dr. Deming.* New York: Carol, 1991.

Almanac of Policy Issues. http://www.policyalmanac.org/social_welfare/archive/unemployment_compensation.shtml.

Anderson, Peggy, ed. *Great Quotes from Great Leaders.* Lombard, IL: Lombard, 1989.

Barbee, Cliff, and Valerie Bott. "Customer Treatment as a Mirror of Employee Treatment," *Advanced Management Journal,* Spring 1991.

Barker, Joel Arthur. *Paradigms: The Business of Discovering the Future.* New York: HarperCollins, 1993.

Becker, Dennis, and Paula Borkum Becker. *Powerful Presentation Skills.* Boston: Mirror Press, 1994.

Belasco, James A. *Teaching the Elephant to Dance.* New York: Crown, 1990.

Bennus, Warren, and Burt Nanus. *Leaders: The Strategies for Taking Charge.* New York: HarperCollins, 1985.

Berne, Eric. *Games People Play.* London: Penguin, 1964.

Bernstein, Charles, and William P. Fisher. *Lessons in Leadership: Perspectives for Hospitality Industry Success.* New York: Van Nostrand Reinhold, 1991.

Berta, Dina. *Nation's Restaurant News – HR & Services.* "People Report: Worker Turnover Rate Continues to Climb." November 2006. http://www.peoplereport.com/newsclippings/200611_NRN_PostConferenceCoverage.pdf

Berta, Dina. "Diversity at the Top: Quick-Service Outshines Other Segments with the Highest Percentage of Women and Minorities in Management Positions: Segment Study: QSR & Diversity." Nation's Restaurant News. February 6, 2006, Vol. 40, Issue 6, 33.

Blanchard, Ken, John Carlos, and Alan Randolph. *Empowerment Takes More Than a Minute.* San Francisco: Berrett-Koehler Publishers, 1996.

Blanchard, Ken, and Michael O'Connor. *Managing By Values*: San Francisco: Berrett Koehler Publishers, 1997.

Blanchard, Kenneth, Patricia Zigarni, and Drea Zigarni. *Leadership and the One Minute Manager.* New York: Morrow, 1985.

Byars, Lloyd L., and Leslie W. Rue. *Human Resource Management,* 4th ed. Boston: Irwin, 1994.

Cain, Herman. *Leadership Is Common Sense.* New York: Van Nostrand Reinhold, 1996.

California Department of Industrial Relations. http://www.dir.ca.gov/sip/sip.html, 2011.

Carlzon, Jan. *Moments of Truth.* Cambridge, MA: Ballinger, Harper & Row, 1987.

Casio, Wayne F. *Applied Psychology in Human Resources Management,* 5th ed. Upper Saddle River, NJ: Prentice Hall, 1998.

Centers for Disease Control and Prevention, *Morbidity and Mortality Weekly Report: Surveillance for Foodborne Disease Outbreaks—United States, 2007.* 59(31): 973–979, http://www.cdc.gov/mmwr/preview/mmwrhtml/mm5931a1.htm?s_cid=mm5931a1_w

C.E.R.T. *Customer Relations.* Dublin, Ireland: CERT, 1990.

Cherrington, David J. *The Management of Human Resources,* 4th ed. Englewood Cliffs, NJ: Prentice Hall, 1995.

Christensen, Julia. "The Diversity Dynamics: Implications for Organizations in 2005." *Hospitality Research Journal* 17, no. 1 (1993).

Cichy, Ronald, Martin P. Sciarini, and Mark E. Patton. "Food-Service Leadership: Could Attila Run a Restaurant?" *The Cornell Hotel and Restaurant Administration Quarterly* 33, no. 1 (1992).

Clonz, Angela, and Neil H. Snyder. *The Will to Lead: Managing with Courage and Conviction in the Age of Uncertainty.* New York: Irwin, 1997.

Cohen, William A. *The Art of the Leader.* Englewood Cliffs, NJ: Prentice Hall, 1990.

Crosby, Philip. *Quality Is Free.* New York: McGraw-Hill, 1978.

Crosby, Philip. *Quality Is Free: The Art of Making Quality Certain.* New York: John Wiley, 1989.

Cullen, Noel C. "Reengineering the Executive Chef." *Chef Magazine,* October 1993.

Cullen, Noel C. "Total Quality Management for the Modern Chef." *National Culinary Review,* August 1996.

Dale, Barrie G., Cary L. Cooper, and Adrian Wilkinson, *Managing Quality & Human Resources: A Guide to Continuous Improvement.* Oxford, England: Blackwell, 1997.

Davidow, William H., and Bro Utall. *Total Customer Service: The Ultimate Weapon.* New York: Harper Perennial, 1990.

Deming, W. Edwards. *Out of Crisis.* Cambridge, MA: MIT Center for Advanced Engineering Study, 1989.

DePree, Max. *Leadership Is an Art.* New York: Dell, 1989.

Dessler, Gary. *Human Resources Management,* 7th ed. Upper Saddle River, NJ: Prentice Hall, 1997.

Drucker Foundation. *Leader of the Future.* San Francisco: Jossey-Bass, 1996.

Drummond, Karen Eich. *Human Resources Management for the Hospitality Industry.* New York: Van Nostrand Reinhold, 1990.

Drummond, Karen Eich. *The Restaurant Training Program.* New York: John Wiley, 1992.

Dumont, Raymond, and John M. Lannon. *Business Communications,* 2nd ed. Boston: Brown, 1987.

Eade, Vincent H. *Human Resources Management in the Hospitality Industry.* Scottsdale, AZ: Garsuch Sciarisbrick, 1993.

E Notes, Encyclopedia of Management, http://www.enotes.com/management-encyclopedia/theory-z, 2011.

Equal Employment Opportunity Commission. *Sexual Harassment Charges EEOC & FEPAs Combined: FY 1992–FY 2002.* http//:www.eeoc.gov/stats/harass.html.

Fernandez, John P. *Managing a Diverse Work Force: Regaining the Competitive Edge.* Lexington, MA: Heath, 1991.

Ferris, Gerald R., and M. Ronald Buckley. *Human Resources Management: Perspectives, Context, Functions, and Outcomes,* 3rd ed. Englewood Cliffs, NJ: Prentice Hall, 1995.

Fisher, Cynthia D., Lyle F. Schoenfeldt, and James B. Shaw. *Human Resources Management,* 3rd ed. Boston: Houghton Mifflin, 1996.

Francis, Dave, and Don Young. *Improving Work Groups: A Practical Manual for Team Building.* San Diego: Pfeiffer, 1993.

Frumkin, Paul. "At Your Service: Dining and Diversity: Catering to a Multicultural Clientele: As the U.S. Population Becomes Increasingly Diverse, Training Servers to be Sensitive to the Distinct Desires of Different Groups Becomes More Important than Ever." *Nation's Restaurant News,* September 2005, Vol. 39, Issue 38, 110.

Gallos, Joan V., Jean Ramsey, and associates. *Teaching Diversity.* San Francisco: Jossey-Bass, 1997.

Gatewood, Robert D., and Hubert S. Field. *Human Resource Selection,* 4th ed. Fort Worth, TX: Dryden Press, 1998.

Go, Frank M., Mary L. Monachello, and Tom Baum. *Human Resources Management in the Hospitality Industry.* New York: John Wiley, 1996.

Goad, Tom W. *Delivering Effective Training.* San Diego: Pfeiffer, 1982.

Gomez-Mejia, Luis R., David Balkin, and Robert L. Cardy. *Managing Human Resources,* 2nd ed. Upper Saddle River, NJ: Prentice Hall, 1998.

Hammer, Michael, and James Champy. *Reengineering the Corporation: A Manifesto for Business Revolution.* New York: HarperCollins, 1993.

Hargrove, Robert. *Masterful Coaching.* San Francisco: Pfeiffer, 1995.

Harris, Thomas. *I'm OK, You're OK.* London: Pan, 1978.

Hart, Lois B. *Training Methods That Work.* London: Crisp, 1991.

Hay, Julie. *Transactional Analysis for Trainers.* Berkshire, England: McGraw-Hill, 1992.

Heneman, Herbert G., Robert L. Heneman, and Timothy A. Judge. *Staffing Organizations,* 2nd ed. Boston: Irwin, 1997.

Herzberg, Frederick. "One More Time: How Do You Motivate Employees?" *Harvard Business Review* 46, no. 1 (1968).

Herzberg, Frederick. *Work and the Nature of Man.* Cleveland: World, 1966.

Hilgert, Raymond L., and Cyril C. Ling. *Cases and Experiential Exercises in Human Resources Management.* Upper Saddle River, NJ: Prentice Hall, 1996.

Hobson, Barrie, and Mike Scally. *Time Management: Conquering the Clock.* San Diego: Pfeiffer, 1993.

Keiser, James R. *Principles and Practices of Management in the Hospitality Industry,* 2nd ed. New York: Van Nostrand Reinhold, 1989.

Kets de Vries, Manfred F. R. *Leaders, Fools and Imposters.* San Francisco: Jossey-Bass, 1993.

Kinlaw, Dennis C. *Coaching for Commitment.* San Diego: Pfeiffer, 1993.

Kleiman, Lawrence S. *Human Resources Management: A Tool for Competitive Advantage.* San Francisco: West, 1997.

Klein, Allen. *Quotations to Cheer You Up.* New York: Wings Books, 1991.

Koonce, Richard. "Redefining Diversity: It's Not Just the Right Thing to Do. It Also Makes Good Business Sense." *Training & Development,* December 2001, http//:www.findarticles. com/cf_ntrstnws/m4467/12_55/83045836/print.jhtml, 1.

Kotschevar, Lendal H. *Management by Menu.* Dubuque, IA: Brown, 1987.

Kouzes, James M., and Barry Z. Posner. *Credibility: How Leaders Gain and Lose It, Why People Demand It.* San Francisco: Jossey-Bass, 1993.

Leeds, Dorothy. *Marketing Yourself: The Ultimate Job-Seeker's Guide.* New York: HarperCollins, 1991.

Levinson, Charles. *Food and Beverage Operation Cost Control and Systems Management.* Englewood Cliffs, NJ: Prentice Hall, 1989.

Lewis, Pamela S., Stephen H. Goodman, and Patricia M. Fandt. *Management: Challenges in the 21st Century.* San Francisco: West, 1995.

Maddux, Robert B. *Team Building: An Exercise in Leadership.* Menlo Park, CA: Crisp, 1992.

Mager, Robert F. *Preparing Instructional Objectives,* 2nd ed. Belmont, CA: Fearon, 1971.

Marvin, Bill. *The Foolproof Foodservice Selection System.* New York: John Wiley, 1993.

Maslow, Abraham. *Motivation and Personality,* 2nd ed. New York: Harper & Row, 1970.

Maxwell, John C. *The 21 Irrefutable Laws of Leadership: Follow Them and People Will Follow You.* Nashville, TN: Thomas Nelson Publishers, 1998.

Maxwell, John C. *Developing the Leader Within You.* Nashville, TN: Nelson, 1993.

McGregor, Douglas. *The Human Side of Enterprise.* New York: McGraw-Hill, 1960.

McNamara, Carter. *Brief Overview of Contemporary Theories in Management,* http://www.managementhelp.org/mgmnt/cntmpory.htm, 2007.

Merriam-Webster Online. http://www.merriam-webster.com/dictionary/management, 2011.

Merritt, Edward. *Strategic Leadership: Essential Concepts.* Aventine Press, 2008.

Milkovich, George T., and John W. Boudreau. *Human Resources Management,* 8th ed. Boston: Irwin, 1997.

Milkovich, Michael E. *Improving Service Quality.* Delray Beach, FL: St. Lucie Press, 1995.

Miller, Jack E., Mary Porter, and Karen E. Drummond. *Supervision in the Hospitality Industry,* 2nd ed. New York: John Wiley, 1992.

Mondy, Wayne R., and Robert M. Noe. *Human Resource Management.* Upper Saddle River, NJ: Prentice Hall, 1996.

Morgan, William J., Jr. *Food and Beverage Management and Service.* Lansing, MI: Educational Institute of the American Hotel and Motel Association, 1981.

Morgan, William J., Jr. *Supervision and Management of Quality Food Production: Principles and Procedures,* 4th ed. Berkeley, CA: McCutchan, 1995.

Morris, Daniel, and Joel Brandon. *Re-engineering Your Business.* New York: McGraw-Hill, 1993.

National Institutes of Health, National Institute on Drug Abuse. http://www.drugabuse.gov/infofacts/workplace.html, 2011.

National Restaurant Association. *Industry at a Glance.* http//:www.restaurant.org/research/ind_glance.cfm, 2003.

National Restaurant Association. *Legal Monitor: Grocer Settles HIV-Discrimination Lawsuit with EEOC for $80,000.* http//:www.restaurant.org/legal/lm/lm2001_06.cfm, 2001.

National Restaurant Association. *Research and Insights – Facts at a Glance, 2011.* http://www.restaurant.org/research/facts/.

National Restaurant Association. *State of the Restaurant Industry Workforce: An Overview.* Chicago: National Restaurant Association, 2006. http//:www.restaurant.org/research/ind_glance.cfm.

Noe, Raymond A., John R. Hollenbeck, Barry Gerhart, and Patrick M. Wright. *Human Resources Management: Gaining a Competitive Advantage.* Boston: Irwin, 1997.

Patel, Shyam, Sr. "Just Published People Report Survey of Unit Level Employment Practices Highlights Rapid Shifts in the Workforce." January 2007. http//:www.peoplereport.com. http://www.enewsbuilder.net/peoplereport/e_article000733019.cfm?x=b8Rr58S,b520tHgk

Peters, Thomas, and Nancy Austin. *A Passion for Excellence: The Leadership Difference.* New York: Random House, 1985.

Peters, Tom. *Thriving on Chaos: Handbook for a Management Revolution.* New York: Harper & Row, 1988.

Peterson, Jim L. "Self-Esteem Is Essential to Building a Team." In *Lessons in Leadership.* New York: Van Nostrand Reinhold, 1991.

Picogna, Joseph L. *Total Quality Leadership: A Training Approach.* Morrisville, PA: International Information Associates, 1993.

Quick, Thomas J. "The Art of Time Management." *Training,* January 1989.

Restaurant Opportunities Centers United. http://www.rocunited.org/files/roc_servingwhilesick_v06%20%281%29.pdf, September 30, 2010.

Riley, Michael. *Human Resources Management.* London: Butterworth-Heinemann, 1992.

Rinke, Wolf J. *The Winning Foodservice Manager: Strategies for Doing More with Less,* 2nd ed. Rockville, MD: Achievement, 1992.

Roberts, Wess. *Leadership Secrets of Attila the Hun.* New York: Warner Books, 1987.

Roosevelt, Thomas R., Jr. *Beyond Race and Gender.* New York: AMACOM, 1991.

Ryan, Kathleen, and Daniel K. Oestreich. *Driving Fear out of the Workplace.* San Francisco: Jossey-Bass, 1991.

Schwartz, Andrew E. *Delegating Authority.* New York: Barron's, 1992.

Scorza, John. "Benefits Can Boost Employee Loyalty," Society for Human Resource Management, http://www.shrm.org/hrdisciplines/benefits/Articles/Pages/Benefits_Loyalty.aspx, April 1, 2011.

Scott, Cynthia D., and Dennis T. Jaffe. *Empowerment.* London: Crisp, 1991.

Sherman, Arthur, George Bohlander, and Herbert Crudden. *Managing Human Resources,* 9th ed. Cincinnati, OH: South-Western, 1997.

Shiba, Shoji, Alan Graham, and David Walden. *A New American TQM, Four Practical Revolutions in Management.* Portland, OR: Productivity Press, 1993.

Shriver, Stephen, J. *Managing Quality Services.* East Lansing, MI: The Educational Institute of the American Hotel & Motel Association, 1998.

Smith, Steve. *Build That Team.* London: Kogan Page, 1997.

Social Security Administration. http://www.ssa.gov/oact/cola/cbb.html (last reviewed December 29, 2010).

Stamatis, D. H. *Total Quality Services: Principles, Practices, and Implementation.* Delray Beach, FL: St. Lucie Press, 1996.

Sullivan, Richard. *The H.I.T. Man (Humor in Teaching).* Edmund, OK: Central State University, 1990.

Swift, Jill A., Joel E. Ross, and Vincent K. Omachonu. *Principles of Total Quality Management,* 2nd ed. Boca Raton, FL: St. Lucie Press, 1998.

Tanke, Mary L. *Human Resources Management for the Hospitality Industry.* Albany, NY: Delmar, 1990.

Taylor, Lisa Y. "Recipe for Retention," *San Antonio Business Journal,* October 10, 2004. http://www.enewsbuilder.net/peoplereport/e_article000326611.cfm?x=b11,0,w.

Tepper, Bruce B. *The New Supervisor: Skills for Success.* New York: Irwin, 1994.

Thomas, Brain. *Total Quality Training: The Quality Culture and Quality Trainer.* Berkshire, England: McGraw-Hill, 1992.

Toler Sachs, Randi. *Productive Performance Appraisals.* New York: AMACOM, 1992.

Travers, Alfred W. *Supervision, Techniques and New Dimensions.* Englewood Cliffs, NJ: Prentice Hall, 1993.

United States Department of Labor. *Employment Law Guide,* http://www.dol.gov/elaws/elg/.

United States Department of Labor. http://www.ows.doleta.gov/unemploy/uifactsheet.asp (updated January 13, 2010).

United States Department of Labor, Bureau of Labor Statistics. http://www.bls.gov/news.release/ecec.nr0.htm, March 9, 2011.

United States Department of Labor, Occupational Safety and Health Administration. http://www.osha.gov/pls/oshaweb/owadisp.show_document?p_table=OSHACT&p_id=3371, 2011.

United States Department of Labor, Wage and Hour Division. http://www.dol.gov/whd/regs/compliance/fairpay/fs17a_overview.pdf (revised July, 2008).

United States Department of Labor, Wage and Hour Division. http://www.dol.gov/whd/regs/compliance/whdfs14.htm (revised July, 2009).

United States Government Printing Office. *United States Code,* http://www.gpoaccess.gov/uscode/.

U.S. Equal Employment Opportunity Commission. *Sexual Harassment Charges EEOC & FEPAs Combined: FY 1997 – FY 2006.* http://www.eeoc.gov/stats/harass.html.

Van Hoof, Hubert B., Marilyn E. McDonald, Lawrence Yu, and Gary K. Vallen. *A Host of Opportunities: An Introduction to Hospitality.* New York: Irwin, 1996.

Vroom, Victor H. *Work and Motivation.* New York: John Wiley, 1964.

Walker, John R. *Introduction to Hospitality.* Upper Saddle River, NJ: Prentice Hall, 1996.

Walton, Mary. *The Deming Management Method.* New York: Putnam, 1986.

Walton, Sally J. *Cultural Diversity in the Workplace.* New York: Irwin, 1994.

Werther, William B., and Keith Davis. *Human Resources and Personnel Management,* 5th ed. New York: McGraw-Hill, 1996.

Wilson, Robert F. *Conducting Better Job Interviews.* New York: Barron's, 1991.

Woods, John A. *Teams and Teamwork.* New York: Macmillan, 1998.

Woods, Robert H., and Judy Z. King. *Quality Leadership and Management in the Hospitality Industry.* East Lansing, MI: The Educational Institute of the American Hotel & Motel Association, 1996.

Worthington, E. R., and Anita E. Worthington. *People Investment.* Central Point, OR: Oasis Press, 1993.

Wyoming Department of Employment, Research & Planning. http://wydoe.state.wy.us/lmi/0203/a2.htm, 2003.

Index